Pocket
Menu Guide ™

Chinese, Korean and Japanese Foods

Volume 1

CONTEX
Tokyo, Japan

Pocket Menu Guide™
to Enjoyable Restaurant Dining

Published by	Contex Corporation	発行所	コンテックス株式会社
Suzuki Bldg., 1-13-14 Akebono-cho		〒 190-0012	東京都立川市曙町
Tachikawa, Tokyo 190-0012, Japan			1-13-14 鈴木ビル
Fax +81-42-528-2411		Fax	(042) 528-2411
http://www.cydoc.co.jp/contex/		振替	0016-0-32844

Publisher	Shigeru Tsukakoshi	発行人	塚越 繁
Editor	Shigeru Tsukakoshi	編集人	塚越 繁
Editorial Staff	Yuko Tsukakoshi	編集スタッフ	塚越祐子
	Yoshie Miura		三浦良江
	Noyo Ochi		越智野世
	Eric B. Falk		エリック・ビー・フォーク
	Kaoru Seki		関 薫
	Ayumi Hori		堀あゆみ
	Kimie Yamamoto		山本喜三枝
Calorie Calculation	Yoko Kobayashi	カロリー計算	小林陽子

Photographer	Fumiko Sugawara	写真撮影	菅原史子
Copyright Adviser	Japan Uni Copyright Center	著作権顧問	日本ユニ著作権センター
Copyright	©1998 by Shigeru Tsukakoshi	著作権者	©1998 塚越 繁

ISBN 4-907653-00-X

Trademark	POCKET MENU GUIDE is a trademark of Contex Corporation.		
Patent	International Patent Pending	国際特許出願中	
Printed in Japan	(Printed simultaneously in Singapore and published by Contex Corporation, Tokyo, Japan.)		

First Edition Published in Japan on August 28, 1998　初版第 1 刷発行 1998 年 8 月 28 日

CONTENTS

U. S. Library of Congress Cataloging-in-Publication Data:
Pending certificate of registration.

Introduction

Anyone who has ever traveled overseas and eaten at a restaurant has probably- at one time or another- experienced the confusion of not knowing what to order, having not understood the contents of the menu, or having felt a little uneasy because of unfamiliar ingredients used in a particular dish. It is precisely at times like these that this book will be an invaluable partner in helping you to select what you want to eat, as well as get the most enjoyment from your meal. This book contains brief explanations in 10 languages along with color photographs of some of the more popular dishes served at restaurants in East Asia featuring 75 Chinese dishes, 39 Korean dishes and 80 Japanese dishes.

The act of eating and enjoying food goes beyond national boundaries. What is more, the dishes and foods which are enjoyed in each country provide a glimpse into the culture and history of that particular country. I hope that this book will give you the motivation to try different foods from various countries. It is also my desire that this book will contribute to mutual understanding between people of different countries while enjoying the intricate and lavish food culture of East Asia.

I would also like to take this opportunity to express my sincere appreciation to Chef Eiko Setsu, who supervised the Chinese cuisine; Mrs. Kamyon Cho, an expert in the field of Korean cuisine, Chef Kikuo Takada, who supervised the Japanese cuisine, those people who assisted in conducting surveys when selecting the dishes to be introduced in this book, as well as the many other people who contributed to the production of this book, for their generous and invaluable assistance and cooperation.

Shigeru Tsukakoshi

前言

在國外的餐廳，您是否有過這樣的經曆？當一份您所不懂得的異國語言的菜譜送到您的眼前時，您會由於不知道點什麼而不知所措，或者因為不知道某種菜中使用了什麼材料而感到困惑。遇到這種情況，本書一定會成為各位選擇菜譜的良朋益友，在這裡我們收錄了東亞各國的主要菜譜（中國菜75道、韓國・朝鮮菜39道、日本菜80道）10國語言的簡單介紹及彩色照片。

"食"無國界。各種"食"中凝縮著該國家的文化和曆史。難道您不想通過本書向各種各樣的"食"發起挑戰嗎？我們希望各位能夠在充分品嘗東亞食文化韻味的同時，加深相互的理解。

本書在編寫中，曾得到了中國菜廚師長勢津榮興先生、韓國、朝鮮菜等研究專家曹甲連先生、日本菜廚師長高田喜久雄先生等對菜譜的選擇提供意見，對各位先生以及其他眾多朋友的大力協助，在此我們深表謝意。

塚越　繁

前言

在国外的餐厅，您是否有过这样的经历？当一份您所不懂得的异国语言的菜谱送到您的眼前时，您会由于不知道点什么而不知所措，或者因为不知道某种菜中使用了什么材料而感到困惑。遇到这种情况，本书一定会成为各位选择菜谱的良朋益友，在这里我们收录了东亚各国的主要菜谱（中国菜75道、韩国・朝鲜菜39道、日本菜80道）10国语言的简单介绍及彩色照片。

"食"无国界。各种"食"中凝缩着该国家的文化和历史。难道您不想通过本书向各种各样的"食"发起挑战吗？我们希望各位能够在充分品尝东亚食文化韵味的同时，加深相互的理解。

本书在编写中，曾得到了中国菜厨师长势津荣兴先生、韩国、朝鲜菜等研究专家曹甲连先生、日本菜厨师长高田喜久雄先生等对菜谱的选择提供意见，对各位先生以及其他众多朋友的大力协助，在此我们深表谢意。

塚越　繁

머리말

 해외의 레스토랑에서 읽지 못하는 메뉴를 눈앞에 두고, 무엇을 주문해야 좋을지 망설이거나 어떤 재료를 사용한 요리인지 불안했던 경험은 없으십니까? 그럴 때에 이 책자가 여러분의 메뉴 선정에 좋은 안내자 역할을 할 것입니다. 여기에는 동아시아의 주요 요리 (중국요리 75점, 한국·조선요리 39점, 일본요리 80점)를 10개 국어로, 간단한 설명과 컬러 사진을 함께 수록하고 있습니다.

 먹는 것에는 국경이 없습니다. 또한 음식에는 그 나라의 문화와 역사가 응축되어 있습니다. 여러분도 이 책으로 여러 가지 '음식'에 도전해 보시지 않겠습니까? 그렇게 해서 동아시아인의 음식문화를 마음껏 즐기며 상호간의 이해를 깊이해 가는 것, 그것이 제 소망입니다.

 이 책을 위해서 중국요리 요리사 세쓰 에이코 씨, 한국·조선요리 연구가 조갑연 씨, 일본요리 요리사 다카다 기쿠오 씨를 비롯하여 요리 선택을 위한 앙케이트에 협력하여 주신 분들과 그 밖의 많은 여러분들께 깊은 감사를 드립니다.

쓰카고시 시게루

はじめに

 海外のレストランで、言葉のわからないメニューを目の前にして、何を注文したらよいかとまどったり、どんな素材を使った料理なのか、不安になったりした経験はありませんか。そんなとき、本書はきっと、皆様のメニュー選びの良きガイド役となるでしょう。ここには、東アジアの主な料理 (中国料理75点、韓国・朝鮮料理39点、日本料理80点)が、10カ国語の簡単な説明とカラー写真で収録されています。

 「食べる」ということには国境がありません。またそれぞれの「食」には、その国の文化と歴史が凝縮されています。あなたもこの本によって、さまざまな「食」に挑戦しませんか。そして、東アジアの食文化を存分に楽しみながら、相互の理解を深めていただくこと、それが私の願いです。

 本書をまとめるにあたり、中国料理のシェフ勢津栄興氏、韓国・朝鮮料理研究家チョ・カムヨン氏、日本料理シェフ高田喜久雄氏をはじめ、料理を選ぶ際のアンケートに協力していただいた方々、また、その他多くの皆様から多大なご協力をいただきました。厚くお礼申し上げます。

塚越　繁

مقدمة

من الطبيعي لكل فرد أتيح له أن يسافر للخارج ويأكل في بعض المطاعم الاجنبية أن يتعرض في لحظة أو أخرى لذلك الموقف المحير، حيث يقف عاجزاً عن تحديد ما يرغب في تناوله أمام قائمة للمأكولات يعجز عن فك رموزها، أوأطباق يقلقه عدم معرفة محتوياتها، تلك هي اللحظات التي يصبح فيها هذا الكتيب رفيقاً قيماً يساعدك على اختيار طعامك والاستمتاع الكامل بوجبتك، وهو يضم شرحاً موجزاً بعشر لغات مع صور ملونة لأشهر الأطباق التي تقدم في مطاعم شرق آسيا، من بينها ٧٥ طبقاً صينياً، و٣٩ طبقاً كورياً، و ٨٠ طبقاً يابانياً.

والواقع أن تناول الطعام والاستمتاع به هو أمر يتعدى الحدود الدولية للبلاد المختلفة، فتلك الأطباق والأطعمة التي تتذوقها في كل بلد تزودك بلمحة من ثقافة وتاريخ هذا البلد، ومن ثم يحدونا الأمل في أن يصبح هذا الدليل حافزاً يدفعكم إلي تذوق العديد من الأطباق المختلفة لتلك الدول، كما نطمح في أن يساهم في تحقيق نوع من التفاهم المتبادل بين أفراد من شعوب مختلفة مع الاستمتاع بثراء وسخاء الثقافة الغذائية لشعوب شرق آسيا.

وهنا نود أن نعبر عن خالص تقديرنا للطباخ المحترف السيد إيكو ستنسو الذي أشرف على قائمة الطعام الصيني، والسيدة كاميون تشو الخبيرة في مجال الطعام الكوري، والطباخ المحترف السيد كيكو تاكادا الذي أشرف على قائمة الطعام الياباني ، والأفراد الذين ساهموا في عمل المسح الاستفتائي لاختيار الأطباق التي نقدمها في هذا الكتيب وللكثيرين الآخرين الذين ساهموا في إخراجه ... لكل هؤلاء نتقدم بخالص شكرنا على معونتهم الكريمة ومساهمتهم الثمينة .

شيجيرو تسوكاكوشي

Einleitung

Jeder, der schon einmal ins Ausland gereist ist und dort in einem Restaurant gegessen hat, hat sicherlich das eine oder andere Mal bereits die verwirrende Erfahrung gemacht, daß er nicht wußte, was er bestellen sollte, ihm der Inhalt der Speisekarte unverständlich war oder er sich nicht ganz wohl gefühlt hat, weil ihm bestimmte in der betreffenden Speise verwendete Zutaten nicht bekannt waren. Für diese Fälle soll dieses Buch Hilfe leisten und Ihnen ein unschätzbarer Partner bei der Wahl Ihrer Speisen sein, damit Sie Ihr Mahl unbeschwert genießen können. Dieses Buch enthält kurze Erläuterungen in 10 Sprachen zusammen mit Farbfotografien von populären Speisen, die in Restaurants in Ostasien serviert werden. Insgesamt enthält es 75 chinesische, 39 koreanische und 80 japanische Gerichte.

Das Vergnügen ein gutes Mahl zu genießen kennt keine nationalen Grenzen. Doch darüber hinaus bieten Speisen und Gerichte der einzelnen Länder einen Eindruck in deren Kultur und Geschichte. Ich hoffe, daß dieses Buch Ihnen Motivation sein wird, Speisen aus verschiedenen Ländern zu kosten und sich nicht "sicherheitshalber" in Fast-Food-Restaurants zu flüchten . Außerdem hoffe ich, daß dieses Buch einen Beitrag zum gegenseitigen Verständnis zwischen den Menschen aus verschiedenen Regionen leisten wird, während sie die vielfältige und üppige Speisekultur Ostasiens genießen.

Ich möchte diese Gelegenheit auch dazu nutzen, folgenden Personen meinen Dank auszusprechen:
Chef Eiko Setsu, der die Zubereitung der chinesischen Gerichte überwacht hat; Herrn Kamyon Cho, einem Experten der koreanischen Küche sowie Chef Kikuo Takada, der für die japanischen Gerichte verantwortlich zeichnet. Mein Dank gilt ferner allen, die bei den Umfragen geholfen haben, die zur Auswahl der in diesem Buch vorgestellten Gerichte geführt haben, sowie den vielen Menschen, die mich bei der Produktion dieses Buches unterstützt haben für ihre selbstlose und wertvolle Hilfe und Kooperation.

Shigeru Tsukakoshi

Introduction

Tout voyageur en pays étranger ayant pris son repas dans un restaurant local a probablement déjà éprouvé - à un moment ou à un autre - un sentiment de confusion à la lecture du menu et du contenu peu familier des ingrédients composant un plat particulier. C'est justement dans ces moments-là que ce livre sera le compagnon idéal et qu'il vous aidera à choisir les plats que vous désirez manger, vous permettant ainsi de retirer le plus grand plaisir de vos expériences culinaires. Ce guide contient de brèves explications en dix langues ainsi que des photographies en couleur de quelques plats les plus populaires servis dans les restaurants est-asiatiques. Il comprend 75 plats chinois, 39 plats coréens et 80 plats japonais.

Manger et apprécier la gastronomie sont des pratiques universelles. En outre, les mets et les aliments consommés dans un pays permettent de comprendre la culture et l'histoire de ce pays particulier. J'espère que ce livre vous incitera à goûter les différentes cuisines de divers pays. Je souhaite également qu'il contribue à une meilleure entente mutuelle entre les peuples des différents pays et qu'il permette d'apprécier l'abondante gastronomie ethnique de l'Asie orientale.

Je voudrais également profiter de cette occasion pour adresser mes sincères remerciements au Chef Eiko Setsu, qui a dirigé la préparation des plats chinois, à Madame Kamyon Cho, spécialiste de cuisine coréenne, au Chef Kikuo Takada chargé de la préparation des plats japonais, à toutes les personnes qui ont prêté leur concours lors de la sélection des plats présentés dans ce guide, ainsi qu'à toutes les autres personnes - et elles sont nombreuses - qui ont contribué à la publication de ce livre, qu'elles soient remerciées pour leur aide généreuse et leur précieuse collaboration.

Shigeru Tsukakoshi

Introducción

Cualquier persona que haya viajado a ultramar y comido en un restaurante habrá experimentado –en un momento dado- la confusión de no saber qué ordenar, no entender el contenido del menú o se habrá sentido un poco indispuesta a causa de que no conoce los ingredientes de un platillo en particular. Precisamente, éstos son los momentos en los que este libro será un compañero insustituible para ayudarle a Usted a seleccionar lo que desea comer y disfrutar al máximo los alimentos. Este libro contiene breves explicaciones en 10 idiomas acompañadas de fotografías a color de algunos de los platillos más populares que se sirven en los restaurantes de Asia Oriental. Ello incluye 75 platillos chinos, 39 platillos coreanos y 80 platillos japoneses.

Comer y disfrutar los alimentos trasciende las fronteras nacionales. Además, los platillos y alimentos que se disfrutan en cada país proporcionan una breve perspectiva de la cultura y la historia de cada lugar en particular. Espero que este libro le ofrezca a Usted una razón para paladear los alimentos de distintos países. Asimismo, deseo que contribuya a la comprensión mutua entre la gente de distintas culturas en el momento de disfrutar la variada y exuberante cultura gastronómica de Asia Oriental.

Quisiera aprovechar esta oportunidad para expresar mi más sincero agradecimiento a la generosa e inapreciable ayuda y colaboración del cocinero Eiko Setsu -quien supervisó la cocina china, a la Sra. Kamyon Cho -experta en el campo de la cocina coreana, al cocinero Kikuo Takada -quien revisó la cocina japonesa, a las personas que me ayudaron a realizar los estudios de selección de los platillos presentados en este libro y a muchas otras personas que contribuyeron a la producción de este libro.

Shigeru Tsukakoshi

Introduzione

A chi non è capitato, in un ristorante all'estero, di non saper che cosa ordinare perché non capisce il menu o di sentirsi disorientato perché non conosce gli ingredienti dei piatti? È proprio in tal caso che questo libro sarà un prezioso aiuto per la scelta del menu. Corredata di semplici spiegazioni in dieci lingue e di foto a colori, questa guida presenta infatti i piatti più importanti dell'Asia Orientale: 75 cinesi, 39 coreani e 80 giapponesi.

Cibarsi e godere il cibo è un'azione umana senza frontiere e in ogni cucina si condensano la cultura e la storia del paese stesso. Mi auguro che questa guida sia uno stimolo a provare cucine diverse e che apprezzando la ricca cultura del cibo dell'Asia Orientale i lettori pervengano ad una più approfondita comprensione reciproca.

Nella preparazione di questo libro ho avuto la grandissima collaborazione dello chef Eiko Setsu per la cucina cinese, della ricercatrice Kamyon Cho per la cucina coreana, sia del sud che del nord, dello chef Kikuo Takada per la cucina giapponese, e inoltre di coloro che hanno risposto al questionario per la scelta dei piatti e, in vario modo, di molte altre persone. A tutti i miei più vivi e sentiti ringraziamenti.

Shigeru Tsukakoshi

Introdução

Qualquer um que, em viagem ao exterior, já tenha ido a restaurantes quase certamente viu-se uma vez ou outra na situação embaraçosa de não saber o que pedir, em razão de não entender o cardápio ou de se sentir desconfortável com os ingredientes desconhecidos de um determinado prato. Precisamente nessas ocasiões, é que este livro será um companheiro inestimável para ajudá-lo a decidir o que comer e a apreciar ao máximo a refeição. Ele contém breves descrições em dez idiomas, com fotos em cores, de alguns dos pratos mais servidos em restaurantes no Leste da Ásia. São apresentados 75 pratos chineses, 39 coreanos e 80 japoneses.

O ato de comer e desfrutar a comida transcende as fronteiras nacionais. Além disso, os pratos e alimentos apreciados em vários países representam uma amostra da cultura e da história dessas nações em particular. Espero que este livro dê ao leitor a motivação para experimentar comidas diferentes de vários países. Também é meu desejo que o presente guia contribua para a compreensão mútua entre indivíduos de diferentes países, ao mesmo tempo em que permita desfrutar a pródiga e complexa cultura alimentar do Leste da Ásia.

Aproveito a oportunidade para expressar o meu agradecimento sincero ao chef Eiko Setsu, que supervisionou a cozinha chinesa; à senhora Kamyon Cho, especialista em pratos coreanos; ao chef Kikuo Takada, que supervisionou a cozinha japonesa; àqueles que ajudaram a realizar pesquisas para a seleção dos pratos incluídos neste livro; bem como aos muitos outros que contribuíram para a produção deste guia, por sua generosa e inestimável assistência e cooperação.

Shigeru Tsukakoshi

How to Use This Book

The List of Dishes on pages 21 to 43 provides a complete list of the dishes introduced in this guide so that you can point to them when ordering. Please refer to the page numbers shown in the photographs for a more detailed explanation of each dish. The main ingredients used in each dish, price and calorie indicators and whether or not a particular dish is spicy are shown in graphic form one each page in the manner shown below for easier reference. In addition, examples of basic phrases and conversation frequently used in restaurants are described in each language on pages 44 to 53 to ensure that your dining experience is more enjoyable.

Name of dish in English

Name of dish in corresponding country

Price Indicator

- Inexpensive Dishes
- Moderately Priced Dishes
- Expensive Dishes

Ingredient symbols

- Beef
- Pork
- Beef or Pork
- Chicken
- Fowl (other than chicken)
- Fish
- Shrimp
- Crab
- Squid
- Shellfish
- Tofu (Bean curd)
- Vegetables

Spicy Dishes

Calorie Indicator (per person)

kcal
- 0kcal ~ 200kcal
- 200kcal ~ 400kcal
- 400kcal ~ 600kcal
- 600kcal ~

88 Braised Bean Curd with Chili Sauce

麻婆豆腐（Ma Po Dou Fu）

Braised Bean Curd with Chili Sauce
This typical Szechwan dish features braised tofu and stir-fried ground meat
Explanation in English
cornstarch for a spicy combination that brings out the appetite.

kcal

麻婆豆腐
Explanation in Chinese
(Traditional Chinese Characters)

Geschmorter Tofu mit Chili-Soße
Dies ist ein typisches Gericht der Szechwan-Küche.
Explanation in German
Stärke gebunden werden, bieten eine Kombination, die so richtig Appetit macht.

麻婆豆腐
Explanation in Chinese
(Simplified Chinese Characters)

Pâte de soja braisée à la sauce pimentée
Cette spécialité du Sichuan se compose de tofu braisé
Explanation in French
mélange piquant qui ouvre l'appétit.

마파두부
Explanation in Korean

Salteado de Cuajada de Soja con Salsa Picante
Este platillo típico de Szechwan se caracteriza por el
Explanation in Spanish
salsa picante y otros condimentos.

マーボー豆腐
Explanation in Japanese

Brasato di tofu in salsa piccante doban djan
Questo piatto tipico della regione di Szechwan viene
Explanation in Italian
stuzzica l'appetito.

توفو مطهو مع صلصة الفلفل الأحمر
Explanation in Arabic

Queijo de soja refogado com molho de pimenta
Este prato típico de Szech Wan é feito com tofu e
Explanation in Portuguese
iguaria picante, que desperta o apetite.

Types of Foods

- Meat Dishes
- Seafood Dishes
- Vegetable Dishes
- Soups
- Rice Dishes
- Noodle Dishes
- Side Dishes (Dim Sum)
- One-Pot Dishes
- Desserts
- Beverages

The ingredients used and prices tend to vary depending on the particular restaurant. We recommend that you find out about ingredients and prices from the waiter before ordering. The number of calories contained in a certain dish also may vary according to the kinds and amounts of ingredients used. The calorie indicators contained in this book are intended to provide you with a general indication of the calorie count of a particular dish.

本書的使用方法

菜譜單（21～43頁）上登載了本書介紹的菜、可用手指著點菜詳細內容請參看登有照片的地方。菜譜單的每頁上記載有使用的主要材料、價格及大致熱量，辣菜如下圖所示可一目了然，此外，用於餐廳的各國語言基礎會話範例。編排在44-53頁上，請實際應用。

英文菜名

相應國的菜名 ── 麻婆豆腐（Ma Po Dou Fu）

參考價格
- 🫛 廉價菜
- 🫛🫛 普通菜
- 🫛🫛🫛 貴重菜

材料的圖片
- 🐄 牛
- 🐖 豬
- 🐄 牛或豬
- 🐔 雞
- （雞以外的）禽類
- 🐟 魚
- 🦐 蝦
- 🦀 蟹
- 烏賊
- 貝類
- 豆腐
- 蔬菜

🌶 辣味菜

熱量標準（每人）

kcal	
●	0kcal ～ 200kcal
●●	200kcal ～ 400kcal
●●●	400kcal ～ 600kcal
●●●●	600kcal ～

菜的種類
- 肉類菜
- 魚貝菜
- 蔬菜
- 湯
- 主食
- 面類
- 點心
- 火鍋
- 甜食
- 飲料

88 Braised Bean Curd with Chili Sauce

Braised Bean Curd with Chili Sauce

This typical Szechwan dish features braised ⬜⬜⬜⬜⬜⬜ and meat flavored ⬜⬜⬜⬜⬜⬜ nd other spices 英文介紹 ⬜⬜ ed with cornstarch for a spicy combination that brings out the appetite.

1 kcal ●●

麻婆豆腐

將豆⬜⬜⬜⬜⬜⬜ ⬜⬜⬜⬜調 味，⬜⬜⬜⬜⬜⬜ 中文（繁體字） 的四川 菜。 介紹

Geschmorter Tofu mit Chili-Soße

Dies ist ein typisches Gericht der Szechwan-Küche. Geschmor⬜⬜⬜⬜⬜⬜ uark) und pfannengerü⬜⬜⬜⬜ 德文介紹 ili-Soße und anderen Ge⬜⬜⬜⬜ d dann mit Stärke gebunden werden, bieten eine Kombination, die so richtig Appetit macht.

麻婆豆腐

將豆⬜⬜和⬜⬜⬜⬜ ⬜⬜⬜⬜ 用⬜⬜醬調 味，⬜⬜⬜⬜⬜⬜ 中文（簡體字） 川菜。 麻辣 介紹

Pâte de soja braisée à la sauce pimentée

Cette spécialité du Sichuan se compose de tofu braisé et de viande ⬜⬜⬜⬜⬜⬜ d'une sauce à base de pi⬜⬜⬜⬜⬜ 法文介紹 , que l'on a épaissie ave⬜⬜⬜⬜⬜ d'obtenir un mélange piquant qui ouvre l'appétit.

마파두부

두부와 다진 고기를 볶아서 또반장으로 맛 을 내고 고⬜⬜⬜⬜ 韓文介紹 대표적인 사천요리. 구이 준다.

Salteado de Cuajada de Soja con Salsa Picante

Este platillo típico de Szechwan se caracteriza por el queso ⬜⬜⬜⬜⬜⬜ dos con esta ap⬜⬜⬜⬜ 西班牙文介紹 ase de un ado⬜⬜⬜⬜ salsa picante y otros condimentos.

マーボー豆腐

豆腐、ひき肉を炒めて豆板醤などで味付けし、片栗粉⬜⬜⬜⬜ 的四川料 理。ピリ辛 日文介紹

Brasato di tofu in salsa piccante doban djan

Questo piatto tipico della regione di Szechwan viene prepara⬜⬜⬜⬜⬜⬜ do con salsa ⬜⬜⬜⬜⬜ 意大利文介紹 , e poi addens⬜⬜⬜⬜⬜ iccante stuzzica l'appetito.

توفو مطهو مع صلصة الفلفل الأحمر

هذا الطبق الشعبي من إقليم سشتشوان يتكون من قطع من التوفو 阿拉伯文介紹 و

Queijo de soja refogado com molho de pimenta

Este prato típico de Szech Wan é feito com tofu e carne ⬜⬜⬜⬜⬜⬜ nês e condin⬜⬜⬜⬜⬜ 葡萄牙文介紹 outros temper⬜⬜⬜⬜⬜ ar uma iguaria picante, que desperta o apetite.

菜譜的材料及價格會由於餐廳的不同而有所不同，您應當向餐廳人員進行確認。熱量由於材料的種類及量的不同也會有所變化，因此，本書將僅供您作為參考使用。

本书的使用方法

菜谱单（21～43页）上登载了本书介绍的菜、可用手指着点菜详细内容请参看登有照片的地方。菜谱单的每页上记载有使用的主要材料、价格及大致热量，辣菜如下图所示可一目了然，此外，用于餐厅的各国语言基础会话范例。编排在44～53页上，请实际应用。

英文菜名 ——————

相应国的菜名 ——————

参考价格 ——————
- 🟡 廉价菜
- 🟡🟡 普通菜
- 🟡🟡🟡 贵重菜

材料的图片 ——————
- 🐮 牛
- 🐷 猪
- 🐂 牛或猪
- 🐔 鸡
- 🐦 （鸡以外的）禽类
- 🐟 鱼
- 🦐 虾
- 🦀 蟹
- 🦑 乌贼
- 🐚 贝类
- ⬜ 豆腐
- 🥬 蔬菜

🔥 辣味菜

热量标准（每人）

kcal
- 🔴 0kcal ～ 200kcal
- 🔴🔴 200kcal ～ 400kcal
- 🔴🔴🔴 400kcal ～ 600kcal
- 🔴🔴🔴🔴 600kcal ～

88 Braised Bean Curd with Chili Sauce

麻婆豆腐（Ma Po Dou Fu）

Braised Bean Curd with Chili Sauce
This typical Szechwan dish features braised t... ...und meat flavored ... and other spices ... ...d with cornstarch for a spicy combination that brings out the appetite.

英文介绍

1 kcal ●●

麻婆豆腐
中文（繁体字）介绍

Geschmorter Tofu mit Chili-Soße
Dies ist ein typisches Gericht der Szechwan-Küche. Geschmor... ...uark) und pfannengü... ...anderen Ge... ...d dann mit Stärke gebunden werden, bieten eine Kombination, die so richtig Appetit macht.

德文介绍

麻婆豆腐
中文（简体字）介绍

Pâte de soja braisée à la sauce pimentée
Cette spécialité du Sichuan se compose de tofu braisé et de viande ... ...d'une sauce à base de p... ...que l'on a épaissie ave... ...d'obtenir un mélange piquant qui ouvre l'appétit.

法文介绍

마파두부
韩文介绍

Salteado de Cuajada de Soja con Salsa Picante
Este platillo típico de Szechwan se caracteriza por el queso... ...da. En esta ap... ...dos con un ado... ...ase de salsa picante y otros condimentos.

西班牙文介绍

マーボー豆腐
日文介绍

Brasato di tofu in salsa piccante doban djan
Questo piatto tipico della regione di Szechwan viene prepar... ...e poi adden... ...iccante stuzzica l'appetito.

意大利文介绍

توفو مطهو مع صلصة الفلفل الأحمر
阿拉伯文介绍

Queijo de soja refogado com molho de pimenta
Este prato típico de Szech Wan é feito com tofu e carne ... ...nês e condim... ...outros temper... ...ar uma iguaria picante, que desperta o apetite.

葡萄牙文介绍

菜的种类 ——————

| 🟥 肉类菜 | 🐟 鱼贝菜 | 🥬 蔬菜 | 🍲 汤 | 🍚 主食 |
| 🟫 面类 | 🟧 点心 | 🔥 火锅 | 🟦 甜食 | 🟨 饮料 |

菜谱的材料及价格会由于餐厅的不同而有所不同，您应当向餐厅人员进行确认。热量由于材料的种类及量的不同也会有变化，因此，本书将仅供您作为参考使用。

본 책자의 사용 방법

요리 일람(P.21~P.43)에는 본 책자에 소개된 요리를 손으로 가르키면서 주문할 수 있도록 한자리에 게재하였습니다. 자세한 내용은 사진 안에 기입된 페이지를 참조하여 주십시오. 각 요리의 페이지에는 사용된 주요 재료, 가격과 칼로리, 특히 매운 요리를 한 눈에 알 수 있도록 아래와 같이 그림으로 나타냈습니다. 또 레스토랑에서 사용하는 각 언어의 기본적인 회화 예를 P.44~P.53에 수록하고 있으므로 참조하시기 바랍니다.

영어 요리명

해당 각 나라의 요리명

참고 가격
- 저가
- 보통
- 고가

주요 재료
- 쇠고기
- 돼지고기
- 쇠고기 또는 돼지고기
- 닭고기
- (닭 이외의)새고기
- 생선
- 새우
- 게
- 오징어
- 조개류
- 두부
- 채소

특히 매운 요리

칼로리 기준 (1인분)

kcal
- 0kcal ~ 200kcal
- 200kcal ~ 400kcal
- 400kcal ~ 600kcal
- 600kcal 이상

88 Braised Bean Curd with Chili Sauce

麻婆豆腐（Ma Po Dou Fu）

Braised Bean Curd with Chili Sauce
영어 해설

麻婆豆腐 중국어(굉동어) 해설 / **Geschmorter Tofu mit Chili-Soße** 독일어 해설

麻婆豆腐 중국어(북경어) 해설 / **Pâte de soja braisée à la sauce pimentée** 불어 해설

마파두부 한국어 해설 / **Salteado de Cuajada de Soja con Salsa Picante** 스페인어 해설

マーボー豆腐 일본어 해설 / **Brasato di tofu in salsa piccante doban djan** 이탈리아 해설

توفو مطهو مع صلصة الفلفل الأحمر 아라비아어 해설 / **Queijo de soja refogado com molho de pimenta** 포르투갈어 해설

요리의 장르
- 고기요리
- 어패요리
- 야채요리
- 수프
- 백반요리
- 면요리
- 딤섬(점심)요리
- 냄비요리
- 디저트
- 음료수

요리의 재료와 가격은 레스토랑에 따라 다를 경우가 있으므로 식당 주인에게 확인하시기 바랍니다. 그리고 칼로리는 재료의 종류와 음식의 양에 따라 달라지므로 어디까지나 참고 정도로 이용하여 주십시오.

本書の使い方

料理一覧（P.21〜P.43）には、本書で紹介した料理を指さしでも注文できるように、写真を一挙に掲載しました。詳しい料理の内容は、写真に記したページをご覧ください。それぞれの料理のページには、使われている主な材料、価格とカロリーの目安、辛い料理が一目でわかるように、下記のように図で示してあります。また、レストランで使う各言語の基本的な会話例を、P.44〜P.53に収録しましので、お役立てください。

英語の料理名 ————

対応国の料理名 ————

価格の目安 ————
- 🪙 安い
- 🪙🪙 普通
- 🪙🪙🪙 高い

主な材料 ————
- 🐄 牛
- 🐷 豚
- 🐄 牛か豚
- 🐔 鶏
- 🦆 （鶏以外の）鳥
- 🐟 魚
- 🦐 えび
- 🦀 かに
- 🦑 いか
- 🐚 貝類
- 🍲 豆腐
- 🥬 野菜

🌶 特に辛い料理 ————

カロリーの目安（1人分）

kcal
- ● 0kcal 〜 200kcal
- ●● 200kcal 〜 400kcal
- ●●● 400kcal 〜 600kcal
- ●●●● 600kcal 以上

料理のジャンル ————

🍖 肉料理　　🐟 魚介料理　　🥬 野菜料理　　🥣 スープ　　🍚 ご飯料理

🍜 麺料理　　🥟 点心　　🍲 鍋料理　　🍮 デザート　　☕ 飲みもの

---

88 Braised Bean Curd with Chili Sauce

麻婆豆腐（Ma Po Dou Fu）

Braised Bean Curd with Chili Sauce
This typical Szechwan dish features braised 〔 〕 d meat flavore 〔 〕 l other spices 〔英語の解説〕 d with cornstarch for a spicy combination that brings out the appetite.

🌶 kcal ●●

麻婆豆腐 中国語（繁体字）の解説	**Geschmorter Tofu mit Chili-Soße** Dies ist ein typisches Gericht der Szechwan-Küche. Ges〔 〕und pfann〔 〕und ande〔 〕n mit Stärke gebunden werden, bieten eine Kombination, die so richtig Appetit macht. ドイツ語の解説
麻婆豆腐 中国語（簡体字）の解説	**Pâte de soja braisée à la sauce pimentée** Cette spécialité du Sichuan se compose de tofu braisé et〔 〕a ép〔 〕un mélange piquant qui ouvre l'appétit. フランス語の解説
마파두부 두부와 다진 고기를 볶아서 두반장으로 맛〔 〕적인 시푼〔 〕준다. 韓国語の解説	**Salteado de Cuajada de Soja con Salsa Picante** Este platillo típico de Szechwan se caracteriza por el qu〔 〕on es〔 〕n un salsa picante y otros condimentos. スペイン語の解説
マーボー豆腐 豆腐、ひき肉を炒めて豆板醤などで味付けし〔 〕料理。 日本語の解説	**Brasato di tofu in salsa piccante doban djan** Questo piatto tipico della regione di Szechwan viene sa〔 〕oi ac〔 〕a stuzzica l'appetito. イタリア語の解説
توفو مطهو مع صلصة الفلفل الأحمر هذا الطبق الشعبي من إقليم سشتشوان يتكون من قطع من التوفو 〔 〕 نظ〔 〕 اشه〔 〕 أراビア語の解説	**Queijo de soja refogado com molho de pimenta** Este prato típico de Szech Wan é feito com tofu e〔 〕 iguaria picante, que desperta o apetite. ポルトガル語の解説

料理の素材と価格はレストランによって異なる場合がありますので、お店の人に確認を。また、カロリーは材料の種類や量によって変化するので、あくまでも目安としてご利用ください。

كيف تستخدم هذا الكتيب

تضم الصفحات من ١٥ إلى ٣٧ قائمة لبعض المأكولات الشعبية في كل من الصين وكوريا الجنوبية والشمالية واليابان. يرجى الرجوع إلى أرقام الصفحات المبينة في الصور للحصول على تفاصيل أكثر حول كل طبق، وتسهيلاً للأمر تم توضيح المحتويات الرئيسية لكل طبق باستخدام الصور، وخاصة الأطباق الحريفة، مع مؤشرات بالأسعار والسعرات الحرارية .

اسم الطبق باللغة الإنجليزية

88 Braised Bean Curd with Chili Sauce

اسم الطبق في بلده الأصلي

麻婆豆腐（Ma Po Dou Fu）

مؤشر السعر

Braised Bean Curd with Chili Sauce

This typical Szechwan dish features braised tofu and stir-fried ground meat ... شرح باللغة الإنجليزية ... cornstarch for a spicy combination that brings out the appetite.

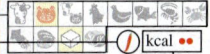

- أطباق رخيصة
- أطباق معتدلة السعر
- أطباق غالية

kcal ●●

رموز محتويات الطبق

麻婆豆腐

شرح باللغة الصينية

（ باستخدام الحروف الصينية التقليدية ）

Geschmorter Tofu mit Chili-Soße

Dies ist ein typisches Gericht der Szechwan-Küche. Ges ...) und
pfann ... شرح باللغة الألمانية ...ße und
ander ... mit
Stärke gebunden werden, bieten eine Kombination, die so richtig Appetit macht.

- لحم بقري
- لحم خنزير
- لحم بقري أو خنزير
- دجاج
- طيور (فيما عدا الدجاج)
- سمك
- جمبري (روبيان)
- كابوريا (سرطان)
- سبيط (حبار)
- محار
- توفو (جبن من فول الصويا)
- خضر

麻婆豆腐

شرح باللغة الصينية

（ باستخدام الحروف الصينية المبسطة ）

Pâte de soja braisée à la sauce pimentée

Cette spécialité du Sichuan se compose de tofu braisé et d ...auce
à b ... شرح باللغة الفرنسية ...on a
épa ...ir un
mélange piquant qui ouvre l'appétit.

마파두부

두부와 다진 고기를 볶아서 두반장으로 맛 ...적인
시찬... 던다. شرح باللغة الكورية

Salteado de Cuajada de Soja con Salsa Picante

Este platillo típico de Szechwan se caracteriza por el que ...a. En
esta ... شرح باللغة الاسبانية ...os con
un a ...se de
salsa picante y otros condimentos.

マーボー豆腐

豆腐、ひき肉を炒めて豆板醤などで味付け し、片...れ
味...شرح باللغة اليابانية

Brasato di tofu in salsa piccante doban djan

Questo piatto tipico della regione di Szechwan viene prep ...e con
sals ... شرح باللغة الإيطالية ...e poi
add ...cante
stuzzica l'appetito.

توفو مطهو مع صلصة الفلفل الأحمر

هذا الطبق الشعبي من إقليم سشتوان يتكون من قطع من التوفو تطهى مع ...أحمر وتقلى مع ... شرح باللغة العربية ...مملأ في النهاية

Queijo de soja refogado com molho de pimenta

Este prato típico de Szech Wan é feito com tofu e ca ... s e
co ...tros
ter ...ma
iguana picante, que desperta o apetite.

أطباق حارة (حريفة)

مؤشر السعرات الحرارية (للفرد الواحد)

kcal
- ● 0kcal ～ 200kcal
- ●● 200kcal ～ 400kcal
- ●●● 400kcal ～ 600kcal
- ●●●● 600kcal ～

أنواع الأطعمة

أطباق من اللحوم　　أطباق من الخضر　　أنواع من الحساء　　أطباق من الأسماك　　أطباق من الأرز

المشروبات　　الحلوى والفطائر　　طواجن من خليط من المكونات　　أطباق جانبية ومكملات　　أطباق من الشعرية

عادة تختلف محتويات الطبق وسعره من مطعم لآخر، لذا ننصح بسؤال عامل المطعم للتأكد من ذلك قبل تحديد الطلب، وقد تختلف السعرات الحرارية أيضاً تبعاً لأنواع وكميات المقادير المختلفة، وهنا ننوه بأن مؤشرات السعرات الحرارية الموضحة في هذا الكتيب تهدف إلى إعطاء فكرة تقريبية عن السعرات الحرارية لكل طبق .

ملاحظة: بعض المطاعم الصينية والكورية واليابانية الموجودة في البلاد الإسلامية تحرص على استخدام لحم البقر أو الضأن بدلاً من لحم الخنزير، في الوقت نفسه قد يستخدم المطعم لحم الخنزير بدلاً من لحم البقر في بلاد أخرى، لذا ينصح دائماً بسؤال عامل المطعم للتأكد من مكونات الطبق قبل طلبه.

Verwendungsweise dieses Buchs

Die Liste der Gerichte auf den Seiten 21 bis 43 gibt Ihnen einen vollständige Überblick über die in diesem Führer vorgestellten Gerichte, so daß Sie bei der Bestellung einfach darauf zeigen können. Eine genauere Beschreibung der einzelnen Gerichte finden Sie auf den Seiten, die in den Fotografien angegeben sind. Zur leichteren Orientierung sind, wie in nachfolgendem Beispiel gezeigt, jeweils auf einer Seite in graphischer Form die Hauptzutaten angegeben, die in den einzelnen Gerichten verwendet werden, insbesondere bei scharf gewürzten Speisen. Außerdem erhalten Sie Auskunft über die darin enthaltenen Kalorien und ein ungefähres Preisniveau. Schließlich finden Sie auf den Seiten 44 bis 53 Beispiele in jeder Sprache für grundlegende Redewendungen und Gespräche, die häufig in Restaurants verwendet werden, damit Ihr Essen zu einem wirklich angenehmen Erlebnis wird.

Bezeichnung des Gerichtes auf englisch

Bezeichnung des Gerichtes in der jeweiligen Landessprache

Preisangaben

Preisgünstige Gerichte
Gerichte der mittleren Preisklasse
Teure Gerichte

Symbole der Zutaten

Rind
Schwein
Rind oder Schwein
Huhn
Geflügel, (außer Huhn)
Fisch
Garnelen
Krebs
Tintenfisch
Muscheln
Tofu (Sojabohnenquark)
Gemüse

Scharf gewürzte Gerichte

Kalorienangaben (pro Person)

kcal
● 0kcal ～ 200kcal
●● 200kcal ～ 400kcal
●●● 400kcal ～ 600kcal
●●●● 600kcal ～

Arten von Gerichten

Gerichte mit Fleisch
Gerichte mit Seefrüchten
Gerichte mit Gemüse
Suppen
Gerichte mit Reis
Gerichte mit Nudeln
Beilagen (Dim Sum)
Eintopfgerichte
Nachspeisen
Getränke

88 Braised Bean Curd with Chili Sauce

麻婆豆腐（Ma Po Dou Fu）

Braised Bean Curd with Chili Sauce
This typical Szechwan dish features
brai... Erläuterungen auf ...at
flav... englisch ...er
spi... ...ith
corr... ...at
brings out the appetite.

kcal ●●

麻婆豆腐
Erläuterung auf chinesisch
(traditionelle chinesische Schriftzeichen)

Geschmorter Tofu mit Chili-Soße
Dies ist ein typisches Gericht der Szechwan-Küche.
G... Erläuterung auf deutsch ...d
ar... Stärke gebunden werden, bieten eine Kombination,
die so richtig Appetit macht.

麻婆豆腐
Erläuterung auf chinesisch
(vereinfachte chinesische Schriftzeichen)

Pâte de soja braisée à la sauce pimentée
Cette spécialité du Sichuan se compose de tofu braisé
et de vi... sauce
à base Erläuterung auf l'on a
épaissi français ...enir un
mélang...

마파두부
두부와 다진 고기를 볶어어 두반장으로 맛
Erläuterung auf koreanisch

Salteado de Cuajada de Soja con Salsa Picante
Este platillo típico de Szechwan se caracteriza por el
... Erläuterung auf spanisch ...n
... salsa picante y otros condimentos.

マーボー豆腐
豆腐、ひき肉を炒めて豆板醤などで味付け
Erläuterung auf japanisch

Brasato di tofu in salsa piccante doban djan
Questo piatto tipico della regione di Szechwan viene
pre... Erläuterung auf italienisch ...on
sal... ...poi
aggiungendo il tutto con fecola, il suo sapore piccante
stuzzica l'appetito.

توفو مطهو مع صلصة الفلفل الأحمر
هذا الطبق الشعبي من إقليم سشسوان يتكون من قطع من التوفو
ظا... Erläuterung auf arabisch ...ط
ح... ...
في اسهله على ضوء مريح جريب يبجر سهله...

Queijo de soja refogado com molho de pimenta
Este prato típico de Szech Wan é feito com tofu e
carne Erläuterung auf nês e
condim... portugiesisch outros
temper... ...ar uma
iguaria picante, que despertá o apetite.

Die verwendeten Zutaten und Preise hängen in starkem Maße vom jeweiligen Restaurant ab. Wir empfehlen Ihnen, daß Sie - falls möglich - Einzelheiten über die Zutaten und Preise vom Kellner erfragen, ehe Sie Ihre Bestellung aufgeben. Die in der jeweiligen Speise enthaltene Kalorienzahl kann ebenfalls entsprechend der Art und der Menge der verwendeten Zutaten abweichen. Die Kalorienangaben in diesem Buch haben lediglich den Zweck, Ihnen einen allgemeinen Eindruck vom Kaloriengehalt des jeweiligen Gerichtes zu verschaffen.

Comment utiliser ce guide

Les pages 21 à 43 sont consacrées à une liste complète des plats présentés dans ce guide pour vous permettre de passer plus facilement votre commande. Pour une explication plus détaillée des plats de cette liste, se reporter au numéro de page indiqué sur la photo. Les principaux ingrédients composant chacun des plats, le prix, la valeur calorique et le degré d'assaisonnement en épices sont résumés dans un tableau graphique après chaque page comme illustré ci-dessous. De plus, en pages 44 à 53, nous avons rassemblé les phrases et les mots élémentaires généralement utilisés dans les restaurants pour vous faciliter les relations avec vos hôtes.

Nom du plat en anglais

Nom du plat dans le pays correspondant

Index des prix

- Plats bon marché
- Plats à prix moyen
- Plats onéreux

Symboles des ingrédients

- Bœuf
- Porc
- Bœuf ou porc
- Poulet
- Volaille (autre que le poulet)
- Poisson
- Crevettes
- Crabe
- Calmars
- Crustacés
- Tofu (pâté de soja)
- Légumes

- Plats épicés

Indicateur de calories (par personne)

kcal
- 0kcal ～ 200kcal
- 200kcal ～ 400kcal
- 400kcal ～ 600kcal
- 600kcal ～

Types de plats

- Viande
- Fruits de mer
- Légumes
- Soupes
- Riz
- Nouilles
- Accompagnement (Dim Sum)
- Plats complets
- Desserts
- Boissons

---

88 Braised Bean Curd with Chili Sauce

麻婆豆腐 （Ma Po Dou Fu）

Braised Bean Curd with Chili Sauce

This typical Szechwan dish features braised tofu and stir-fried ground meat Explications en anglais cornstarch for a spicy combination that brings out the appetite.

kcal ••

麻婆豆腐
Explications en chinois
(caractères chinois traditionnels)

Geschmorter Tofu mit Chili-Soße
Dies ist ein typisches Gericht der Szechwan-Küche. Explications en allemand Stärke gebunden werden, bieten eine Kombination, die so richtig Appetit macht.

麻婆豆腐
Explications en chinois
(caractères chinois simplifiés)

Pâte de soja braisée à la sauce pimentée
Cette spécialité du Sichuan se compose de tofu braisé à l Explications en français mélange piquant qui ouvre l'appétit.

마파두부
Explications en coréen

Salteado de Cuajada de Soja con Salsa Picante
Este platillo típico de Szechwan se caracteriza por el Explications en espagnol salsa picante y otros condimentos.

マーボー豆腐
Explications en japonais

Brasato di tofu in salsa piccante doban djan
Questo piatto tipico della regione di Szechwan viene Explications en italien stuzzica l'appetito.

توفو مطهو مع صلصة الفلفل الإحمر
Explications en arabe

Queijo de soja refogado com molho de pimenta
Este prato típico de Szech Wan é feito com tofu e Explications en portugais iguaria picante, que desperta o apetite.

Les ingrédients utilisés ainsi que les prix pratiqués ont tendance à varier selon les restaurants. Nous vous recommandons de vous informer auprès du serveur sur les ingrédients et les prix avant de passer votre commande. Le nombre de calories contenues dans un plat particulier peut également varier suivant la quantité d'ingrédients employés. Les indicateurs de calories contenus dans ce livre ont pour but de vous fournir des indications générales sur le nombre de calories contenues dans chaque plat.

Cómo usar este libro

En la Lista de Platillos de las páginas 21 a 43 se encuentra una lista completa de los platillos presentados en esta guía para que Usted pueda señalarlos en el momento de ordenar. Haga el favor de consultar los números de página escritos al pie de las fotografías para obtener una explicación más detallada de cada platillo. Para hacer más fácil la consulta, se muestran en forma gráfica los principales ingredientes empleados en cada comida, especialmente los alimentos aromáticos, así como su precio e indicadores de calorías. Del mismo modo, para garantizar una experiencia fabulosa al cenar en un restaurante, las páginas 44 a 53 contienen ejemplos en cada idioma sobre las frases básicas y el tipo de conversación que se emplea frecuentemente en los restaurantes.

Nombre del platillo en inglés ——

Nombre del platillo en el país correspondiente ——

Indicador de Precios ——

- Platillos Económicos
- Platillos de Precio Moderado
- Platillos Caros

Símbolos de los ingredientes ——

- Res
- Cerdo
- Res o Cerdo
- Pollo
- Aves de Corral (excepto el pollo)
- Pescado
- Camarón
- Cangrejo
- Calamar
- Mariscos
- Tofu (Queso de Soja)
- Verduras

Platillos Fragantes

Indicador de Calorías (por persona) ——

kcal
- 0kcal ~ 200kcal
- 200kcal ~ 400kcal
- 400kcal ~ 600kcal
- 600kcal ~

Clases de Alimentos ——

88 Braised Bean Curd with Chili Sauce

麻婆豆腐（Ma Po Dou Fu）

Braised Bean Curd with Chili Sauce
This typical Szechwan dish features braised tofu and stir-fried ground meat... Explicación en inglés ... cornstarch for a spicy combination that brings out the appetite.

kcal ●●

麻婆豆腐
将味菜 Explicación en chino (caracteres chinos tradicionales)

Geschmorter Tofu mit Chili-Soße
Dies ist ein typisches Gericht der Szechwan-Küche. Ge... Explicación en alemán ...und pfa... anderen Gewürzen abgeschmeckt und dann mit Stärke gebunden werden, bieten eine Kombination, die so richtig Appetit macht.

麻婆豆腐
将味麻 Explicación en chino (caracteres chinos simplificados)

Pâte de soja braisée à la sauce pimentée
Cette spécialité du Sichuan se compose de tofu braisé et... Explicación en francés ...uce à l... épaisse avec de la farine de maïs, afin d'obtenir un mélange piquant qui ouvre l'appétit.

마파두부
Explicación en coreano

Salteado de Cuajada de Soja con Salsa Picante
Este platillo típico de Szechwan se caracteriza por lo es... Explicación en español ...on un adobo concentrado de maicena, hecho a base de salsa picante y otros condimentos.

マーボー豆腐
豆腐、ひき肉を炒めて豆板醤などで味付け Explicación en japonés

Brasato di tofu in salsa piccante doban djan
Questo piatto tipico della regione di Szechwan viene pre... Explicación en italiano ...con sal... adensan... il tutto con fecola. Il suo sapore piccante stuzzica l'appetito.

توفو مطهو مع صلصة الفلفل الأحمر
هذا الطبق الشعبي من إقليم سشتشوان يتكون من قطع من التوفو Explicación en árabe تطهى في النهاية على مزيج خفيف حريف يثير الشهية.

Queijo de soja refogado com molho de pimenta
Este prato típico de Szech Wan é feito com tofu e... Explicación en portugués ...s temperos. Engrossa-se com amido para tornar uma iguaria picante, que desperta o apetite.

- Platillos de Carne
- Platillos de Mariscos
- Platillos de Verduras
- Sopas
- Platillos de Arroz
- Platillos de Fideos Chinos
- Platillos de Acompañamiento (Dim Sum)
- Platillos en cazuela
- Postres
- Bebidas

Los ingredientes usados y los precios tienden a cambiar según el restaurante que se visite. Le recomendamos que pregunte al camarero los ingredientes y los precios antes de ordenar. Del mismo modo, la cantidad de calorías que contiene un platillo en particular puede variar según el tipo y la cantidad de ingredientes usados. Los indicadores de calorías en este libro tienen la intención de proporcionar a usted una observación general de la cantidad de calorías que contiene un platillo en particular.

Come usare questa guida

Nelle liste dei piatti (P.21-P.43) abbiamo inserito tutti i piatti presentati in questa guida in modo che sia possibile ordinarli indicandoli con il dito. Per i particolari, vedere la pagina indicata in calce alle foto. Nella pagina di ogni piatto sono graficamente indicati nel modo seguente, comprensibile a colpo d'occhio, i principali ingredienti usati, il prezzo, le calorie, i piatti piccanti. Da P.44 a P.53 abbiamo poi riportato delle frasi di conversazione elementare da usare nei ristoranti, che Vi preghiamo di voler utilizzare.

Nome del piatto in inglese

Nome del piatto nel corrispondente paese

Prezzi indicativi

- Piatti economici
- Piatti mediamente cari
- Piatti cari

Ingredienti principali

- Carne bovina
- Maiale
- Carne bovina o maiale
- Pollo
- Altri volatili
- Pesce
- Gamberetti
- Granchi
- Seppie
- Molluschi e crostacei
- Tofu (latte di soia cagliato)
- Verdure
- Piatti particolarmente piccanti

Calorie indicative (per persona)

kcal
- 0kcal ~ 200kcal
- •• 200kcal ~ 400kcal
- ••• 400kcal ~ 600kcal
- •••• 600kcal ~

Generi ci cucina

---

88 Braised Bean Curd with Chili Sauce

麻婆豆腐（Ma Po Dou Fu）

Braised Bean Curd with Chili Sauce

This typical Szechwan dish features braised tofu and stir-fried ground meat
Spiegazione in inglese
cornstarch for a spicy combination that brings out the appetite.

kcal ••

麻婆豆腐
將豆腐和肉末炒在一起爆炒後，用豆瓣醬調
味菜
Spiegazione in cinese
(ideogrammi tradizionali)
四川

Geschmorter Tofu mit Chili-Soße

Dies ist ein typisches Gericht der Szechwan-Küche.
Spiegazione in tedesco
anderen Gewürzen abgeschmeckt und dann mit
Stärke gebunden werden, bieten eine Kombination,
die so richtig Appetit macht.

麻婆豆腐
將豆腐和肉末炒在一起爆炒後，用豆瓣醬調
味麻
Spiegazione in cinese
(ideogrammi semplificati)

Pâte de soja braisée à la sauce pimentée

Cette spécialité du Sichuan se compose de tofu braisé
et
à t
Spiegazione in francese
épaissie avec de la farine de maïs, afin d'obtenir un
mélange piquant qui ouvre l'appétit.

마파두부
도브어 다진 고기를 보아다 드바자으 아
Spiegazione in coreano

Salteado de Cuajada de Soja con Salsa Picante

Este platillo típico de Szechwan se caracteriza por el
Spiegazione in spagnolo
un adobo concentrado de maicena, hecho a base de
salsa picante y otros condimentos.

マーボー豆腐
豆腐。ひき肉を炒めて豆板醤などで味付け
Spiegazione in giapponese

Brasato di tofu in salsa piccante doban djan

Questo piatto tipico della regione di Szechwan viene
sal
Spiegazione in italiano
addensando il tutto con fecola, ha un sapore piccante
stuzzica l'appetito.

توفو مطهو مع صلصة الفلفل الأحمر
Spiegazione in arabo

Queijo de soja refogado com molho de pimenta

Este prato típico de Szech Wan é feito com tofu e
Spiegazione in portoghese
temperos. Engrossa-se com amido para formar uma
iguaria picante, que desperta o apetite.

- Piatti di carne
- Piatti di pesce e frutti di mare
- Piatti di verdura
- Minestre
- Piatti di riso
- Piatti di pasta
- Spuntini
- Piatti in pignatta
- Dessert
- Bevande

Ingredienti e prezzi possono variare a seconda del ristorante. Consigliamo di accertarsi con il personale. Poiché il contenuto calorico varia a seconda del tipo e della quantità degli ingredienti, i valori sono puramente indicativi.

Como usar este guia

A "Lista de pratos", da página 21 à 43, relaciona todos os pratos apresentados neste guia, para que você possa indicá-los ao fazer seu pedido. Veja nas fotos o número da página que traz mais informações detalhadas sobre cada prato. Os ingredientes principais utilizados, os indicadores de preço e calorias, e o sabor especialmente picante de determinado prato, são mostrados de forma gráfica em cada página, como aparece aqui abaixo, para facilitar a consulta. Além disso, exemplos de expressões básicas e diálogos freqüentemente usados em restaurantes são apresentados em cada idioma, da página 44 à 53, para assegurar que seu maior prazer à mesa.

Nome do prato em inglês —

Nome do prato no país de origem —

Indicador de preço —

- Pratos baratos
- Pratos de preço médio
- Pratos caros

Símbolos dos ingredientes —

- Carne bovina
- Carne de porco
- Carne de gado ou de porco
- Frango
- Ave (excetuando-se frango)
- Peixe
- Camarão
- Caranguejo
- Lula
- Mariscos
- Tofu (queijo de soja)
- Vegetais

Pratos picantes

Indicador de calorias (por pessoa) —

kcal		
••	0kcal	~ 200kcal
••	200kcal	~ 400kcal
•••	400kcal	~ 600kcal
••••	600kcal	~

88 Braised Bean Curd with Chili Sauce

麻婆豆腐（Ma Po Dou Fu）

Braised Bean Curd with Chili Sauce
This typical Szechwan dish features braised tofu and stir-fried ground meat
fla Descrição em inglês er
sp th
cornstarch for a spicy combination that brings out the appetite.

kcal ••

麻婆豆腐
将豆腐和肉末放在一起爆炒後，用豆瓣醬調 四川
味菜
Descrição em chinês
(caracteres chineses tradicionais)

麻婆豆腐
将豆腐和肉末放在一起爆炒后，用豆瓣酱调 [菜‧
味麻
Descrição em chinês
(caracteres chineses simplificados)

마파두부
두부와 다진 고기를 볶아서 두반장으로 맛
Descrição em coreano 인 다.

マーボー豆腐
豆腐、ひき肉を炒めて豆板醤などで味付け
Descrição em japonês

توفو مطهو مع صلصة الفلفل الأحمر
هذا الطبق الشعبي من إقليم سشنوان يتكون من قطع من التوفو
المطهي
Descrição em árabe
في النهاية على مزيج حريف يثير شهية.

Geschmorter Tofu mit Chili-Soße
Dies ist ein typisches Gericht der Szechwan-Küche.
Ge nd
pfa Descrição em alemão und
anderen Gewürzen abgeschmeckt und dann mit
Stärke gebunden werden, bieten eine Kombination,
die so richtig Appetit macht.

Pâte de soja braisée à la sauce pimentée
Cette spécialité du Sichuan se compose de tofu braisé
et c uce
à b Descrição em francês n a
épaisse avec de la farine de maïs, qui d obtient un
mélange piquant qui ouvre l'appétit.

Salteado de Cuajada de Soja con Salsa Picante
Este platillo típico de Szechwan se caracteriza por el
qu on
un Descrição em espanhol
un adobo concentrado de maicena, hecho a base de
salsa picante y otros condimentos.

Brasato di tofu in salsa piccante doban djan
Questo piatto tipico della regione di Szechwan viene
pre con
sal Descrição em italiano poi
addensando il tutto con fecola. Il suo sapore piccante
stuzzica l'appetito.

Queijo de soja refogado com molho de pimenta
Este prato típico de Szech Wan é feito com tofu e
s
Descrição em português
temperos. Engrossa-se com amido para formar uma
iguaria picante, que desperta o apetite.

Tipos de pratos —

- Pratos com carne
- Pratos com frutos do mar
- Pratos com vegetais
- Sopas
- Pratos com arroz
- Pratos com macarrão oriental
- Pratos secundários (Dim Sum)
- Pratos de caçarola
- Sobremesas
- Bebidas

Os ingredientes utilizados nas iguarias e o seu preço costumam variar segundo cada restaurante. Recomendamos ao leitor que se informe sobre os ingredientes e o preço com o garçom, antes de fazer o pedido. Também o número de calorias de cada prato varia conforme o tipo e a quantidade de ingredientes utilizados. O indicador de calorias apresentado neste guia visa oferecer uma referência aproximada sobre o número de calorias que cada prato contém.

LIST OF CHINESE FOODS

中國菜菜單
中国菜菜单
중국요리 일람
中国料理一覧
قائمة المأكولات الصينية
Liste der chinesischen Gerichte
Liste des plats chinois
Lista de Platillos Chinos
Lista di piatti cinesi
Lista de pratos chineses

---

56 青椒牛肉絲

- **Stir-Fried Shredded Beef and Green Peppers**
- 青椒牛肉絲 ● 青椒牛肉丝
- 피망쇠고기볶음
- ピーマンと牛肉の細切り炒め
- شرائح محمرة من اللحم البقري والفلفل الأخضر
- Pfannengerührtes, kleingeschnittenes Rindfleisch und grüne Paprikaschoten
- Sauté de bœuf et de poivrons verts en lamelles
- Salteado de Carne de Res y Pimiento Morrón
- Sauté di striscioline di manzo e peperoni verdi
- Tiras finas de carne e pimentão refogadas

---

57 蠔油牛肉

- **Stir-Fried Beef and Vegetables in Oyster Sauce**
- 蠔油牛肉 ● 蚝油牛肉
- 쇠고기와 야채의 굴소스볶음
- 牛肉と野菜のオイスターソース炒め
- لحم بقري وخضر محمرة في صلصة المحار
- Pfannengerührtes Rindfleisch und Gemüse in Austernsoße
- Sauté de bœuf et de légumes à la sauce d'huîtres
- Salteado de Carne de Res y Verduras en Salsa de Ostras
- Sauté di manzo e verdure in salsa di ostriche
- Carne e vegetais refogados com molho de ostra

---

58 洋蔥牛肉絲

- **Stir-Fried Beef and Onions**
- 洋蔥牛肉絲
- 洋葱牛肉絲
- 쇠고기양파볶음
- 牛肉と玉ねぎの炒めもの
- خليط محمر من اللحم البقري والبصل
- Pfannengerührtes Rindfleisch mit Zwiebeln
- Sauté de bœuf et d'oignons
- Salteado de Carne de Res y Cebollas
- Sauté di manzo e cipolle
- Carne e cebolas refogados

---

59 紅燒牛肉

- **Simmered Beef in Soy Sauce**
- 紅燒牛肉
- 红烧牛肉
- 쇠고기간장조림
- 牛肉のしょうゆ煮込み
- لحم بقري مطهر مع صلصة الصويا
- Gesottenes Rindfleisch in Sojasoße
- Bœuf mijoté dans une sauce de soja
- Guisado de Carne de Res en Salsa de Soja
- Manzo bollito in salsa di soia
- Carne cozida com molho de soja

---

60 咕老肉

- **Sweet and Sour Pork**
- 咕老肉
- 咕老肉
- 탕수육
- 酢豚
- طبق حلو حامض من اللحم
- Süßsaures Schweinefleisch
- Porc à l'aigre-doux
- Cerdo Agridulce
- Maiale in agrodolce
- Carne de porco agridoce

---

61 回鍋肉

- **Stir-Fried Boiled Pork and Cabbage in Spicy Fermented Bean Paste**
- 回鍋肉 ● 回锅肉
- 삶은 돼지고기와 양배추의 매운 장볶음
- ゆで豚肉とキャベツの辛みそ炒め
- لحم محمر مع الكرنب في معجن الصويا
- Pfannengerührtes, gekochtes Schweinefleisch und Kohl in würziger Paste aus fermentierten Bohnen
- Sauté de porc et de chou bouilli à la pâte de soja fermenté parfumé au piment rouge
- Salteado de Cerdo y Col en Pasta Aromática de Soja Fermentada
- Sauté di maiale bollito con miso piccante
- Carne de porco e repolho refogados com molho picante

62

榨菜肉絲

- **Stir-Fried Meat with Szechwan Pickles**
- 榨菜肉絲　　　● 榨菜肉丝
- 짜새고기볶음
- ザーサイと肉の炒めもの
- لحم محمر مع مخلل ستشوان
- Pfannengerührtes Fleisch mit nach Szechwan Art eingelegten Senfwurzelknollen
- Sauté de viande accompagné de légumes au vinaigre de Sichuan
- Salteado de Carne con Tallo de Mostaza
- Sauté di carne con radice di senape in salamoia di szechwan
- Carne refogada ao estilo chinês com picles de Szech Wan

63

螞蟻上樹

- **Stir-Fried Bean Threads with Ground Pork**
- 螞蟻上樹　　　● 蚂蚁上树
- 당면과 다진 고기볶음
- 春雨とひき肉の炒めもの
- عيدان اللوبيا المحمرة مع اللحم المفري
- Pfannengerührte Glasnudeln mit Schweinehackfleisch
- Sauté de porc haché et de nouilles de haricots d'Orient
- Salteado de Fideos con Carne de Cerdo
- Sauté di vermicelli di fecola e carne di maiale tritata
- Fios gelatinosos refogados com carne de porco moída

64

炸肉丸子

- **Deep-Fried Ground Pork Dumplings**
- 炸肉丸子
- 炸肉丸子
- 고기완자튀김
- 揚げ肉団子
- كرات محمرة من اللحم المفري
- Fritierte Schweinehackfleischbällchen
- Boulettes de porc haché frites
- Albóndigas Chinas de Cerdo
- Polpettine di maiale fritte
- Almôndegas fritas de carne de porco

65

叉燒肉

- **Chinese Roast Pork**
- 叉燒肉
- 叉燒肉
- 구운 돼지고기
- 焼き豚
- روستو اللحم على الطريقة الصينية
- Geröstetes chinesisches Schweinefleisch
- Porc rôti à la chinoise
- Cerdo Chino Tostado
- Arrosto di maiale
- Carne de porco assada

66

雲白肉片

- **Boiled Pork with Garlic Sauce**
- 雲白肉片
- 云白肉片
- 마늘소스를 끼얹은 삶은 돼지고기
- ゆで豚のにんにくソースがけ
- لحم مسلوق مع صلصة الثوم
- Gekochtes Schweinefleisch mit Knoblauchsoße
- Porc bouilli à la sauce à l'ail
- Cocido de Cerdo con Salsa de Ajo
- Bollito di maiale con salsa all'aglio
- Carne de porco fervida com molho de alho

67

北京烤鴨

- **Peking Duck**
- 北京烤鴨
- 北京烤鸭
- 북경식 오리구이
- アヒルの直火焼き（ペキンダック）
- البط البكيني
- Peking-Ente
- Canard à la pékinoise
- Pato Pequinés
- Anatra alla pechinese
- Pato de Pequim

68

腰果雞丁

- **Stir-Fried Chicken and Cashews**
- 腰果雞丁
- 腰果鸡丁
- 닭고기캐슈너트볶음
- 鶏とカシューナッツの炒めもの
- دجاج محمر مع الكاشوناتا
- Pfannengerührtes Hühnerfleisch mit Cashew-Nüssen
- Sauté de poulet et de noix de cajou
- Salteado de Pollo y Nueces de Acajú
- Sauté di pollo e mandorle indiane
- Frango xadrez

69

油淋子雞

- **Crispy Fried Chicken with Fragrant Sauce**
- 油淋子雞
- 油淋子鸡
- 양념소스를 끼얹은 닭튀김(깐풍기)
- 揚げ鶏の香味ソースがけ
- دجاج محمر هش مع صلصة طيبة الرائحة
- Kroß gebratenes Hühnerfleisch mit würziger Soße
- Poulet frit croustillant à la sauce parfumée
- Pollo Frito en Salsa Fragante
- Pollo fritto in salsa aromatica
- Frango frito crocante com molho aromático

70

棒棒雞

- **Steamed Cold Chicken with Sesame Sauce**
- 棒棒雞
- 棒棒鸡
- 참깨소스를 끼얹은 삶은 닭고기
- 蒸し鶏のごまダレがけ
- دجاج بارد مغلي بصلصة السمسم
- Gedünstetes kaltes Huhn mit Sesamsoße
- Poulet froid cuit à la vapeur aromatisé à la sauce au sésame
- Pollu al Vapor en Salsa de Sésamo
- Pollo cotto a vapore in salsa di sesamo
- Frango frio cozido em vapor com molho de gergelim

71 炸雞塊

Chinese-Style Fried Chicken
- 炸雞塊
- 炸鸡块
- 닭튀김
- 鶏の唐揚げ
- دجاج محمر على الطريقة الصينية
- Gebratenes Hühnchen nach chinesischer Art
- Poulet frit à la chinoise
- Pollo Frito al Estilo Chino
- Pollo fritto alla cinese
- Frango frito ao estilo chinês

72 三色拼盆

Assorted Cold Plate Appetizer
- 三色拼盆
- 三色拼盆
- 삼품전채 (삼품냉채)
- 三種前菜の盛り合わせ
- تشكيلة من المشهيات الباردة
- Appetitanregende gemischte kalte Platte
- Hors-d'œuvre variés
- Entremés Combinado
- Misto di antipasti freddi
- Entrada sortida servida fria

73 清蒸鮮魚

Steamed Fish
- 清蒸鮮魚
- 清蒸鲜鱼
- 생선찜
- 魚の姿蒸し
- سمك مطهو على البخار
- Gedünsteter Fisch mit weißem Fleisch
- Poisson vapeur
- Pescado al Vapor
- Pesce intero cotto a vapore
- Peixe cozido em vapor

74 幹燒蝦仁

Shrimp with Spicy Tomato Sauce
- 幹燒蝦仁
- 干烧虾仁
- 새우칠리소스
- えびのチリソース
- جمبري بصلصة الطماطم الحريفة
- Garnelen mit scharfer Tomatensoße
- Crevettes à la sauce tomate piquante
- Langostinos con Salsa Picante de Tomate
- Gamberetti in salsa piccante di pomodoro
- Camarão com molho de tomate picante

75 青豆蝦仁

Stir-Fried Shrimp with Green Peas
- 青豆蝦仁
- 青豆虾仁
- 보리새우와 그린피스볶음
- 芝えびとグリンピースの炒めもの
- جمبري محمر مع البازلاء الخضراء
- Pfannengerührte Garnelen mit grünen Erbsen
- Sauté de crevettes accompagnées de petits pois
- Salteado de Langostinos con Guisantes
- Gamberetti saltati con piselli
- Camarões refogados com ervilhas

76 高麗蝦仁

Batter-Fried Shrimp
- 高麗蝦仁
- 高丽虾仁
- 새우 달걀흰자튀김
- えびの卵白揚げ
- جمبري مغلف ومحمر
- In Teig fritierte Garnelen
- Crevettes frites
- Langostinos Rebozados
- Gamberetti fritti in albume
- Camarões empanados

77 海蜇皮

Jellyfish Salad
- 海蜇皮
- 海蜇皮
- 중국식 해파리무침
- くらげの中華風あえもの
- سلطة قنديل البحر
- Quallensalat
- Salade de méduse
- Medusa a la Vinagreta
- Insalata di meduse
- Salada de medusa

78 海鮮粉絲

Stir-Fried Seafood and Bean Threads
- 海鮮粉絲
- 海鲜粉丝
- 해산물 당면볶음
- 海の幸と春雨の炒め煮
- قواقع البحر المحمرة مع عيدان اللوبيا
- Pfannengerührte Seefrüchte mit Glasnudeln
- Sauté de fruits de mer et de nouilles de haricots d'Orient
- Salteado de Mariscos con Fideos de Soja
- Sauté di frutti di mare e vermicelli di fecola
- Frutos do mar e fios gelatinosos refogados

79 芙蓉蟹

Egg Foo Yung
- 芙蓉蟹
- 芙蓉蟹
- 게살을 넣은 달걀부침
- かに玉
- بيض فو يون
- Foo Yung-Eier
- Foo Yung aux œufs
- Tortilla de Cangrejo
- Uova foo yung
- Caranguejo com ovos

80

八寶菜

- Stir-Fried Combination
- 八寶菜
- 八宝菜
- 꽐보채
- 八宝菜
- طبق من خليط محضر
- Pfannengerührte Kombination
- Mélange sauté
- Combinación Salteada
- Sauté misto
- Refogado de carne, frutos do mar e vegetais

81

炒青菜

- Sauteed Vegetables
- 炒青菜
- 炒青菜
- 푸른채소볶음
- 青菜の炒めもの
- خضر سوتيه
- Sautiertes Gemüse
- Sauté de légumes
- Verduras Salteadas
- Sauté di verdure
- Verduras ligeiramente refogadas

82

奶油白菜

- Chinese Cabbage in Cream Sauce
- 奶油白菜
- 奶油白菜
- 배추의 크림수프
- 白菜のクリーム煮
- كرنب صيني مع صلصة بيضاء
- Chinakohl in Sahnesoße
- Chou chinois à la crème
- Col China en Salsa Cremosa
- Cavolo cinese in salsa cremosa
- Repolho-chinês em molho cremoso

83

木樨肉

- Stir-Fried Egg and Vegetables
- 木樨肉
- 木樨肉
- 달걀과 야채볶음
- 炒り卵と野菜の炒めもの
- بيض مقلي مع الخضروات
- Pfannengerührte Eier und Gemüse
- Sauté d'œufs et de légumes
- Revuelto de Huevo con Verduras
- Uova strapazzate con verdure
- Ovos e vegetais refogados

84

魚香茄子

- Szechwan-Style Stir-Fried Eggplant
- 魚香茄子
- 鱼香茄子
- 사천풍 가지볶음
- なすの四川風炒め
- باذنجان محمر على طريقة ستشوان
- Pfannengerührte Auberginen nach Szechwan-Art
- Sauté d'aubergines à la mode du Sichuan
- Salteado de Berenjena al Estilo Szechwan
- Melanzane saltate alla szechwan
- Beringela refogada ao estilo Szech Wan

85

油淋茄子

- Deep-Fried Eggplant with Fragrant Sauce
- 油淋茄子
- 油淋茄子
- 양념소스를 끼얹은 가지튀김
- 揚げなすの香味ソースがけ
- باذنجان مقلي مع صلصة طيبة الرائحة
- Fritierte Auberginen mit duftender Soße
- Aubergines frites en sauce parfumée
- Berenjena Frita en la Salsa Fragante
- Melanzane fritte in salsa odorosa
- Beringela frita com molho aromático

86

辣黃瓜

- Szechwan Cucumber Slices
- 辣黃瓜
- 辣黃瓜
- 중국식 오이김치
- きゅうりのピリ辛漬け
- شرائح الخيار على طريقة ستشوان
- Gurkenscheiben nach Szechwan-Art
- Concombres du Sichuan en lamelles
- Adobado de Pepino
- Cetrioli piccanti alla szechwan
- Pepino ao estilo de Szech Wan fatiado

87

涼拌豆腐

- Chinese-Style Cold Seasoned Bean Curd
- 涼拌豆腐
- 涼拌豆腐
- 중국식 냉두부
- 中華風冷や奴
- توفر بارد متبل على الطريقة الصينية
- Kalter gewürzter Tofu nach chinesischer Art
- Pâte de soja à la chinoise
- Queso de Soja al Estilo Chino
- Tofu freddo alla cinese
- Queijo de soja frio, condimentado

88

麻婆豆腐

- Braised Bean Curd with Chili Sauce
- 麻婆豆腐
- 麻婆豆腐
- 마파두부
- マーボー豆腐
- توفر مطهر مع صلصة الفلفل الاحمر
- Geschmorter Tofu mit Chili-Soße
- Pâte de soja braisée à la sauce pimentée
- Salteado de Cuajada de Soja con Salsa Picante
- Brasato di tofu in salsa piccante doban djan
- Queijo de soja refogado com molho de pimenta

89

家常豆腐

- **Fried Bean Curd with Meat and Vegetables**
- 家常豆腐
- 家常豆腐
- 뛰긴 두부종임
- 揚げ豆腐の炒め煮
- توفو محمر مع لحم وخضر
- Gebratener Tofu mit Fleisch und Gemüse
- Pâte de soja frite accompagnée de viande et de légumes
- Queso de Soja Frito con Carne y Verduras
- Tofu fritto con carne e verdure
- Queijo de soja frito com carne e vegetais

90

什錦鍋巴

- **Crispy Rice with Meat and Vegetable Sauce**
- 什錦鍋巴
- 什锦锅巴
- 삼선 누룽지탕
- おこげの五目あんかけ
- أرز محمص مع صلصة اللحم والخضروات
- Knspriger Reis mit Fleisch und Gemüsesoße
- Riz croustillant accompagné d'une sauce à la viande et aux légumes
- Arroz Tostado con Salsa de Carne y Verduras
- Riso fritto croccante in salsa di carne e verdure
- Arroz frito com molho de carne e vegetais

91

蛋花湯

- **Egg Drop Soup**
- 蛋花湯
- 蛋花汤
- 달걀수프
- かき卵のスープ
- حساء فطرات البيض
- Suppe mit Eieinlage
- Soupe aux œufs filés
- Sopa de Gotas de Huevo
- Stracciatella
- Sopa com ovos escaldados

92

玉米羹

- **Chinese-Style Corn Soup**
- 玉米羹
- 玉米羹
- 중국식 옥수수수프
- 中華風コーンスープ
- حساء كريمة الذرة على الطريقة الصينية
- Maissuppe nach chinesischer Art
- Soupe de maïs à la chinoise
- Crema de Maíz Estilo Chino
- Minestra di mais alla cinese
- Sopa de milho ao estilo chinês

93

酸辣湯

- **Szechwan Hot and Sour Soup**
- 酸辣湯
- 酸辣汤
- 사천풍 산미수프
- 四川風酸味スープ
- حساء ستشوان الحار بنكهة الخل
- Scharfsaure Suppe nach Szechwan-Art
- Soupe aigre et piquante à la Sichuan
- Sopa Agridulce de Szechwan
- Minestra all'agro di szechwan
- Sopa picante e azedinha de Szech Wan

94

榨菜肉絲湯

- **Szechwan Pickles and Pork Soup**
- 榨菜肉絲湯
- 榨菜肉丝汤
- 짝제 돼지고기수프
- ザーサイと豚肉のスープ
- حساء اللحم مع مخلل ستشوان
- Suppe mit nach Szechwan-Art eingelegten Senfwurzelknollen und Schweinefleisch
- Soupe de porc et de légumes au vinaigre du Sichuan marinés
- Sopa de Cerdo con Tallos de Mostaza Adobados
- Minestra di maiale e radice di senape in salamoia di szechwan
- Sopa de picles de Szech Wan e carne de porco

95

蟹粉魚翅湯

- **Shark's Fin Soup with Crab Meat**
- 蟹粉魚翅湯
- 蟹粉鱼翅汤
- 게살샤스펜수프
- かに入りふかひれスープ
- حساء زعانف القرش مع لحم الكابوريا
- Haifischflossensuppe mit Krebsfleisch
- Soupe aux ailerons de requin et au crabe
- Sopa de Aleta de Tiburón con Carne de Cangrejo
- Zuppa di pinne di pescecane e polpa di granchi
- Sopa de barbatana de tubarão com carne de caranguejo

96

什錦炒飯

- **Fried Rice**
- 什錦炒飯
- 什锦炒饭
- 볶음밥
- チャーハン
- أرز محمر
- Gebratener Reis
- Riz sauté
- Arroz Frito
- Riso fritto
- Arroz frito

97

牛肉燴飯

- **Beef and Vegetables in Oyster Sauce over Rice**
- 牛肉燴飯
- 牛肉烩饭
- 쇠고기덮밥
- 牛肉あんかけご飯
- لحم بقري وخضر بصلصة المحار مع الارز
- Rindfleisch und Gemüse in Austernsoße über Reis
- Bœuf et légumes à la sauce d'huîtres servis sur du riz
- Salteado de Carne de Res
- Riso coperto di manzo e verdure in salsa di ostriche
- Carne e vegetais em molho de ostra sobre arroz

98
什錦粥

- Assorted Rice Gruel
- 什錦粥
- 什锦粥
- 잡탕죽
- 五目がゆ
- أنواع من ثريد الارز
- Reissuppe mit verschiedenen Zutaten
- Gruau mixte de riz
- Puches de Arroz Combinado
- Minestra di riso con carne e verdure
- Mingau de arroz com ingredientes variados

99
什錦湯面

- Assorted Meat and Vegetable Stew with Noodles
- 什錦湯面
- 什锦汤面
- 잡탕면
- 五目そば
- ياخني اللحم والخضر مع حساء الشعرية
- Fleisch- und Gemüseeintopf mit Nudeln
- Ragoût de viande et de légumes mixtes accompagnés de nouilles
- Caldo de Fideos con Carne y Verduras
- Spaghettini in brodo con carne e verdure
- Sopa de macarrão chinês com molho de carne e vegetais cozidos

100
叉燒湯面

- Roasted Pork and Noodles
- 叉燒湯面
- 叉烧汤面
- 구운 돼지고기면
- チャーシュー麺
- روستو اللحم مع الشعرية
- Schweinerostbraten und Nudeln
- Porc rôti et nouilles
- Caldo de Fideos con Cerdo Asado
- Spaghettini con maiale arrosto
- Sopa de macarrão com porco assado

101
牛腩面（五花牛肉面）

- Szechwan-Style Beef and Noodles
- 牛腩面（五花牛肉面）
- 牛腩面（五花牛肉面）
- 쇠고기 중화면
- 牛バラ肉そば
- لحم بقري على طريقة ستشوان مع الشعرية
- Rindfleisch und Nudeln nach Szechwan-Art
- Bœuf et nouilles à la mode du Sichuan
- Caldo de Fideos con Carne de Res al Estilo Szechwan
- Spaghettini con pancetta di manzo
- Sopa de macarrão e carne ao estilo Szech Wan

102
排骨湯面

- Deep-Fried Pork Rib and Noodles
- 排骨湯面
- 排骨汤面
- 돼지갈비튀김 중화면
- 豚骨付き肉の唐揚げそば
- ضلع اللحم المحمر والشعرية
- Fritierte Schweinerippen und Nudeln
- Côte de porc frite et nouilles
- Caldo de Fideos con Costilla Frita de Cerdo
- Spaghettini con costolette di maiale fritte
- Sopa de macarrão chinês e costela de porco frita

103
雪菜肉絲面

- Mustard Greens and Shredded Pork Noodle Soup
- 雪菜肉絲面
- 雪菜肉丝面
- 갓과 채썬 돼지고기 중화면
- カラシ菜入り豚細切りそば
- حساء الشعرية مع اللحم وخيران المستردة
- Nudelsuppe mit eingelegten Senfwurzelknollen und kleingeschnittenem Schweinefleisch
- Soupe de nouilles et de lamelles de porc accompagnées de feuilles de moutarde
- Sopa de Fideos con Tallo de Mostaza y Cerdo
- Spaghettini con striscioline di maiale e cime di senape
- Sopa de macarrão chinês com folhas de mostarda e tiras finas de porco

104
擔擔面

- Szechwan Spicy Noodles
- 擔擔面
- 担担面
- 사천풍 매운맛 중화면
- 四川風辛味そば
- حساء الحريف مع الشعرية
- Scharfe Nudeln nach Szechwan-Art
- Nouilles du Sichuan relevées
- Caldo de Fideos Aromáticos de Szechwan
- Spaghettini piccanti alla szechwan
- Macarrão picante de Szech Wan

105
餛飩面

- Wonton Noodle Soup
- 餛飩面
- 馄饨面
- 완탕면
- ワンタン麺
- حساء الشعرية بالوانتان
- Wan-Tan-Nudelsuppe
- Soupe de nouilles au wonton
- Sopa de Fideos y Ravioles Chinos
- Spaghettini con won ton
- Sopa de macarrão com wonton

106
什錦炒面

- Fried Noodles with Meat and Vegetables
- 什錦炒面
- 什锦炒面
- 잡탕볶음면
- 五目あんかけ焼きそば
- شعرية محمرة مع لحم وخضر
- Gebratene Nudeln mit Fleisch und Gemüse
- Nouilles frites accompagnées de viande et de légumes
- Salteado de Fideos Chinos con Carne y Verduras
- Spaghettini fritti con carne e verdure in sugo denso
- Macarrão frito com carne e vegetais

107

廣東炒麵

- **Canton-Style Fried Noodles**
- 廣東炒麵
- 广东炒面
- 광둥식 볶음면
- 広東風炒めそば
- شعرية محمرة على طريقة الكانتون
- Gebratene Nudeln nach kantonesischer Art
- Nouilles frites à la cantonaise
- Fideos Fritos al Estilo Cantonés
- Spaghetti fritti alla cantonese
- Macarrão chinês frito ao estilo de Cantão

108

什錦炸麵

- **Deep-Fried Noodles with Meat and Vegetables in a Thick Sauce**
- 什錦炸麵
- 什錦炸麵
- 잡탕뒤김면
- 五目かた焼きそば
- شعرية محمرة مع لحم وخضر في صلصة سميكة
- Fritierte Nudeln mit Fleisch und Gemüse in dicker Soße
- Nouilles frites accompagnées d'une sauce épaisse à la viande et aux légumes
- Fideos Fritos con Carne y Verduras en una Salsa Espesa
- Spaghettini croccanti con carne e verdure in sugo denso
- Macarrão chinês frito com carne e vegetais em molho grosso

109

炒米粉

- **Stir-Fried Rice Vermicelli with Meat and Vegetables**
- 炒米粉
- 炒米粉
- 잡탕 쌀국수볶음
- 五目焼きビーフン
- شعرية الارز المحمرة مع اللحم والخضر
- Pfannengerührte Reis-Fadennudeln mit Fleisch und Gemüse
- Sauté de vermicelle de riz accompagné de viande et de légumes
- Salteado de Fideos Vermicelli con Carne y Verduras
- Vermicelli di riso saltati con carne e verdure
- Aletria de arroz com carnes e vegetais refogados

110

涼拌麵

- **Mixed Cold Noodles**
- 涼拌麵
- 涼拌麵
- 중국식 냉면
- 冷やし中華そば
- شعرية باردة مع خليط متبل
- Gemischte kalte Nudeln
- Mélange de nouilles froides
- Surtido de Fideos Chinos Fríos
- Spaghettini freddi
- Macarrão chinês misto, servido frio

111

春卷

- **Deep-Fried Spring Rolls**
- 春卷
- 春卷
- 춘권 (春卷)
- 春巻き
- ملفوف الرقاق المحمر
- Ausgebackene Frühlingsrollen
- Rouleaux de printemps frits
- Rollos Fritos
- Involtini primavera
- Rolinhos-primavera fritos

112

蛋皮春卷

- **Fried Egg Roll**
- 蛋皮春卷
- 蛋皮春卷
- 달걀말이튀김
- 薄焼き卵の巻き揚げ
- ملفوف البيض المقلي
- Gebratene Omelettrolle
- Rouleaux frits aux œufs
- Rollo Frito de Huevo
- Involtini di crespelle di uova ripieni
- Enrolado frito de ovos

113

燒賣

- **Steamed Dumplings**
- 燒賣
- 烧卖
- 슈마이
- シュウマイ
- محشوات مطهوة على البخار
- Gedünstete Fleischklößchen
- Petites poches de pâte farcies cuites à la vapeur
- Rellenos al Vapor
- Ravioli cotti a vapore
- Embrulhinhos cozidos em vapor

114

鍋貼餃子

- **Fried Dumplings**
- 鍋貼餃子
- 锅贴饺子
- 군만두
- 焼き餃子
- محشوات محمرة
- Gebratene Fleischklöße
- Raviolis frits
- Relleno Asado
- Ravioli fritti
- Pasteizinhos recheados ao estilo chinês

115

蝦餃

- **Steamed Shrimp Dumplings**
- 蝦餃
- 虾饺
- 새우만두
- えび入り蒸し餃子
- محشو الجمبري المطهو على البخار
- Gedünstete Garnelenklöße in Teigtaschen
- Boulettes de crevettes à la vapeur
- Relleno de Langostino al Vapor
- Ravioli di gamberetti cotti a vapore
- Pasteizinhos de camarão assados em vapor

116 韭菜餃

- **Chive Dumplings**
- 韭菜餃
- 韭菜饺
- 부추만두
- ニラ餃子
- محشوات الكرات
- Schnittlauchklößchen in Teigtaschen
- Boulettes à la ciboulette
- Relleno de Puerro
- Ravioli di verdura agliacea
- Pasteizinhos de alho-poró

117 小籠包

- **Steamed Juicy Pork Buns**
- 小籠包
- 小笼包
- 수프가 든 고기만두
- スープ入り肉まんじゅう
- محشو اللحم المطهو على البخار
- Gedünstete Teigtaschen mit saftigem Schweinefleisch
- Brioches de porc moelleux cuites à la vapeur
- Relleno Jugosos de Cerdo al Vapor
- Pagnottelle con ripieno di maiale al sugo
- Bolinhos suculentos de porco, assados em vapor

118 蘿蔔糕

- **Steamed Radish Cakes**
- 蘿蔔糕
- 萝卜糕
- 무떡
- 大根もち
- فطائر الفجل المطهوة على البخار
- Gedünsteter Rettichkuchen
- Gâteaux de radis à la vapeur
- Tortas de nabo al vapor
- Focaccine di rapa
- Tortas de nabo preparadas em vapor

119 叉燒包

- **Roasted Pork Buns**
- 叉燒包
- 叉烧包
- 구운 돼지고기만두
- チャーシューまん
- خبز محشو بروستو اللحم
- Teigtaschen mit Schweinerostbraten
- Brioches de porc rôti
- Relleno de Cerdo Asado
- Pagnottelle con ripieno di maiale arrosto
- Pão chinês recheado com porco assado

120 鹹水角

- **Glutinuous Rice Fried Dumplings**
- 鹹水角
- 咸水角
- 찹쌀튀김만두
- もち米粉の揚げ餃子
- محشوات مقلية من الارز اللدن
- Gefüllte gebratene Reisteigtaschen
- Boulettes frites de riz gluant
- Relleno Frito
- Ravioli di farina di riso fritti
- Bolinhos de arroz glutinoso fritos

121 腸粉

- **Steamed Rice Flour Sheets**
- 腸粉
- 肠粉
- 쩐 크레이프
- 米粉のクレープ蒸し
- رقائق دقيق الارز المحشوة والمطهوة على البخار
- Gedünstete Reisteigtaschen
- Feuilletés de farine de riz à la vapeur
- Crepa di Harina de Arroz
- Crespelle di farina di riso cotte a vapore
- Crepes de farinha de arroz assadas em vapor

122 珍珠丸子

- **Pearl Balls**
- 珍珠丸子
- 珍珠丸子
- 찹쌀경단
- もち米団子
- كرات اللؤلؤ
- Perlenkugeln
- Boules perlées
- Bolas Perla
- Palline di riso glutinoso
- Bolinhos de pérolas

123 豆豉排骨

- **Steamed Spareribs with Fermented Black Beans**
- 豆豉排骨　　　　　● 豆豉排骨
- 돼지갈비찜
- 豚スペアリブの豆豉蒸し
- ريش اللحم المطهوة على البخار مع الفول المتخمر
- Gedünsteter Rippenspeer mit fermentierten schwarzen Bohnen
- Côtelettes de porc et haricots noirs fermentés cuits à la vapeur
- Puntas de Costilla y Frijoles Negros al Vapor
- Costolette di maiale cotte a vapore
- Costela de porco com feijão preto fermentado, cozidos em vapor

124 花卷

- **Steamed Bread Rolls**
- 花卷
- 花卷
- 꽃빵
- 花巻き
- لفائف الخبز المطهوة على البخار
- Gedünstete Teigrollen
- Petits pains ronds à la vapeur
- Pan Chino
- Panini a forma di fiore
- Pãezinhos assados em vapor

125

西米露

- **Coconut Milk with Tapioca**
- 西米露
- 西米露
- 타피오카가 들어간 코코넛밀크
- タピオカ入りココナッツミルク
- لبن جوز الهند بالتابيوكة
- Kokosnußmilch mit Tapioca
- Lait de coco accompagné de tapioca
- Leche de Coco con Tapioca
- Latte di cocco con tapioca
- Leite de coco com tapioca

126

杏仁豆腐

- **Almond Jelly with Fruit**
- 杏仁豆腐
- 杏仁豆腐
- 안닝두부
- 杏仁豆腐
- جيلي اللوز بالفاكهة
- Mandelgelee mit Früchten
- Gelée d'amandes aux fruits
- Gelatina de Almendra con Fruta
- Gelatina di mandorle con frutta
- Gelatina de amêndoa com frutas

127

炸芝麻團

- **Deep-Fried Sesame Balls**
- 炸芝麻團
- 炸芝麻团
- 튀긴 참깨경단
- 揚げごま団子
- كرات السمسم المقلية
- Fritierte Sesambällchen
- Boules de sésame frites
- Bolas de sésamo fritas
- Palline fritte al sesamo
- Bolinhos de gergelim fritos

128

馬拉糕

- **Chinese Sponge Cake**
- 馬拉糕
- 马拉糕
- 중국식 카스델라
- 中国風蒸しカステラ
- كعكة اسفنجية على الطريقة الصينية
- Chinesischer Bisquitkuchen
- Gâteau chinois moelleux
- Biscocho Chino
- Pan di spagna cinese cotto a vapore
- Pão-de-ló chinês

129

芒果布丁

- **Mango Pudding**
- 芒果布丁
- 芒果布丁
- 망고 푸딩
- マンゴープリン
- بودنج المانجو
- Mango-Pudding
- Pudding à la mangue
- Budín de Mango
- Budino di mango
- Pudim de manga

130

蛋撻

- **Egg Tart**
- 蛋撻
- 蛋挞
- 에그 타르트
- エッグタルト
- كعك البيض
- Eiertörtchen
- Tarte aux œufs
- Tarta de Huevo
- Crostata di uova
- Torta de ovos

LIST OF KOREAN FOODS

韓國・朝鮮菜菜單
韩国・朝鲜菜菜单
한국・조선요리 일람
韓国・朝鮮料理一覧
قائمة المأكولات الكورية
Liste der koreanischen Gerichte
Liste des plats coréens
Lista de Platillos Coreanos
Lista di piatti sudcoreani e nordcoreani
Lista de pratos coreanos

142 불고기

Stir-Fried Beef Slices
- 炒牛肉片
- 炒牛肉片
- **불고기**
- 牛薄切り肉の炒め焼き
- شرائح اللحم المحمرة
- Pfannengerührte Rindfleisch-Scheiben
- Sauté d'émincé de bœuf
- Salteado de Carne de Res
- Fettine di carne bovina saltate
- Fatias de carne refogadas

143 고기구이

Grilled Beef
- 烤牛肉
- 烤牛肉
- **고기구이**
- 焼肉
- لحم البقر المشوي
- Gegrilltes Rindfleisch
- Bœuf grillé
- Carne de Res Asada a la Parrilla
- Carne alla griglia
- Carne grelhada

144 갈비구이

Grilled Beef Short Ribs
- 烤牛排
- 烤牛排
- **갈비구이**
- 牛骨付きカルビ焼き
- ريش البقر المشوية
- Gegrillte kurze Rippen vom Rind
- Travers de bœuf grillés
- Agujas de Res Asadas a la Parilla
- Costicine con l'osso alla griglia
- Falsa costela de gado grelhada

145 갈비찜

Braised Beef Short Ribs
- 炖五花牛肉
- 炖五花牛肉
- **갈비찜**
- 牛バラ肉の煮もの
- ضلع البقر المطهر على نار هادئة
- Geschmorte Kurze Rippe vom Rind
- Poitrine de bœuf braisée
- Guisado de Pecho de Res Dorado
- Punta di petto in umido
- Falsa costela cozida

146 육회

Seasoned Raw Beef
- 生牛肉片
- 生牛肉片
- **육회**
- 牛肉のさしみ
- لحم البقر المتبل النيئ
- Gewürztes rohes Rindfleisch
- Bœuf cru aromatisé
- Carne Cruda de Res Sazonada
- Striscioline di carne cruda in salsa
- Carne crua condimentada

147 김치볶음

Stir-Fried Pork with Kimchee
- 朝鮮腌菜炒豬肉
- 朝鲜腌菜炒猪肉
- **김치볶음**
- キムチと豚肉の炒めもの
- لحم محمر مع الكيمتشي
- Pfannengerührtes Schweinefleisch mit Kimchee
- Sauté de porc avec du kimchee
- Salteado de Cerdo con Kimchee
- Sauté di maiale con kimchi
- Porco refogado com kimchee

148

족발

● **Boiled Pig's Feet**
● 豬蹄
● 猪蹄
● 족발
● 豚足
● الكوارع المسلوقة
● Gekochte Schweinefüße
● Pieds de porc bouillis
● Cocido de Pata de Cerdo
● Bollito di zampa di maiale
● Pés de porco fervidos

149

삼계탕

● **Whole Boiled Chicken with Ginseng Soup**
● 全雞參湯
● 全鸡参汤
● 삼계탕
● 丸鶏と朝鮮人参のスープ
● حساء دجاجة مسلوقة مع الارالية
● Suppe mit einem ganzen gekochten Hühnchen und Ginseng
● Soupe de poulet entier bouilli avec du ginseng
● Pollo Relleno en Sopa de Ginseng
● Pollo intero bollito con ginseng
● Frango inteiro cozido com sopa de ginseng

150

생선조림

● **Spicy Boiled Fish**
● 辣椒燉魚
● 辣椒炖鱼
● 생선조림
● 魚の唐辛子煮
● سمك مسلوق حريف
● Scharfer gekochter Fisch
● Poisson bouilli aux épices
● Guisado de Pescado Aromático
● Pesce in umido piccante
● Peixe cozido picante

151

오징어회 무침

● **Vinegared Squid**
● 酸甜醬涼拌生烏賊
● 酸甜酱凉拌生乌贼
● 오징어회 무침
● いかのさしみの酢みそあえ
● سبيط بالخل
● Mit Essig gesäuerter Tintenfisch
● Calmars au vinaigre
● Calamar Avinagrado
● Seppia in salsa agra
● Lula avinagrada

152

전

● **Fried Meat and Vegetables in Egg Batter**
● 烤蛋拖
● 烤蛋拖
● 전
● 卵のつけ焼き
● لحم وخضر محمرة بالبيض والدقيق
● Gebratenes Fleisch und Gemüse in Eierpanade
● Viande et légumes à l'œuf grillé
● Carne y Verduras con Huevo a la Plancha
● Fritto misto all'uovo
● Fritura de carne e vegetais com massa mole de ovo

153

아구찜

● **Braised Angler with Hot Red Pepper**
● 辣椒燉老頭魚
● 辣椒炖老头鱼
● 아구찜
● あんこうの唐辛子煮
● سمك مطهو مع الفلفل الاحمر الحار
● Geschmorter Seeteufel mit scharfem spanischen Pfeffer
● Lotte de mer braisée au piment rouge piquant
● Cocido de Pejesapo Dorado en Salsa Chile
● Coda di rospo in umido con peperoncino rosso
● Cozido de xarroco-maior com pimenta-malagueta

154

김치

● **Kimchee**
● 朝鮮腌菜
● 朝鮮腌菜
● 김치
● キムチ
● الكيمتشي
● Kimchee
● Kimchee
● Kimchee
● Kimchi
● Kimchee

155

나물

● **Assorted Sesame-Flavored Vegetables**
● 拌蔬菜
● 拌蔬菜
● 나물
● 野菜のあえもの（ナムル）
● خضر مشكلة بنكهة السمسم
● Gemischtes, mit Sesam gewürztes Gemüse
● Légumes mixtes agrémentés de sésame
● Verduras Mixtas en Sésamo
● Verdure in salsa al sesamo
● Vegetais sortidos condimentados com gergelim

156

상추 생채

● **Korean Lettuce Salad**
● 萵苣沙拉
● 萵苣沙拉
● 상추 생채
● サンチュのサラダ
● سلطة الخس الكورية
● Koreanischer Eisbergsalat
● Salade de laitue coréenne
● Ensalada de Lechuga Coreana
● Insalata coreana
● Salada de alface coreana

157

잡채

- **Gelatin Noodles with Stir-Fried Meat and Vegetables**
- 粉絲拌菜
- 粉丝拌菜
- 잡채
- 春雨と野菜の炒めあえ
- شعرية جيلاتينية مع اللحم والخضر المحمرة
- Glasnudeln mit pfannengerührtem Fleisch und Gemüse
- Nouilles collantes accompagnées d'un sauté de viande et de légumes
- Salteado de Fideos Gelatinosos de Soja con Carne y Verduras
- Vermicelli di fecola e verdure
- Fios gelatinosos com carne e vegetais refogados

158

파전

- **Leek Pancakes**
- 蔥烤餅
- 葱烤饼
- 파전
- ねぎのお好み焼き
- فطيرة البصل الأخضر
- Schnittlauch-Omelett
- Crêpes de poireaux
- Panqueques de Puerro
- Tortini di porri
- Panquecas de cebolinha

159

감자지짐

- **Fried Potato**
- 燒馬鈴薯
- 烧马铃薯
- 감자지짐
- じゃがいものおやき
- بطاطس محمرة
- Gebratene Kartoffeln
- Pommes de terre frites
- Patatas Fritas
- Frittelle di patate
- Batata frita

160

김구이

- **Toasted Nori**
- 烤紫菜
- 烤紫菜
- 김 구이
- 焼きのり
- نوري محمص
- Gerösteter Nori-Seetang
- Nori grillé
- Nori Tostado
- Alghe nori tostate
- Alga nori tostada

161

미역국

- **Wakame Soup**
- 裙帶菜什錦湯
- 裙带菜什锦汤
- 미역국
- わかめスープ
- حساء الواكامي
- Wakame-Suppe
- Soupe de wakame
- Sopa de Wakame
- Minestra di alghe wakame
- Sopa de alga wakame

162

갈비탕

- **Beef Short Rib Soup**
- 五花牛肉湯
- 五花牛肉汤
- 갈비탕
- 牛バラ肉のスープ
- حساء ريش البقر
- Suppe aus kurzer Rinderrippe
- Soupe de travers de bœuf
- Sopa de Agujas de Res
- Minestra di costolette di manzo
- Sopa de falsa costela

163

곰탕

- **Oxtail Soup**
- 牛尾湯
- 牛尾汤
- 곰탕
- 牛テールスープ
- حساء ذيل الثور
- Ochsenschwanzsuppe
- Queue de bœuf en soupe
- Sopa de Rabo de Buey
- Minestra di coda di bue
- Sopa de rabada

164

육계장

- **Spicy Beef and Vegetable Soup**
- 辣味牛肉菜湯
- 辣味牛肉菜汤
- 육계장
- 牛肉と野菜の辛味スープ
- حساء حريف من لحم البقر والخضر
- Scharfe Suppe mit Rindfleisch und Gemüse
- Soupe épicée aux légumes et au bœuf
- Sopa Aromática de Res y Verduras
- Minestra piccante di manzo e verdure
- Sopa picante com carne e vegetais

165

떡국

- **Korean Rice Cake Soup**
- 韓國朝鮮特色燴年糕
- 韩国朝鲜特色烩年糕
- 떡국
- 韓国・朝鮮風雑煮
- حساء كعك الارز الكوري
- Koreanische Reiskuchensuppe
- Soupe de petits gâteaux de riz coréens
- Sopa de Pastel de Arroz Coreano
- Minestra con gnocchi di riso alla coreana
- Sopa de bolinhos de arroz ao estilo coreano

166

만두국

- **Dumpling Soup**
- 餃子湯
- 饺子汤
- **만두국**
- 餃子スープ
- حساء المحشوات
- Suppe mit Teigtaschen
- Soupe de boulettes
- Sopa de Relleno de Carne
- Minestra con ravioli cinesi
- Sopa de pasteizinhos recheados

167

비빔밥

- **Mixed Vegetables over Rice**
- 什錦蓋飯
- 什锦盖饭
- **비빔밥**
- ビビンバ
- خضر متنوعة فوق الارز
- Gemischtes Gemüse auf Reis
- Légumes mixtes servis sur du riz
- Verduras Surtidas sobre Arroz
- Riso con copertura di verdure miste
- Misto de vegetais sobre arroz

168

돌솥비빔밥

- **Stone-Baked Mixed Vegetables over Rice**
- 石烤什錦蓋飯   石烤什锦盖饭
- **돌솥비빔밥**
- 石焼きビビンバ
- طاجن من الخضر المختلفة فوق الارز
- Im Steintopf gebackenes Mischgemüse auf Reis
- Légumes mixtes cuits à la pierre et servis sur du riz
- Verduras Cocinadas sobre Arroz en una Vasija de Piedra
- Riso e verdure miste cotti in tegame di pietra
- Misto de vegetais sobre arroz, cozidos em tigela de pedra

169

김치볶음밥

- **Fried Rice with Kimchee**
- 朝鮮腌菜炒飯
- 朝鲜腌菜炒饭
- **김치볶음밥**
- キムチ入り炒めご飯
- أرز محمر مع الكيمتشي
- Gebratener Reis mit Kimchee
- Riz sauté accompagné de kimchee
- Arroz Frito con Kimchee
- Riso fritto con kimchi
- Arroz refogado com kimchee

170

전복죽

- **Abalone Gruel**
- 鮑魚粥
- 鲍鱼粥
- **전복죽**
- あわびがゆ
- ثريد أذن البحر
- Sämige Reissuppe mit Abalone
- Gruau d'ormeaux
- Puches de Oreja Marina
- Minestra di riso con orecchia di mare
- Haliotes em mingau de arroz

171

국밥

- **Cooked Rice in Hot Broth**
- 滾湯飯
- 浇汤饭
- **국밥**
- スープかけご飯
- أرز مطبوخ في حساء ساخن
- Gekochter Reis in heißem Sud
- Riz cuit dans un bouillon chaud
- Arroz Cocido en Caldo
- Riso affogato
- Arroz cozido em sopa de verduras

172

비빔냉면

- **Cold Noodles with Hot Sauce**
- 拌面
- 拌面
- **비빔냉면**
- 混ぜ麺
- شعرية باردة في صلصة حريفة
- Kalte Nudeln mit scharfer Soße
- Nouilles froides à la sauce piquante
- Fideos Fríos con Salsa Picante
- Spaghettini asciutti con sugo piccante
- Macarrão frio com molho picante

173

물냉면

- **Cold Noodle Dish**
- 冷面
- 冷面
- **물냉면**
- 冷麺
- طبق من الشعرية الباردة
- Kaltes Nudelgericht
- Plat de nouilles froides
- Fideos Fríos
- Spaghettini freddi
- Macarrão servido frio

174

온면

- **Hot Noodle Dish**
- 溫面
- 温面
- **온면**
- 温麺
- طبق من الشعرية الساخنة
- Heißes Nudelgericht
- Plat de nouilles chaudes
- Fideos Calientes
- Pasta in brodo caldo
- Macarrão quente

175 김치찌개

- **Pork and Kimchee Casserole**
- 朝鮮腌菜火鍋
- 朝鲜腌菜火锅
- **김치찌개**
- キムチ鍋
- طاجن اللحم مع الكيمتشي
- Schweinefleisch- und Kimchee Kasserolle
- Cocotte de porc et de kimchee
- Cacerola de Cerdo y Kimchee
- Pignatta con kimchi
- Caçarola de porco e kimchee

176 생선찌개

- **Hot and Spicy Fish Stew**
- 魚類火鍋
- 鱼类火锅
- **생선찌개**
- 魚の鍋
- ياخني ساخن من السمك الحريف
- Scharfer und würziger Fischeintopf
- Ragoût de poisson chaud épicé
- Cacerola de Pescado Aromático
- Pignatta di pesce
- Ensopado de peixe apimentado e condimentado

177 곱창전골

- **Beef Entrails Stew**
- 雜燴火鍋
- 杂烩火锅
- **곱창전골**
- もつ鍋
- ياخني أحشاء البقر
- Eintopf aus Rinderinnereien
- Ragoût de tripes de bœuf
- Cacerola de Vísceras
- Pignatta di interiora di manzo
- Ensopado de miúdos

178 약식

- **Steamed Sweet Rice**
- 藥膳
- 药膳
- **약식**
- 薬食
- أرز حلو مطهو على البخار
- Gedämpfter süßer Reis
- Riz sucré cuit à la vapeur
- Arroz Dulce
- Dolce di riso con frutta secca
- Bolinhos de arroz doce cozidos em vapor

179 떡

- **Rice Cake Sweets**
- 糕餅
- 糕饼
- **떡**
- 餅菓子
- كعكات الارز الحلوة
- Süßigkeiten aus Reiskuchen
- Dessert de gâteaux de riz
- Golosinas de Arroz Glutinoso
- Dolcetti di mochi
- Doces de bolinhos de arroz glutinoso

180 강정

- **Confections**
- 各色點心
- 各色点心
- **강정**
- 菓子
- أنواع من الحلوي
- Konfekt
- Sucreries
- Confituras
- Dolcetti vari
- Confeitos

LIST OF JAPANESE FOODS

日本菜菜單
日本菜菜单
일본요리 일람
日本料理一覧
قائمة المأكولات اليابانية
Liste der japanischen Gerichte
Liste des plats japonais
Lista de Platillos Japoneses
Lista di piatti giapponesi
Lista de pratos japoneses

---

188 牛たたき

- **Rare-Broiled Beef Sashimi**
- 拍牛肉
- 拍牛肉
- 쇠고기다짐
- **牛たたき**
- لحم بقري نيء بلمسة من الشواء
- Sashimi aus rohem leicht angebratenem Rindfleisch
- Sashimi de bœuf grillé saignant
- Sashimi de Res Ligeramente Asada a la Parrilla
- Manzo leggermente arrostito
- Sashimi de carne levemente grelhada

189 豚肉のしょうが焼き

- **Stir-Fried Pork with Ginger**
- 姜汁烤肉
- 姜汁烤肉
- 돼지고기 생강볶음
- **豚肉のしょうが焼き**
- لحم محمر مع الزنجبيل
- Pfannengerührtes Schweinefleisch mit Ingwer
- Sauté de porc au gingembre
- Cerdo Salteado con Jengibre
- Maiale in padella allo zenzero
- Porco refogado com gengibre

190 トンカツ

- **Breaded Pork Cutlet**
- 炸猪排
- 炸猪排
- 포크 커틀렛
- **トンカツ**
- ريش اللحم البانيه
- Paniertes Schweinekotelett
- Escalope de porc panée
- Chuleta de Cerdo Rebozada
- Cotolette di maiale impanate
- Milanesa de carne de porco ao estilo japonês

---

191 串カツ

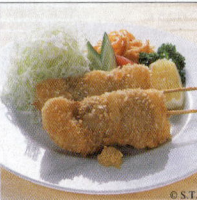

- **Deep-Fried Pork on Skewers**
- 炸肉菜串
- 炸肉菜串
- 꼬치 포크커틀렛
- **串カツ**
- لحم محمر بالاسياخ
- Fritierte Schweinefleisch-Spießchen
- Brochettes de porc frit
- Brochetas de Cerdo Fritas en Aceite
- Spiedini fritti di maiale
- Porco frito em espetinhos

192 豚の角煮

- **Simmered Pork**
- 炖猪肉塊
- 炖猪肉块
- 돼지고기찜
- **豚の角煮**
- لحم مطهو على نار هادئة
- Gedünstetes Schweinefleisch
- Porc mijoté
- Carne de Cerdo Cocida a Fuego Lento
- Bollito di maiale
- Carne de porco cozida

193 焼きとり

- **Japanese Broiled Chicken**
- 烤雞肉串
- 烤鸡肉串
- 닭꼬치구이
- **焼きとり**
- دجاج مشوي على الطريقة اليابانية
- Japanisches Brathühnchen
- Brochettes de poulet
- Brochetas de Pollo Japonés Asado
- Spiedini di pollo
- Frango em espetinhos

194

とりの唐揚げ

- **Deep-Fried Chicken**
- 日式炸子雞
- 日式炸子鸡
- 닭튀김
- とりの唐揚げ
- دجاج مقلي
- Fritiertes Hühnchen
- Poulet frit
- Pollo Frito en Aceite
- Pollo fritto alla giapponese
- Frango frito

195

とりの照り焼き

- **Chicken Teriyaki**
- 日式醬烤雞
- 日式酱烤鸡
- 닭고기양념구이
- とりの照り焼き
- ترياكي الدجاج
- Hühnchen-Teriyaki
- Teriyaki de poulet
- Pollo Teriyaki
- Pollo "laccato" (teriyaki)
- Frango teriyaki

196

さしみの盛り合わせ

- **Assorted Sashimi**
- 生魚片拼盆
- 生鱼片拼盆
- 모듬회
- さしみの盛り合わせ
- تشكيلة من السمك النيء
- Gemischtes Sashimi
- Assortiment de sashimi
- Sashimi Surtido
- Misto di fettine di pesce crudo (sashimi)
- Sashimi sortido

197

天ぷらの盛り合わせ

- **Assorted Tempura**
- 天婦羅拼盆(酥炸拼盆)
- 天妇罗拼盆(酥炸拼盆)
- 모듬튀김
- 天ぷらの盛り合わせ
- منوعات من التمبورا
- Gemischtes Tempura
- Assortiment de tempura
- Tempura Surtido
- Fritto misto alla giapponese (tempura)
- Tempura sortido

198

えびフライ

- **Deep-Fried Breaded Shrimp**
- 炸蝦
- 炸虾
- 새우튀김
- えびフライ
- جمبري بانيه مقلي
- Panierte fritierte Garnelen
- Crevettes panées frites
- Langostinos Rebosados
- Gamberi impanati
- Camarões empanados

199

魚の塩焼き

- **Broiled Salted Fish**
- 鹽烤魚
- 盐烤鱼
- 생선소금구이
- 魚の塩焼き
- سمك مشوي بالملح
- Gegrillter gesalzener Fisch
- Grillade de poissons salés
- Pescado Salado a las Brasas
- Pesce grigliato con sale
- Peixe grelhado com sal

200

魚の照り焼き

- **Grilled Teriyaki-Style Fish**
- 醬烤魚
- 酱烤鱼
- 생선양념구이
- 魚の照り焼き
- ترياكي السمك المشوي
- Gegrillter Fisch nach Teriyaki-Art
- Teriyaki de poisson
- Pescado a la Brasa al Estilo Teriyaki
- Pesce grigliato laccato (teriyaki)
- Peixe assado ao estilo teriyaki

201

さばのみそ煮

- **Simmered Mackerel in Miso Sauce**
- 炖面醬鮐魚
- 炖面酱鲐鱼
- 고등어 된장조림
- さばのみそ煮
- سمك مطهو في صلصة الميسو
- Gedünstete Makrele in Miso-Soße
- Maquereau mijoté dans une sauce de miso
- Caballa Cocida a Fuego Lento en Salsa de Miso
- Sgombro in umido con miso
- Cavala cozida em fogo brando com molho de miso

202

まぐろの山かけ

- **Raw Tuna Topped with Ground Yam**
- 山芋淺蓋金槍魚
- 山芋淡盖金枪鱼
- 참치와 참마 무침
- まぐろの山かけ
- سمك التونة النيء مع اليام المغري
- Roher Thunfisch mit geriebener Jamswurzel
- Thon cru parsemé d'ignames râpées
- Atún Crudo Cubierto con Ñame Molido
- Tonno crudo con copertura di patata yam grattugiata
- Atum cru coberto com inhame-da-china ralado

203 ししゃも

© S.T.

- **Broiled Smelt with Roe**
- 鬍瓜魚
- 胡瓜鱼
- 별빙어
- ししゃも
- سمك مشوي بالبطارخ
- Gegrillter Stint mit Rogen
- Eperlans grillés accompagnés d'œufs de poisson
- Eperlano Seco con Huevas Asado
- Sperlani alla griglia
- Eperlano com ovas grelhado

204 あさりの酒蒸し

© S.T.

- **Steamed Short- Necked Clams in Sake**
- 酒蒸蛤蜊
- 酒蒸蛤蜊
- 모시조개 찜
- あさりの酒蒸し
- قواقع مطهوة على البخار في الساكي
- Gedünstete kleine Miesmuscheln in Sake
- Palourdes cuites à la vapeur dans du saké
- Almejas Cocidas al Vapor en Sake
- Vongole cotte a vapore con sakè
- Mariscos ao vapor de saquê

205 いくらおろし

© S.T.

- **Salmon Roe with Grated Radish**
- 鹽漬大馬哈魚子醬
- 盐渍大马哈鱼子酱
- 연어알과 간 무우무침
- いくらおろし
- بيض السلمون مع الفجل المبشور
- Lachsrogen mit geriebenem Rettich
- Œufs de saumon servis sur du radis râpé
- Huevas de Salmón con Rábano Rallado
- Uova di salmone con rapa giapponese grattugiata
- Ovas de salmão com nabo-japonês ralado

206 肉じゃが

© S.T.

- **Simmered Beef and Potatoes**
- 土豆燒牛肉
- 土豆烧牛肉
- 쇠고기 감자조림
- 肉じゃが
- لحم البقر المطهو مع البطاطس
- Gekochtes Rindfleisch und Kartoffeln
- Bœuf mijoté avec des pommes de terre
- Carne de Res con Patatas Cocidas a Fuego Lento
- Stufato di manzo e patate
- Carne e batata cozidas

207 コロッケ

© S.T.

- **Potato Croquettes**
- 酥炸土豆肉餅
- 酥炸土豆肉饼
- 크로켓
- コロッケ
- بطاطس باللحم المفري والبقسماط
- Kartoffelkroketten
- Croquettes de pommes de terre
- Croquetas de Patata
- Crocchette
- Croquetes de batata

208 筑前煮

© S.T.

- **Braised Vegetables with Chicken**
- 築前炖
- 筑前炖
- 닭고기 야채조림
- 筑前煮
- خضر مطهوة مع الدجاج
- Geschmortes Gemüse mit Huhn
- Légumes braisés accompagnés de poulet
- Pollo y Verduras Dorados a Fuego Lento
- Verdure e pollo in umido
- Vegetais com frango cozidos

209 野菜の煮もの

© S.T.

- **Boiled Vegetables**
- 炖煨蔬菜
- 炖煨蔬菜
- 야채조림
- 野菜の煮もの
- خضر مسلوقة
- Gekochtes Gemüse
- Légumes bouillis
- Verduras Cocidas
- Verdure in umido
- Vegetais cozidos

210 きんぴらごぼう

© S.T.

- **Stir-Fried Burdock**
- 牛蒡絲
- 牛蒡丝
- 우엉조림
- きんぴらごぼう
- الجوبو المحمر
- Pfannengerührte Schwarzwurzeln
- Sauté de bardane
- Lampazo Salteado
- Bardana saltata in padella
- Bardana refogada

211 ひじきの煮もの

© S.T.

- **Simmered Hijiki**
- 炖羊棲菜
- 炖羊栖菜
- 녹미채(해초)조림
- ひじきの煮もの
- هيجيكي مطهو على نار هادئة
- Gekochter Hijiki
- Hijiki mijoté
- Hijiki Cocido a Fuego Lento
- Alghe hijiki in umido
- Hijiki cozida em fogo brando

212

おひたし

- **Boiled Spinach with Bonito Shavings**
- 凉拌菠菜
- 凉拌菠菜
- 일식 시금치나물
- おひたし
- سبانخ مسلوقة مع مبشور السمك
- Gekochter Spinat mit Bonitfisch-Flocken
- Epinards bouillis accompagnés de bonite séchée râpée
- Espinacas Cocidas con Hojuelas de Bonito Seco
- Spinaci con fiocchi di bonito essiccato
- Espinafre fervido com flocos de bonito seco

213

ごまあえ

- **Vegetables in Sesame Dressing**
- 芝麻拌凉菜
- 芝麻拌凉菜
- 깨소금무침
- ごまあえ
- خضر منتبلة بمحلول السمسم
- Gemüse mit Sesamsoße
- Légumes servis avec un assaisonnement au sésame
- Verduras en Salsa de Sésamo (ajonjoli)
- Verdura al sesamo
- Vegetais em molho de gergelim

214

酢のもの

- **Seaweed and Cucumber Salad**
- 醋拌凉菜
- 醋拌凉菜
- 초무침
- 酢のもの
- سلطة الخيار والاعشاب البحرية
- Salat aus Seetang und Gurken
- Salade d'algues et de concombres
- Ensalada de Algas y Pepinos
- Insalata di alghe e cetrioli
- Salada de algas e pepinos

215

漬けもの

- **Salt-Pickled Vegetables**
- 腌菜
- 腌菜
- 야채절임
- 漬けもの
- خضر مخللة في الملح
- In Salz eingelegtes Gemüse
- Légumes marinés dans du sel
- Verduras en Salmuera
- Verdure in salamoia
- Vegetais em conserva de sal

216

枝豆

- **Salted Green Soybeans Boiled in the Pod**
- 煮毛豆
- 煮毛豆
- 삶은 콩
- 枝豆
- فول الصويا الملح المسلوق
- Gesalzene grüne Sojabohnenschoten
- Haricots de soja vert salés bouillis avec leurs cosses
- Frijoles de Soja Verdes en Vaina Cocidos en Agua Salada
- Fagioli verdi di soia
- Feijão-soja verde fervido, na vagem

217

冷や奴

- **Chilled Tofu**
- 涼拌豆腐
- 涼拌豆腐
- 냉두부
- 冷や奴
- التوفر البارد
- Gekühlter Tofu
- Tofu froid
- Tofu Helado (Queso de Soja)
- Tofu freddo
- Queijo de soja gelado

218

揚げだし豆腐

- **Deep-Fried Tofu**
- 油炸豆腐
- 油炸豆腐
- 튀김두부
- 揚げだし豆腐
- التوفر المقلي
- Fritierter Tofu
- Tofu frit
- Tofu Frito en Aceite
- Tofu fritto
- Queijo de soja frito por mergulho em óleo

219

豆腐ステーキ

- **Pan-Fried Tofu**
- 油煎豆腐
- 油煎豆腐
- 두부스테이크
- 豆腐ステーキ
- توفو محمر في المقلاة
- In der Pfanne gebratener Tofu
- Steak de tofu
- Tofu Frito en Sartén
- Bistecca di tofu
- Queijo de soja frito

220

だし巻き卵

- **Japanese Style Omelet**
- 湯汁蛋卷
- 汤汁蛋卷
- 달걀부침
- だし巻き卵
- أومليت على الطريقة اليابانية
- Japanisches Omelett
- Omelette à la japonaise
- Tortilla de Huevo al Estilo Japonés
- Omelette alla giapponese
- Omelete ao estilo japonês

221

茶碗蒸し

- Savory Egg Custard
- 蒸雞蛋羹
- 蒸鸡蛋羹
- 달걀찜
- **茶碗蒸し**
- بودنغ البيض المملح
- Pikanter Eierstich mit Einlage
- Crème onctueuse aux œufs
- Flan de Huevo Aderezado
- Budino salato in tazza
- Creme de ovos suculento

222

みそ汁

- Miso Soup
- 日本式醬湯
- 日本式酱汤
- 된장국
- **みそ汁**
- حساء الميسو
- Miso-Suppe
- Soupe de miso
- Sopa de Miso
- Minestra di miso
- Sopa de miso

223

すまし汁

- Clear Soup
- 清湯
- 清汤
- 맑은 국
- **すまし汁**
- الحساء الشفاف
- Klare Suppe
- Soupe claire
- Sopa Clara
- Consommé alla giapponese
- Sopa clara

224

豚汁

- Pork and Vegetable Miso Soup
- 豬肉醬湯
- 猪肉酱汤
- 돼지고기국
- **豚汁**
- حساء ميسو مع اللحم والخضر
- Miso-Suppe mit Schweinefleisch und Gemüse
- Soupe de miso au porc et aux légumes
- Sopa de Miso con Carne de Cerdo y Verduras
- Minestra di miso e maiale
- Sopa de miso com porco e vegetais

225

けんちん汁

- Vegetable Chowder
- （日式）雜燴湯
- （日式）杂烩汤
- 일식 두부국
- **けんちん汁**
- حساء الخضر
- Dicke Gemüsesuppe
- Potée de légumes
- Guisado de Verduras
- Minestra di verdura
- Ensopado de vegetais

226

ちらし寿司

- Mixed Sushi
- 拼盆壽司
- 拼盆寿司
- 일식 회덮밥
- **ちらし寿司**
- تشكيلة متبلة فوق أرز السوشي
- Gemischtes Sushi
- Sushi décoré
- Sushi mixto
- Insalata di riso alla giapponese
- Sushi misto

227

にぎり寿司

- Sushi
- 壽司
- 寿司
- 초밥
- **にぎり寿司**
- السوشي
- Sushi
- Sushi
- Sushi
- Sushi
- Sushi

232

太巻き寿司

- Thick Sushi Rolls
- 粗卷壽司
- 粗卷寿司
- 굵은 김초밥
- **太巻き寿司**
- ملفوف السوشي السميك
- Dicke Sushi-Rollen
- Sushi en rouleaux épais
- Rollos de Sushi Gruesos
- Sushi in rotolo grosso
- Rolos grossos de sushi

233

細巻き寿司

- Thin Sushi Rolls
- 細卷壽司
- 细卷寿司
- 가는 김초밥
- **細巻き寿司**
- ملفوف السوشي الرفيع
- Dünne Sushi-Rollen
- Sushi en rouleaux fins
- Rollos de Sushi Delgados
- Sushi in rotolo sottile
- Rolos finos de sushi

234

手巻き寿司

- **Hand-Rolled Sushi**
- 手巻壽司
- 手巻寿司
- 즉석김초밥
- **手巻き寿司**
- يدوياً الملفوف السوشي
- Handgerolltes Sushi
- Sushi roulés à la main
- Sushi Enrollado a Mano
- Sushi avvolti a piacere
- Sushi enrolado à mão

235

いなり寿司

- **Stuffed Deep-Fried Tofu Pouches**
- 油豆腐壽司
- 油豆腐寿司
- 유부초밥
- **いなり寿司**
- أكياس التوفو المحمرة المحشوة
- Gefüllte fritierte Tofu-Taschen
- Petites poches de tofu frit farcies
- Bolsitas de Tofu Fritas en Aceite y Rellenas
- Fagottini ripieni di sushi
- Bolsinhas de tofu frito com recheio

236

牛丼

- **Beef over Rice**
- 牛肉蓋飯
- 牛肉盖饭
- 쇠고기덮밥
- **牛丼**
- لحم بقري فوق الأرز
- Rindfleisch über Reis
- Bœuf servi sur du riz
- Tazón de Arroz con Carne de Res
- Scodella di riso con manzo
- Carne sobre arroz

237

カツ丼

- **Deep-Fried Pork Cutlet over Rice**
- 豬排蓋飯
- 猪排盖饭
- 포크카츠덮밥
- **カツ丼**
- ضلع اللحم المحمر فوق الأرز
- Fritiertes Schweinekotelett auf Reis
- Côtelette de porc frite servie sur du riz
- Tazón de Arroz con Chuleta de Cerdo Rebozada
- Scodella di riso con maiale impanato
- Porco empanado sobre arroz

238

親子丼

- **Chicken and Eggs over Rice**
- 母子蓋飯
- 母子盖饭
- 닭고기 달걀덮밥
- **親子丼**
- دجاج وبيض فوق الأرز
- Huhn und Eier auf Reis
- Poulet et œufs servis sur du riz
- Tazón de Arroz con Pollo y Huevos
- Scodella di pollo e uova
- Frango e ovos sobre arroz

239

天丼

- **Tempura Rice Bowl**
- 炸蝦蓋飯
- 炸虾盖饭
- 튀김덮밥
- **天丼**
- وعاء الأرز بالتمبورا
- Tempura-Reisschale
- Tempura servis sur du riz
- Tazón de Arroz con Tempura
- Scodella di riso con tempura
- Tempura em tigela de arroz

240

うな重

- **Broiled Eel over Rice**
- 鰻魚盒飯
- 鳗鱼盒饭
- 장어덮밥
- **うな重**
- سمك الثعبان المشوي فوق الأرز
- Gegrillter Aal auf Reis
- Anguilles grillées servies sur du riz
- Anguila de Mar Asada sobre Arroz
- Riso con anguilla
- Enguia grelhada sobre arroz

241

鉄火丼

- **Raw Tuna over Rice**
- 生金槍魚片蓋飯
- 生金枪鱼片盖饭
- 참치덮밥
- **鉄火丼**
- سمك التونة النيء فوق الأرز
- Roher Thunfisch auf Reis
- Thon cru servi sur du riz
- Atún Crudo sobre Arroz
- Scodella di riso con tonno crudo
- Atum cru sobre arroz

242

カレーライス

- **Curry with Rice**
- 咖喱飯
- 咖喱饭
- 카레라이스
- **カレーライス**
- أرز بالكاري
- Curry mit Reis
- Riz au curry
- Cari con Arroz
- Riso al curry
- Curry com arroz

243

オムライス

- **Seasoned Fried Rice Omelet**
- 蛋包飯
- 蛋包饭
- 오므라이스
- **オムライス**
- أومليت الأرز المحمر بالتوابل
- Omelett mit gewürztem gebratenen Reis
- Riz à sauté enrobé d'omelette
- Arroz Frito Condimentado
- Omelette ripieno di riso
- Omelete recheada com arroz frito e temperado

244

炊き込みご飯

- **Steamed Rice Flavored with Chicken and Vegetables**
- 十錦菜飯
- 十锦菜饭
- 닭고기야채밥
- **炊き込みご飯**
- أرز مطهو مع الدجاج والخضر
- Gedämpfter Reis mit Huhn und Gemüse
- Riz à la vapeur accompagné de poulet et de légumes
- Arroz con Pollo y Verduras
- Risotto alla giapponese
- Arroz cozido com frango e verduras em vapor

245

お茶漬け

- **Flavored Tea and Rice**
- 茶泡飯
- 茶泡饭
- 차에 만 밥
- **お茶漬け**
- مزيج الشاي والأرز المنتل
- Gewürzter Tee und Reis
- Riz arrosé de thé vert
- Arroz con té aromático
- Riso al tè verde
- Chá e arroz aromatizados

246

おにぎり

- **Rice Balls**
- 飯團子
- 饭团子
- 주먹밥
- **おにぎり**
- كرات الارز المغلفة بعشب البحر
- Reisklöße
- Boulettes de riz
- Bolas de Arroz
- Palle di riso
- Bolinhos de arroz

247

ざるそば

- **Chilled Buckwheat Noodles**
- 蕎麥面條
- 荞麦面条
- 메밀국수
- **ざるそば**
- شعرية باردة من الحنطة السمراء
- Gekühlte Buchweizennudeln
- Nouilles de sarrasin froides
- Fideos de Alforfón Helados
- Soba al setaccio
- Macarrão de trigo-sarraceno servido gelado

248

きつねそば・うどん

- **Buckwheat or Wheat Flour Noodles with Deep-Fried Tofu**
- 油渣豆腐蕎麥面・切面
- 油渣豆腐汤乔麦面・切面
- 유부 메밀국수・우동 ● **きつねそば・うどん**
- شعرية الحنطة البيضاء أو السمراء مع التوفو المقلي
- Buchweizen- oder Weizenmehlnudeln mit frittiertem Tofu
- Nouilles de sarrasin ou de froment avec tofu frit
- Sopa de Fideos de Alforfón o Fideos de Trigo con Tofu Frito
- Soba/udon in brodo con tofu fritto
- Macarrão de trigo-sarraceno ou macarrão japonês com queijo de soja frito

249

たぬきそば・うどん

- **Buckwheat or Wheat Flour Noodles with Tempura Batter Pieces**
- 油渣湯蕎麥面・切面 ● 油渣汤乔麦面・切面
- 메밀국수・우동
- **たぬきそば・うどん**
- شعرية الحنطة البيضاء أو السمراء مع بعض التمبورا
- Buchweizen- oder Weizenmehlnudeln mit ausgebackenen Tempura-Teigteilen
- Nouilles de sarrasin ou de froment saupoudrées de pâte à frire de tempura
- Sopa de Fideos con hojuelas de tempura
- Soba/udon in brodo con palline di pastella fritta
- Macarrão de trigo-sarraceno ou macarrão japonês com floquinhos fritos de tempura

250

天ぷらそば・うどん

- **Tempura and Noodles**
- 天婦麵(酥炸蝦仁面)
- 天妇罗面(酥炸虾仁面)
- 튀김 메밀국수・우동
- **天ぷらそば・うどん**
- تمبورا مع الشعرية
- Tempura und Nudeln
- Nouilles à la tempura
- Sopa de Fideos con Tempura
- Soba/udon in brodo con tempura
- Tempura e macarrão de trigo-sarraceno ou macarrão japonês

251

鍋焼きうどん

- **Wheat Flour Noodle Casserole**
- 砂鍋面條
- 砂锅面条
- 남비우동
- **鍋焼きうどん**
- طاجن شعرية الحنطة البيضاء
- Kasserole mit Weizenmehlnudeln
- Cocotte de nouilles de farine de blé
- Cacerola de Fideos de Harina de Trigo
- Udon cotti in pignatta
- Caçarola de macarrão japonês

252

ラーメン

- **Ramen Noodles**
- 中國湯面
- 中国汤面
- 라면
- **ラーメン**
- شعرية الرامن
- Ramen-Nudelsuppe
- Nouilles ramen
- Sopa de Fideos Chinos (Ramen)
- Ramen
- Sopa de macarrão chinês (Ramen)

253

ラーメン各種

- **Various Kinds of Ramen**
- 各種面
- 各种面
- 각종 라면
- **各種ラーメン**
- أنواع مختلفة من حساء الرامن
- Verschiedene Arten von Ramen
- Différents types de Ramen
- Varias clases de Ramen
- Vari tipi di ramen in brodo
- Vários tipos de sopa de macarrão chinês

254

すき焼き

- **Sukiyaki**
- 日本式牛肉火鍋
- 日本式牛肉火锅
- 스키야키
- **すき焼き**
- سوكياكي
- Sukiyaki
- Sukiyaki
- Sukiyaki
- Sukiyaki
- Sukiyaki

255

しゃぶしゃぶ

- **Shabu-Shabu**
- 涮牛肉
- 涮牛肉
- 샤브샤브
- **しゃぶしゃぶ**
- شابو شابو
- Shabu-Shabu
- Shabu-shabu
- Shabu-Shabu
- Shabu-shabu
- Shabu-shabu

256

寄せ鍋

- **Seafood & Vegetable Casserole**
- 什錦火鍋
- 什锦火锅
- 잡탕냄비
- **寄せ鍋**
- طاجن الخضر والقواقع البحرية
- Kasserole mit Meeresfrüchten und Gemüse
- Cocotte de légumes et de fruits de mer
- Cacerola de Mariscos y Verduras
- Pesce e verdure in pignatta
- Caçarola de frutos do mar e vegetais

257

水炊き

- **Boiled Chicken Casserole**
- 雞肉汆鍋
- 鸡肉汆锅
- 일식 영계백숙
- **水炊き**
- طاجن الدجاج المسلوق
- Kasserole mit gekochtem Huhn
- Cocotte de poulet bouilli
- Cacerola de Pollo Cocido
- Pollo e verdure in pignatta
- Caçarola de frango

258

おでん

- **Fish Cake and Vegetable Casserole**
- 炖雜燴
- 炖杂烩
- 오뎅
- **おでん**
- طاجن الخضر مع كرات السمك
- Kasserole aus Fischpastete und Gemüse
- Cocotte de légumes et de pain de poisson
- Cacerola de Pastas de Pescado y Verduras
- Bollito misto alla giapponese (oden)
- Caçarola de bolinhos de massa de peixe e vegetais

259

湯豆腐

- **Simmered Tofu**
- 豆腐火鍋
- 豆腐火锅
- 두부탕
- **湯豆腐**
- التوفر المطهو على نار هادئة
- Gekochter Tofu
- Tofu mijoté
- Tofu Cocido a Fuego Lento
- Tofu bollito
- Queijo de soja fervido

260

鉄板焼き

- **Mixed Grill**
- 鐵板烤
- 铁板烤
- 철판구이
- **鉄板焼き**
- تشكيلة من المشويات
- Gemischte Grillplatte
- Grillades mixtes
- Surtido a la Plancha
- Misto alla piastra (teppanyaki)
- Misto na chapa

261

お好み焼き

- **Grilled Japanese-Style Pancakes**
- 什錦煎菜餅
- 什錦煎菜饼
- 일식 부침개
- **お好み焼き**
- فطيرة مشوية على الطريقة اليابانية
- Gegrillte japanische Pfannkuchen
- Crêpes épaisses grillées à la japonaise
- Panqueques Asados al Estilo Japonés
- Tortine alla piastra
- Panquecas ao estilo japonês

262

みつ豆

- **Gelatin (Agar-agar) and Fruit Dessert**
- 什錦甜凉粉
- 什锦甜凉粉
- 콩시럽 디저트
- **みつ豆**
- حلوي الفاكهة والجيلي
- Dessert aus Gelatine (Agar-Agar) und Früchten
- Agar-agar accompagné de fruits et de haricots rouges
- Postre de Gelatina con Fruta
- Dessert di gelatina e frutta
- Sobremesa de gelatina (ágar-ágar) e frutas

263

抹茶アイスクリーム

- **Green Tea Ice Cream**
- 末茶冰淇淋
- 末茶冰淇淋
- 녹차 아이스크림
- **抹茶アイスクリーム**
- آيس كريم من الشاي الأخضر
- Eiscreme aus grünem Tee
- Glace au thé vert
- Helado de Té Verde
- Gelato di tè verde
- Sorvete de chá verde

264

小豆アイスクリーム

- **Sweet Bean Ice Cream**
- 小豆冰淇淋
- 小豆冰淇淋
- 단팥 아이스크림
- **小豆アイスクリーム**
- آيس كريم من الفول الحلو
- Eiscreme aus süßen Bohnen
- Glace aux haricots rouges sucrés
- Helado de Judías Azucaradas
- Gelato con fagioli azuki dolci
- Sorvete de feijão doce

265

ようかん

- **Sweet Bean Jelly**
- 羊羹
- 羊羹
- 양갱
- **ようかん**
- جيلي الفول الحلو
- Gelee aus süßen Bohnen
- Gelée de haricots rouges sucrés
- Pasta de Judías Azucaradas
- Gelatina di fagioli azuki dolci
- Gelatina de feijão doce

266

みたらし団子

- **Dessert Dumplings**
- 丸子串
- 丸子串
- 떡꼬치
- **みたらし団子**
- كرات الارز الحلوة
- Dessert-Kugeln
- Brochettes de boulettes sucrées
- Postre de Bolas de Masa
- Palline dolci di farina di riso
- Sobremesa de bolinhos

Restaurant Conversation Aids

This section provides an introduction to some of the more commonly used phrases used in restaurants. You should be able to make use of these phrases from the time you walk in the door and order until you pay your check and leave. Remembering a few of these simple phrases will make your dining experience even more enjoyable.

餐廳常用會話集

餐厅常用会话集

레스토랑에서 금방 도움이 되는 회화집

レストランですぐに役立つ会話集

تعبيرات شائعة في حديث المطاعم

Typische Gespräche in Restaurants

Conversations typiques entendues dans les restaurants

Conversación Típica Empleada en los Restaurantes

Conversazione utile in un ristorante

Expressões usadas em restaurantes

Greetings and Responses

寒喧和應酬 — **Begrüßungsformeln und Antworten**
寒喧和应酬 — **Salutations et réponses**
인사와 대답 — **Saludos y Respuestas**
あいさつと対応 — **Saluti e risposte**
تحيات وردود — **Saudações e respostas**

Good morning
- 早晨好
- 早晨好
- 안녕하십니까?
- おはよう。
- صباح الخير
- Guten Morgen
- Bonjour
- Buenos días.
- Buongiorno
- Bom Dia

Good afternoon (Hello)
- 您好
- 您好
- 안녕하십니까?
- こんにちは。
- (مساء الخير (سعيدة
- Guten Tag (Hallo)
- Bonjour
- Buenas tardes (¡Hola!).
- Buongiorno
- Boa tarde (Olá)

Good evening
- 晚上好
- 晚上好
- 안녕하십니까?
- こんばんは。
- مساء الخير
- Guten Abend
- Bonsoir
- Buenas noches.
- Buona sera
- Boa noite

Good bye

- 再見
- **再见**
- 안녕히 가십시오.
- さようなら。
- مع السلامة
- Auf Wiedersehen
- Au revoir
- Adiós.
- Arrivederci
- Tchau

Excuse me

- 對不起
- **对不起**
- 미안합니다.
- すみません。
- بعد إذنكم
- Entschuldigen Sie bitte
- Excusez-moi
- Disculpe.
- Scusi
- Com licença

Yes/No

- 是的 / 不是
- **是的 / 不是**
- 예 / 아니오.
- はい。／いいえ。
- نعم / لا
- Ja/Nein
- Oui/Non
- Sí/No.
- Si/ No
- Sim/Não

Yes, I understand (Okay)

- 知道了
- **知道了**
- 알겠습니다.
- わかりました。
- نعم ، فهمت (حسناً)
- Ja, ich verstehe (in Ordnung)
- Oui, je comprends (OK)
- Sí, si entiendo.
- Ho capito
- Sim, eu compreendo (O.K.)

Thank you/You're welcome

- 謝謝 / 不客氣
- **谢谢 / 不客气**
- 감사합니다 / 괜찮습니다.
- ありがとう。／どういたしまして。
- شكراً / عفواً
- Vielen Dank/Bitte sehr
- Merci/Je vous en prie
- Gracias/De nada.
- Grazie/Prego
- Obrigado/De nada

Before going to a restaurant

去餐廳之前   **Ehe Sie zu einem Restaurant gehen**

去餐厅之前   **Avant d'aller dans un restaurant**

레스토랑에 가기 전에   **Antes de ir a un restaurante**

レストランへ行く前に   **Scelta del ristorante**

قبل الذهاب إلى المطعم   **Antes de ir ao restaurante**

Is there a good (inexpensive) restaurant nearby?

- 您能否告訴我附近有沒有好喫（便宜）的餐館？
- **您能否告诉我附近有没有好吃（便宜）的餐馆?**
- 이 근처에 (싸고) 맛있게 하는 식당을 가르쳐 주십시오.
- この近くで(安くて)おいしいレストランを教えて下さい。
- هل يوجد مطعم جيد (رخيص) بالقرب من هنا ؟
- Gibt es in der Nähe ein gutes (preiswertes) Restaurant?
- Y a-t-il un bon restaurant (bon marché) près d'ici ?
- ¿Hay algún buen restaurante cerca de aquí (que no sea caro)?
- Può indicarmi un buon ristorante (non caro) qui vicino?
- Conhece um restaurante bom (barato) aqui perto?

I would like to eat___food.

- 我想喫（　）菜
- **我想吃（　）菜**
- ○○요리가 먹고 싶습니다만.
- ○○料理を食べたいのですが。
- أود أن أتناول طعاماً ___.
- Ich würde gern ein___ Gericht essen.
- Je voudrais manger ___.
- Quisiera probar comida ___.
- Vorrei mangiare cucina ___.
- Eu gostaria de ir a um restaurante de comida _____.

Would you please take me there? (to a taxi.)

- 您能帶我去那里嗎？
- **您能带我去那里吗?**
- 그곳으로 안내해 주시겠습니까?
- そこへ連れていってくれませんか？
- هل يمكن أن تأخذني إلى هناك من فضلك ؟
- Könnten Sie mir den Weg dorthin zeigen?
- Pourriez-vous m'y conduire, s'il vous plaît ?
- ¿Podría llevarme a ese sitio?
- Mi potrebbe accompagnare?
- Poderia levar-me até lá?

At a restaurant

在餐廳時　　　レストランで　　Au restaurant
在餐厅时　　　في المطعم　　En un Restaurante
레스토랑에서　Im Restaurant　Al ristorante
　　　　　　　　　　　　　　No restaurante

Is there a table available?

- 有座位嗎?
- 有座位吗?
- 자리가 있습니까?
- 席はありますか?
- هل هناك منضدة خالية؟
- Haben Sie einen Tisch frei?
- Avez-vous une table?
- ¿Hay una mesa libre?
- C'è posto?
- Tem mesa vaga?

(How many of you are there?) I am by myself.

- (幾位?)一個人(Yi Ge Ren)。
- (几位?) 一个人(Yi Ge Ren)。
- 몇 분이세요? 혼자입니다.
  (Honjaimnida).
- (何人ですか?)一人(Hitori)です。
- (كم عددكم؟) واحد فقط(WAHED).
- (Wieviel Personen sind Sie?)
  Ich bin allein(eine Person).
- Vous êtes combien?
  Je suis seul(e).
- ¿Mesa para cuantas parsonas?
  Solo(a).
- (In quanti siete?) Io sono solo
  (sola).
- (Quantas pessoas?) Estou sozinho.

There are 2(two), 3(three), 4(four), 5(five)… of us.

- 我們一共，2(Liang), 3(Shan),
  4(Si), 5(Wu)… 個人。
- 我们一共，2(Liang), 3(Shan),
  4(Si), 5(Wu)… 个人。
- 저희는 2(Du), 3(Se), 4(Ne),
  5(Daseon)… 명입니다.
- 私たちは、2人(Hutari)、3人
  (Sannin)、4人(Yonin)、5人(Gonin)…
  です。
- عددنا ٢(ETHNĀN)، ٣(THALĀTHA)،
  ٤(ARBA´A)، ٥(KHAMSA)…
- Wir sind 2(zwei), 3(drei), 4(vier),
  5(fünf) Personen.
- Nous sommes 2(deux)/3(trois)/
  4(quatre)/5(cinq).
- Somos 2(dos), 3(tres), 4(cuatro),
  5(cinco).
- Siamo 2(due), 3(tre), 4(quattoro),
  5(cinque).
- Somos 2(duas), 3(três), 4(quatro),
  5(cinco) pessoas.

Please show me a menu.

- 請給我看一下菜單
- 请给我看一下菜单
- 메뉴를 보여주세요.
- メニューを見せて下さい。
- أرني قائمة المأكولات من فضلك .
- Bitte geben Sie mir die Speisekarte.
- Veuillez me montrer le menu.
- Por favor, muéstreme el menú (la carta).
- Mi faccia vedere il menu.
- O cardápio, por favor.

I'll have that.

- 請上那個 / 請上這個
- 请上那个 / 请上这个
- 그것을 주십시오. / 이것을 주십시오.
- それを下さい。／これを下さい。
- أريد هذا .
- Ich nehme das.
- Je prendrai ceci.
- Quiero eso.
- Mi dia quello/Mi dia questo.
- Este aqui, por favor.

I'll have the same as that.

- 請上跟那道菜一樣的菜
- 请上跟那道菜一样的菜
- 저것과 같은 것을 주세요.
- あれと同じものを下さい。
- أريد نفس هذا الطبق.
- Ich nehme dasselbe.
- Je prendrai la même chose que cela.
- Deseo aquél mismo platillo.
- Me ne dia uno come quello.
- Vou querer o mesmo também.

Does this take a long time?

- 能馬上做好嗎？
- 能马上做好吗？
- 금방 됩니까?
- すぐできますか？
- هذا الطبق ، هل يحتاج إعداده
- وقتاً طويلاً ؟.
- Dauert dies lange?
- Est-ce que cela prend beaucoup de temps?
- ¿Se tarda mucho en cocinar esto?
- Si può avere subito?
- Leva muito tempo para se preparar este prato?

Please give me today's special.

- 請您推薦一道今天的菜
- 请您推荐一道今天的菜
- 오늘의 추천 요리를 주세요.
- 本日のおすすめを下さい。
- أريد طبق اليوم من فضلك.
- Bitte bringen Sie mir das heutige Tagesgericht.
- Veuillez me donner le plat du jour.
- Por favor, déme el platillo especial de hoy.
- Mi dia i piatti del giorno.
- O prato do dia, por favor.

How much is this？ Please write down the price.

- 多少錢？請寫一下數字
- 多少钱？请写一下数字
- 얼마입니까? 숫자로 써 주세요.
- いくらですか？数字で書いて下さい。
- كم سعر هذا الطبق ؟
- أكتب لي هنا من فضلك .
- Wieviel kostet dies? Bitte schreiben Sie mir den Preis auf.
- Combien ça coûte? Veuillez écrire le prix, s'il vous plaît.
- ¿Cuánto cuesta? Escriba el precio, por favor.
- Quanto fa? Scriva la cifra, per favore.
- Quanto custa este prato? Escreva o preço, por favor.

This is not what I ordered.

- 這和我點的菜不一樣
- 这和我点的菜不一样
- 이것은 제가 주문한 것과 다릅니다.
- これは私の注文したものと違います。
- ليس هذا هو الطبق الذي طلبته.
- Dies habe ich nicht bestellt.
- Ceci n'est pas ce que j'ai commandé.
- Esto no es lo que ordené.
- Non è quello che ho ordinato.
- Não foi isto o que eu pedi.

(Excuse me.) My food has not come.

- 還沒做好
- 还没做好
- 아직 오지 않았습니다.
- まだ料理がきていません。
- إلى الآن لم يأت طلبي .
- Meine Bestellung ist immer noch nicht gekommen.
- Mon plat n'est toujours pas arrivé.
- Todavía no llega lo que pedí.
- Non me l'ha ancora portato.
- Ainda não veio o que pedi.

What kind of meat is used in this dish?

- 這道菜是用什麼肉做的？
- 这道菜是用什么肉做的?
- 이 요리는 무슨 고기로 만들었습니까?
- この料理は何の肉を使っていますか？
- ما نوع اللحم المستخدم في هذا الطبق ؟.
- Welches Fleisch wird in diesem Gericht verwendet?
- Quelle viande y a-t-il dans ce plat?
- ¿Qué clase de carne usan en este platillo?
- Che tipo di carne c'è in questo piatto?
- Que tipo de carne é servida neste prato?

Please leave out the Japanese horseradish (when eating sushi).

- 請不要放入芥茉（喫日本壽司時）
- 请不要放入芥茉（吃日本寿司时）
- 와사비를 빼고 주세요. (일본요리 초밥의 경우)
- わさびをぬいて下さい。 （日本料理の寿司の注文の時に）
- من فضلك لا أريد ميشور الفجل الحار (عند تناول السوشي)
- Bitte lassen Sie den japanischen Meerrettich weg (beim Sushi-Essen)
- Veuillez ne pas mettre de raifort japonais (dans le cas des sushi)
- Por favor, no le ponga mostaza verde japonesa (cuando come sushi).
- Non metta il rafano giapponese (nel caso di sushi).
- Por favor não inclua a raiz-forte-do-japão (ao pedir sushi).

Is it possible to have this made with (beef, pork, chicken, lamb)?

- 能用(牛、豬、雞、羊)肉做嗎？
- **能用(牛、猪、鸡、羊)肉做吗?**
- (소, 돼지, 닭, 양)고기로 만들어 주시겠습니까?
- (牛、豚、鶏、羊) 肉で作っていただけますか？
- هل يمكنكم إعداد هذا الطبق باستخدام
  (لحم البقر / الخنزير / الدجاج / الضأن) ؟
- Könnten Sie mir dies eventuell auch mit (Rindfleisch, Schweinefleisch, Hühnerfleisch, Lammfleisch) zubereiten?
- Serait-il possible de préparer ce plat avec (du bœuf, du porc, du poulet, de l'agneau) ?
- ¿Es posible que me preparen este platillo con (res, cerdo, pollo, cordero)?
- Me lo può fare con carne (bovina, maiale, pollo, agnello)?
- Seria possível servir este prato com (carne de gado, porco, frango, cordeiro)?

Please wrap this up for me to take home.

- 我想帶回去，請包一下
- **我想带回去，请包一下**
- 가져가고 싶은데, 포장해 주세요
- 持ち帰りたいので、包んで下さい。
- غلف هذا من فضلك لأحمله معي.
- Könnten Sie mir dies einpacken? Ich möchte es mitnehmen.
- Veuillez emballer ceci pour que je l'emporte avec moi.
- Por favor envuélvame ésto, para llevar.
- Vorrei portarlo via, me lo può incartare?
- Por favor, coloque isto numa embalagem, para que eu possa levar para casa.

Cheers!

- 幹杯！
- **干杯!**
- 건배!
- 乾杯!
- في صحتك !
- Prost! (Zum Wohl!)
- Santé!
- ¡Salud!
- Alla salute!
- Saúde!

This tastes delicious!

- 真好喫
- **真好吃**
- 맛있습니다.
- おいしい！
- هذا لذيذ الطعم !
- Dies schmeckt wunderbar!
- C'est vraiment délicieux!
- ¡Esto está delicioso!
- Buono!
- Está uma delícia!

Where are the rest rooms?

- 洗手間在哪里？
- **洗手间在哪里?**
- 화장실은 어디입니까?
- トイレはどこですか？
- أين دورة المياه ؟
- Wo sind die Toiletten?
- Où sont les toilettes?
- ¿Dónde están los sanitarios?
- Dov'è la toeletta?
- Onde fica o toalete?

Paying the Check

付款	**Bezahlen der Rechnung**
付款	**Régler l'addition**
지불	**Al Pagar la Cuenta**
支払い	**Il conto**
عند دفع الحساب	**Pagando a conta**

I would like the check, please.

- 請結帳
- **请结帐**
- 계산해 주세요.
- お勘定をお願いします。
- أريد فاتورة الحساب من فضلك ؟
- **Bitte bringen Sie mir die Rechnung.**
- Je voudrais l'addition, s'il vous plaît.
- Por favor, traiga la cuenta.
- Il conto, per favore.
- Poderia trazer a conta, por favor?

Is the tip included?

- 包括小費嗎？
- **包括小费吗?**
- 봉사료가 포함되어 있습니까?
- チップは含まれていますか？
- هل يشتمل الحساب على البقشيش ؟
- **Ist die Bedienung im Preis enthalten?**
- Le pourboire est-il inclus?
- ¿Está incluida la propina?
- Il servizio è compreso?
- Está incluída a gorjeta?

Do you accept credit cards?

- 可以用信用卡嗎？
- **可以用信用卡吗?**
- 신용카드를 사용할 수 있습니까?
- クレジットカードを使えますか？
- هل تقبلون الدفع بالبطاقات البنكية ؟
- **Nehmen Sie Kreditkarten?**
- Acceptez-vous les cartes de crédit?
- ¿Aceptan tarjetas de crédito?
- Posso usare la carta di credito?
- Aceita cartão de crédito?

We would like to pay individually.

- 請分別結賬
- **请分别结账**
- 계산은 따로따로 해 주세요.
- 支払いは一人一人でお願いします。
- نود أن يدفع كل منا على حدة .
- Wir möchten getrennt bezahlen.
- Nous voudrions régler séparément.
- Cada quien desea pagar su cuenta por separado
- Conti separati, per favore.
- Gostaríamos de pagar individualmente.

We would like one check for the whole party.

- 請集中結賬
- **请集中结账**
- 같이 계산해 주세요.
- 支払いはひとつにまとめて下さい。
- نريد فاتورة واحدة للجميع.
- Wir möchten eine Rechnung für die ganze Gruppe.
- Nous voudrions une seule note pour tout le groupe.
- Deseamos una sola cuenta para todo el grupo.
- Faccia un conto solo.
- Gostaríamos de receber uma só conta para todos.

I would like a receipt, please.

- 請給開張收據
- **请给开张收据**
- 영수증을 주세요.
- 領収書を下さい。
- أريد إيصالاً بالحساب من فضلك .
- Bitte geben Sie mir eine Quittung.
- Je voudrais un reçu, s'il vous plaît.
- ¿Podría darme un recibo?
- Mi dia la ricevuta, per favore.
- Poderia dar o recibo, por favor?

CHINESE
FOODS

中國菜

中国菜

중국요리 메뉴

中国料理

أطباق صينية

Chinesische Gerichte

Cuisine Chinoise

Cocina China

Piatti Cinesi

Cozinha Chinesa

青椒牛肉絲（Qing Jiao Niu Rou Si）

© S.T.

Stir-Fried Shredded Beef and Green Peppers

Beef, green peppers, bamboo shoots and other vegetables are cut into thin slices, stir-fried and flavored with soy sauce, sugar and rice wine.

kcal ●●

青椒牛肉絲

這是將牛肉、青椒和筍切成細絲進行煸炒，用醬油、白糖和酒來調味烹飪而成的一道菜肴。

青椒牛肉丝

这是将牛肉、青椒和笋切成细丝进行煸炒，用酱油、白糖和酒来调味烹饪而成的一道菜肴。

피망쇠고기볶음

쇠고기와 피망, 죽순 등을 채썰어 볶은 요리. 간장, 설탕, 술 등으로 맛을 냈다.

ピーマンと牛肉の細切り炒め

牛肉とピーマン、たけのこなどを細切りにして炒めた料理。しょうゆ、砂糖、酒などで味付けしてある。

شرائح محمرة من اللحم البقري والفلفل الأخضر

لحم بقري مع فلفل أخضر وبراعم بامبو وغيرهما من الخضار. يتم تقطيعها جميعا إلى شرائح رفيعة ثم تحمر وتتبل بصلصة الصويا والسكر ونبيذ الأرز.

Pfannengerührtes, kleingeschnittenes Rindfleisch und grüne Paprikaschoten

Rindfleisch, grüne Paprikaschoten, Bambussprossen und andere Gemüse werden in dünne Streifen geschnitten, im Wok scharf angebraten und dann mit Sojasoße, Zucker und Reiswein abgeschmeckt.

Sauté de bœuf et de poivrons verts en lamelles

Du bœuf, des poivrons verts, des pousses de bambou et d'autres légumes coupés en fines lamelles sont assaisonnés à la sauce de soja, au sucre et à l'alcool de riz.

Salteado de Carne de Res y Pimiento Morrón

Se corta carne de res, pimiento morrón, brotes de bambú y otras verduras en pequeñas tiras para saltearse y sazonarse con salsa de soja, azúcar y sake.

Sauté di striscioline di manzo e peperoni verdi

Manzo, peperoni verdi, germogli di bambù e altri ingredienti vengono saltati condendoli con salsa di soia, zucchero, sakè e altro.

Tiras finas de carne e pimentão refogadas

Carne de gado, pimentões, brotos de bambu e outros vegetais são cortados em tiras finas, refogados ao estilo chinês e condimentados com molho de soja, açúcar e vinho de arroz.

蠔油牛肉（Hao You Niu Rou）

Stir-Fried Beef and Vegetables in Oyster Sauce

Beef and vegetables are stir-fried and flavored with rich-tasting oyster sauce resulting in a tasty dish featuring a pleasantly mild, sweet flavor.

kcal ●●

© S.T.

蠔油牛肉

這是將牛肉和蔬菜一起煸炒，用濃蠔油調味而成的菜肴。其特點是清甜爽口，易於品嘗。

Pfannengerührtes Rindfleisch und Gemüse in Austernsoße

Rindfleisch und Gemüse werden im Wok scharf angebraten und dann mit der wohlschmeckenden Austernsoße gewürzt. Das Ergebnis ist ein angenehm mildes, süßlich gewürztes Gericht.

蚝油牛肉

这是将牛肉和蔬菜一起煸炒，用浓蚝油调味而成的菜肴。其特点是清甜爽口，易于品尝。

Sauté de bœuf et de légumes à la sauce d'huîtres

Ce mets savoureux au goût sucré et agréablement léger contient du bœuf et des légumes sautés relevés d'une sauce d'huîtres au goût riche.

쇠고기와 야채의 굴소스볶음

쇠고기와 야채를 볶아서 진한 굴소스로 간을 한 요리. 감칠 맛이 있어 먹기 좋다.

Salteado de Carne de Res y Verduras en Salsa de Ostras

Se saltea y sazona la carne de res y las verduras con una salsa de ostras condimentada para obtener un platillo aromático caracterizado por un suave y dulce sabor.

牛肉と野菜のオイスターソース炒め

牛肉と野菜を炒め、コクのあるオイスターソースで味付けした料理。ほんのり甘味があって食べやすい。

Sauté di manzo e verdure in salsa di ostriche

Manzo e verdure vengono saltati condendoli con saporita salsa di ostriche. È un piatto appetitoso dal gusto leggermente dolce.

لحم بقري وخضر محمرة في صلصة المحار

يحمر اللحم البقري والخضر ويتبل بصلصة محار سخية الطعم لإعداد طبق شهي يتصف بمذاق سكري ممتع ومعتدل.

Carne e vegetais refogados com molho de ostra

Carne de gado e vegetais são refogados ao estilo chinês e condimentados com molho de ostra de fino sabor. O resultado é um prato delicioso, de sabor agradavelmente leve e doce.

洋蔥牛肉絲（Yang Cong Niu Rou Si）

© S.T.

Stir-Fried Beef and Onions

This dish features the perfect combination of beef and onions stir-fried in a sauce flavored with soy sauce, rice wine, sugar and soup stock that allows the sweetness of the onions to bring out the true flavor of the beef.

kcal ●●

洋蔥牛肉絲

將牛肉和於其味覺相融的洋蔥放在一起煸炒，再用醬油、酒、白糖、湯料調味而成。洋蔥的清甜使牛肉清香倍增。

Pfannengerührtes Rindfleisch mit Zwiebeln

Dieses Gericht ist eine perfekte Kombination aus Rindfleisch und Zwiebeln, die im Wok scharf angebraten und in einer Soße aus Sojasoße, Reiswein, Zucker und Brühe pfannengerührt wird. Hierdurch bringt der süßliche Geschmack der Zwiebeln das volle Aroma des Rindfleisches hervor.

洋葱牛肉丝

将牛肉和与其味觉相融的洋葱放在一起煸炒，再用酱油、酒、白糖、汤料调味而成。洋葱的清甜使牛肉清香倍增。

Sauté de bœuf et d'oignons

Ce plat représente un mélange parfait de bœuf et d'oignons que l'on fait revenir dans une sauce agrémentée de sauce de soja, de vin de riz, de sucre et de bouillon de volaille. Le goût légèrement sucré des oignons relève la vraie saveur du bœuf.

쇠고기양파볶음

쇠고기와 잘 어울리는 양파를 볶은 다음 간장, 술, 설탕, 육수 등으로 맛을 낸 요리. 양파의 단맛이 쇠고기 맛을 한층 더 좋게 한다.

Salteado de Carne de Res y Cebollas

Este platillo se caracteriza por la perfecta combinación de carne de res y cebollas salteadas en una pasta compuesta por salsa de soja, sake, azúcar y extracto de sopa. De esta forma, el sabor dulce de las cebollas hace resaltar el verdadero sabor de la carne de res.

牛肉と玉ねぎの炒めもの

牛肉と相性がよい玉ねぎを炒め、しょうゆ、酒、砂糖、スープなどで調味。玉ねぎの甘味とコクで肉のうまみが増す。

Sauté di manzo e cipolle

Manzo e cipolle, che ben si combinano fra di loro, vengono saltati condendoli con salsa di soia, sakè, zucchero, brodo e altro. Il dolce sapido delle cipolle esalta il gusto della carne.

خليط محمر من اللحم البقري والبصل

خليط ممتاز من اللحم البقري والبصل يتم تحميره في صلصة متبلة بصلصة الصويا ونبيذ الأرز والسكر والبهريز بحيث يؤدي الطعم الحلو للبصل إلى إبراز نكهة اللحم الحقيقية .

Carne e cebolas refogados

Este prato apresenta a combinação perfeita de carne de gado com cebolas refogados ao estilo chinês, em um tempero preparado com molho de soja, vinho de arroz, açúcar e concentrado para sopa. É uma iguaria em que a doçura da cebola realça o sabor da carne.

紅燒牛肉（Hong Shao Niu Rou）

Simmered Beef in Soy Sauce

Beef is simmered in soy sauce laden with the flavor of ginger and leeks for several hours to bring out the deep, rich flavor of the meat.

kcal ●●

© S.T.

紅燒牛肉

將牛肉用放入生姜和蔥花的醬油湯汁中長時間燉煮而成的，散發牛肉清香鮮味的一道菜肴。

Gesottenes Rindfleisch in Sojasoße

Rindfleisch wird mehrere Stunden lang in Sojasoße geköchelt, die mit Ingwer und Lauch angereichert ist. Dies bringt den vollen und reichen Geschmack des Fleisches richtig zur Geltung.

红烧牛肉

将牛肉用放入生姜和葱花的酱油汤汁中长时间炖煮而成的，散发牛肉清香鲜味的一道菜肴。

Bœuf mijoté dans une sauce de soja

On fait mijoter du bœuf pendant plusieurs heures dans une sauce de soja enrichie de gingembre et de poireaux, ce qui accentue le goût riche et marqué de la viande.

쇠고기간장조림

생강과 파로 향을 낸 간장조림 국물에 쇠고기를 장시간 조린 요리. 쇠고기 맛이 충분히 우러나 있다.

Guisado de Carne de Res en Salsa de Soja

Se cuece durante varias horas la carne de res a fuego lento en una mezcla de salsa de soja sazonada con jengibre y puerro para extraer el intenso y rico sabor de la carne.

牛肉のしょうゆ煮込み

しょうがとねぎの風味がきいたしょうゆ味の煮汁で、牛肉を長時間煮込んだもの。牛肉のうまみをたっぷり味わえる。

Manzo bollito in salsa di soia

Il manzo viene fatto sobbollire a lungo in un brodo insaporito con salsa di soia e aromatizzato con zenzero e porri, che evidenzia appieno il sapore della carne.

لحم بقري مطهو مع صلصة الصويا

يطهى اللحم البقري فوق نار هادئة في صلصة صويا متبلة بالزنجبيل والبصل الأخضر، وذلك لساعات طويلة، حتى يبرز المذاق القوي للحم بطعمه اللذيذ.

Carne cozida com molho de soja

A carne de gado é cozida durante várias horas em fogo brando, com molho de soja fortemente aromatizado com gengibre e cebolinha. Este cozimento realça o sabor rico e consistente da carne.

咕老肉（Gu Lao Rou）

© S.T

Sweet and Sour Pork

Deep-fried chunks of pork are stir-fried with green peppers, onions and pineapple and then bathed in a sweet and sour sauce for a rich-tasting and satisfying dish.

kcal ●●

咕老肉

將預先炸熟的豬肉與青椒、洋蔥、菠蘿放在一起煸炒，再用甜中帶酸的調味汁勾芡烹飪而成的一道風味濃鬱的菜肴。

Süßsaures Schweinefleisch

Fritierte Schweinefleischstücken werden mit grünen Paprikaschoten, Zwiebeln und Ananas pfannengerührt und anschließend mit einer süßsauren Soße übergossen. Ein Gericht mit vollem Geschmack, das den Gaumen verwöhnt.

咕老肉

将预先炸熟的猪肉与青椒、洋葱、菠萝放在一起煸炒，再用甜中带酸的调味汁勾芡烹饪而成的一道风味浓郁的菜肴。

Porc à l'aigre-doux

On fait sauter de gros morceaux de porc frits avec des poivrons verts, des oignons et de l'ananas que l'on trempe ensuite dans une sauce aigre-douce, ce qui en fait un plat nourrissant au goût riche.

탕수육

튀긴 돼지고기와 피망, 양파, 파인애플 등을 볶아서 새콤달콤한 소스로 버무린 진한 맛이 나는 요리.

Cerdo Agridulce

Este platillo bien condimentado y exquisito se hace salteando pedazos de cerdo refrito con pimientos morrones, cebollas y piña para después bañar el conjunto en una salsa agridulce.

酢豚

揚げた豚肉とピーマン、玉ねぎ、パイナップルなどを炒め、甘酸っぱいソースをからめた濃厚な味の料理。

Maiale in agrodolce

È un piatto dal ricco sapore, preparato con pezzetti di carne di maiale fritti in abbondante olio, saltati poi con peperoni verdi, cipolle, ananas e altri ingredienti e infine legati con una salsa agrodolce.

طبق حلو حامض من اللحم

تحضر قطع مكتنزة من لحم الخنزير مع الفلفل الأخضر والبصل والأناناس ثم تغمر في صلصة حلوة يضاف إليها الخل لتحصل على طبق رائع لذيذ الطعم.

Carne de porco agridoce

Pedaços de carne de porco fritos por mergulho em óleo são refogados na frigideira chinesa com pimentões, cebolas e abacaxi. Em seguida, tudo é regado com um molho agridoce para criar um prato de sabor rico e agradável.

回鍋肉（Hui Guo Rou）

Stir-Fried Boiled Pork and Cabbage in Spicy Fermented Bean Paste

This is a sweet and spicy dish prepared by stir-frying boiled pork and cabbage with Chinese fermented bean paste. This dish is also called twice-cooked pork because the boiled pork is cooked again when it is stir-fried in a wok.

kcal ●●

©S.T.

回鍋肉

將煮熟豬肉片與圓白菜在一起煸炒，再用中國面醬調節鹹甜。由於是將煮過的肉再次放回鍋中進行烹飪，故得其名。

回锅肉

将煮熟猪肉片与圆白菜在一起煸炒，再用中国面酱调节咸甜。由于是将煮过的肉再次放回锅中进行烹饪，故得其名。

삶은 돼지고기와 양배추의 매운 장볶음

삶은 돼지고기와 양배추를 볶아 중국 된장으로 매콤달콤하게 조미한 요리. 한번 삶은 고기를 다시 볶는다는 데서 "回鍋肉"이라 불린다.

ゆで豚肉とキャベツの辛みそ炒め

ゆでた豚肉とキャベツを炒め、中国みそで甘辛く調味。一度ゆでた肉を再び鍋に戻して炒めることから "回鍋肉" と呼ばれる。

لحم محمر مع الكرنب في معجون الميسو

هذا طبق حلو حريف يتم إعداده بسلق لحم الخنزير والكرنب ثم تحميرهما مع الميسو الصيني (مادة تتبيل من فول الصويا)، ويطلق أيضا على هذا الطبق اسم " لحم مطهر مرتين " حيث يعاد طهي الخنزير المسلوق عند تحميره في المقلاة الصينية.

Pfannengerührtes, gekochtes Schweinefleisch und Kohl in würziger Paste aus fermentierten Bohnen

Dies ist ein süß abgeschmecktes und würziges Gericht, bei dem gekochtes Schweinefleisch und Kohl im Wok scharf angebraten und dann mit fermentierter chinesischer Bohnenpaste pfannengerührt wird. Dieses Gericht wird auch zweimal gekochtes Schweinefleisch genannt, da das bereits gekochte Schweinefleisch noch einmal beim Pfannenrühren im Wok gekocht wird.

Sauté de porc et de chou bouilli à la pâte de soja fermenté parfumé au piment rouge

Ce plat sucré et épicé se prépare en faisant revenir du porc bouilli et du chou avec de la pâte de soja fermenté parfumé au piment rouge. Comme ici on a d'abord fait bouillir le porc avant de le faire revenir, cette recette porte également le nom de porc " cuit deux fois ".

Salteado de Cerdo y Col en Pasta Aromática de Soja Fermentada

Este es un dulce y fragante platillo que se prepara salteando carne de cerdo cocido y col con pasta de soja china fermentada. También, se le conoce como plato que se prepara dos veces, por ser la carne de cerdo una vez hervida y luego se vuelve a cocinar cuando se saltea en un sartén chino llamado "wok".

Sauté di maiale bollito con miso piccante

È un piatto dolce-piccante preparato saltando fette di maiale bollito e cavolo con miso (passato di soia fermentato) cinese. È anche chiamato "maiale cotto due volte", in quanto il maiale viene bollito e poi saltato nel wok, la padella cinese multiuso.

Carne de porco e repolho refogados com molho picante

Este é um prato adocicado e picante que se prepara refogando, à moda chinesa, carne de porco fervida e repolho, com pasta de soja fermentada picante. O prato também se chama "carne de porco duplamente cozida", porque a carne de porco fervida é cozida outra vez, ao ser refogada na frigideira chinesa.

榨菜肉絲（Zha Cai Rou Si）

© S.T.

Stir-Fried Meat with Szechwan Pickles

Thinly-sliced Szechwan pickles, meat and vegetables are stir-fried allowing the characteristic flavor of the pickles and salt to accent the taste of the other ingredients.

kcal ●●

榨菜肉絲

這是將切成絲的榨菜同肉和蔬菜放到一起煸炒，形成了以榨菜特有腌制風味為主體的一道菜肴。

榨菜肉丝

这是将切成丝的榨菜同肉和蔬菜放到一起煸炒，形成了以榨菜特有腌制风味为主体的一道菜肴。

착채고기볶음

채썬 착채(중국 무김치의 하나)와 고기, 야채 등을 볶은 것. 착채의 독특한 풍미와 소금기가 요리에 악센트를 준다.

ザーサイと肉の炒めもの

細切りにしたザーサイと肉、野菜などを炒めたもの。ザーサイ特有の風味と塩けが、味のアクセントになる。

لحم محمر مع مخلل ستشوان

تحضر شرائح رقيقة من مخلل ستشوان واللحم والخضر حتى تتخلل النكهة المميزة للملح وعيدان المستردة الخضراء، مذاق المكونات الأخرى.

Pfannengerührtes Fleisch mit nach Szechwan Art eingelegten Senfwurzelknollen

Dünn geschnittene, nach Szechwan Art eingelegte, fermentierte Senfwurzelknollen, Fleisch und Gemüse werden im Wok scharf angebraten, wobei der charakteristische salzige Geschmack der Senfwurzelknollen den Eigengeschmack der anderen Zutaten hervorheben.

Sauté de viande accompagné de légumes au vinaigre de Sichuan

On fait revenir la viande, les légumes et les légumes au vinaigre de Sichuan finement hachés, le goût caractéristique des légumes au vinaigre et du sel relevant ainsi la saveur des autres ingrédients.

Salteado de Carne con Tallo de Mostaza

Se saltea el tallo de mostaza de Szechwan adobado, la carne y las verduras cortadas en tiras, permitiendo que el sabor característico del tallo de mostaza y la sal acentúen el sabor de los demás ingredientes.

Sauté di carne con radice di senape in salamoia di szechwan

La radice di senape in salamoia di szechwan, tagliata sottile e saltata con carne, verdure e altro, accentua con il suo particolare sapore salato il gusto degli altri ingredienti.

Carne refogada ao estilo chinês com picles de Szech Wan

Picles de Szech Wan, carne e vegetais em tiras finas são refogados ao estilo chinês, permitindo que o sabor característico dos picles e o sal realcem o gosto dos demais ingredientes.

螞蟻上樹（Ma Yi Shang Shu）

Stir-Fried Bean Threads with Ground Pork

Stir-fried bean threads, ground pork and vegetables are stir-fried in chili sauce, soy sauce and other seasonings so that the slender bean threads absorb the flavor of the ingredients.

kcal ●

© S.T.

螞蟻上樹

將粉絲和肉末、蔬菜一起煸炒，以豆瓣醬和醬油調味鹹甜。配料的特有鮮味充分浸透於滑溜的粉絲內，是這道菜肴的特色。

Pfannengerührte Glasnudeln mit Schweinehackfleisch

Schweinehackfleisch und Gemüse werden in Chili-Soße, Sojasoße und mit anderen Gewürzen pfannengerührt und dann die Glasnudeln hinzugegeben. Die dünnen Glasnudeln nehmen dadurch den Geschmack aller Zutaten an.

蚂蚁上树

将粉丝和肉末、蔬菜一起煸炒，以豆瓣酱和酱油调味咸甜。配料的特有鲜味充分浸透于滑溜的粉丝内，是这道菜肴的特色。

Sauté de porc haché et de nouilles de haricots d'Orient

Dans une sauce contenant du chili, de la sauce de soja et d'autres ingrédients, on fait revenir du porc haché et des légumes sautés afin que les nouilles de haricots d'Orient absorbent la saveur des ingrédients.

당면과 다진 고기볶음

당면과 다진 돼지고기, 야채를 볶아 두반장과 간장 등으로 맛을 낸 것. 매끈매끈한 당면과 그 밖의 재료의 맛이 잘 어우러져 있다.

Salteado de Fideos con Carne de Cerdo

Se saltean los finos fideos de soja, la carne de cerdo molida y las verduras en salsa picante, salsa de soja y otros condimentos para que los finos fideos de soja absorban el sabor de los ingredientes.

春雨とひき肉の炒めもの

春雨と豚ひき肉、野菜を炒め、豆板醤やしょうゆなどで味付けしたもの。つるつるとした春雨に、材料のうまみがからまって美味。

Sauté di vermicelli di fecola e carne di maiale tritata

Vermicelli di fecola, carne di maiale tritata, verdure e altro vengono saltati con salsa piccante Doban Djan, soia e altri condimenti. Il sapore dei vari ingredienti si amalgama ai vermicelli e ne nasce un piatto prelibato.

عيدان اللوبيا المحمرة مع اللحم المفروي

تخلط عيدان اللوبيا المحمرة مع لحم الخنزير المفري والخضر وتحمر في مزيج من الصلصة الحارة وصلصة الصويا وغيرهما من المتبلات حتى تمتص اللوبيا الرفيعة نكهة شهية من مختلف المكونات.

Fios gelatinosos refogados com carne de porco moída

Fios gelatinosos de amido de feijão refogados ao estilo chinês, carne de porco moída e vegetais são refogados na frigideira com molho apimentado, molho de soja e outros condimentos, de tal modo que os finos fios gelatinosos de amido de feijão absorvam o sabor dos demais ingredientes.

炸肉丸子（Zha Rou Wan Zi）

© S.T.

Deep-Fried Ground Pork Dumplings

Eggs, salt and soy sauce are mixed into ground pork which is then shaped into dumplings and deep-fried in oil to create a kind of Chinese meatball.

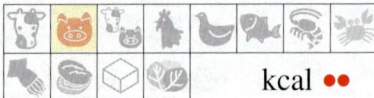

kcal ●●

炸肉丸子

這是在豬肉末內打入雞蛋、放進鹽、醬油，充分拌勻後捏成丸子、用油炸成的中國風味的肉丸子。

Fritierte Schweinehackfleischbällchen

Eier, Salz und Sojasoße werden mit Schweinehackfleisch gemischt und dann zu Fleischbällchen geformt, die anschließend in Öl ausgebacken werden. Eine Art chinesische Frikadelle.

炸肉丸子

这是在猪肉末内打入鸡蛋、放进盐、酱油，充分拌匀后捏成丸子、用油炸成的中国风味的肉丸子。

Boulettes de porc haché frites

Après avoir mélangé des œufs, du sel et de la sauce de soja avec du porc haché, on façonne le tout en boulettes que l'on fait frire dans de l'huile afin de créer une sorte de boulettes de viande à la chinoise.

고기완자튀김

다진 돼지고기에 달걀, 소금, 간장을 섞어서 완자형으로 둥글게 빚어 기름에 튀긴 중국식 미트볼.

Albóndigas Chinas de Cerdo

Se mezcla huevo, sal y salsa de soja con carne de cerdo molida, dando la forma de bolas y se fríen en aceite abundante.

揚げ肉団子

豚ひき肉に卵や塩、しょうゆを混ぜて団子状に丸め、油で揚げた中国風ミートボール。

Polpettine di maiale fritte

Con un impasto di carne di maiale tritata, uova, sale e salsa di soia si preparano delle palline che vengono fritte in abbondante olio; sono l'equivalente cinese delle polpettine occidentali.

كرات محمرة من اللحم المفري

يخلط البيض والملح وصلصة الصويا مع لحم الخنزير المفري ثم يشكل المزيج على هيئة كرات تحمر تحميراً غزيراً لإعداد نوع من الكفتة الصينية.

Almôndegas fritas de carne de porco

Dá-se a forma de bolinhos a uma mistura contendo carne de porco moída, ovos, sal e molho de soja. Fritam-se então as pequenas porções por mergulho em óleo, para criar almôndegas ao estilo chinês.

叉燒肉（Cha Shao Rou）

Chinese Roast Pork

Roast pork is marinated for several hours in a sauce containing a mixture of soy sauce, sugar and fragrant vegetables, and then baked in an oven and served in thin slices.

kcal ●●

© S.T.

叉燒肉

這是將豬肉塊浸漬於用醬油、白糖、香菜拌成的佐料中數小時，用烤箱烘烤後，再切成薄片的一種菜肴。

Geröstetes chinesisches Schweinefleisch

Schweinerostbraten wird mehrere Stunden lang in einer Marinade aus Sojasoße, Zucker und duftendem Gemüse mariniert, im Backofen überbacken und dann in dünnen Scheiben serviert.

叉烧肉

这是将猪肉块浸渍于用酱油、白糖、香菜拌成的佐料中数小时，用烤箱烘烤后，再切成薄片的一种菜肴。

Porc rôti à la chinoise

Le porc rôti est mariné pendant plusieurs heures dans une sauce contenant un mélange de sauce de soja, de sucre et de légumes aromatisés, que l'on fait ensuite cuire au four et que l'on sert en tranches fines.

구운 돼지고기

간장, 설탕, 향미 야채 등을 섞은 양념 국물에 덩이 돼지고기를 수시간 재어 두었다가 오븐에 구워서 얇게 썬 것.

Cerdo Chino Tostado

Es un rosbif chino de cerdo conservado durante varias horas en una mezcla de salsa de soja, azúcar y verduras fragantes. Después se hornea y se sirve en finas rebanadas.

焼き豚

しょうゆ、砂糖、香味野菜などを合わせたタレに、豚のかたまり肉を数時間漬け込み、オーブンで焼いて薄切りにしたもの。

Arrosto di maiale

Un blocco di carne di maiale viene fatto macerare per varie ore in un miscuglio di salsa di soia, zucchero, verdure aromatiche e altri ingredienti. Cotto in forno, viene poi servito tagliato a fette sottili.

روستو اللحم على الطريقة الصينية

يوضع روستو الخنزير لساعات طويلة في صلصة تحوي مزيجاً من صلصة الصويا والسكر والخضر ذات الرائحة القوية، ثم يحمر في الفرن ويقدم بعد تقطيعه إلى شرائح رقيقة .

Carne de porco assada

A carne de porco é marinada durante várias horas em uma mistura de molho de soja, açúcar e vegetais aromáticos. Depois, é assada no forno e servida em fatias finas.

雲白肉片（Yun Bai Rou Pian）

© S.T.

Boiled Pork with Garlic Sauce

Boneless pork is boiled and then cut into thin slices and covered with a garlic sauce. The mildly flavored pork and richly aromatic sauce make an appetizing match.

kcal ●●

雲白肉片

這是將五花豬肉塊煮熟後切成薄片，再加入蒜味調料進行食用的一種菜肴。豬肉的清淡配上濃鬱的調料使菜肴風味恰到好處。

云白肉片

这是将五花猪肉块煮熟后切成薄片，再加入蒜味调料进行食用的一种菜肴。猪肉的清淡配上浓郁的调料使菜肴风味恰到好处。

마늘소스를 끼얹은 삶은 돼지고기

삶은 삼겹살을 얇게 썰어 마늘소스를 끼얹은 요리. 담백한 돼지고기가 진한 맛의 소스와 잘 어울린다.

ゆで豚のにんにくソースがけ

豚バラ肉のかたまりをゆでて薄切りにし、にんにく風味のソースをかけた料理。さっぱりとした豚肉と濃厚なソースがよく合う。

Gekochtes Schweinefleisch mit Knoblauchsoße

Kurze Rippe vom Schwein wird gekocht und dann in dünne Scheiben geschnitten. Anschließend wird es mit einer Knoblauchsoße übergossen. Das mild gewürzte Schweinefleisch und die aromatische Soße bilden einen appetitlichen Kontrast.

Porc bouilli à la sauce à l'ail

On fait bouillir du porc désossé, on le coupe en tranches fines et on l'arrose de sauce à l'ail. Le porc légèrement aromatisé et la sauce fortement aromatique forment un mélange appétissant.

Cocido de Cerdo con Salsa de Ajo

Se cuece el tocino fresco de cerdo y se come esparciendo la salsa de ajo sobre la carne cortada en rebanadas finas. El cerdo suavemente aderezado y el delicioso aroma de la salsa ofrecen una apetitosa combinación.

Bollito di maiale con salsa all'aglio

Un blocco di ventre di maiale viene bollito, tagliato a fette sottili e ricoperto con una salsa all'aglio. Il sapore blando della carne si combina bene con quello forte della salsa.

لحم مسلوق مع صلصة الثوم

يسلق لحم الخنزير الخالي من العظم ثم يقطع إلى شرائح رقيقة تغطى بصلصة الثوم، وهنا نجد أن النكهة المعتدلة للحم الخنزير تتوافق تماما مع النكهة اللذيذة والقوية للصلصة لتكونا معاً طبقاً شهياً.

Carne de porco fervida com molho de alho

A carne de porco desossada é fervida, cortada em fatias e coberta com molho de alho. A carne levemente temperada e o molho ricamente aromatizado combinam-se numa iguaria muito apetitosa.

北京烤鴨（Bei Jing Kao Ya）

Peking Duck

One of the most famous delicacies among Peking cuisine, this dish is enjoyed by placing duck skin, roasted to a golden brown, on a thin rice cake, applying sweet fermented bean paste and then rolling the mixture up with leeks.

© S.T.

kcal ●●

北京烤鴨

將烤成金黃的鴨子皮披成薄片，放在薄餅上、蘸上甜面醬後與蔥裹在一起食用。這是具有代表性的高級北京菜之一。

Peking-Ente

Dies ist eines der berühmtesten Delikatessen der Peking-Küche. Bei diesem Gericht wird goldbraun geröstete Entenhaut auf einen dünnen Reiskuchen gelegt, dann süß fermentierte Bohnenpaste aufgetragen und alles zusammen dann mit Lauch aufgerollt.

北京烤鴨

將烤成金黃的鴨子皮披成薄片，放在薄饼上、蘸上甜面酱后与葱裹在一起食用。这是具有代表性的高级北京菜之一。

Canard à la pékinoise

Ce plat, qui est l'un des mets les plus célèbres de la cuisine pékinoise, se déguste en mettant la peau de canard cuite à point, des poireaux en julienne et de la pâte de soja fermenté sur une mince crêpe roulée.

북경식 오리구이

잘 구워진 오리고기 껍질을 단 맛이 나는 된장에 찍어 파와 같이 전병에 싸서 먹는다. 대표적인 북경고급요리.

Pato Pequinés

Este delicioso platillo es uno de los manjares más famosos del arte culinario de Pekín. La piel del pato tostada hasta el punto dorado oscuro se coloca sobre crepas de pasta de arroz. Se adereza con una dulce pasta de soja fermentada y se enrolla junto con puerros.

アヒルの直火焼き（ペキンダック）

こんがり焼いたアヒルの皮を薄餅の上にのせて甘みそをつけ、ねぎと一緒に包んで食べる。北京料理を代表する高級料理。

Anatra alla pechinese

È un piatto di alta gastronomia, fra i più famosi della cucina di Pekino. Dell'anatra arrostita si mangia la pelle dorata e croccante, spalmandola con miso dolce e avvolgendola con porri in sottili crespelle di farina di riso.

البط البكيني

هذا الطبق هو واحد من أشهر الأطباق اللذيذة في مطبخ العاصمة الصينية، ويتم إعداده بتحمير البط حتى يصبح لونه بنياً غامقاً، ويؤكل بوضع شريحة محمرة من البط فوق رقاقة مصنوعة من الدقيق، ويضاف إليه معجون حلو من الميسو (مادة تنبيل من فول الصويا) ثم يضاف البصل الأخضر وتلف الرقاقة حول المزيج.

Pato de Pequim

Uma das mais renomadas iguarias da cozinha de Pequim, este prato consiste em pele de pato, dourada ao forno, disposta sobre uma massa fina de arroz. Adiciona-se pasta de feijão fermentada e adoçada, e enrola-se então o petisco juntamente com cebolinha.

腰果雞丁（Yao Guo Ji Ding）

© S.T.

Stir-Fried Chicken and Cashews

Aromatic, fried cashew nuts are stir-fried with diced chicken and assorted vegetables and then given a sweet and spicy flavor.

kcal ●●●

腰果雞丁

這是將炸得香熱的腰果與切成丁的雞肉、蔬菜放在一起煸炒後，進行鹹甜調味而制成的一道菜肴。

Pfannengerührtes Hühnerfleisch mit Cashew-Nüssen

Aromatische, geröstete Cashew-Nüsse werden mit in Würfel geschnittenem Hühnerfleisch und verschiedenen Gemüsesorten pfannengerührt und anschließend süßlich und scharf abgeschmeckt.

腰果鸡丁

这是将炸得香热的腰果与切成丁的鸡肉、蔬菜放在一起煸炒后，进行咸甜调味而制成的一道菜肴。

Sauté de poulet et de noix de cajou

Avec des noix de cajou parfumées et frites, on fait revenir du poulet coupé en dés avec un assortiment de légumes que l'on arrose d'une sauce sucrée et piquante.

닭고기캐슈너트볶음

고소하게 튀겨 낸 캐슈너트(cashew nut)와 각썰기를 한 닭고기, 야채 등을 볶아서 매콤새콤하게 맛을 낸 것.

Salteado de Pollo y Nueces de Acajú

Se saltea pollo, nueces fritas de la India y una variedad de verduras y se les da un sabor dulce y fragante.

鶏とカシューナッツの炒めもの

香ばしく揚げたカシューナッツとさいの目に切った鶏肉、野菜などを炒め、甘辛く味付けしたもの。

Sauté di pollo e mandorle indiane

Fragranti mandorle indiane passate in olio bollente, pollo tagliato a dadi, verdure e altri ingredienti vengono saltati e conditi in modo dolce-piccante.

دجاج محمر مع الكاشوناتا

تحمر الكاشوناتا المحمصة (نوع من المكسرات) ذات المذاق القوي مع قطع مكعبة من الدجاج والخضر المختلفة ثم يتبل الخليط بنكهة حلوة حريفة.

Frango xadrez

Aromáticas castanhas-de-caju fritas são refogadas na frigideira chinesa com carne de frango cortada em cubinhos e vegetais diversos. A mistura é condimentada para adquirir um sabor doce e apimentado.

油淋子雞（You Lin Zi Ji）

Crispy Fried Chicken with Fragrant Sauce

This fragrant dish involves deep-frying chicken by applying oil to the skin, frying to a crispy texture, and then serving with an aromatic sauce containing garlic, leeks and ginger.

kcal ●●

油淋子雞

在雞肉的表面上邊淋油邊炸至酥，然後用蒜、蔥、姜調成的調料澆汁而成 。其特點是噴香撲鼻，味鮮宜人。

油淋子鸡

在鸡肉的表面上边淋油边炸至酥，然后用蒜、葱、姜调成的调料浇汁而成 。其特点是喷香扑鼻，味鲜宜人。

양념소스를 끼얹은 닭튀김 (깐풍기)

표면에 기름을 발라가면서 바삭하게 튀긴 닭고기에 마늘, 파, 생강을 넣은 양념소스를 끼얹은 구수한 풍미의 요리.

揚げ鶏の香味ソースがけ

表面に油をかけながら鶏肉をカラリと揚げ、にんにく、ねぎ、しょうが入りの香味ソースをかけた香ばしい料理。

دجاج محمر هش مع صلصة طيبة الرائحة

هذا طبق طيب الرائحة من الدجاج المحمر تحميراً غزيراً، ويتم إعداده بدهان جلد الدجاج بالزيت ثم تحمير الدجاج حتى يصبح هشاً، ويقدم مع صلصة متبلة من الثوم والبصل الأخضر والزنجبيل.

Kroß gebratenes Hühnerfleisch mit würziger Soße

Bei diesem würzigen Gericht wird Öl auf die Haut des Huhns aufgetragen und dies anschließend kroß gebraten. Es wird mit einer aromatischen Soße serviert, die Knoblauch, Lauch und Ingwer enthält.

Poulet frit croustillant à la sauce parfumée

Ce plat parfumé contient du poulet que l'on fait frire en l'arrosant d'huile afin d'obtenir une texture croustillante. Il se sert accompagné d'une sauce aromatisée contenant de l'ail, des poireaux et du gingembre.

Pollo Frito en Salsa Fragante

Este fragante platillo se prepara esparciendo aceite bien caliente sobre la piel del pollo friendo hasta que alcanza una textura crujiente. Se sirve con una salsa aromática que contiene ajo, puerros y jengibre.

Pollo fritto in salsa aromatica

È un piatto dal profumo invitante, costituito da croccante carne di pollo fritta in abbondante olio irrorandone continuamente la pelle e servita in salsa aromatica di aglio, porri e zenzero.

Frango frito crocante com molho aromático

Este prato aromático é feito com pedaços de frango fritos por mergulho em óleo, em cuja pele aplica-se constantemente óleo quente até que a mesma adquira uma textura crocante. Serve-se com um molho aromático contendo alho, cebolinha e gengibre.

棒棒雞（Bang Bang Ji）

© S.T.

Steamed Cold Chicken with Sesame Sauce

This is a cold dish enjoyed by pouring a sesame sauce containing hot pepper oil over cucumbers and steamed, shredded chicken.

kcal ●

棒棒雞

在黃瓜和蒸熟擢碎的雞肉上，澆上含辣椒油的麻醬而食用的一種美味冷菜。

Gedünstetes kaltes Huhn mit Sesamsoße

Dies ist ein kaltes Gericht, bei dem eine Sesamsoße, die mit scharfem Pfefferöl abgeschmeckt ist, über Gurken und gedünstetes, kleingeschnittenes Hühnerfleisch gegossen wird.

棒棒鸡

在黄瓜和蒸熟擢碎的鸡肉上，浇上含辣椒油的麻酱而食用的一种美味冷菜。

Poulet froid cuit à la vapeur aromatisé à la sauce au sésame

C'est un plat froid composé de poulet coupé en lamelles cuit à la vapeur et de concombres, le tout arrosé de sauce au sésame à base d'huile de piment.

참깨소스를 끼얹은 삶은 닭고기

삶아서 살을 발라 놓은 닭고기와 오이 위에 고추기름을 넣은 참깨소스를 끼얹은 냉채.

Pollo al Vapor en Salsa de Sésamo

Este es un tipo de entremés que se sirve frío. Se disfruta esparciendo la salsa de sésamo (ajonjolí) con aceite picante sobre pepinos y pollo cocido desmenuzado.

蒸し鶏のごまダレがけ

きゅうりや蒸してほぐした鶏肉などの上に、ラー油入りのごまダレをかけた冷菜。

Pollo cotto a vapore in salsa di sesamo

È un piatto freddo di pollo cotto a vapore, sminuzzato e mescolato con cetrioli e una salsa fatta di sesamo e olio al peperoncino.

دجاج بارد مغطى بصلصة السمسم

هذا الطبق يقدم بارداً ويعد بسكب صلصة سمسم محتوي على زيت فلفل حار فوق مزيج من خيار وشرائح رفيعة من الدجاج المطهو على البخار.

Frango frio cozido em vapor com molho de gergelim

Este é um prato frio, que se saboreia despejando molho de gergelim com óleo picante sobre pepino fatiado e frango desfiado, cozido a vapor.

炸雞塊（Zha Ji Kuai）

Chinese-Style Fried Chicken

This popular and satisfying dish is prepared by flavoring chicken with spices, rice wine and soy sauce, coating it with flour and deep-frying in oil to a golden brown color.

kcal ●●

© S.T.

炸雞塊

將雞肉用香料、酒和醬油腌制調味後，裹上面粉用油炸至呈金黃色澤。雞香誘人，是一道深受人們喜愛的菜肴。

Gebratenes Hühnchen nach chinesischer Art

Bei diesem populären und wohlschmeckenden Gericht wird Hühnerfleisch mit Gewürzen, Reiswein und Sojasoße gewürzt, das Fleisch in Mehl gewendet und anschließend in Öl goldbraun ausgebacken.

炸鸡块

将鸡肉用香料、酒和酱油腌制调味后，裹上面粉用油炸至呈金黄色泽。鸡香诱人，是一道深受人们喜爱的菜肴。

Poulet frit à la chinoise

Ce plat populaire et nourrissant se prépare en assaisonnant du poulet avec des épices, du vin de riz et de la sauce de soja, en l'enrobant de farine et en le faisant frire dans l'huile jusqu'à ce qu'il ait une jolie couleur dorée.

닭튀김

닭고기에 향신료 또는 술, 간장으로 조미하여 튀김가루를 입혀 기름에 튀긴 것. 구수한 맛으로 인기있는 요리.

Pollo Frito al Estilo Chino

Este popular y delicioso platillo se prepara condimentando al pollo con especias, vino de arroz y salsa de soja; después se cubre con harina y se fríe en abundante aceite hasta que adquiere un color dorado oscuro.

鶏の唐揚げ

鶏肉に香辛料や酒、しょうゆで下味をつけ、粉をまぶして油でこんがり揚げたもの。香ばしい味で人気の一品。

Pollo fritto alla cinese

È un piatto appetitoso e popolare, preparato insaporendo pezzetti di pollo con spezie, sakè e salsa di soia, infarinandoli e friggendoli in abbondante olio fino a che diventano dorati.

دجاج محمر على الطريقة الصينية

يعد هذا الطبق الشعبي اللذيذ بتتبيل الدجاج بالبهارات ونبيذ الأرز وصلصة الصويا ثم يغطى بالدقيق ويحمر تحميراً غزيراً حتي يكتسب لوناً ذهبياً.

Frango frito ao estilo chinês

Muito apreciado, este prato saboroso é preparado condimentando-se o frango com temperos, vinho de arroz e molho de soja, passando-o na farinha e fritando-o por mergulho em óleo até dourar.

三色拼盆（San Se Pin Pen）

© S.T.

Assorted Cold Plate Appetizer

Three kinds of cold appetizers are attractively arranged on a plate. A wide range of ingredients are used including meat, chicken and jellyfish, which are arranged in various assortments.

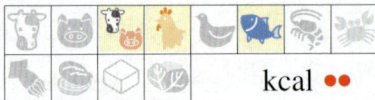

kcal ●●

三色拼盆

這是一道將三種涼菜精美擺放的冷盆。用有肉、雞肉、海蜇等各種材料，拼擺樣式也為觀賞興趣之一。

Appetitanregende gemischte kalte Platte

Drei Sorten kalter Appetitshäppchen werden auf einem Teller attraktiv arrangiert. Hierbei können zahlreiche verschiedene Zutaten verwendet werden, einschließlich Fleisch, Hühnchen und Quallen, die auf verschiedene Art zubereitet und angeordnet werden.

三色拼盆

这是一道将三种凉菜精美摆放的冷盆。用有肉、鸡肉、海蜇等各种材料，拼摆样式也为观赏兴趣之一。

Hors-d'œuvre variés

Ce plat offre trois sortes de hors-d'œuvre froids arrangés de façon décorative sur une assiette. Il est composé d'une large palette d'ingrédients tels que de la viande, du poulet et de la méduse joliment présentés en divers assortiments.

삼품전채 (삼품냉채)

세 종류의 차가운 요리를 접시에 예쁘게 담은 전채요리. 고기, 닭고기, 해파리 등 여러 가지 재료를 사용하여 보기좋게 담은 모양도 또 하나의 즐거움.

Entremés Combinado

Un entremés que se colocan los tres ingredientes básicos en forma atractiva sobre un plato. Además, se puede disfrutar las distintas combinaciones utilizando diversos ingredientes, como carne de res, cerdo, pollo, medusa, etc.

三種前菜の盛り合わせ

３種類の冷たい料理を皿にきれいに並べた前菜。牛肉や豚肉、鶏肉、くらげなどさまざまな材料を使い、盛り付けも楽しみのひとつ。

Misto di antipasti freddi

Tre tipi di antipasti freddi vengono disposti in modo attraente sul piatto di portata. Si usano ingredienti vari, tra i quali carne, pollo, meduse, e anche la presentazione è una piacevole componente del piatto.

تشكيلة من المشهيات الباردة

ترتب ثلاثة أنواع من المشهيات الباردة بشكل جميل فوق صحن الطعام، ويستخدم لإعداد هذا الطبق العديد من المكونات من بنها اللحم والدجاج وقنديل البحر، في تشكيلة متنوعة.

Entrada sortida servida fria

Três tipos de iguarias frias são dispostos de modo atraente num prato. Utiliza-se uma grande variedade de ingredientes, entre os quais carne, frango e medusa, dispostos no prato em vários arranjos.

清蒸鮮魚（Qing Zheng Xian Yu）

Steamed Fish

Fresh fish is steamed whole with leeks and ginger and then coated with a sauce of hot oil and soy sauce just prior to serving.

kcal ●

© S.T.

清蒸鮮魚

在整條新鮮的白肉魚上放蔥、姜後，用水清蒸，然後再用燒熱的油和醬油調料進行澆汁。

Gedünsteter Fisch mit weißem Fleisch

Ein ganzer frischer, weißfleischiger Fisch wird mit Lauch und Ingwer gedünstet und dann kurz vor dem Servieren mit einer Soße aus heißem Öl und Sojasoße übergossen.

清蒸鲜鱼

在整条新鲜的白肉鱼上放葱、姜后，用水清蒸，然后再用烧热的油和酱油调料进行浇汁。

Poisson vapeur

On fait cuire à la vapeur un poisson frais entier que l'on agrémente de poireaux et de gingembre ; on arrose ensuite le tout d'une sauce à base de soja et d'huile piquante juste avant de servir.

생선찜

신선한 흰살 생선에 파, 생강을 얹어 통째로 쪄낸 다음 뜨거운 기름과 간장소스를 끼얹은 생선요리.

Pescado al Vapor

Se cuece al vapor el pescado fresco junto con puerros y jengibre y justo antes de servir se baña en un condimento preparado con aceite caliente y salsa de soja.

魚の姿蒸し

新鮮な白身魚にねぎ、しょうがをのせてまるごと蒸し、熱した油としょうゆのソースをかけた魚料理。

Pesce intero cotto a vapore

Un pesce fresco e di carne bianca, cotto a vapore cosparso di porri e zenzero tagliuzzati, viene presentato intero, irrorandolo di olio bollente misto a salsa di soia poco prima di servire.

سمك مطهو على البخار

تطهى السمكة كاملة مع البصل الأخضر والزنجبيل ثم تغطى قبل التقديم مباشرة بصلصة من الزيت الحار وصلصة الصويا.

Peixe cozido em vapor

O peixe fresco é cozido por inteiro em vapor, com cebolinha e gengibre, e coberto com óleo quente e molho de soja pouco antes de ser servido.

幹燒蝦仁（Gan Shao Xia Ren）

© S.T.

Shrimp with Spicy Tomato Sauce

This typical Chinese-style shrimp dish is prepared by stir-frying shrimp in a spicy sauce containing tomato ketchup and chili sauce.

kcal ●●

幹燒蝦仁

這是一道將蝦用番茄醬、含豆瓣醬的辣味調料進行煸炒而成的中國傳統蝦類菜。辣甜適中、深受大眾歡迎。

干烧虾仁

这是一道将虾用番茄酱、含豆瓣酱的辣味调料进行煸炒而成的中国传统虾类菜。辣甜适中、深受大众欢迎。

새우칠리소스

새우를 토마토케첩과 두반장을 넣은 소스로 볶은 대표적인 중국의 새우요리. 매운 맛과 단 맛이 잘 조화된 인기 높은 메뉴.

えびのチリソース

えびをトマトケチャップ、豆板醤入りのソースで炒めた、代表的な中華のえび料理。辛味と甘味のバランスがよく、人気の高いメニュー。

جمبري بصلصة الطماطم الحريفة

طبق شعبي من الجمبري (الروبيان) على الطريقة الصينية يتم إعداده بتحمير الجمبري في صلصة حريفة تشتمل على صلصة طماطم من نوع الكاتشوب وصلصة الفلفل الأحمر.

Garnelen mit scharfer Tomatensoße

Dieses typische chinesische Garnelengericht besteht aus Garnelen, die in einer würzigen Soße aus Tomaten-Ketchup und Chili-Soße pfannengerührt wird.

Crevettes à la sauce tomate piquante

Ce plat de crevettes typiquement chinois se prépare en faisant revenir des crevettes dans une sauce piquante contenant de la sauce tomate et de la sauce pimentée.

Langostinos con Salsa Picante de Tomate

Este típico platillo de langostino al estilo chino se prepara salteando los langostinos en salsa catsup y salsa picante, que brindan un armonioso sabor dulce y picante.

Gamberetti in salsa piccante di pomodoro

Questo tipico piatto cinese viene preparato cuocendo i gamberetti a fuoco vivo con una salsa piccante di ketchup e salsa piccante Doban Djan. Per il suo equilibrio di gusto dolce e piccante, è un piatto assai richiesto.

Camarão com molho de tomate picante

Este prato tipicamente chinês prepara-se refogando camarão ao estilo chinês em um molho contendo ketchup e pimenta-malagueta.

青豆蝦仁 (Qing Dou Xia Ren)

Stir-Fried Shrimp with Green Peas

This colorful dish features the combination of green peas and shrimp stir-fried to bring out the unique texture of the shrimp.

kcal ●●

© S.T.

青豆蝦仁

將新鮮蝦仁和青豆放在一起燜炒而成的這道菜肴，蝦肉質地滑溜，色香誘人，使您無法拒絕。

Pfannengerührte Garnelen mit grünen Erbsen

Diese farbenfrohe Gericht besteht aus einer Kombination von grünen Erbsen und Garnelen, die im Wok scharf angebraten werden, wodurch die Garnelen einen ganz charakteristischen Biß erhalten.

青豆虾仁

将新鲜虾仁和青豆放在一起燜炒而成的这道菜肴，虾肉质地滑溜，色香诱人，使您无法拒绝。

Sauté de crevettes accompagnées de petits pois

Ce plat coloré associe un mélange de petits pois et de crevettes que l'on fait sauter afin de souligner la texture particulière des crevettes.

보리새우와 그린피스볶음

색깔이 고운 새우와 그린피스를 볶은 것. 새우의 톡 터지는 듯한 맛이 일품이다.

Salteado de Langostinos con Guisantes

Este platillo lleno de colorido se caracteriza por la combinación de los guisantes y los langostinos salteados que brindan una textura original a los langostinos.

芝えびとグリンピースの炒めもの

色どりがきれいな、えびとグリンピースの炒めもの。えびのプリッとした食感がたまらない。

Gamberetti saltati con piselli

Gli ingredienti costituiscono una bella combinazione di colori e la netta sensazione dei gamberetti in bocca è irresistibile.

جمبري محمر مع البازلاء الخضراء

هذا الطبق بلونه الجميل يتكون من مزيج من البازلاء الخضراء والجمبري (الروبيان) يتم تحميرهما معاً إلى أن يبرز الشكل المميز للجمبري.

Camarões refogados com ervilhas

Este prato de cores vivas apresenta uma combinação de ervilhas com camarões refogados ao estilo chinês, em que se destaca a textura singular do camarão.

高麗蝦仁（Gao Li Xia Ren）

© S.T.

Batter-Fried Shrimp

Shelled shrimp are coated with a mixture of flour, egg white and salt, deep-fried to a fluffy texture and served with Szechwan salt and pepper and ketchup.

kcal ●●

高麗蝦仁

將蝦裹上用面粉、蛋白、鹽調成的漿糊後，放入鍋中油炸，將炸後的蝦蘸著花椒鹽和甜面醬食用，松軟脆香，鮮美可口。

In Teig fritierte Garnelen

Die Garnelen werden mit Schale in einem Gemisch aus Mehl, Eiweiss und Salz gewendet und dann fritiert. Auf der Oberfläche bildet sich so eine lockere Textur. Die Garnelen werden dann mit Czechwan-Salz und Pfeffer sowie Ketchup serviert.

高丽虾仁

将虾裹上用面粉、蛋白、盐调成的浆糊后，放入锅中油炸，将炸后的虾蘸着花椒盐和甜面酱食用，松软脆香，鲜美可口。

Crevettes frites

Après avoir été décortiquées, les crevettes sont enrobées d'un mélange de farine, de blanc d'œuf et de sel que l'on fait frire jusqu'à l'obtention d'une texture légère et que l'on sert ensuite avec du sel et du poivre de Sichuan ainsi que du ketchup.

새우 달걀흰자튀김

새우에 밀가루, 달걀 흰자, 소금을 섞어 만든 튀김옷을 입혀 가볍게 튀겨 낸 것. 소금이나 케첩에 찍어 먹는다.

Langostinos Rebozados

Se rebozan los langostinos con cáscara en una mezcla de harina, clara de huevo y sal y se fríen hasta alcanzar una textura esponjosa. Se sirven con sal, pimienta y salsa catsup de Szechwan.

えびの卵白揚げ

えびに小麦粉、卵白、塩を混ぜ合わせた衣をつけ、フワッと揚げたもの。花椒塩やケチャップをつけて食べる。

Gamberetti fritti in albume

I gamberetti vengono passati in una pastella di farina, albume e sale e poi fritti in abbondante olio con un risultato di soffice consistenza; si mangiano con sale e pepe di Szechwan o con ketchup.

جمبري مغلف ومحمر

يغطى الجمبري (الروبيان) دون تقشيره بمزيج مخفوق من الدقيق وبياض البيض والملح ثم يحمر تحميراً غزيراً حتى ينفش الغطاء، ويقدم مع صلصة السشوان والملح والفلفل والكاتشوب.

Camarões empanados

Camarões parcialmente com casca são cobertos com uma mistura de farinha de trigo, clara de ovo e sal. Fritos por mergulho em óleo até adquirir uma textura fofa, são servidos com uma mistura de sal e pimenta de Szech Wan, e ketchup.

海蜇皮（Hai Zhe Pi）

Jellyfish Salad

This appetizer features jellyfish and vegetables bathed in a sesame-flavored, sweet and sour dressing to bring out the characteristic flavor of the chewy jellyfish.

kcal ●

© S.T.

海蜇皮

這是將海蜇和蔬菜用帶有香油味的甜醋拌成的冷菜。海蜇獨特的咀嚼口感增添了這道菜肴的美味。

Quallensalat

Dieses appetitanregende Gericht besteht aus Quallen und Gemüse, die mit einem süßsauren Dressing, das mit Sesam gewürzt ist, übergossen werden. Dies akzentuiert den charakteristischen Geschmack der etwas bißfesten Quallen.

海蜇皮

这是将海蜇和蔬菜用带有香油味的甜醋拌成的冷菜。海蜇独特的咀嚼口感增添了这道菜肴的美味。

Salade de méduse

Cet hors-d'œuvre se compose de méduse et de légumes que l'on fait tremper dans un assaisonnement aigre-doux au parfum de sésame afin de relever la saveur caractéristique de la méduse, dont la texture est un peu dure.

중국식 해파리무침

해파리와 야채를 새콤달콤한 참깨맛 소스로 버무린 전채요리. 해파리 특유의 꼬들꼬들한 맛이 난다.

Medusa a la Vinagreta

En este sabroso entremés se baña a la medusa y las verduras en un aderezo agridulce con sabor a sésamo que realza el peculiar sabor de la medusa comestible.

くらげの中華風あえもの

くらげと野菜をごま風味の甘酢ダレであえた前菜。歯ごたえのよいくらげには、特有のうまみがある。

Insalata di meduse

È un antipasto di striscioline di meduse e verdure condite con salsa agrodolce all'aroma di sesamo. Le meduse hanno una consistenza "al dente" e un sapore particolare.

سلطة قنديل البحر

هذا الصنف من المشهيات هو عبارة عن شرائح من قنديل البحر والخضر مغموسة في سائل حلو حمضي متبل بالسمسم يبرز النكهة المميزة لقنديل البحر بقوامه اللدن.

Salada de medusa

Esta entrada consiste em medusa e vegetais regados com molho agridoce condimentado com gergelim. Sente-se o sabor característico e a consistência firme da medusa ao se mastigar.

海鮮粉絲（Hai Xian Fen Si）

© S.T

Stir-Fried Seafood and Bean Threads

This simple stir-fried dish is enjoyed by practically everyone, featuring the appealing combination of seafood and bean threads mildly flavored with salt.

kcal ●●

海鮮粉絲

是魚貝類與粉絲一起煸炒烹成的鹹味菜肴，兩種材料的美味互相融和，是大眾喜愛的菜譜之一。

Pfannengerührte Seefrüchte mit Glasnudeln

Dieses einfache, pfannengerührte Gericht schmeckt wirklich fast jedem. Es ist eine ansprechende Kombination aus Meeresfrüchten und Glasnudeln, die leicht mit Salz gewürzt sind.

海鲜粉丝

是鱼贝类与粉丝一起煸炒烹成的咸味菜肴，两种材料的美味互相融和，是大众喜爱的菜谱之一。

Sauté de fruits de mer et de nouilles de haricots d'Orient

Ce sauté simple est apprécié de tout le monde ; il présente un appétissant mélange de fruits de mer et de nouilles de haricots d'Orient légèrement assaisonnés de sel.

해산물 당면볶음

어패류와 당면이 잘 어울리며, 소금으로 간을 한 심플한 볶음요리. 누구 입에나 잘 맞는 요리.

Salteado de Mariscos con Fideos de Soja

Este sencillo platillo salteado es disfrutado prácticamente en todos los sitios. Se caracteriza por la apetecible combinación de los mariscos y fideos de soja, suavemente condimentada con sal.

海の幸と春雨の炒め煮

魚介類のうまみと春雨がよくマッチした、塩味のシンプルな炒めもの。誰にでも好まれる一品。

Sauté di frutti di mare e vermicelli di fecola

È un piatto semplice e gradito da tutti, in cui il sapore dei frutti di mare esaltato dal sale ben si accompagna ai vermicelli di fecola.

قواقع البحر المحمرة مع عيدان اللوبيا

هذا الطبق البسيط من الطعام المحمر يتصف بمذاق يرضي كل الأذواق حيث يشتمل على مزيج جذاب من الكائنات البحرية وعيدان اللوبيا ويعبق بقليل من الملح .

Frutos do mar e fios gelatinosos refogados

Este refogado simples, ao estilo chinês, é apreciado praticamente por todos. Apresenta uma agradável combinação de frutos do mar com fios gelatinosos de amido de feijão, suavemente condimentados com sal.

芙蓉蟹（Fu Rong Xie）

Egg Foo Yung

Crab, vegetables and other ingredients are mixed together with eggs and then fried into a fluffy delicacy. The sweet and sour sauce made with soy sauce and other flavorings goes well with the eggs.

kcal ●●

© S.T.

芙蓉蟹

這是一道在雞蛋中摻入螃蟹和蔬菜末烹飪制出的菜肴。帶醬油味的甜酸芡汁，與雞蛋的自然風味摻合，相映成輝。

芙蓉蟹

这是一道在鸡蛋中掺入螃蟹和蔬菜末烹饪制出的菜肴。带酱油味的甜酸芡汁，与鸡蛋的自然风味掺合，相映成辉。

게살을 넣은 달걀부침

달걀에 게살과 야채 등을 넣어 부드럽게 부쳐 낸 달걀 부침. 새콤달콤한 간장소스가 달걀과 잘 어울린다.

かに玉

卵に、かにや野菜などの具を混ぜてフワッと焼き上げた料理。しょうゆ味の甘酸っぱいあんが卵によく合う。

بيض فو يون

تخلط الكابوريا (السرطان) والخضر وغيرها مع البيض ثم يقلى الخليط حتى ينفش قوامه، وتضاف إلى البيض صلصة تلائمه ذات مذاق حلو حامض معدة من صلصة الصويا مع متبلات أخرى.

Foo Yung-Eier

Krebsfleisch, Gemüse und andere Zutaten werden mit Eiern gemischt und dann zu einer lockeren Delikatesse gebraten. Die süßsaure Soße, die aus Sojasoße und anderen Gewürzen hergestellt wird, ist die perfekte Ergänzung zu den Eiern.

Foo Yung aux œufs

Après avoir mélangé du crabe, des légumes et d'autres ingrédients avec des œufs, on fait frire le tout jusqu'à obtention d'une texture légère. La sauce aigre-douce à base de sauce de soja et d'autres condiments se marie bien avec les œufs.

Tortilla de Cangrejo

Se combinan cangrejo, verduras y otros ingredientes junto con huevos y se fríen como una golosina esponjosa. La salsa agridulce hecha con salsa de soja y otros condimentos hace una magnífica combinación con los huevos.

Uova foo yung

Preparato un composto di uova, polpa di granchi e verdure, lo si frigge ottenendo una soffice consistenza. Il piatto viene servito con una salsina agrodolce addensata con fecola che ben si sposa alle uova.

Caranguejo com ovos

Carne de caranguejo, vegetais e outros ingredientes são misturados com ovos e fritos para formar uma iguaria fofa. O caldo agridoce, preparado com molho de soja e vários condimentos, e o sabor dos ovos formam uma agradável combinação.

八寶菜（Ba Bao Cai）

Stir-Fried Combination

Meat, seafood and various kinds of vegetables are stir-fried and lightly flavored to create a dish that is nutritiously balanced and healthy.

kcal ●●

八寶菜

這是一道將肉、魚貝類及各種蔬菜放在一起煸炒而成，味道清淡，營養全面的健康菜肴。

Pfannengerührte Kombination

Fleisch, Meeresfrüchte und verschiedene Arten Gemüse werden pfannengerührt und mild gewürzt. Ein nahrhaftes, ausgewogenes und gesundes Gericht.

八宝菜

这是一道将肉、鱼贝类及各种蔬菜放在一起煸炒而成，味道清淡，营养全面的健康菜肴。

Mélange sauté

Ce mets équilibré et sain se compose de viande, de fruits de mer et de diverses sortes de légumes sautés puis légèrement aromatisés.

팔보채

고기, 어패류, 여러 가지 야채를 볶아서 담백한 맛을 낸 것. 여러 가지 재료를 사용하므로 영양 밸런스도 좋은 건강음식.

Combinación Salteada

Se saltea carne, mariscos y distintas clases de verduras y se les condimenta ligeramente para crear un platillo que además de nutritivo es saludable.

八宝菜

肉、魚介類、いろいろな野菜を炒め、さっぱり味付け。具だくさんで栄養バランスのよい、ヘルシーな料理。

Sauté misto

Carne, frutti di mare e vari tipi di verdure vengono saltati e conditi leggermente; si ottiene così un piatto assai vario, sano e dieteticamente ben bilanciato.

طبق من خليط محمر

هو طبق من اللحم والكائنات البحرية والخضر المختلفة يتم تحميرها معاً مع تتبيل خفيف لتحصل على طبق من طعام صحي ومتوازن غذائياً.

Refogado de carne, frutos do mar e vegetais

Carne, frutos do mar e várias espécies de vegetais são refogados ao estilo chinês e levemente temperados, para criar um prato que é nutritivamente balanceado e saudável.

炒青菜（Chao Qing Cai）

Sauteed Vegetables

A combination of green Chinese vegetables are briskly stir-fried in oil and flavored with salt to create a dish that is an enjoyable substitute for salad.

kcal ●

©S.T.

炒青菜

其烹飪方法是將中國的蔬菜用油略煸炒後，用鹽進行調味。它與沙拉一樣是人們喜歡點的一道菜。

Sautiertes Gemüse

Eine Kombination von grünem chinesischen Gemüse, das rasch in sehr heißem Öl pfannengerührt und dann mit Salz gewürzt wird, ergibt ein Gericht, das sich hervorragend als Ersatz für einen Salat eignet.

炒青菜

其烹饪方法是将中国的蔬菜用油略煸炒后，用盐进行调味。它与沙拉一样是人们喜欢点的一道菜。

Sauté de légumes

Ce plat, pouvant facilement remplacer la salade, contient un mélange de légumes verts chinois que l'on fait revenir vivement dans l'huile et que l'on assaisonne de sel.

푸른채소볶음

중국야채를 기름에 재빨리 볶아 소금으로 조미한 것. 샐러드 대용으로 주문해도 좋은 요리.

Verduras Salteadas

Es una combinación de legumbres verdes chinas salteadas rápidamente en aceite y condimentadas con sal para crear un delicioso platillo que puede sustituir a la ensalada.

青菜の炒めもの

中国野菜を油で手早く炒め、塩で調味。サラダがわりに注文したい一品。

Sauté di verdure

È un piatto di verdure cinesi cotte velocemente a fuoco vivo nell'olio e insaporite soltanto con sale, un'alternativa alle insalate che consigliamo di provare.

خضر سوتيه

مجموعة من الخضر المختلفة تحمر تحميراً خفيفاً في الزيت وتتبل بالملح لإعداد طبق لذيذ يحل محل السلطة.

Verduras ligeiramente refogadas

Uma variedade de verduras chinesas é refogada ligeiramente em óleo e condimentada com sal no preparo deste prato, que é um ótimo substituto para saladas.

奶油白菜（Nai You Bai Cai）

© S.T.

Chinese Cabbage in Cream Sauce

Chinese cabbage is boiled until just tender and then covered with a tasty cream sauce. This dish brings out the flavor of the chicken broth and dried shrimp, creating a taste that is much lighter than traditional Western cream sauce dishes.

kcal ●●

奶油白菜

將白菜用小火煮熟後，再加入生奶油調味。由與菜的風味保持著雞湯和乾蝦的香味，同西餐的奶油蔬菜相比，口感更是清淡。

Chinakohl in Sahnesoße

Chinakohl wird gekocht, bis er gerade weich zu werden beginnt, und dann mit einer schmackhaften Sahnesoße übergossen. Dieses Gericht bringt den Geschmack von Hühnerbrühe und getrockneten Krabben hervor und kreiert einen Geschmack, der viel milder ist, als traditionelle westliche Gerichte mit Sahnesoßen.

奶油白菜

将白菜用小火煮熟后，再加入生奶油调味。由于菜的风味保持着鸡汤和干虾的香味，同西餐的奶油蔬菜相比，口感更是清淡。

Chou chinois à la crème

Après avoir fait bouillir le chou chinois jusqu'à ce qu'il soit tendre, on l'arrose d'une sauce onctueuse à la crème. Cette préparation relève le goût du bouillon de poulet et des crevettes séchées, ce qui lui confère une saveur beaucoup plus légère que celle des plats occidentaux traditionnels à base de crème.

배추의 크림수프

배추를 부드럽게 삶아서 생크림으로 맛을 낸다. 닭국물과 말린 새우의 맛이 살아있는 서양풍의 크림수프보다 담백한 맛이 난다.

Col China en Salsa Cremosa

Se hierve la col china hasta que queda suave y se cubre con una aromática salsa cremosa. Este platillo destaca el sabor del caldo de pollo y el langostino seco, creando un gusto mucho más ligero que el de los platillos tradicionales de crema en Occidente.

白菜のクリーム煮

白菜を柔らかく煮て生クリームで風味づけ。とりがらスープや干しえびのうまみが生き、洋風のクリーム煮よりさっぱりした味。

Cavolo cinese in salsa cremosa

Il cavolo cinese viene bollito fino a farlo diventare tenero e insaporito con una salsa cremosa, nella quale risaltano i sapori del brodo di pollo e dei gamberetti secchi. Risulta più leggero di un analogo piatto occidentale.

كرنب صيني مع صلصة بيضاء

يسلق الكرنب الصيني حتى يلين قليلاً فقط ثم يغطى بصلصة بيضاء لذيذة الطعم، وتبرز في هذا الطبق نكهة حساء الدجاج والجمبري (الروبيان) المجفف مما يمنحه مذاقاً أخف بكثير من الأطباق الغربية التقليدية المعدة من الصلصة البيضاء.

Repolho-chinês em molho cremoso

O repolho-chinês, fervido até ficar tenro, é coberto com um saboroso molho cremoso. Neste prato, destaca-se o aroma do caldo de galinha e do camarão seco, num sabor bem mais suave do que o dos pratos convencionais com molho branco do Ocidente.

木樨肉（Mu Xi Rou）

Stir-Fried Egg and Vegetables

This attractive and colorful dish features the combination of fluffy scrambled eggs mixed with stir-fried meat and vegetables.

kcal ●●

©S.T.

木樨肉

先將雞蛋嫩炒一下，然後拌入另外炒好的肉和蔬菜。這道菜的特點是色澤美觀。

Pfannengerührte Eier und Gemüse

Dieses attraktive und farbenfrohe Gericht besteht aus einer Kombination von lockerem Rührei, das mit pfannengerührtem Fleisch und Gemüse gemischt ist.

木樨肉

先将鸡蛋嫩炒一下，然后拌入另外炒好的肉和蔬菜。这道菜的特点是色泽美观。

Sauté d'œufs et de légumes

Ce plat coloré et attrayant se compose d'un mélange d'œufs légèrement sautés, de viande et de légumes sautés à part.

달걀과 야채볶음

살짝 볶은 달걀에 따로 볶은 고기나 야채를 섞어 색깔의 배합이 산뜻한 요리.

Revuelto de Huevo con Verduras

Este atractivo platillo lleno de color se caracteriza por la combinación del huevo revuelto esponjoso junto con la carne salteada y las verduras.

炒り卵と野菜の炒めもの

フワッと炒めた卵と、別に炒めた肉や野菜を合わせた色どりのきれいな料理。

Uova strapazzate con verdure

Questo piatto dagli attraenti colori viene preparato mescolando soffici uova strapazzate con carne e verdure saltate a parte.

بيض مقلي مع الخضروات

هذا الطبق الجذاب بألوانه الجميلة هو عبارة عن مزيج من بيض مخفوق مقلي مع لحم وخضر محمرة.

Ovos e vegetais refogados

Este prato de cores atraentes combina ovos mexidos em consistência fofa com carne e vegetais refogados ao estilo chinês.

魚香茄子（Yu Xiang Qie Zi）

© S.T.

Szechwan-Style Stir-Fried Eggplant

Deep-fried eggplant and ground meat are stir-fried with chili sauce, soy sauce and other flavorings to create a dish that brings out the flavor of the eggplant in a spicy base that whets the appetite.

kcal ●●

魚香茄子

這是一道將油炸好的茄子和肉末用豆瓣醬和醬油等佐料煸炒而成的菜肴。茄子的香味和辛辣的刺激會使您的食欲頓開。

鱼香茄子

这是一道将油炸好的茄子和肉末用豆瓣酱和酱油等佐料煸炒而成的菜肴。茄子的香味和辛辣的刺激会使您的食欲顿开。

사천풍 가지볶음

튀긴 가지와 다진 고기를 두반장, 간장 등으로 볶은 요리. 가지의 맛과 매운맛이 어우러져 식욕을 돋구어 준다.

なすの四川風炒め

揚げたなすとひき肉を豆板醤、しょうゆなどで炒めた料理。なすのうまみとピリッとした辛味が食欲をそそる。

باذنجان محمر على طريقة ستشوان

يقلى الباذنجان ثم يضاف إليه اللحم المفري ويحمران معاً في صلصة الفلفل الأحمر الحار وصلصة الصويا وغيرهما من المتبلات لصنع طبق تبرز فيه نكهة الباذنجان بمذاق حريف مثير للشهية.

Pfannengerührte Auberginen nach Szechwan-Art

Fritierte Auberginen und Hackfleisch werden mit Chili-Soße, Sojasoße und anderen Gewürzen pfannengerührt. Dieses Gericht kombiniert den milden Geschmack der Auberginen mit einer würzigen Grundlage, so daß einem förmlich das Wasser im Munde zusammenläuft.

Sauté d'aubergines à la mode du Sichuan

Ce plat qui éveille l'appétit contient des aubergines frites et de la viande hachée que l'on fait revenir dans une sauce au piment, sauce de soja et autres condiments afin de relever la saveur des aubergines baignant dans une sauce épicée.

Salteado de Berenjena al Estilo Szechwan

La berenjena previamente frita se saltea junto con carne molida en una combinación de salsa picante con salsa de soja y otros condimentos para crear un platillo que destaca el sabor de la berenjena en un guiso aromático que excita el apetito.

Melanzane saltate alla szechwan

Le melanzane, fritte in abbondante olio, vengono saltate con carne tritata e un condimento di salsa di soia, salsa piccante Doban Djan e altri ingredienti. Il sapore delle melanzane e il gusto piccante stimolano l'appetito.

Beringela refogada ao estilo Szech Wan

Beringela frita por mergulho em óleo e carne moída são refogadas na frigideira chinesa com molho apimentado, molho de soja e outros condimentos. É um prato que apresenta um sabor de beringela com teor picante, plenamente capaz de despertar o apetite.

油淋茄子（You Lin Qie Zi）

Deep-Fried Eggplant with Fragrant Sauce

This dish is prepared by making shallow cuts in the eggplant, deep-frying in oil and pouring a fragrant sauce of garlic and leeks over the eggplant. It is delicious either hot or cold.

kcal ●●

© S.T.

油淋茄子

先在茄子表面劃上幾道刀痕，放入油中煎炸，然後用蒜和蔥製成的香味調料澆汁。這道菜不論是趁熱還是涼後品嘗，都鮮美可口。

Fritierte Auberginen mit duftender Soße

Bei der Zubereitung dieses Gerichts werden die Auberginen flach angeschnitten, dann in Öl ausgebacken und mit einer duftenden Soße aus Knoblauch und Lauch übergossen. Heiß oder kalt eine wirkliche Delikatesse.

油淋茄子

先在茄子表面划上几道刀痕，放入油中煎炸，然后用蒜和蔥制成的香味调料浇汁。这道菜不论是趁热还是凉后品尝，都鲜美可口。

Aubergines frites en sauce parfumée

Ce mets se prépare en éminçant des aubergines, en les faisant frire dans l'huile puis en les arrosant d'une sauce parfumée à base d'ail et de poireaux. Il se déguste aussi bien chaud que froid.

양념소스를 끼얹은 가지튀김

칼집을 넣은 가지를 기름에 튀겨 마늘, 파를 넣은 양념소스를 끼얹은 요리. 뜨거울 때 그대로 먹어도 좋고 차갑게 해서 먹어도 좋다.

Berenjena Frita en la Salsa Fragante

Este platillo se prepara haciendo cortes superficiales a la berenjena, friéndola en aceite y recubriéndola en una salsa fragante de ajo y puerro. Frío o caliente, este platillo es delicioso.

揚げなすの香味ソースがけ

なすに切り目を入れて油で揚げ、にんにくやねぎ入りの香味ソースをかけた料理。温かいままでも冷たくしてもおいしい。

Melanzane fritte in salsa odorosa

Le melanzane, leggermente incise, vengono fritte in abbondante olio e servite ricoperte di una salsa odorosa contenente aglio e porro. Ottime sia calde che fredde.

باذنجان مقلي مع صلصة طيبة الرائحة

يتم إعداد هذا الطبق بعمل بضعة شقوق في الباذنجان ثم يقلى في الزيت وتسكب فوقه بعد ذلك صلصة قوية الرائحة من الثوم والبصل الأخضر، وهو طبق لذيذ الطعم سواء تناولته ساخناً أم بارداً.

Beringela frita com molho aromático

Este prato é preparado fazendo-se cortes superficiais na beringela, fritando-a por mergulho em óleo e regando-a com um molho aromático de alho e cebolinha. É delicioso tanto quente como frio.

辣黄瓜（La Huang Gua）

© S.T.

Szechwan Cucumber Slices

These pickled cucumber slices are flavored with red pepper and hot pepper oil for a spicy hot taste that stimulates the appetite.

kcal ●

辣黄瓜

這是一種用紅辣椒和辣椒油腌制的黃瓜，食後可使您的食欲增加。

Gurkenscheiben nach Szechwan-Art

Diese Scheiben von eingelegten Gurken sind mit spanischem Pfeffer und scharfem Pfefferöl gewürzt. Sie haben einen scharf-würzigen Geschmack, der den Appetit anregt.

辣黄瓜

这是一种用红辣椒和辣椒油腌制的黄瓜，食后可使您的食欲增加。

Concombres du Sichuan en lamelles

Ces lamelles de concombres marinées sont aromatisées avec de l'huile de poivron rouge et de piment afin d'en rehausser la saveur par un goût fort et relevé qui stimule l'appétit.

중국식 오이김치

빨간 고추와 고추기름의 매운맛이 식욕을 돋구어 주는 오이절임.

Adobado de Pepino

Estas rebanadas de pepino adobado son sazonadas con chile y aceite picante para crear un aromático sabor picante que estimula el apetito.

きゅうりのピリ辛漬け

赤唐辛子とラー油の辛味が食欲をそそる、きゅうりの漬けもの。

Cetrioli piccanti alla szechwan

Si tratta di cetrioli in conserva, dal piccante gusto di paprica e olio al peperoncino rosso che stimola l'appetito.

شرائح الخيار على طريقة ستشوان

هذه الشرائح الرفيعة من الخيار المخلل تتبل بالفلفل الأحمر وزيت الفلفل الحار لإضفاء، طعم حريف يفتح الشهية.

Pepino ao estilo de Szech Wan fatiado

Fatias de pepino em conserva, condimentadas com pimonta malagueta e óleo picante. O sabor apimentado estimula o apetite.

涼拌豆腐（Liang Ban Dou Fu）

Chinese-Style Cold Seasoned Bean Curd

Various seasonings are sprinkled over bean curd followed by pouring over a sauce flavored with sesame oil and hot pepper oil for a tasty and healthy treat.

kcal ●

涼拌豆腐

這是一道在豆腐上盛放各種配料的增進健康的菜肴。調味的關鍵在於香油和辣椒油。

涼拌豆腐

这是一道在豆腐上盛放各种配料的增进健康的菜肴。调味的关键在于香油和辣椒油。

중국식 냉두부

두부 위에 여러 가지 양념을 고명한 건강요리. 참기름과 고추기름이 들어간 양념장이 맛을 좌우한다.

中華風冷や奴

豆腐の上にさまざまな薬味をのせたヘルシーな料理。ごま油やラー油入りのタレが味の決め手。

توفو بارد متبل على الطريقة الصينية

تنثر مجموعة من التوابل فوق قطعة من التوفو ثم تسكب فوقها صلصة منكهة بزيت السمسم وزيت الفلفل الحار لإعداد طبق صحي لذيذ الطعم.

Kalter gewürzter Tofu nach chinesischer Art

Verschiedene Gewürze werden über Tofu (Sojabohnenquark) gestreut. Danach wird dieser mit einer Soße übergossen, die mit Sesamöl und scharfem Pfefferöl gewürzt ist. Ein schmackhaftes und gesundes Gericht.

Pâte de soja à la chinoise

Ce mets sain et savoureux contient de la pâte de soja que l'on a saupoudrée de divers condiments et arrosée d'une sauce aromatisée à l'huile de sésame et de piment.

Queso de Soja al Estilo Chino

Después de esparcir varios condimentos sobre el queso de soja, se recubre con una salsa compuesta por aceite de sésamo (ajonjolí) y aceite picante para crear un aromático y saludable convite.

Tofu freddo alla cinese

È un piatto sano di tofu ricoperto di vari gusti, in cui il tono base del sapore è dato dalla salsina che vi si versa sopra, composta di olio di sesamo e olio al peperoncino rosso.

Queijo de soja frio, condimentado

Vários condimentos são salpicados sobre o tofu. Rega-se então com um molho condimentado com óleo de gergelim e óleo picante. É uma iguaria saborosa e saudável.

麻婆豆腐（Ma Po Dou Fu）

© S.T.

Braised Bean Curd with Chili Sauce

This typical Szechwan dish features braised tofu and stir-fried ground meat flavored with chili sauce and other spices which is thickened with cornstarch for a spicy combination that brings out the appetite.

kcal ●●

麻婆豆腐

將豆腐和肉末放在一起煸炒後，用豆瓣醬調味，最後用澱粉勾芡。這是一道典型的四川菜。麻辣味會使您的食欲大開。

麻婆豆腐

将豆腐和肉末放在一起煸炒后，用豆瓣酱调味，最后用淀粉勾芡。这是一道典型的四川菜。麻辣味会使您的食欲大开。

마파두부

두부와 다진 고기를 볶아서 두반장으로 맛을 내고 녹말가루로 걸쭉하게 한 대표적인 사천요리. 매콤한 맛이 식욕을 돋구어 준다.

マーボー豆腐

豆腐、ひき肉を炒めて豆板醤などで味付けし、片栗粉でとろみをつけた代表的な四川料理。ピリ辛味が食欲をそそる。

Geschmorter Tofu mit Chili-Soße

Dies ist ein typisches Gericht der Szechwan-Küche. Geschmorter Tofu (Sojabohnenquark) und pfannengerührtes Hackfleisch, die mit Chili-Soße und anderen Gewürzen abgeschmeckt und dann mit Stärke gebunden werden, bieten eine Kombination, die so richtig Appetit macht.

Pâte de soja braisée à la sauce pimentée

Cette spécialité du Sichuan se compose de tofu braisé et de viande hachée sautée agrémentés d'une sauce à base de piment chili et d'autres épices, que l'on a épaissie avec de la farine de maïs, afin d'obtenir un mélange piquant qui ouvre l'appétit.

Salteado de Cuajada de Soja con Salsa Picante

Este platillo típico de Szechwan se caracteriza por el queso de soja dorado y la carne molida salteada. En esta apetitosa combinación, se adereza a ambos con un adobo concentrado de maicena, hecho a base de salsa picante y otros condimentos.

Brasato di tofu in salsa piccante doban djan

Questo piatto tipico della regione di Szechwan viene preparato saltando tofu e carne tritata, condendo con salsa piccante Doban Djan e altre spezie, e poi addensando il tutto con fecola. Il suo sapore piccante stuzzica l'appetito.

Queijo de soja refogado com molho de pimenta

Este prato típico de Szech Wan é feito com tofu e carne moída, retogados ao estilo chinês e condimentados com molho de pimenta e outros temperos. Engrossa-se com amido para formar uma iguaria picante, que desperta o apetite.

توفو مطهو مع صلصة الفلفل الأحمر

هذا الطبق الشعبي من إقليم ستشوان يتكون من قطع من التوفو تطهى على نار هادئة مع لحم مفري محمر في صلصة فلفل أحمر وتوابل أخرى، ويضاف للصلصة نشا الذرة ليثخن قوامها فتتحصل في النهاية على مزيج حريف يثير الشهية.

家常豆腐（Jia Chan Dou Fu）

Fried Bean Curd with Meat and Vegetables

This family-style dish goes great with rice, having just the right amount of spicy taste produced by simmering fried bean curd with leeks, mushrooms and meat.

kcal ●●

© S.T.

家常豆腐

這是一道將油炸豆腐、蔥、香菇和肉放在一起略煸炒後加水煮熟的家常菜。由於辣味適度，非常適合於下飯。

家常豆腐

这是一道将油炸豆腐、葱、香菇和肉放在一起略煸炒后加水煮熟的家常菜。由于辣味适度，非常适合于下饭。

튀긴 두부졸임

튀긴 두부, 파, 표고버섯, 고기를 볶아서 조린 가정요리. 적당한 매운 맛이 밥반찬으로 적격.

揚げ豆腐の炒め煮

揚げた豆腐、ねぎ、しいたけ、肉を炒め煮にした家庭料理。ほどよい辛味で、ご飯のおかずに格好。

توفو مـحـمـر مع لحم وخضر

هذا الطبق المناسب للعائلات يكون وجبة لذيذة إذا تناولته مع الأرز ، حيث يتمتع بقدر مناسب تماماً من المذاق الحريف الذي يتم الحصول عليه بطهي التوفو على نار هادئة مع اللحم والبصل الأخضر وعش الغراب.

Gebratener Tofu mit Fleisch und Gemüse

Dieses Gericht ist typische chinesische Hausmannskost und paßt gut zu Reis. Es hat gerade die richtige Würze, die durch Kochen des gebratenen Tofus (Sojabohnenquark) mit Lauch, Pilzen (Shiitake) und Fleisch entsteht.

Pâte de soja frite accompagnée de viande et de légumes

Ce plat familial s'harmonise bien avec du riz par son arôme suffisamment piquant obtenu en faisant mijoter de la pâte de tofu frite avec des poireaux, des champignons et de la viande.

Queso de Soja Frito con Carne y Verduras

Este platillo casero se lleva bastante bien con el arroz, pues logra un equilibrado sabor fragante cuando se cuece a fuego lento el queso de soja con puerros, champiñones y carne.

Tofu fritto con carne e verdure

Questo piatto di cucina casalinga preparato con tofu fritto in abbondante olio e poi cotto con porri, funghi shiitake e carne, ha un giusto grado di piccantezza, che ne fa un'ottima pietanza per accompagnare il riso in bianco.

Queijo de soja frito com carne e vegetais

Este prato caseiro faz um ótimo acompanhamento ao arroz. O sabor picante na medida certa resulta do cozimento em fogo alto de tofu frito, acompanhado de cebolinha, cogumelos e carne.

什錦鍋巴（Shi Jin Guo Ba）

© S.T.

Crispy Rice with Meat and Vegetable Sauce

This fragrant dish is prepared by covering rice fried to a crisp with a delicious, piping hot sauce containing meat and vegetables. It is famous for the hissing sound produced when the sauce is poured over the deep-fried rice.

kcal ●●●

什錦鍋巴

這是在剛炸好的鍋巴上澆上熱的什錦調味汁烹飪而成的一種菜肴。 澆汁瞬間發出的聲響，會給您的進餐增添不少樂趣。

什锦锅巴

这是在刚炸好的锅巴上浇上热的什锦调味汁烹饪而成的一种菜肴。浇汁瞬间发出的声响，会给您的进餐增添不少乐趣。

삼선 누룽지탕

금방 튀겨 낸 누룽지에 걸쭉한 소스를 부어 먹는 고소한 요리. 뜨거운 소스를 부을 때의 "치지직" 하는 소리가 재미있다.

おこげの五目あんかけ

揚げたてのおこげに熱い五目あんをかけた香ばしい料理。あんをかけた瞬間、ジュッと音が立つのも楽しみのひとつ。

ارز محمص مع صلصة اللحم والخضروات

هذا طبق طيب الرائحة يتم إعداده من أرز يحمر جيداً حتى يتحمص ثم تسكب فوقه صلصة حريفة ساخنة لذيذة الطعم من اللحم والخضر، ويشتهر هذا الطبق بالصوت المميز الذي تحدثه الصلصة المسكبة فوق الأرز المحمص.

Knuspriger Reis mit Fleisch und Gemüsesoße

Bei diesem duftendem Gericht wird kroß gebratener Reis mit einer köstlichen, siedendheißen Soße übergossen, die Fleisch und Gemüse enthält. Diese Speise ist insbesondere durch das zischende Geräusch bekannt, das entsteht, wenn die Soße über den knusprig gebratenen Reis gegossen wird.

Riz croustillant accompagné d'une sauce à la viande et aux légumes

Ce plat parfumé se prépare en versant sur du riz frit croustillant une délicieuse sauce bouillante à base de viande et de légumes. Ce plat est célèbre pour le bruit frémissant produit par la sauce lorsqu'on la verse sur le riz.

Arroz Tostado con Salsa de Carne y Verduras

Este fragante platillo se prepara esparciendo sobre el arroz tostado una deliciosa salsa espesa hirviente que contiene carne y verduras. Es famoso por el sonido silbante que produce cuando se baña con la salsa al arroz bien frito.

Riso fritto croccante in salsa di carne e verdure

Sul riso croccante, appena fritto in molto olio, viene versata una salsa bollente di carne e verdure legate con fecola. Il profumo che ne emana e lo sfriglio prodotto dalla salsa rendono il piatto ancor più gradito.

Arroz frito com molho de carne e vegetais

Este prato aromático é preparado cobrindo-se o arroz, frito por mergulho em óleo até ficar crocante, com um denso molho de carne e vegetais muito picante. É famoso pelo som característico que se produz quando o molho é despejado sobre o arroz frito, um pouco antes de ser servido.

蛋花湯（Dan Hua Tang）

Egg Drop Soup

This salt-based soup is flavored with light and airy shreds of lightly beaten egg that give the appearance of yellow flowers.

© S.T.

kcal ●

蛋花湯

飄浮在湯上的雞蛋花松軟，散發出陣陣清香。其形狀看上去好似黃色的花朵。 烹飪特點是時間短暫，用鹽調味。

蛋花汤

飄浮在汤上的鸡蛋花松软，散发出阵阵清香。其形状看上去好似黄色的花朵。烹饪特点是时间短暂，用盐调味。

달걀수프

살짝 익힌 달걀이 먹기좋은 소금간의 수프. 달걀은 노란색 꽃을 연상시킨다.

かき卵のスープ

ふんわりと火を通した卵がやさしい味わいの塩味のスープ。卵は黄色い花に見立てられている。

حساء قطرات البيض

هذا حساء، يتبل أساساً بالملح ويكتسب نكهته من البيض الذي يخفق قليلاً فيتشكل في الحساء، في خيوط خفيفة هشة تبدو كوردات من اللون الأصفر.

Suppe mit Eieinlage

Der Geschmack dieser Suppe basiert in erster Linie auf Salz. Der besondere Reiz liegt in den leichten und luftigen Fäden von geschlagenem Ei, die aussehen wie gelbe Blumen.

Soupe aux œufs filés

Cette soupe à base de sel est agrémentée de minces filets d'œufs légèrement battus, ce qui lui donne l'apparence de fleurs jaunes.

Sopa de Gotas de Huevo

Esta sopa de ligero sabor salado se cocina con sutiles y graciosas pizcas de huevo batido que dan la apariencia de flores amarillas.

Stracciatella

È una minestra dal semplice sapore dato dal sale e dalle uova sbattute, che cuocendo sembrano diventare soffici fiori gialli.

Sopa com ovos escaldados

Esta sopa à base de sal é enriquecida com tênues tiras de ovos ligeiramente batidos, que se assemelham a flores amarelas.

玉米羹（Yu Mi Geng）

© S.T.

Chinese-Style Corn Soup

This thick and rich soup contains creamed corn and lightly beaten eggs. The chicken broth base gives this soup a flavor that is somewhat different from its Western-style cousin, corn soup.

kcal ●

玉米羹

這是將奶油玉米和雞蛋煮湯後勾芡制成的一種菜肴。由於是以雞湯味為主，與西餐相比，有著不同的風味。

玉米羹

这是将奶油玉米和鸡蛋煮汤后勾芡制成的一种菜肴。由于是以鸡汤味为主，与西餐相比，有着不同的风味。

중국식 옥수수수프

크림상태의 옥수수와 달걀이 들어간 걸쭉한 수프. 닭고기수프를 베이스로 하므로 양식과는 또 다른 맛이 있다.

中華風コーンスープ

クリームコーンと卵が入ったとろみのあるスープ。とりがらスープがベースなので、洋風とは違ったおいしさ。

حساء كريمة الذرة على الطريقة الصينية

حساء ، شهي ثخين القوام من كريمة الذرة والبيض المخفوق قليلاً ، وهنا يمنح بهيز الدجاج نكهة للحساء تجعله يختلف بشكل ما عن حساء كريمة الذرة على الطريقة الغربية .

Maissuppe nach chinesischer Art

Diese dickflüssige und nahrhafte Suppe enthält passierten Mais und leicht geschlagene Eier. Die Basis aus Hühnerbrühe gibt der Suppe einen etwas anderen Geschmack als man es von westlichen Maissuppen her gewohnt ist.

Soupe de maïs à la chinoise

Cette soupe riche et épaisse contient de la crème de maïs et des œufs légèrement battus. Le bouillon de poulet utilisé donne à cette soupe une saveur quelque peu différente de celle de son pendant, la soupe de maïs à l'occidentale.

Crema de Maíz Estilo Chino

Esta espesa y rica sopa contiene maíz cremoso y huevos ligeramente batidos. La base de caldo de pollo le da a esta sopa un sabor ligeramente diferente al de su prima occidental, la sopa de maíz.

Minestra di mais alla cinese

È una minestra alquanto densa di crema di mais e uova sbattute. A base di brodo di pollo, ha un sapore diverso dalle minestre di mais occidentali.

Sopa de milho ao estilo chinês

Esta sopa rica, densa e suculenta contém milho cremoso e ovos ligeiramente batidos. A base do caldo de galinha dá a esta sopa um sabor diferente do oferecido pela sopa de milho ocidental.

酸辣湯（Suan La Tang）

Szechwan Hot and Sour Soup

This spicy soup features the flavors of pepper and vinegar accented with meat, eggs, bean curd, bamboo shoots and other hearty ingredients.

© S.T.

kcal ●

酸辣湯

這種湯帶有鬍椒和醋風味。湯內加入了許多肉、蛋、豆腐、竹筍等材料。

Scharfsaure Suppe nach Szechwan-Art

Diese würzige Suppe kombiniert den Geschmack von Pfeffer und Essig, akzentuiert mit Fleisch, Eiern, Tofu (Sojabohnenquark), Bambussprossen und anderer herzhafter Zutaten.

酸辣汤

这种汤带有胡椒和醋风味。汤内加入了许多肉、蛋、豆腐、竹笋等材料。

Soupe aigre et piquante à la Sichuan

Cette soupe épicée se compose de viande, d'œufs, de pâte de soja, de pousses de bambou et d'autres ingrédients copieusement agrémentés de poivre et de vinaigre.

사천풍 산미수프

후추, 식초가 들어간 스파이시한 수프. 고기, 달걀, 두부, 죽순 등의 재료가 많이 들어 있다.

Sopa Agridulce de Szechwan

Esta aromática sopa se caracteriza por los sabores del pimiento y el vinagre acentuados por la carne, huevos, cuajada de soja, brotes de bambú y otros nutritivos ingredientes.

四川風酸味スープ

こしょうと酢がきいたスパイシーなスープ。肉、卵、豆腐、たけのこなどの具がたくさん入っている。

Minestra all'agro di szechwan

È una minestra piuttosto piccante, in cui spicca il gusto del pepe e dell'aceto; ha molti ingredienti, quali carne, uova, tofu, germogli di bambù, ecc.

حساء ستشوان الحار بنكهة الخل

هذا الحساء الحريف يتميز بنكهة الخل والفلفل الحار بالإضافة إلى طعم اللحم والبيض والتوفو وبراعم البامبو وباقي المكونات اللذيذة التي يحتوي عليها الطبق.

Sopa picante e azedinha de Szech Wan

Esta sopa picante tem os sabores da pimenta e do vinagre, enriquecidos com carne, ovos, tofu, brotos de bambu e outros ingredientes apetitosos.

榨菜肉絲湯（Zha Cai Rou Si Tang）

© S.T.

Szechwan Pickles and Pork Soup

Shredded pork, Szechwan pickles and bamboo shoots are blended together to create an appetizing soup enhanced by the aroma and salty flavor of the pickles.

kcal ●

榨菜肉絲湯

這是用切成細絲的榨菜、竹筍、豬肉作成的湯。榨菜特有的腌鹹風味使湯美味無比。

Suppe mit nach Szechwan-Art eingelegten Senfwurzelknollen und Schweinefleisch

Schweinefleisch, nach Szechwan-Art eingelegte, fermentierte Senfwurzelknollen und Bambussprossen werden miteinander vermischt und ergeben eine appetitanregende Suppe, die durch das Aroma und den salzigen Geschmack der eingelegten Senfwurzelknollen bereichert wird.

榨菜肉丝汤

这是用切成细丝的榨菜、竹笋、猪肉作成的汤。榨菜特有的腌咸风味使汤美味无比。

Soupe de porc et de légumes au vinaigre du Sichuan marinés

Ce mélange de lamelles de porc, de légumes au vinaigre du Sichuan marinés et de pousses de bambou forme une soupe appétissante relevée par la saveur aromatique et salée des légumes au vinaigre.

착채 돼지고기수프

채썬 착채(중국 무김치의 하나), 죽순, 돼지고기가 들어간 수프. 착채의 풍미와 소금기가 수프의 맛을 한층 더해 준다.

Sopa de Cerdo con Tallos de Mostaza Adobados

El cerdo cocido a fuego lento se combina con tallo de mostaza de Szechwan adobadas y brotes de bambú cortadas en tiras para crear una apetitosa sopa realzada por el aroma y el agudo sabor del tallo de mostaza adobadas.

ザーサイと豚肉のスープ

細切りにしたザーサイ、たけのこ、豚肉が入ったスープ。ザーサイの風味と塩けがスープを味わい豊かにしている。

Minestra di maiale e radice di senape in salamoia di szechwan

È una minestra di radice di senape in salamoia, germogli di bambù e carne di maiale sminuzzati, il cui sapore è accentuato dal particolare gusto salato della radice in salamoia.

حساء اللحم مع مخلل ستشوان

يخلط لحم الخنزير مع مخلل ستشوان وبراعم البامبو لعمل حساء شهي يحمل رائحة المخلل وطعمه المملح.

Sopa de picles de Szech Wan e carne de porco

Tiras finas de carne de porco, picles de Szech Wan e brotos de bambu são combinados para criar uma sopa apetitosa, que é enriquecida pelo aroma e o sabor dos picles.

蟹粉魚翅湯（Xie Fen Yu Chi Tang）

Shark's Fin Soup with Crab Meat

This richly-flavored delicacy contains shark's fin, crab meat, mushrooms, bamboo shoots and other mouth-watering favorites that accent the slippery texture of the shark's fin.

kcal ●

© S.T.

蟹粉魚翅湯

這是用魚翅、蟹肉、香菇、竹筍等材料烹飪而成的香味濃鬱的上等湯。品嘗滑溜的魚翅，給人一種高雅不凡的口感享受。

Haifischflossensuppe mit Krebsfleisch

Diese üppig gewürzte Delikatesse enthält Haifischflossen, Krebsfleisch, Pilze (Shiitake), Bambussprossen und andere appetitliche Zutaten, die die etwas glibberige Textur der Haifischflossen akzentuieren.

蟹粉鱼翅汤

这是用鱼翅、蟹肉、香菇、竹笋等材料烹饪而成的香味浓郁的上等汤。品尝滑溜的鱼翅，给人一种高雅不凡的口感享受。

Soupe aux ailerons de requin et au crabe

Ce mets fortement aromatisé contient des ailerons de requin, de la chair de crabe, des champignons, des pousses de bambou et d'autres ingrédients alléchants qui rehaussent la texture glissante des ailerons de requin.

게살삭스핀수프

상어 지느러미, 게살, 표고버섯, 죽순 등이 들어간 고급 수프. 매끄러운 상어 지느러미의 맛이 고급스럽다.

Sopa de Aleta de Tiburón con Carne de Cangrejo

En este manjar deliciosamente aderezado se acentúa la tersa textura de la aleta de tiburón con la carne de cangrejo, champiñones, brotes de bambú y otras delicias.

かに入りふかひれスープ

ふかひれ、かに肉、しいたけ、たけのこなどが入った味わい深い高級なスープ。ツルリとしたふかひれの食感がぜいたく。

Zuppa di pinne di pescecane e polpa di granchi

È un piatto di alta gastronomia dal ricco sapore, preparato con pinne di pescecane, polpa di granchi, funghi shiitake, germogli di bambù e altri ingredienti. Le pinne di pescecane, dalla consistenza gelatinosa, sono un ingrediente di lusso.

حساء زعانف القرش مع لحم الكابوريا

طبق غني بنكهته يحتوي على زعانف سمك القرش ولحم الكابوريا وعش الغراب وبراعم البامبو وغير ذلك من مكونات شهية تضفي مذاقها على زعانف القرش التى تنزلق بسرعة في الفم عند تناولها.

Sopa de barbatana de tubarão com carne de caranguejo

Esta iguaria de rico sabor contém barbatana de tubarão, carne de caranguejo, cogumelos, brotos de bambu e outros ingredientes apetitosos, que realçam a consistência lisa da barbatana de tubarão.

什錦炒飯（Shi Jin Chao Fan）

Fried Rice

Roasted pork, vegetables, scrambled eggs and various other ingredients are stir-fried with rice in a well-heated wok for a rich and aromatic flavor.

kcal ●●

什錦炒飯

這是用燒熱的中國鍋將切細的叉燒、蔬菜、雞蛋和飯一起燜炒而成的、香氣撲鼻、美味炒飯。

Gebratener Reis

Geröstetes Schweinefleisch, Gemüse, Rührei und verschiedene andere Zutaten werden mit Reis in einem sehr heißem Wok pfannengerührt und ergeben ein Gericht mit vollem und aromatischem Geschmack.

什锦炒饭

这是用烧热的中国锅将切细的叉烧、蔬菜、鸡蛋和饭一起燜炒而成的、香气扑鼻、美味炒饭。

Riz sauté

Dans un wok bien chaud, on fait revenir du riz, du porc rôti, des légumes, des œufs brouillés et divers autres ingrédients afin d'obtenir une riche saveur aromatique.

볶음밥

구운 돼지고기, 야채, 달걀 등의 재료가 들어간 볶음밥. 뜨겁게 달군 중화냄비에 볶아 구수한 맛이 난다.

Arroz Frito

Se saltea cerdo tostado, verduras, huevos revueltos y otros ingredientes con arroz en un wok bien caliente para crear un aromático sabor.

チャーハン

焼き豚、野菜、卵などの具が入った炒めご飯。よく熱した中華鍋で炒めたご飯は、パラッとして香ばしい。

Riso fritto

Maiale arrosto e verdure tritate, uova sbattute e altri ingredienti vengono saltati con il riso in una fonda padella cinese (wok) ben riscaldata, creando un piatto dall'invitante profumo.

أرز محمر

يضاف لحم الخنزير الناضج والخضر المقلي والبيض المخفوق وغيرها إلى الأرز ويتم تحميرها معاً في مقلاة صينية على نار قوية للحصول على نكهة غنية طيبة الرائحة.

Arroz frito

Porco assado, vegetais, ovos mexidos e vários outros ingredientes são refogados com arroz na frigideira chinesa bem aquecida, para a produção de um sabor intenso e aromático.

牛肉燴飯（Niu Rou Hui Fan）

Beef and Vegetables in Oyster Sauce over Rice

Beef and vegetables are flavored with oyster sauce and soy sauce, thickened, and then served over hot rice.

kcal ●●●●

©S.T.

牛肉燴飯

烹飪方法是將牛肉和蔬菜等用蠔油、醬油等調味、勾芡成稠狀後再澆到熱飯上。

Rindfleisch und Gemüse in Austernsoße über Reis

Rindfleisch und Gemüse werden mit Austernsoße und Sojasoße gewürzt, angedickt und dann über heißem Reis serviert.

牛肉烩饭

烹饪方法是将牛肉和蔬菜等用蚝油、酱油等调味、勾芡成稠状后再浇到热饭上。

Bœuf et légumes à la sauce d'huîtres servis sur du riz

Bœuf et légumes sont agrémentés d'une sauce d'huîtres et de soja que l'on épaissit et que l'on sert sur du riz chaud.

쇠고기덮밥

쇠고기와 야채를 굴소스, 간장 등으로 맛을 내어 걸쭉하게 끓인 것을 뜨거운 밥 위에 끼얹은 것.

Salteado de Carne de Res

Se sazonan la carne de res y las verduras con salsa de ostras y salsa de soja, y se sirve sobre arroz caliente.

牛肉あんかけご飯

牛肉と野菜をオイスターソース、しょうゆなどで味付けしてとろみをつけ、温かいご飯の上にかけたもの。

Riso coperto di manzo e verdure in salsa di ostriche

Manzo e verdure vengono insaporiti con salsa di ostriche e salsa di soia, il tutto viene fatto addensare con fecola e poi versato sul riso caldo.

لحم بقري وخضر بصلصة المحار مع الأرز

يطهى اللحم البقري والخضر مع صلصة المحار وصلصة الصويا، وعند التقديم يسكب الخليط بصلصته الثخينة فوق الأرز الساخن.

Carne e vegetais em molho de ostra sobre arroz

Carne de gado e vegetais são aromatizados com molhos de ostra e de soja, engrossados e servidos sobre arroz quente.

什錦粥（Shi Jin Zhou）

©S.T

Assorted Rice Gruel

This healthy rice dish is prepared by slowly boiling rice until it is very soft, and then adding a wide assortment of ingredients such as meat, seafood and vegetables for a mild, pleasant flavor.

kcal ●

什錦粥

這是將大米煮至柔熟而成的有益健康的飯食佳肴，其特點是松軟適口。　配料有肉、魚貝類、蔬菜等許多種類切碎的菜。

什锦粥

这是将大米煮至柔熟而成的有益健康的饭食佳肴，其特点是松软适口。配料有肉、鱼贝类、蔬菜等许多种类切碎的菜。

잡탕죽

쌀을 부드러워 질 때까지 푹 끓인 죽. 부드러워 먹기도 좋다. 재료는 고기, 어패류, 야채 등 여러 가지.

五目がゆ

米を柔らかくなるまで煮たヘルシーなご飯料理。口当たりがよく、肉、魚介類、野菜など、さまざまな具を混ぜたり、上にのせたりする。

انواع من شريد الأرز

هذا الطبق الصحي من الأرز يتم إعداده بسلق الأرز على نار هادئة حتى يصبح ليناً تماماً، ثم تضاف إليه تشكيلة كبيرة من الأطعمة كاللحم أوالسمك أوالقواقع البحرية أوالخضر للحصول على نكهة معتدلة لذيذة.

Reissuppe mit verschiedenen Zutaten

Bei diesem gesunden Reisgericht wird zunächst der Reis bei schwacher Hitze gekocht, bis er sehr weich ist. Dann werden verschiedene Zutaten ergänzt, wie z.B. Fleisch, Meeresfrüchte und Gemüse, die einen milden und angenehmen Geschmack ergeben.

Gruau mixte de riz

Ce plat sain à base de riz se prépare en faisant bouillir du riz à petit feu jusqu'à ce qu'il devienne moelleux, puis en y ajoutant une large variété d'ingrédients tels que de la viande, des fruits de mer et des légumes, ce qui lui donne une saveur légère et agréable.

Puches de Arroz Combinado

Este saludable platillo de arroz se prepara hirviendo a fuego lento el arroz hasta que queda bien suave; después se agrega un amplio surtido de ingredientes tales como carne, mariscos y verduras, dándole un sabor ligero y agradable.

Minestra di riso con carne e verdure

È un piatto sano e gradevole al palato, preparato bollendo il riso fino a che diventa molto tenero e aggiungendovi svariati ingredienti sminuzzati, quali carne, frutti di mare, verdure e così via.

Mingau de arroz com ingredientes variados

Prepara-se este prato saudável fervendo lentamente o arroz até que este fique bastante tenro. Adiciona-se então uma grande variedade de ingredientes, tais como carne, frutos do mar e vegetais, para produzir um sabor leve e agradável.

什錦湯面（Shi Jin Tang Mian）

Assorted Meat and Vegetable Stew with Noodles

A delicious broth containing meat, seafood and various vegetables flavored with soy sauce is served with Chinese noodles.

kcal ●●●●

© S.T.

什錦湯面

這是將肉、魚貝類、蔬菜煸炒、勾芡澆在面條上而做成的帶醬油風味的湯面。

Fleisch- und Gemüseeintopf mit Nudeln

Ein köstlicher Sud mit Fleisch, Meeresfrüchten und verschiedenen Gemüsen wird mit Sojasoße abgeschmeckt und mit chinesischen Nudeln serviert.

什锦汤面

这是将肉、鱼贝类、蔬菜煸炒、勾芡浇在面条上而做成的带酱油风味的汤面。

Ragoût de viande et de légumes mixtes accompagnés de nouilles

Ce délicieux bouillon contenant de la viande, des fruits de mer et divers légumes agrémentés d'une sauce de soja est servi avec des nouilles chinoises.

잡탕면

고기, 어패류, 야채를 넣어 만든 걸쭉한 국물을 중화면 위에 끼얹은 것으로, 간장으로 간을 한 국물있는 면.

Caldo de Fideos con Carne y Verduras

Este delicioso caldo, que contiene carne, mariscos y varias verduras sazonadas con salsa de soja, se sirve con fideos chinos.

五目汁そば

肉、魚介類、野菜の入ったあんを中華麺の上にかけた、しょうゆ味の汁そば。

Spaghettini in brodo con carne e verdure

Sugli spaghettini in brodo insaporito con salsa di soia viene versato un sugo denso con dentro carne, frutti di mare e verdure.

ياخني اللحم والخضر مع حساء الشعرية

حساء لذيذ الطعم يشتمل على اللحم والقواقع البحرية والعديد من الخضر مع صلصة الصويا، وتضاف إليه الشعرية الصينية.

Sopa de macarrão chinês com molho de carne e vegetais cozidos

Um caldo denso e delicioso, que contém carne, frutos do mar e vários vegetais condimentados com molho de soja, é servido com macarrão chinês.

叉燒湯面（Cha Shao Tang Mian）

Roasted Pork and Noodles

This hearty dish is filled with roasted pork and noodles and flavored with soy sauce.

kcal ●●●●

叉燒湯面

這是一種在其上面放有叉燒肉、味美量多的醬油風味湯面。

Schweinerostbraten und Nudeln

Dieses herzhafte Gericht besteht aus geröstetem Schweinefleisch und Nudeln und ist mit Sojasoße gewürzt.

叉烧汤面

这是一种在其上面放有叉烧肉、味美量多的酱油风味汤面。

Porc rôti et nouilles

Ce plat copieux se compose de porc rôti et de nouilles aromatisés avec de la sauce de soja.

구운 돼지고기면

잘 구운 돼지고기를 얹은 볼륨있는 간장국물 맛의 중화면.

Caldo de Fideos con Cerdo Asado

Este substancioso platillo se prepara sirviendo el cerdo asado y los fideos chinos sazonados con salsa de soja.

チャーシュー麺

焼き豚をのせたボリュームのあるしょうゆ味の汁そば。

Spaghettini con maiale arrosto

È un piatto sostanzioso di spaghettini cinesi con fette di maiale arrosto in un brodo insaporito con salsa di soia.

روستو اللحم مع الشعرية

هذا الحساء الشهي يتكون من روستو الخنزير مع الشعرية الصينية ونضاف إليه صلصة الصويا لإعطائه نكهة طيبة.

Sopa de macarrão com porco assado

Este prato apetitoso contém uma generosa porção de fatias de porco assado sobre a sopa de macarrão chinês. É condimentado com molho de soja.

牛腩面（五花牛肉面）(Niu Pu Mian（Wu Hua Niu Rou Mian）)

Szechwan-Style Beef and Noodles

Boneless beef flank is boiled in soy sauce and spices and served with noodles.

© S.T.

kcal ●●●●

牛腩面（五花牛肉面）

這種面因內有用醬油及香料炖得噴香的五花牛肉而得名。

牛腩面（五花牛肉面）

这种面因内有用酱油及香料炖得喷香的五花牛肉而得名。

쇠고기 중화면

간장과 향신료로 조린 쇠고기가 들어있는 국물있는 중화면.

牛バラ肉そば

しょうゆと香辛料で煮込んだ牛バラ肉のかたまりが入っている汁そば。

لحم بقري على طريقة ستشوان مع الشعرية

تسلق قطع لحم خالية العظم من الخاصرة مع التوابل وصلصة الصويا وتقدم كحساء مضاف إليه الشعرية الصينية.

Rindfleisch und Nudeln nach Szechwan-Art

Kurze Rippe vom Rind ohne Knochen wird in Sojasoße und Gewürzen gekocht und dann mit Nudeln serviert.

Bœuf et nouilles à la mode du Sichuan

On fait bouillir du flanchet de bœuf désossé dans une sauce de soja contenant des épices que l'on sert avec des nouilles.

Caldo de Fideos con Carne de Res al Estilo Szechwan

La espaldilla de res deshuesada en salsa de soja se cuece con especias para servirse con fideos chinos.

Spaghettini con pancetta di manzo

Spaghettini in brodo con un pezzo di pancetta di manzo cotta in umido con salsa di soia e spezie.

Sopa de macarrão e carne ao estilo Szech Wan

A paleta de gado sem osso é fervida com molho de soja e temperos, e servida com macarrão chinês.

排骨湯面（Pai Gu Tang Mian）

Deep-Fried Pork Rib and Noodles

Deep-fried pork rib and boiled green vegetables are served with noodles in a soup flavored with soy sauce for a light-tasting treat.

kcal ●●●●

排骨湯面

這是一種面上放有油炸排骨及青菜的湯面。湯帶有醬油味，清淡可口。

Fritierte Schweinerippen und Nudeln

In Öl ausgebackene Schweinerippen und gekochtes grünes Gemüse wird mit Nudeln in einer Suppe serviert, die mit Sojasoße gewürzt ist. Ein wohlschmeckendes Gericht mit mildem Geschmack.

排骨汤面

这是一种面上放有油炸排骨及青菜的汤面。汤带有酱油味，清淡可口。

Côte de porc frite et nouilles

Ce mets plaisant au goût léger contient une côte de porc frite et des légumes bouillis que l'on sert avec des nouilles dans une soupe aromatisée à la sauce de soja.

돼지갈비튀김 중화면

튀긴 돼지갈비와 데친 야채를 얹은 국물있는 중화면. 국물은 담백한 간장맛.

Caldo de Fideos con Costilla Frita de Cerdo

La costilla de cerdo asada y las legumbres cocidas se sirven con fideos chinos en una deliciosa sopa de sabor ligero guisada con salsa de soja.

豚骨付き肉の唐揚げそば

唐揚げにした豚の骨付きロース肉と、ゆでた野菜をのせた汁そば。スープはしょうゆ味でさっぱりしている。

Spaghettini con costolette di maiale fritte

Spaghettini in brodo con sopra lombatine di maiale fritte in abbondante olio e verdure bollite. Il brodo è leggero e insaporito con salsa di soia.

ضلع اللحم المحمر والشعرية

يحمر لحم الخنزير تحميراً غزيراً ويقدم مع الخضر المسلوقة والشعرية الصينية في حساء متبل بصلصة الصويا ينسم بطعمه المعتدل.

Sopa de macarrão chinês e costela de porco frita

Costela de porco frita por mergulho em óleo e vegetais fervidos são servidos com macarrão chinês, em uma sopa condimentada com molho de soja, numa iguaria de leve sabor.

雪菜肉絲面（Xue Cai Rou Si Mian）

Mustard Greens and Shredded Pork Noodle Soup

Stir-fried shredded pork and mustard greens are served with noodles in a mild, salt-flavored soup.

© S.T.

kcal ●●●●

雪菜肉絲面

這是一種面上盛有煸炒過的豬肉絲和雪菜的湯面。湯帶有鹹味，清淡鮮美。

Nudelsuppe mit eingelegten Senfwurzelknollen und kleingeschnittenem Schweinefleisch

In Öl ausgebackenes, kleingeschnittenes Schweinefleisch und eingelegte, fermentierte Senfwurzelknollen werden mit Nudeln in einer milden, mit Salz gewürzten Suppe serviert.

雪菜肉丝面

这是一种面上盛有煸炒过的猪肉丝和雪菜的汤面。汤带有咸味，清淡鲜美。

Soupe de nouilles et de lamelles de porc accompagnées de feuilles de moutarde

Cette soupe au goût léger et salé se compose de lamelles de porc et de feuilles de moutarde sautées que l'on sert avec des nouilles.

갓과 채썬 돼지고기 중화면

채썬 돼지고기와 갓을 볶아 얹은 국물있는 중화면. 국물은 담백한 소금맛.

Sopa de Fideos con Tallo de Mostaza y Cerdo

Se fríe la carne cerdo y los tallos de mostaza cortados en tiras y se sirven con fideos chinos en una sopa suave con ligero sabor a sal.

カラシ菜入り豚細切りそば

豚肉の細切りとカラシ菜の炒めものをのせた汁そば。スープは塩味であっさりしている。

Spaghettini con striscioline di maiale e cime di senape

Spaghettini in brodo con sopra striscioline di maiale saltate con cime di senape. Il brodo e leggero e insaporito soltanto con sale.

حساء الشعرية مع اللحم وعيدان المستردة

حساء متبل بالملح يتكون من شرائح طولية من لحم الخنزير المحمر مع عيدان المستردة الخضراء ويقدم مضافاً إليه الشعرية الصينية.

Sopa de macarrão chinês com folhas de mostarda e tiras finas de porco

Tiras finas de carne de porco e folhas de mostarda refogadas são servidas em uma sopa de sabor levemente salgado.

擔擔面（Dan Dan Mian）

© S.T.

Szechwan Spicy Noodles

Chinese noodles covered with stir-fried ground beef are served in a spicy soup flavored with hot pepper oil.

kcal ●●●●

擔擔面

這是一種在其上面放有煸炒過的豬肉末，然後澆上加有辣椒油的辛辣的汁而制成的面。

Scharfe Nudeln nach Szechwan-Art

Pfannengerührtes Schweinehackfleisch wird über chinesische Nudeln gegeben und in einer würzigen, mit scharfem Pfefferöl gewürzten Suppe serviert.

担担面

这是一种在其上面放有煸炒过的猪肉末，然后浇上加有辣椒油的辛辣的汁而制成的面。

Nouilles du Sichuan relevées

Des nouilles chinoises recouvertes de bœuf haché sauté sont servies dans une soupe épicée aromatisée avec de l'huile de piment.

사천풍 매운맛 중화면

다진 돼지고기를 볶아 중화면 위에 얹은 다음 고추기름을 넣은 매운 양념장을 끼얹은 것.

Caldo de Fideos Aromáticos de Szechwan

Se cubre a los fideos chinos con carne de cerdo o res molida salteada y se sirven en un caldo picante condimentado con aceite de chile.

四川風辛味そば

中華麺に炒めた豚ひき肉をのせ、ラー油を加えた辛いタレをかけたもの。

Spaghettini piccanti alla szechwan

Sugli spaghettini viene messa della carne di maiale tritata e rosolata e sul tutto viene versato un sugo piccante all'olio con peperoncino rosso.

حساء ستشوان الحريف مع الشعرية

حساء حريف بنكهة زيت الفلفل الأحمر توضع فيه الشعرية الصينية وتغطى بلحم بقري مقري ومحمر.

Macarrão picante de Szech Wan

O macarrão chinês, coberto com carne moída refogada, é servido numa sopa condimentada a que se adiciona óleo picante.

餛飩面（Hun Tun Mian）

Wonton Noodle Soup

This noodle soup is prepared by using a soy sauce base and contains wontons prepared by stuffing wonton skins made of flour with ground pork, shrimp or other tasty ingredients.

kcal ●●●●

© S.T.

餛飩面

這是因餛飩放在湯面上而得其名。用小麥皮包上豬肉末及蝦仁而做成的餛飩美味可口。

Wan-Tan-Nudelsuppe

Diese Nudelsuppe wird mit einer Sojasoßen-Grundlage gekocht und enthält Wan-Tans. Bei Wan-Tans (oder Wontons) handelt es sich um Nudeltaschen, die mit Schweinehackfleisch, Garnelen oder anderen wohlschmeckenden Zutaten gefüllt werden.

馄饨面

这是因馄饨放在汤面上而得其名。用小麦皮包上猪肉末及虾仁而做成的馄饨美味可口。

Soupe de nouilles au wonton

Cette soupe de nouilles préparée à base de sauce de soja contient des wontons que l'on prépare en farcissant des feuilles de wonton à base de farine avec du porc haché, des crevettes et d'autres ingrédients savoureux.

완탕면

완탕을 넣고 간장으로 간을 한 국물있는 중화면. 밀가루를 반죽하여 만든 만두피에 다진 돼지고기와 새우 등을 넣어 만든 완탕이 일품이다.

Sopa de Fideos y Ravioles Chinos

Esta sopa de fideos chinos se prepara usando una base de salsa de soja. Los ravioles chinos se preparan rellenando las hojas de wonton con carne de cerdo molida, langostinos u otros apetitosos ingredientes.

ワンタン麺

ワンタン入りのしょうゆ風味の汁そば。小麦粉を練った皮に豚ひき肉やえびなどを詰めたワンタンが美味。

Spaghettini con won ton

In un brodo insaporito con salsa di soia, gli spaghettini sono uniti ai deliziosi won ton, sorta di ravioli di pasta sottile ripieni di carne di maiale tritata o di gamberetti e altri ingredienti.

حساء الشعرية بالوانتان

هذا الحساء، من الشعرية الصينية يتم إعداده بنكهة صلصة الصويا ويحتوي على وحدات من محشي الوانتان الذي يعد بملء رقائق الوانتان المصنوعة من الدقيق بلحم الخنزير أو الجمبري (الروبيان) أو غير ذلك من أنواع الحشو اللذيذة.

Sopa de macarrão com wonton

Sopa de macarrão feita à base de molho de soja. Contém wontons, que são preparados recheando-se a massa de farinha de trigo wonton com carne de porco moída, camarão ou outros ingredientes saborosos.

什錦炒面（Shi Jin Chao Mian）

© S.T.

Fried Noodles with Meat and Vegetables

A thickened sauce containing meat and vegetables is poured over fried noodles.

kcal ●●●●

什錦炒面

是一種在面上澆有由肉、魚貝類及蔬菜煸炒勾芡澆汁的炒面。

Gebratene Nudeln mit Fleisch und Gemüse

Gebratene Nudeln werden mit einer angedickten Soße übergossen, die Fleisch und Gemüse enthält.

什锦炒面

是一种在面上浇有由肉、鱼贝类及蔬菜煸炒勾芡浇汁的炒面。

Nouilles frites accompagnées de viande et de légumes

On verse une sauce épaisse contenant de la viande, du poisson, et des légumes sur des nouilles frites.

잡탕볶음면

볶은 중화면 위에 고기 또는 어패류, 야채 등이 들어있는 걸쭉한 국물을 끼얹은 것.

Salteado de Fideos Chinos con Carne y Verduras

Sobre los fideos salteados se esparce una espesa salsa que contiene carne y verduras.

五目あんかけ焼きそば

炒めた麺の上に、肉や魚介類、野菜などが入ったあんをトロリとかけた焼きそば。

Spaghettini fritti con carne e verdure in sugo denso

Sono spaghettini fritti, sui quali viene versato un sugo addensato con fecola e contenente carne o frutti di mare, verdure e altri ingredienti.

شعرية محمرة مع لحم وخضر

تسكب صلصة سميكة القوام من لحم وخضر فوق الشعرية الصينية المحمرة.

Macarrão frito com carne e vegetais

Um molho engrossado, que contém carne e vegetais, é despejado sobre macarrão frito.

廣東炒面（Guang Dong Chao Mian）

Canton-Style Fried Noodles

Chinese noodles are first deep-fried in oil and boiled, then stir-fried with pork, shrimp, chives and other ingredients and then accented with the flavor of soy sauce.

© S.T.

kcal ●●●

廣東炒面

這種面是把面條用油炸完後再煮熟，然後同豬肉、蝦仁、韭黃等一起煸炒而成的、具有醬油風味。

Gebratene Nudeln nach kantonesischer Art

Chinesische Nudeln werden zunächst in Öl ausgebacken und dann gekocht. Anschließend werden sie mit Schweinefleisch, Garnelen, Schnittlauch und anderen Zutaten im Wok scharf angebraten und dann mit Sojasoße fertiggewürzt.

广东炒面

这种面是把面条用油炸完后再煮熟，然后同猪肉、虾仁、韭黄等一起煸炒而成的、具有酱油风味。

Nouilles frites à la cantonaise

Après avoir fait frire dans l'huile puis bouillir des nouilles chinoises, on les fait revenir avec du porc, des crevettes, de la ciboulette et d'autres ingrédients que l'on accompagne avec une sauce de soja.

광동식 볶음면

기름에 튀겨낸 면을 삶아 돼지고기, 새우, 노란색 부추 등의 재료와 함께 볶은 간장으로 간을 한 면.

Fideos Fritos al Estilo Cantonés

Primero, los fideos chinos se fríen en aceite abundante y se cuecen, después se saltean con cerdo, langostinos, cebollinos y otros ingredientes y por último se acentúa su sabor con la salsa de soja.

広東風炒めそば

麺を油で揚げてからゆで、豚肉、えび、黄ニラなどの具と一緒に炒めた、しょうゆ味の焼きそば。

Spaghettini fritti alla cantonese

Gli spaghettini vengono prima fritti in abbondante olio e bolliti, quindi saltati con carne di maiale, gamberetti, erba agliacea e altri ingredienti conditi con salsa di soia.

شعرية محمرة على طريقة الكانتون

تحمص الشعرية الصينية في الزيت ثم تسلق وبعد ذلك تحمر مع لحم الخنزير والجمبري (الروبيان) والكراث وغيرها وتتبل بصلصة الصويا.

Macarrão chinês frito ao estilo de Cantão

O macarrão chinês primeiramente é frito por mergulho em óleo e em seguida fervido. Depois, é refogado na frigideira, com porco, camarão, alho-poró e outros ingredientes. Por fim, realça-se o sabor com molho de soja.

什錦炸面（Shi Jin Zha Mian）

© S.T.

Deep-Fried Noodles with Meat and Vegetables in a Thick Sauce

This fragrant dish features meat, seafood and vegetables mixed into a thickened sauce and poured over crunchy, deep-fried noodles.

kcal ●●●●

什錦炸面

這種面是在炸好的面上澆上用肉、魚貝類、蔬菜煸炒勾芡成的汁。面條香脆、誘人食欲。

Fritierte Nudeln mit Fleisch und Gemüse in dicker Soße

Dieses duftende Gericht besteht aus Fleisch, Meeresfrüchten und Gemüse in einer angedickten Soße, die über knusprige ausgebackene Nudeln gegossen wird.

什锦炸面

这种面是在炸好的面上浇上用肉、鱼贝类、蔬菜煸炒勾芡成的汁。面条香脆、诱人食欲。

Nouilles frites accompagnées d'une sauce épaisse à la viande et aux légumes

Ce plat parfumé contient de la viande, des fruits mer et des légumes mélangés à une sauce épaisse que l'on verse sur des nouilles frites croustillantes.

잡탕튀김면

튀긴 면 위에 고기, 어패류, 야채 등을 넣고 끓인 걸쭉한 국물을 끼얹은 것. 바삭바삭한 면맛이 구수하다.

Fideos Fritos con Carne y Verduras en una Salsa Espesa

Este fragante platillo se caracteriza por la mezcla de carne, mariscos y verduras en una espesa salsa que se esparce sobre fideos fritos y crujientes.

五目かた焼きそば

揚げた麺の上に、肉、魚介類、野菜の入ったあんをかけたもの。パリパリの麺が香ばしい。

Spaghettini croccanti con carne e verdure in sugo denso

Sugli spaghettini, fritti in abbondante olio fino a renderli croccanti, viene versato un sugo addensato con fecola e contenente carne, frutti di mare e verdure.

شعرية محمرة مع لحم وخضر في صلصة سميكة

هذا الطبق برائحته الطيبة يحتوي على مزيج من اللحم والقواقع البحرية والخضر في صلصة سميكة تسكب فوق شعرية صينية محمرة لدرجة التحميص.

Macarrão chinês frito com carne e vegetais em molho grosso

Este prato aromático apresenta carne, frutos do mar e vegetais misturados num molho grosso, que é despejado sobre o macarrão, frito por mergulho em óleo até ficar crocante.

炒米粉（Chao Mi Fen）

© S.T.

Stir-Fried Rice Vermicelli with Meat and Vegetables

Meat, dried prawns and vegetables are stir-fried with rice vermicelli, made from rice powder, for a taste that is lighter than Chinese noodles.

kcal ●●●

炒米粉

將肉、蝦米、蔬菜等垜成細末與米粉一起炒熟。這種用米做出的米粉與中國面條相比，味道清淡。

Pfannengerührte Reis-Fadennudeln mit Fleisch und Gemüse

Fleisch, getrocknete Krabben und Gemüse werden mit Reis-Fadennudeln, die aus Reismehl hergestellt sind, im Wok scharf angebraten. Der Geschmack der Reis-Fadennudeln ist milder als bei chinesischen Nudeln.

炒米粉

将肉、虾米、蔬菜等垜成细末与米粉一起炒熟。这种用米做出的米粉与中国面条相比，味道清淡。

Sauté de vermicelle de riz accompagné de viande et de légumes

Ce sauté contient de la viande, des crevettes roses séchées et des légumes ainsi que du vermicelle de riz à base de poudre de riz, qui confère au tout un goût plus léger que celui des nouilles chinoises.

잡탕 쌀국수볶음

고기, 말린새우, 야채 등의 재료와 쌀국수를 볶은 것. 쌀로 만든 면으로 중화면보다 가볍다.

Salteado de Fideos Vermicelli con Carne y Verduras

Se saltea carne, langostino seco y verduras con fideos vermicelli hechos de harina de arroz para crear un sabor más ligero que el de los fideos chinos.

五目焼きビーフン

肉、干しえび、野菜などの具とビーフンを炒めたもの。米の粉で作られたビーフンは中華麺より軽い味。

Vermicelli di riso saltati con carne e verdure

È un piatto di pasta saltata in padella con carne, gamberetti essiccati, verdure e altri ingredienti. I vermicelli di farina di riso sono più leggeri dei comuni spaghetti cinesi.

شعرية الأرز المحمرة مع اللحم والخضر

تحمر الشعرية المصنوعة من الأرز المسحوق مع مزيج من لحم وخضر ونوع من الجمبري (الروبيان) الجاف لإعداد طبق يتميز بمذاق أخف من الشعرية الصينية العادية.

Aletria de arroz com carnes e vegetais refogados

Carne, camarões grandes secos e vegetais são refogados ao estilo chinês com aletria de farinha de arroz, produzindo um sabor mais leve do que o do macarrão chinês comum.

涼拌面（Liang Ban Mian）

© S.T.

Mixed Cold Noodles

This cold noodle dish is prepared by serving shredded roasted pork and vegetables over cold noodles, then flavoring with sweet and sour soy sauce.

kcal ●●●

涼拌面

這是一種在面條上放上切細的叉燒和蔬菜，再用甜醋和醬油澆汁而拌成的冷面。

Gemischte kalte Nudeln

Dieses kalte Nudelgericht wird so zubereitet, daß kleingeschnittener Schweinerostbraten und Gemüse über kalte Nudeln gegeben und dann mit einer süßsauren Sojasoße gewürzt werden.

凉拌面

这是一种在面条上放上切细的叉烧和蔬菜,再用甜醋和酱油浇汁而拌成的冷面。

Mélange de nouilles froides

Ce plat de nouilles froides se prépare avec du porc rôti coupé en lamelles et des légumes que l'on verse sur des nouilles froides, le tout étant assaisonné d'une sauce de soja aigre-douce.

중국식 냉면

중화면 위에 채썬 구운 돼지고기, 야채 등을 얹고 새콤달콤한 간장 양념장을 끼얹은 차가운 면.

Surtido de Fideos Chinos Fríos

Este platillo frío de fideos chinos se prepara sirviendo sobre fideos fríos la carne de cerdo asado y verduras cortadas en tiras para después condimentarlos con salsa de soja agridulce fría.

冷やし中華そば

中華麺の上に細切りにした焼き豚、野菜などをのせ、甘酢っぱいしょうゆ味のタレをかけた冷麺。

Spaghettini freddi

È un piatto di spaghettini freddi ricoperti di sottili fette di arrosto di maiale, verdure e altri ingredienti e conditi con un sugo agrodolce dal gusto di salsa di soia.

شعرية باردة مع خليط متبل

هذا الطبق البارد من الشعرية الصينية يتم إعداده بوضع شرائح طولية رفيعة من روستو الخنزير والخضر فوق الشعرية الباردة ثم تسكب فوقه صلصة صويا ذات طعم حلو حامض.

Macarrão chinês misto, servido frio

Este prato consiste em tiras finas de carne de porco assada e vegetais dispostos sobre o macarrão chinês frio. É condimentado com molho de soja agridoce.

春巻（Chun Juan）

Deep-Fried Spring Rolls

Spring roll skins are filled with meat, bamboo shoots, mushrooms and other ingredients and then deep-fried to a crispy, golden-brown.

kcal ●●

春卷

春卷皮中包入切碎的肉、香菇、竹筍等，然後用油炸成金黄色澤。

Ausgebackene Frühlingsrollen

Teigplatten für Frühlingsrollen werden mit Fleisch, Bambussprossen, Pilzen (Shiitake) und anderen Zutaten gefüllt und zu Rollen geformt. Diese werden dann anschließend in Öl ausgebacken, bis sie knusprig und goldbraun sind.

春卷

春卷皮中包入切碎的肉、香菇、竹笋等，然后用油炸成金黄色泽。

Rouleaux de printemps frits

Après avoir farci des crêpes chinoises avec de la viande, des pousses de bambou, des champignons et d'autres ingrédients, on fait rissoler les rouleaux de printemps jusqu'à ce qu'ils deviennent dorés et croustillants.

춘권 （春卷）

춘권피에 고기, 죽순, 표고버섯 등이 들어있는 소를 싸서 기름에 노릇노릇하게 튀겨 낸 것.

Rollos Fritos

Se envuelven en las hojas de crepa los ingredientes tales como carne, brotes de bambú, hongos, etc. y después se fríen en aceite abundante hasta que quedan crujientes y bien dorados.

春巻き

春巻きの皮に肉、たけのこ、しいたけなどが入った具を包み、油でカリッと色よく揚げたもの。

Involtini primavera

Sono involtini di pasta, contenenti un ripieno di carne, germogli di bambù, funghi shiitake e altri ingredienti, fritti in abbondante olio fino a farli diventare croccanti e di un bel colore dorato.

ملفوف الرقاق المحمر

يتم ملء الرقائق بحشو من اللحم وبراعم البامبو وعش الغراب وغيرها ثم تحمر تحميراً غزيراً حتى تصبح مقرمشة بلون ذهبي.

Rolinhos-primavera fritos

Carne, brotos de bambu, cogumelos e outros ingredientes enrolados em massa fina especial. Fritam-se os rolinhos por mergulho em óleo até que fiquem dourados e crocantes.

蛋皮春卷（Dan Pi Chun Juan）

© S.T.

Fried Egg Roll
Crab meat, leeks, mushrooms and bamboo shoots are wrapped in very thin sheets of egg and then deep-fried.

kcal ●●●

蛋皮春卷
其制作方法是在攤好的、極薄的雞蛋皮中包上蟹肉、蔥、香菇、竹筍用油炸熟而成。

Gebratene Omelettrolle
Krebsfleisch, Lauch, Pilze (Shiitake) und Bambussprossen werden mit einem sehr dünnen Omelett umwickelt und dann in Öl ausgebacken.

蛋皮春卷
其制作方法是在摊好的、极薄的鸡蛋皮中包上蟹肉、葱、香菇、竹笋用油炸熟而成。

Rouleaux frits aux œufs
On enrobe du crabe, des poireaux, des champignons et des pousses de bambou de très minces filets d'œufs que l'on fait ensuite frire.

달걀말이튀김
아주 얇게 부친 달걀에 게살, 파, 표고버섯, 죽순 등을 싸서 튀겨 낸 것.

Rollo Frito de Huevo
Se envuelve ingredientes tales como carne de cangrejo, puerros, hongos y brotes de bambú en hojas muy delgadas de huevo y se fríen en aceite abundante.

薄焼き卵の巻き揚げ
ごく薄く焼いた卵に、かに、ねぎ、しいたけ、たけのこを包んで揚げたもの。

Involtini di crespelle di uova ripieni
Polpa di granchio, porri, funghi shiitake e germogli di bambù vengono avvolti in sottilissime crespelle di uova e poi fritti in abbondante olio.

ملفوف البيض المقلي
شرائح رقيقة من البيض يتم ملؤها بحشو من لحم الكابوريا والبصل الأخضر وعش الغراب وبراعم البامبو ثم تحمر في المقلاة.

Enrolado frito de ovos
Carne de caranguejo, cebolinha, cogumelos e brotos de bambu são enrolados em finas camadas de ovos e fritos por mergulho em óleo.

燒賣（Shao Mai）

Steamed Dumplings

Various ingredients such as ground pork and shrimp are wrapped in wonton skins and cooked in a steaming basket that enhances the flavor of the meat and fish for a taste that really satisfies the palate.

kcal ●●

© S.T.

燒賣

將切碎的豬肉末、蝦仁等包進燒賣皮中，再上屜蒸熟。您可充分品嘗到肉和魚貝的美味。

Gedünstete Fleischklößchen

Verschiedene Zutaten, wie z.B. Schweinehackfleisch und Garnelen werden in Wan-Tan-Hüllen eingewickelt und dann in heißem Wasserdampf gedämpft. Dies hebt den Eigengeschmack des Fleischs und Fischs hervor und ergibt einen runden Geschmack, der auch den anspruchvollsten Gourmet befriedigt.

烧卖

将切碎的猪肉末、虾仁等包进烧卖皮中，再上屜蒸熟。您可充分品尝到肉和鱼贝的美味。

Petites poches de pâte farcies cuites à la vapeur

Après avoir farci des feuilles de wonton, on les fait cuire dans un cuiseur à vapeur en bambou, ce qui rehausse l'arôme de la viande et du poisson et offre une saveur qui enchante le palais.

슈마이

다진 돼지고기, 새우 등을 슈마이피에 싸서 중국식 찜통에 찐 것. 고기와 어패류 맛의 조화가 일품이다.

Rellenos al Vapor

En hojas de crepa se envuelven varios ingredientes, tales como carne de cerdo molida y langostinos y se cocinan en una canasta de vapor que realza el sabor de la carne y el pescado, dándole un sazón que realmente satisface el paladar.

シュウマイ

豚ひき肉、えびなどの具をシュウマイの皮で包み、セイロで蒸したもの。肉と魚介のおいしさがギュッと詰まっている。

Ravioli cotti a vapore

Carne di maiale tritata, gamberetti e altri ingredienti vengono avvolti in un sottile strato di pasta e cotti a vapore, imprigionando tutto il buon sapore della carne e dei frutti di mare.

محشوات مطهوة على البخار

يغلف لحم الخنزير أوالجمبري (الروبيان) أوغيرها برقائق الوانتان ثم تطهى في سلة الطهي على البخار التي تبرز نكهة اللحم أوالجمبري وتعطي مذاقاً لذيذاً رائعاً.

Embrulhinhos cozidos em vapor

Vários ingredientes, como carne de porco moída e camarão, são envoltos em massa fina de wonton e cozidos em vapor, em recipiente especial, realçando assim o sabor da carne e do pescado, e satisfazendo plenamente o paladar.

鍋貼餃子（Guo Tie Jiao Zi）

© S.T.

Fried Dumplings

These crescent-shaped dumplings contain a mixture of ground pork and vegetables wrapped in a wonton skin and then fried in oil to a golden brown.

kcal ●●●

鍋貼餃子

將切碎的蔬菜拌入豬肉末、包進餃子皮中，然後用油煎至呈金黃色而成。

Gebratene Fleischklöße

Diese halbmondförmigen Fleischklöße enthalten eine Mischung aus Schweinehackfleisch und Gemüse, die in einer Wan-Tan-Hülle eingewickelt und anschließend in Öl goldbraun ausgebacken wird.

锅贴饺子

将切碎的蔬菜拌入猪肉末、包进饺子皮中，然后用油煎至呈金黄色而成。

Raviolis frits

Ces raviolis en forme de croissant contiennent un mélange de porc haché et de légumes enrobés dans des feuilles de wonton que l'on fait frire jusqu'à ce qu'ils soient dorés.

군만두

만두피에 다진 돼지고기, 야채 등을 섞어 만든 소를 넣고 싸서 기름으로 노릇노릇하게 구워 낸 것.

Relleno Asado

Este relleno con apariencia de media luna contiene una combinación de carne de cerdo molida y verduras picadas envuelta en hojas de crepa. Después de preparar, se asa en un sartén hasta que quedan doradas.

焼き餃子

餃子の皮で豚ひき肉、野菜などを混ぜ合わせた具を包み、油でこんがりと焼いたもの。

Ravioli fritti

Questi ravioli a forma di spicchio sono ripieni di carne di maiale tritata, verdure e altri ingredienti; fritti in abbondante olio, assumono un colore dorato.

محشوات محمرة

هذه المحشوات على شكل الهلال هي عبارة عن مزيج من لحم الخنزير المفري والخضر يغلف بغشاء من الوانتان ثم يحمر في الزيت حتى يكتسب لوناً ذهبياً.

Pasteizinhos recheados ao estilo chinês

Estas iguarias chinesas em forma de pastel contêm uma mistura de carne de porco moída e vegetais, envolta em massa fina de farinha de arroz. São fritas até dourar.

蝦餃（Xia Jiao）

Steamed Shrimp Dumplings

These dumplings are stuffed with fresh shrimp wrapped in wonton skins that become transparent when steamed to accentuate the luscious taste of the shrimp.

kcal ●

© S.T.

蝦餃

將新鮮的蝦仁包進餃子皮中蒸熟。品嘗透明的餃子皮、和鮮嫩的蝦仁、將使您的口福大開。

Gedünstete Garnelenklöße in Teigtaschen

Teigtaschen werden mit frischen Garnelen gefüllt und dann im Wasserdampf gedünstet. Hierbei werden die Hüllen durchsichtig und betonen den saftigen Geschmack der Garnelen.

虾饺

将新鲜的虾仁包进饺子皮中蒸熟。品尝透明的饺子皮、和鲜嫩的虾仁、将使您的口福大开。

Boulettes de crevettes à la vapeur

Ces boulettes sont garnies de crevettes fraîches enveloppées dans des feuilles de wonton qui deviennent transparentes à la vapeur, ce qui rehausse la saveur exquise des crevettes.

새우만두

만두피에 신선한 새우를 넣고 싸서 찐 것. 찐 만두피의 투명감과 새우의 톡 터지는 듯한 맛이 고급스럽다.

Relleno de Langostino al Vapor

Es un relleno de langostinos frescos envueltos en hojas de crepa, las cuales se vuelven transparentes cuando se cocinan, acentuando el seductor sabor de los langostinos.

えび入り蒸し餃子

餃子の皮に新鮮なえびを包んで蒸したもの。蒸すと皮が透き通ってえびの赤が美しく見え、プリッとしたえびの食感がぜいたく。

Ravioli di gamberetti cotti a vapore

Contengono un ripieno di gamberetti freschi e il sottile involucro di pasta con la cottura a vapore diventa semitrasparente. La netta sensazione dei gamberetti in bocca è da buongustai.

محشو الجمبري المطهو على البخار

يتم حشو الجمبري (الروبيان) الطازج في رقائق الوانتان التي تصبح شفافة اللون بعد أن تطهي على البخار ويبرز فيها المذاق الطيب للجمبري.

Pasteizinhos de camarão assados em vapor

São feitos com massa fina de farinha de arroz, recheada com camarão fresco. Tornando-se transparente ao ser assada em vapor, a massa fina realça o delicioso sabor do camarão.

韮菜餃（Jiu Cai Jiao）

©S.T.

Chive Dumplings

These attractive, green dumplings are filled with Chinese chives and steamed for a surprisingly mild flavor that brings out the characteristic pungent aroma of the Chinese chives.

kcal ●●

韮菜餃

這是內包韮菜的蒸餃。看上去呈淡綠色，雖然蒸後散發著韮菜特有的香味，但喫口很清淡。

韭菜饺

这是内包韭菜的蒸饺。看上去呈淡绿色，虽然蒸后散发着韭菜特有的香味，但吃口很清淡。

부추만두

부추를 듬뿍 넣은 찐만두. 미관상 고운 초록색과, 부추 특유의 강한 향기가 의외로 담백한 맛을 낸다.

ニラ餃子

ニラがたっぷり入った蒸し餃子。見た目はきれいな緑色で、ニラ特有の香りはするが意外にあっさりした味。

محشوات الكراث

هذه المحشوات الجميلة ذات اللون الأخضر تحتوي على الكراث الصيني وتطهى على البخار فتكتسب مذاقا معتدلاً مدهشاً وتبرز النكهة القوية المميزة للكراث الصيني.

Schnittlauchklößchen in Teigtaschen

Diese attraktiven Teigtaschen sehen grün aus, weil sie mit chinesischem Schnittlauch gefüllt und dann gedämpft werden. Sie haben einen überraschend milden Geschmack, der das charakteristische scharfe Aroma des chinesischen Schnittlauchs angenehm betont.

Boulettes à la ciboulette

Ces appétissantes boulettes vertes sont fourrées avec de la ciboulette japonaise puis cuites à la vapeur, ce qui leur confère une saveur agréablement douce qui relève l'arôme âcre caractéristique de la ciboulette japonaise.

Relleno de Puerro

Este atractivo plato de color jade, se rellenan con puerro y se cocinan al vapor para extraer un sabor sorprendentemente suave que realza el fuerte aroma característico del puerro.

Ravioli di verdura agliacea

Sono come i precedenti per forma e cottura, ma ripieni di una verdura cinese di gusto agliaceo. Sono di un bel colore verde e l'odore è piuttosto forte, ma il gusto è leggero.

Pasteizinhos de alho-poró

Estes atraentes pasteizinhos verdes são recheados com alho-poró e cozidos em vapor. Têm um sabor surpreendentemente suave, caracterizado pelo aroma marcante do alho-poró.

小籠包（Xiao Long Bao）

Steamed Juicy Pork Buns

Ground pork is wrapped in wonton skins and steamed so that the flavory juice of the pork fills the mouth when eaten. Be careful though, it can easily burn the tongue!

© S.T.

kcal ●●

小籠包

用由面粉揉成的餃子皮包上餡蒸熟。喫時，肉味十足的湯汁會散溢整個口中。由於很燙，喫起來要小心。

Gedünstete Teigtaschen mit saftigem Schweinefleisch

Wan-Tan-Hüllen werden mit Schweinehackfleisch gefüllt und dann im Wasserdampf so gedünstet, daß der wohlschmeckende Fleischsaft des Schweinefleischs sich beim Essen im Mund verteilt. Seien Sie jedoch vorsichtig, da Sie sich leicht die Zunge verbrennen können!

小笼包

用由面粉揉成的饺子皮包上馅蒸熟。吃时，肉味十足的汤汁会散溢整个口中。由于很烫，吃起来要小心。

Brioches de porc moelleux cuites à la vapeur

On fait cuire à la vapeur des feuilles de wonton après les avoir farcies de porc haché. Quand on déguste ces brioches, le jus parfumé du porc se répand pleinement dans la bouche. Attention toutefois à ne pas vous brûler la langue!

수프가 든 고기만두

만두피에 다진 돼지고기를 싸서 찐 것. 먹는 순간 고기 맛이 우러난 국물이 입안에서 확 퍼진다. 뜨거우므로 주의할 것.

Relleno Jugosos de Cerdo al Vapor

Primero, la carne de cerdo molido es envuelta en hojas de crepa; después se cocina al vapor para que el suculento jugo del cerdo penetre por todos los rincones de la boca en el momento de saborear. ¡Tenga cuidado porque puede quemarse la lengua con facilidad!

スープ入り肉まんじゅう

小麦粉を練った皮に豚ひき肉を包んで蒸したもの。食べた時、肉のうまみが溶け出したスープが口の中に広がる。熱いので注意。

Pagnottelle con ripieno di maiale al sugo

Queste pagnottelle di farina di grano cotte a vapore hanno un succoso ripieno di carne di maiale tritata. Quando le si mangia, il sugo saporito si diffonde in bocca. Ma attenti a non scottarsi!

محشو اللحم المطهو على البخار

يتم حشو رقائق مصنوعة من عجينة دقيق بلحم الخنزير المفري ثم تطهى على البخار فيمتلئ الفم عند تناولها بعصارة اللحم اللذيذة، ولكن احترس حتى لايحترق لسانك.

Bolinhos suculentos de porco, assados em vapor

A carne de porco moída, envolta em massa fina de farinha de arroz, é preparada em vapor, para que o caldo suculento da carne encha a boca à primeira mordida. Mas cuidado! É muito fácil queimar a língua.

蘿蔔糕（Luo Bu Gao）

©S.T.

Steamed Radish Cakes

Glutinous rice flour, Japanese radish, leeks, dried shrimp and other ingredients are blended together and steamed, and then cut into pieces and browned on both sides for a mild, salty flavor.

kcal ●

蘿蔔糕

將糯米粉與蘿蔔、蔥、蝦米等攪拌在一起後蒸熟，再將兩面烤黃。味道清爽，略帶鹹味。

Gedünsteter Rettichkuchen

Klebriges Reismehl, Riesenrettich, Lauch, getrocknete Krabben und andere Zutaten werden gemischt und dann gedünstet. Der so entstandene Kuchen wird anschließend in Stücke geschnitten und auf beiden Seiten braun gebraten. Ein milder, leicht salziger Geschmack.

萝卜糕

将糯米粉与萝卜、葱、虾米等搅拌在一起后蒸熟，再将两面烤黄。味道清爽，略带咸味。

Gâteaux de radis à la vapeur

On mélange de la farine de riz gluant, des radis japonais, des poireaux, des crevettes séchées et d'autres ingrédients que l'on fait cuire à la vapeur ; on les découpe ensuite en morceaux et on les fait bien dorer des deux côtés afin d'obtenir une saveur salée et légère.

무떡

찹쌀가루와 무, 파, 말린 새우 등을 섞어 반죽하여 찐 다음 적당한 크기로 썰어서 양면을 구운 것. 담백한 소금맛.

Tortas de nabo al vapor

Se mezclan harina de arroz glutinoso, rábano japonés, puerros, langostinos secos y otros ingredientes y se cocinan al vapor, después se cortan en trozos y se tuestan por ambos lados, creando un suave y ligero sabor a sal.

大根もち

もち米粉と大根、ねぎ、干しえびなどを練り合わせて蒸し、切り分けて両面を焼いたもの。さっぱりした塩味。

Focaccine di rapa

Un impasto di farina di riso glutinoso, rapa cinese, porri, gamberetti essiccati e altri ingredienti viene cotto a vapore e tagliato a fette. Le focaccine così ottenute vengono poi dorate in padella da entrambe le parti. Hanno un leggero sapore di sale.

فطائر الفجل المطهوة على البخار

يمزج دقيق الأرز اللدن مع الفجل الياباني والبصل الأخضر والجمبري (الروبيان) الجاف وغيرها ثم يطهى على البخار ويقطع إلى أجزاء، تحمر على الجانبين للحصول على مذاق مملح معتدل.

Tortas de nabo preparadas em vapor

Massa de arroz glutinoso, nabo-japonês, cebolinha, camarão seco e outros ingredientes são misturados e cozidos em vapor. A mistura é então cortada em pedaços e tostada nos dois lados, adquirindo um sabor levemente salgado.

叉燒包（Cha Shao Bao）

Roasted Pork Buns

These Chinese steamed buns are prepared by stuffing roasted pork into fluffy pastry and steaming to seal in the flavor.

kcal ●

©S.T.

叉燒包

在發好的面粉中包上叉燒肉蒸出的包子。

Teigtaschen mit Schweinerostbraten

Diese gedünsteten chinesischen Teigtaschen bestehen aus einem lockeren Gebäck, das mit kleingeschnittenem Schweinerostbraten gefüllt ist. Durch das Dämpfen bleibt der volle Geschmack erhalten.

叉烧包

在发好的面粉中包上叉烧肉蒸出的包子。

Brioches de porc rôti

Ces raviolis chinois cuits à la vapeur se préparent en farcissant une pâte légère avec du porc rôti que l'on fait ensuite cuire à la vapeur afin d'en préserver toute la saveur.

구운 돼지고기만두

부드럽게 부푼 빵 속에 구운 돼지고기가 듬뿍 들어있는 중화만두.

Relleno de Cerdo Asado

Este relleno chino al vapor se preparan envolviendo carne de cerdo endulzado en una esponjosa masa que se cocina al vapor hasta que queda impregnada con el sabor.

チャーシューまん

ふっくらとした皮の中にチャーシューがたっぷり入った中華まんじゅう。

Pagnottelle con ripieno di maiale arrosto

Queste soffici pagnottelle cotte a vapore contengono un abbondante ripieno di maiale arrosto.

خبز محشو بروستو اللحم

يتم إعداد هذا الصنف بحشو الخبز المنفوش اللين بلحم الخنزير المحمر ثم طهيه على البخار للحصول على طعم لذيذ.

Pão chinês recheado com porco assado

Estes pãezinhos chineses consistem em massa fofa recheada com pedaços de porco assado. São assados em vapor para conservar o sabor dos ingredientes.

鹹水角（Xian Shui Jiao）

©S.T.

Glutinuous Rice Fried Dumplings

A sauce containing meat, shrimp and vegetables is sealed in glutinous rice skin and then deep-fried to create the marvelous combination of a crispy outside and rich filling.

kcal ●●

鹹水角

將肉、蝦仁、蔬菜餡包進糯米皮中，然後炸熟。香脆的皮與黏稠的餡成為絕妙的組合。

Gefüllte gebratene Reisteigtaschen

Klebrige Reisteigtaschen werden mit einer Soße gefüllt, die Fleisch, Garnelen und Gemüse enthält. Anschließend werden diese Taschen ausgebacken und ergeben eine phantastische Kombination aus einer krossen äußeren Hülle und einer wohlschmeckenden, sämigen Füllung.

咸水角

将肉、虾仁、蔬菜馅包进糯米皮中，然后炸熟。香脆的皮与黏稠的馅成为绝妙的组合。

Boulettes frites de riz gluant

Une pâte de riz gluant est farcie avec une sauce à base de viande, de crevettes et de légumes que l'on fait frire afin d'obtenir un succulent mélange croquant à l'extérieur et une riche garniture intérieure.

찹쌀튀김만두

고기 또는 새우, 야채로 걸쭉하게 만든 소를 찹쌀만두피로 싸서 튀긴 것. 바삭한 껍질과 걸쭉한 소의 맛이 별미.

Relleno Frito

Se fríe en aceite abundante el caldo con los ingredientes tales como carne de cerdo, langostinos y verduras envueltos en hojas de crepa de arroz glutinoso, creando la maravillosa combinación de una capa externa crujiente y un delicioso relleno.

もち米粉の揚げ餃子

肉やえび、野菜入りのあんをもち米粉の皮で包み、揚げたもの。カリッとした皮とトロリとした具の組み合わせが絶妙。

Ravioli di farina di riso fritti

L'esterno è di farina di riso glutinoso e il ripieno è un sugo denso contenente carne di maiale o gamberetti e verdure. Fritti in abbondante olio, ne risulta un'ottima combinazione di esterno croccante e interno cremoso.

محشوات مقلية من الأرز اللدن

يتم حشو رقائق من الأرز اللدن بصلصة من اللحم والجمبري (الروبيان) والخضر وتغلف جيدا، ثم تحمر الرقائق المحشوة تحميراً غزيراً. يحصل على طبق يجمع بين غشاء هش وحشو شهي.

Bolinhos de arroz glutinoso fritos

Um preparado de carne, camarão e vegetais serve de recheio a uma massa fina de arroz glutinoso. Fritos por mergulho em óleo, os bolinhos formam uma excelente iguaria, com consistência exterior crocante e farto recheio.

腸粉（Chang Fen）

Steamed Rice Flour Sheets

Beef, roasted pork or shrimp is wrapped in thin sheets made of rice flour, and then steamed for an attractive appearance.

kcal ●

© S.T.

腸粉

在米粉做成的薄皮中包進牛肉及叉燒肉、蝦仁等，然後蒸熟。

Gedünstete Reisteigtaschen

Dünne Nudelteigplatten aus Reismehl werden mit Rindfleisch, geröstetem Schweinefleisch oder Garnelen gefüllt und anschließend in Wasserdampf gedünstet. Aufgeschnitten sehen sie sehr attraktiv aus.

肠粉

在米粉做成的薄皮中包进牛肉及叉烧肉、虾仁等，然后蒸熟。

Feuilletés de farine de riz à la vapeur

Après avoir enrobé du bœuf, du porc rôti ou des crevettes dans de fines feuilles à base de farine de riz, on les fait cuire à la vapeur, ce qui donne à ce plat une apparence attrayante.

찐 크레이프

쌀가루로 만든 얇은 껍질에 쇠고기, 돼지고기, 새우 등을 싸서 찐 것.

Crepa de Harina de Arroz

Se envuelve carne de res, cerdo o langostino en finas hojas de crepa de arroz que se cocinan al vapor hasta que obtienen una apariencia atractiva.

米粉のクレープ蒸し

米の粉で作った薄い皮で、牛肉やチャーシュー、えびなどを包み、蒸したもの。

Crespelle di farina di riso cotte a vapore

Carne bovina o maiale arrosto, gamberetti e altri ingredienti vengono avvolti in un sottile involucro fatto con farina di riso e il tutto viene cotto a vapore.

رقائق دقيق الأرز المحشوة والمطهوة على البخار

يغلف اللحم البقري وروستو الخنزير والجمبري (الروبيان) بعجينة رقيقة من دقيق الأرز ثم يطهى على البخار فيكتسب شكلاً جميلاً.

Crepes de farinha de arroz assadas em vapor

Pedaços de carne de gado, porco assado ou camarão enrolados em crepes de farinha de arroz. Assado em vapor, este prato adquire uma aparência apetitosa.

珍珠丸子（Zhen Zhu Wan Zi）

©S.T.

Pearl Balls

Ground pork and minced vegetables are thoroughly blended and formed into dumplings that are sprinkled with glutinous rice and steamed.

kcal ●●

珍珠丸子

將肉末及蔬菜拌勻後做成丸子，然後黏上糯米蒸熟。

Perlenkugeln

Schweinehackfleisch und kleingehacktes Gemüse werden sorgfältig miteinander vermischt und zu Klößen geformt. Diese werden anschließend mit klebrigem Reis bestreut und dann in Wasserdampf gedünstet.

珍珠丸子

將肉末及蔬菜拌勻后做成丸子,然后黏上糯米蒸熟。

Boules perlées

Après avoir complètement mélangé le porc haché et les légumes émincés, on façonne le tout en boulettes que l'on recouvre de riz gluant et que l'on fait cuire à la vapeur.

찹쌀경단

다진 고기와 야채를 잘 버무려서 경단 모양으로 빚은 다음 찹쌀을 입혀 찐 것.

Bolas Perla

Se mezcla bien la carne molida de cerdo con las verduras picadas y se envuelve en bolas de masa espolvoreadas con arroz glutinoso para después cocinarlas al vapor.

もち米団子

ひき肉と野菜をよく練って団子状にし、まわりにもち米をまぶして蒸したもの。

Palline di riso glutinoso

Palline di carne tritata e verdure ben impastate vengono coperte di riso glutinoso e cotte a vapore.

كرات اللؤلؤ

يمزج لحم الخنزير المفري مع خضر مفرية ويشكل المزيج على هيئة كرات تنثر فوقها حبات من الأرز اللدن ثم تطهى على البخار.

Bolinhos de pérolas

Dá-se a forma de bolinhos a uma mistura de carne de porco moída e vegetais picadinhos. Uma vez salpicados com arroz glutinoso, os bolinhos são assados em vapor.

豆豉排骨 (Dou Chi Pai Gu)

Steamed Spareribs with Fermented Black Beans

Pork spareribs are flavored with fermented black beans and red pepper and then steamed until the flavor penetrates throughout the tender meat.

kcal ●●●●

© S.T.

豆豉排骨

將豬排骨加上豆豉和辣椒一起蒸熟。由於調料浸透到肉的內部，因此風味十足。

Gedünsteter Rippenspeer mit fermentierten schwarzen Bohnen

Schweine-Rippenspeer wird mit fermentierten schwarzen Bohnen und spanischem Pfeffer gewürzt und dann so lange gedünstet, bis der Geschmack das zarte Fleisch vollständig durchzogen hat.

豆豉排骨

将猪排骨加上豆豉和辣椒一起蒸熟。由于调料浸透到肉的内部，因此风味十足。

Côtelettes de porc et haricots noirs fermentés cuits à la vapeur

On fait cuire à la vapeur des côtelettes de porc agrémentées de haricots noirs fermentés et de poivrons rouges jusqu'à ce que la saveur imprègne toute la viande tendre.

돼지갈비찜

돼지갈비를 도우치(중국 조미료의 하나)와 고추양념에 재었다가 찐 요리. 연하고 부드러우며 고깃속까지 양념이 배어있어 풍미가 좋다.

Puntas de Costilla y Frijoles Negros al Vapor

Las puntas de costilla de cerdo se aderezan con frijoles negros y chile para cocinar al vapor hasta que el sabor penetra completamente a través de la suave carne.

豚スペアリブの豆豉蒸し

豚のスペアリブを豆豉と唐辛子で味付けし、蒸したもの。柔らかい肉の中まで味がしみ込んで、風味豊か。

Costolette di maiale cotte a vapore

Le costolette vengono macerate in un particolare condimento, fatto di semi di soia cotti a vapore, fermentati e poi essiccati, e di peperoncino rosso. Cotte in seguito a vapore, il gusto penetra fin dentro la carne tenera e ne risulta un piatto assai saporito.

ريش اللحم المطهوة على البخار مع الفول المتخمر

تتبل ريش الخنزير بالفلفل الأحمر والفول الأسود المتخمر ثم تطهى على البخار حتى تنتشر النكهة الطيبة في أنحاء اللحم اللين.

Costela de porco com feijão preto fermentado, cozidos em vapor

As costelas de porco são enriquecidas com feijão preto fermentado e pimenta-malagueta, e cozidas em vapor até que o sabor dos temperos penetre bem na carne tenra.

花卷（Hua Juan）

Steamed Bread Rolls

Bread rolls are formed into the shape of flowers and then steamed for a mild flavor that goes well with rich foods.

kcal ●

花卷

將饅頭做成花狀蒸熟。由於沒有特殊味道，它適合於味道濃厚的菜一起食用。

Gedünstete Teigrollen

Weißbrotteig wird zu Blüten geformt und dann im Wasserdampf gedünstet. Dieses Gebäck hat einen milden Geschmack und paßt gut zu Gerichten mit sehr üppigem Geschmack.

花卷

将馒头做成花状蒸熟。由于没有特殊味道，它适合与味道浓厚的菜一起食用。

Petits pains ronds à la vapeur

Des petits pains ronds préalablement façonnés en forme de fleurs sont cuits à la vapeur afin d'obtenir un goût léger qui s'harmonise bien avec les plats riches.

꽃빵

빵 반죽으로 꽃 모양을 만들어 쪄 낸 중국 빵. 담백하므로 맛이 진한 요리와 잘 어울린다.

Pan Chino

El pan chino se moldean en forma de flores y después se cocinan al vapor hasta que adquieren un sabor que se lleva bien con los alimentos substanciosos.

花巻き

パン生地を花のような形にまとめて蒸した中国パン。くせのない味なので、濃い味付けの料理によく合う。

Panini a forma di fiore

Pane cinese a forma di fiore cotto a vapore. Non avendo un gusto specifico, si accompagna bene con i piatti di sapore accentuato.

لفائف الخبز المطهوة على البخار

تشكل لفائف الخبز على هيئة وردات وتطهى على البخار لتكتسب نكهة معتدلة تصلح للتناول مع الأطعمة الدسمة.

Pãezinhos assados em vapor

Pãezinhos chineses são amassados no formato do flor e assados em vapor para adquirir um aroma suave, que faz boa companhia a outros pratos saborosos.

西米露（Xi Mi Lu）

Coconut Milk with Tapioca

This sweet and creamy desert is served cold, and is prepared by adding sugar to coconut milk and then blending in tapioca.

kcal ●

西米露

椰子汁加糖後再攪拌進木薯澱粉，從而做成奶油色的冰涼甜點心。

Kokosnußmilch mit Tapioca

Diese süße und cremige Nachspeise wird kalt serviert. Bei der Zubereitung wird Kokosnußmilch mit Zucker versetzt und dann Tapioca hineingegeben.

西米露

椰子汁加糖后再搅拌进木薯淀粉，从而做成奶油色的冰凉甜点心。

Lait de coco accompagné de tapioca

Ce dessert sucré et onctueux est servi froid ; il se prépare en ajoutant du sucre à du lait de coco et en mélangeant le tout dans du tapioca.

타피오카가 들어간 코코넛밀크

코코넛 밀크에 설탕과 타피오카를 넣은 달고 부드러운 맛의 찬 디저트.

Leche de Coco con Tapioca

Este dulce y cremoso postre se sirve frío y se prepara añadiendo azúcar a la leche de coco para después mezclarla con tapioca.

タピオカ入りココナッツミルク

ココナッツミルクに砂糖を加え、タピオカを合わせた甘くてクリーミーな冷たいデザート。

Latte di cocco con tapioca

Questo dolce cremoso servito freddo è fatto di latte di cocco zuccherato con l'aggiunta di tapioca.

لبن جوز الهند بالتابيوكة

هذا الصنف الحلو يقدم بارداً ويتم إعداده بإضافة السكر إلى لبن جوز الهند الذي يمزج بعد ذلك مع التابيوكة (حبيبات نشوية من جذور التابيوكة) .

Leite de coco com tapioca

Esta sobremesa adocicada e cremosa, servida fria, é feita adicionando-se açúcar e tapioca ao leite de coco.

杏仁豆腐（Xing Ren Dou Fu）

Almond Jelly with Fruit

Almond milk is formed into a jelly followed by the addition of various fruits and a sweet syrup to create a refreshing dessert.

kcal ●

杏仁豆腐

在杏仁味的膠狀物中加進水果並澆上甜果汁，這是一道爽口的飯後甜點心。

Mandelgelee mit Früchten

Mandelmilch wird zu einem Gelee verarbeitet und dann mit verschiedenen Früchten und süßem Sirup ergänzt. Ein erfrischender Nachtisch.

杏仁豆腐

在杏仁味的胶状物中加进水果并浇上甜果汁，这是一道爽口的饭后甜点心。

Gelée d'amandes aux fruits

Ce dessert rafraîchissant contient du lait d'amandes gélifié que l'on accompagne de divers fruits et d'un sirop sucré.

안닝두부

아몬드밀크 맛의 젤리에 과일을 곁들여 달콤한 시럽을 끼얹은 산뜻한 디저트.

Gelatina de Almendra con Fruta

Se prepara una gelatina cremosa de almendra a la que se agregan diversas frutas y un jarabe dulce para crear un refrescante postre.

杏仁豆腐

アーモンドミルク風味のゼリーにフルーツを添え、甘いシロップをかけたさわやかなデザート。

Gelatina di mandorle con frutta

È un fresco dessert di gelatina al gusto di latte di mandorle e frutta con sciroppo dolce.

جيلي اللوز بالفاكهة

يعد الجيلي من لبن اللوز وتضاف إليه الفاكهه بأنواعها مع شراب حلو لتحصل على طبق بارد منعش.

Gelatina de amêndoa com frutas

O leite de amêndoa é preparado em forma de gelatina. Em seguida, adicionam-se várias frutas e um xarope adocicado. O resultado é uma sobremesa refrescante.

炸芝麻團（Zha Zhi Ma Tuan）

Deep-Fried Sesame Balls

Sweet bean jam is packed into dumplings that are sprinkled with white sesame seeds and deep-fried into a dessert that combines the aroma of the sesame seeds with the sweetness of the sweet bean jam.

© S.T.

kcal ●

炸芝麻團

這是帶餡的糯米團子蘸上白芝麻後、用油炸出的點心。芝麻的香味和餡的甜味互相摻和、相映添輝。

Fritierte Sesambällchen

Ein Mus aus süßen Bohnen wird in Teigtaschen gefüllt, die anschließend in weißer Sesamsaat gerollt und in Öl ausgebacken werden. Eine Nachspeise, die das Aroma der Sesamsaat mit der Süße des Bohnenmußes angenehm kombiniert.

炸芝麻团

这是带馅的糯米团子蘸上白芝麻后、用油炸出的点心。芝麻的香味和馅的甜味互相掺和、相映添辉。

Boules de sésame frites

Ce dessert qui associe l'arôme des graines de sésame avec la douceur de la confiture de haricots sucrés se prépare en fourrant des boulettes avec de la confiture de haricots sucrés que l'on fait ensuite frire.

튀긴 참깨경단

팥소를 넣은 찹쌀경단에 참깨를 묻혀 튀긴 과자. 참깨의 고소한 맛과 팥소의 단 맛이 잘 어울린다.

Bolas de sésamo fritas

Las bolas de masa de arroz rellenas de masa dulce de soja se espolvorean con semillas de sésamo (ajonjolí) blanco y se fríen en aceite abundante para crear un postre que combina el aroma de las semillas de sésamo y la dulzura de la masa de soja.

揚げごま団子

あんこの入った白玉団子に白ごまをまぶして揚げたお菓子。ごまの香ばしさとあんこの甘さがよく合っている。

Palline fritte al sesamo

Sono palline di farina di riso, contenenti marmellata dolce di fagioli azuki e ricoperte di semi di sesamo bianco, che vengono fritte in abbondante olio. L'aroma del sesamo ben si combina con il dolce della marmellata di fagioli.

كرات السمسم المقلية

ينثر السمسم الأبيض فوق كرات محشوة بمربى حلوة من الفول ثم تقلى الكرات للحصول على طبق حلو يجمع بين رائحة السمسم وحلاوة مربى الفول.

Bolinhos de gergelim fritos

A geléia de feijão doce é o recheio de bolinhos, salpicados com sementes brancas de gergelim e fritos por mergulho em óleo. É uma sobremesa que combina o aroma das sementes de gergelim com a doçura da geléia de feijão.

馬拉糕（Ma La Gao）

© S.T.

Chinese Sponge Cake

This sweet sponge cake is prepared by combining wheat flour, eggs, brown sugar and oil and then steaming to create a satisfying dessert.

kcal ●●

馬拉糕

這是將小麥粉、雞蛋、紅糖和油拌和一起蒸出的甜蛋糕。馬拉是指馬來西亞。

Chinesischer Bisquitkuchen

Für diesen süßen Bisquitkuchen werden Weizenmehl, Eier, brauner Zucker und Öl miteinander vermischt und anschließend in heißem Wasserdampf gedünstet. Ein sehr wohlschmeckender Nachtisch.

马拉糕

这是将小麦粉、鸡蛋、红糖和油拌和一起蒸出的甜蛋糕。马拉是指马来西亚。

Gâteau chinois moelleux

Cette génoise sucrée se prépare en mélangeant de la farine de blé, des œufs, du sucre brun et de l'huile. Le mélangé est ensuite cuit à la vapeur afin d'obtenir un dessert substantiel.

중국식 카스텔라

밀가루, 달걀, 흑설탕, 기름 등을 섞어 부드럽게 찐 먹기 좋은 카스텔라.

Biscocho Chino

Este dulce biscocho se prepara cocinando al vapor una mezcla de harina de trigo, huevos, azúcar morena y aceite, lo cual da como resultado un delicioso postre.

中国風蒸しカステラ

小麦粉、卵、黒砂糖、油を混ぜ、ふんわりと蒸した口当たりのよいカステラ。

Pan di spagna cinese cotto a vapore

È un soffice pan di Spagna cotto a vapore e di gusto gradevole, fatto di farina di frumento, uova, zucchero di canna e olio.

كعكة اسفنجية على الطريقة الصينية

تصنع هذه الكعكة الحلوة بخلط دقيق القمح مع البيض والزيت والسكر غير المكرر، ثم تنضج الكعكة على البخار لتحصل على صنف لذيذ من الحلويات.

Pão-de-ló chinês

Este pão-de-ló é feito com farinha de trigo, ovos, açúcar mascavo e azeite. É assado em vapor, criando uma sobremesa muito saborosa.

芒果布丁（Mang Guo Bu Ding）

Mango Pudding

Fresh mango, eggs and milk are solidified with gelatin for a cool, soft dessert that offers a smooth texture and fruity taste.

kcal ●

© S.T.

芒果布丁

這是將新鮮的芒果、雞蛋和牛奶一起凝固而做成的飯後涼點心。喫起來感覺滑爽。

Mango-Pudding

Frische Mangofrüchte, Eier und Milch werden mit Gelatine zu einer Sülze verarbeitet. Eine weiche Nachspeise, die einen angenehmen Biß und fruchtigen Geschmack bietet.

芒果布丁

这是将新鲜的芒果、鸡蛋和牛奶一起凝固而做成的饭后凉点心。吃起来感觉滑爽。

Pudding à la mangue

Ce dessert doux et frais à la texture lisse et au goût fruité se compose de mangues fraîches, d'œufs et de lait solidifiés avec de la gélatine.

망고 푸딩

신선한 망고, 달걀, 밀크를 젤라틴으로 굳힌 찬 디저트. 부드러운 감칠 맛의 과일향.

Budín de Mango

Se agrega mango, huevos y leche a una gelatina y se deja cuajar hasta que se transforma en un fresco y suave postre de textura uniforme y sabor delicioso.

マンゴープリン

新鮮なマンゴー、卵、ミルクを混ぜ、ゼラチンで固めた冷たいデザート。なめらかな舌ざわりでフルーティー。

Budino di mango

È un dessert freddo fatto di mango fresco, uova, latte e gelatina. Piacevole al palato per la consistenza e il gusto fruttato.

بودنج المـانجو

يضاف الجيلاتين إلى المانجو والبيض واللبن لإعداد صنف حلو بارد يجمع بين قوام البودنج الناعم والمذاق الحلو للفاكهة.

Pudim de manga

Manga, ovos e leite frescos são solidificados em forma de gelatina. É uma sobremesa suave, de consistência agradável e com sabor de fruta.

蛋撻（Dan Da）

© S.T.

Egg Tart

This popular dessert features a crunchy tart outside and creamy egg pudding inside that makes the perfect after-meal treat.

kcal ●●

蛋撻

這是外側用水果餡餅、中間用雞蛋布丁做成的甜味素點心。

Eiertörtchen

Diese populäre Nachspeise hat außen eine knusprige Teighülle, der mit einem cremigen Eierpudding gefüllt ist. Dieses Dessert verwöhnt Sie nach der Hauptmahlzeit.

蛋挞

这是外侧用水果馅饼、中间用鸡蛋布丁做成的甜味素点心。

Tarte aux œufs

Ce dessert populaire se compose d'une croûte croustillante à l'extérieur et d'un onctueux pudding aux œufs à l'intérieur, ce qui en fait une parfaite friandise de fin de repas.

에그 타르트

바삭한 타르트로 만든 바깥부분과 부드러운 달걀 푸딩이 잘 조화된 달콤하고 소박한 맛의 과자.

Tarta de Huevo

Este popular postre se caracteriza por el crujiente exterior de la tarta y el cremoso budín de huevo en el relleno que lo convierten en el perfecto manjar de sobremesa.

エッグタルト

外側のさっくりとしたタルト生地と中の卵プリンがマッチした、甘く素朴な味のお菓子。

Crostata di uova

È un dessert dal gusto schietto, in cui la croccante pasta frolla esterna ben si combina con la crema di uova all'interno.

كعك البيض

هذا صنف محبوب من الحلويات عبارة عن كعك لذيذ يوضع بداخله بودنج لبن من البيض لتحصل على نوع مثالي من الحلويات بعد الأكل.

Torta de ovos

Esta apreciada sobremesa consiste em torta de massa crocante com pudim cremoso de ovos no interior. É o quitute perfeito para depois da refeição.

茶（Cha）

Tea

Chinese tea, which boasts a history that goes back many centuries, comes in a wide range of types and flavors and can be enjoyed all day long - before, during and after every meal.

kcal

茶

具有悠久曆史的中國茶種類多、風味各異。其中、凍頂烏龍茶、鐵觀音、茉莉花茶、普洱茶等比較有名。

Tee

Chinesischer Tee, dessen Geschichte viele Jahrhunderte zurückreicht, gibt es in verschiedenen Arten und Geschmacksrichtungen. Man kann ihn den ganzen Tag lang trinken - vor, während und nach den Mahlzeiten.

茶

具有悠久历史的中国茶种类多、风味各异。其中、冻顶乌龙茶、铁观音、茉莉花茶、普洱茶等比较有名。

Thé

Le thé chinois, dont l'histoire remonte à plusieurs siècles, offre un large choix de variétés et de parfums et peut être dégusté tout au long de la journée - avant, pendant et après chaque repas.

차

오랜 역사가 있는 중국차는 종류도 많고 맛도 풍부하다. 동정우롱차, 철관음차, 재스민차, 부아르차 등이 유명.

Té

El té chino tiene una milenaria historia que se remonta a la antigüedad. Se produce en una extensa variedad de clases y sabores y todo el año puede ser disfrutado antes, durante y después de cada comida.

茶

古い歴史を持つ中国茶は、種類が多く風味も豊か。凍頂烏龍茶、鉄観音茶、茉莉花茶、普洱茶などが有名。

Tè

Il tè cinese ha una storia antica, i tipi sono numerosi e i gusti ricchi. Parecchie qualità sono famose anche all'estero.

الشاي

يرجع تاريخ الشاي الصيني إلى قرون عديدة ويضم العديد من الأنواع والنكهات التي يمكن تناولها في أي وقت من اليوم، مع كل وجبة أو قبلها أو بعدها.

Chá

O chá chinês, cuja história remonta há muitos séculos, apresenta-se em muitas variedades e sabores. Pode ser saboreado o dia todo - antes, durante e após as refeições.

酒（Jiu）

© S.T.

Rice Wine

Chinese rice wines have a diverse assortment of characteristic aromas and flavors, and are consumed not only as alcoholic beverages but also for medicinal purposes.

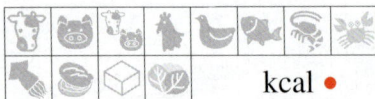

kcal ●

酒

中國酒具有獨特的芳香、豐富多彩且各具特色。其中有代表性的為紹興酒和茅臺酒等。

Reiswein

Chinesische Reisweine gibt es großer Vielfalt. Aroma und Geschmack sind oft sehr charakteristisch. Sie werden nicht nur als alkoholisches Getränk sondern auch für medizinische Zwecke getrunken.

酒

中国酒具有独特的芳香、丰富多彩且各具特色。其中有代表性的为绍兴酒和茅台酒等。

Vin de riz

Les vins de riz chinois présentent un assortiment divers d'arômes et de saveurs caractéristiques, et se consomment non seulement comme boissons alcoolisées mais aussi à des fins médicinales.

술

독특한 향과 개성을 지닌 다양한 중국술. 대표적인 것으로는 소흥주, 모대주(마호타이) 등.

Vino de Arroz

Los vinos chinos de arroz tienen una gran variedad de aromas y sabores característicos y se consumen no solo como bebidas alcohólicas sino también con fines medicinales.

酒

独特の香りがある個性的でバラエティーに富んだ中国酒。代表的なものは、紹興酒、茅台酒など。

Vino di riso

Il vino di riso cinese vanta un assortimento di svariati sapori ed aromi, e viene consumato non solo come bevanda alcolica, ma anche come medicinale.

نبيذ الأرز

يضم نبيذ الأرز الصيني كماً متنوعاً من النكهات والروائح، والصينيون لا يتناولونه فقط باعتباره شراباً كحولياً بل أيضاً كدواً، في العديد من الأحيان.

Vinho de arroz

Os vinhos de arroz chineses são produzidos em uma grande variedade de aromas e sabores. São consumidos não somente como bebidas alcoólicas, mas também como substâncias medicinais.

啤酒（Pi Jiu）

Beer

Beers that are enjoyed with Chinese food include Chinese beers as well as beer brewed in Hong Kong, Taiwan and Singapore. Some major brands are, from left to right, Anchor, Tiger Lager, Taiwan, San Miguel, Tsingtao, Panda and Dinghu Ginseng.

kcal ●

© S.T.

啤酒

中國料理店除了供應中國產的啤酒以外，還有香港、臺灣、新加坡產等的啤酒。從左到右依次為 Anchor 、 Tiger Lager 、 Taiwan 、 San Miguel 、 Tsingtao 、 Panda 、 Dinghu Ginseng 。

Bier

Zu den Bieren, die gut zu chinesischem Essen passen, gehört in China gebrautes Bier, aber auch Marken aus Hong Kong, Taiwan und Singapur. Hier sehen Sie einige wichtige Marken von links nach rechts: Anchor, Tiger Lager, Taiwan, San Miguel, Tsingtao, Panda und Dinghu Ginseng.

啤酒

中国料理店除了供应中国产的啤酒以外，还有香港、台湾、新加坡产等的啤酒。从左到右依次为 Anchor、Tiger Lager、Taiwan、San Miguel、Tsingtao、Panda、Dinghu Ginseng。

Bière

Les bières que l'on peut consommer avec la cuisine chinoise comprennent les bières chinoises ainsi que celles brassées à Hong-Kong, Taiwan et Singapour. Les principales marques sont, de gauche à droite, Anchor, Tiger Lager, Taiwan, San Miguel, Tsingtao, Panda et Dinghu Ginseng.

맥주

중국 요리점에서 마실 수 있는 맥주에는 중국산 외에도 홍콩, 대만, 싱가포르산 등이 있다. 왼쪽부터 Anchor, Tiger Lager, Taiwan, San Miguel, Tsingtao, Panda, Dinghu Ginseng.

Cerveza

Entre las cervezas que se disfrutan con la comida china se encuentran no sólo las que se producen en China, sino también las elaboradas en Hong Kong, Taiwan y Singapur. Algunas de las marcas más conocidas son, de izquierda a derecha: Anchor, Tiger Lager, Taiwan, San Miguel, Tsingtao, Panda y Dinghu Ginseng.

ビール

中国料理店で飲めるビールには、中国産のほかに香港、台湾、シンガポール産などがある。左から Anchor、Tiger Lager、Taiwan、San Miguel、Tsingtao、Panda、Dinghu Ginseng。

Birra

Le birre servite nei ristoranti cinesi sono prodotte in Cina, a Hong Kong, a Taiwan o a Singapore. Le marche più conosciute sono: Anchor, Tiger Lager, Taiwan, San Miguel, Tsingtao, Panda e Dinghu Ginseng.

البيرة

يتناول الصينيون مع طعامهم البيرة المصنوعة في الصين الشعبية وهونج كونج وتايوان وسنغافورة، ونرفق هنا بعض الماركات الشهيرة وهي - من اليسار لليمين: أنكور، تايجر لاجر، تايوان، سان ميجيل، تسينتاو، باندا، دنجو جينسن.

Cerveja

As cervejas apreciadas com comida chinesa incluem tanto as fabricadas na China, como também as produzidas em Hong Kong, Taiwan e Cingapura. Entre as principais estão (da esquerda para a direita): Anchor, Tiger Lager, Taiwan, San Miguel, Tsingtao, Panda e Dinghu Ginseng.

The following provides an introduction to some examples of appetizing combinations of typical Chinese dishes according to the number of people being served.

For 1 person A
1. Fried Rice(p.96)
2. Steamed Dumplings (p.113)

For 1 person B
1. Assorted Meat and Vegetable Stew with Noodles (p.99)
2. Fried Dumplings (p.114)

1個人時 A
1. 什錦炒飯 (p.96)
2. 燒賣 (p.113)

1個人時 B
1. 什錦湯面 (p.99)
2. 鍋貼餃子 (p.114)

1个人时 A
1. 什锦炒饭 (p.96)
2. 烧卖 (p.113)

1个人时 B
1. 什锦汤面 (p.99)
2. 锅贴饺子 (p.114)

1 명의경우 A
1. 볶음밥 (p.96)
2. 슈마이 (p.113)

1 명의 경우 B
1. 잡탕면 (p.99)
2. 군만두 (p.114)

1人の場合 A
1. チャーハン (p.96)
2. シュウマイ (p.113)

1人の場合 B
1. 五目汁そば (p.99)
2. 焼き餃子 (p.114)

لشخص واحد (أ)
١. أرز محمر (ص ٩٦)
٢. محشوات مطهوة على البخار (ص ١١٣)

لشخص واحد (ب)
١. ياخني اللحم والخضر مع حساء الشعرية (ص ٩٩)
٢. محشوات محمرة (ص ١١٤)

Menü für 1 Person A
1. Gebratener Reis (S. 96)
2. Gedünstete Fleischklößchen (S. 113)

Menü für 1 Person B
1. Fleisch- und Gemüseeintopf mit Nudeln (S. 99)
2. Gebratene Fleischklöße (S. 114)

Pour 1 personne A
1. Riz sauté (p.96)
2. Petites poches de pâte farcies cuites à la vapeur (p.113)

Pour 1 personne B
1. Ragoût de viande et de légumes mixtes accompagné de nouilles (p.99)
2. Raviolis frits (p.114)

Para 1 persona A
1. Arroz Frito (p.96)
2. Rellenos al Vapor (p.113)

Para 1 persona B
1. Caldo de Fideos con Carne y Verduras (p.99)
2. Relleno Asado (p.114)

Per 1 persona A
1. Riso fritto (pag. 96)
2. Ravioli cotti a vapore (pag. 113)

Per 1 persona B
1. Spaghettini in brodo con carne e verdure (pag. 99)
2. Ravioli fritti (pag.114)

Para 1 pessoa A
1. Arroz frito (pág. 96)
2. Embrulhinhos cozidos em vapor (pág. 113)

Para 1 pessoa B
1. Sopa de macarrão chinês com molho de carne e vegetais cozidos (pág. 99)
2. Pasteizinhos recheados ao estilo chinês (pág. 114)

© S.T.

For 2 people C

1. Shrimp with Spicy Tomato Sauce (p.74)
2. Steamed Juicy Pork Buns (p.117)
3. Shark's Fin Soup with Crab Meat (p.95)
4. Stir-Fried Chicken and Cashews (p.68)

2 個人時 C

1. 幹燒蝦仁 (p.74)
2. 小籠包 (p.117)
3. 蟹粉魚翅湯 (p.95)
4. 腰果雞丁 (p.68)

2 个人时 C

1. 干烧虾仁 (p.74)
2. 小笼包 (p.117)
3. 蟹粉鱼翅汤 (p.95)
4. 腰果鸡丁 (p.68)

2 명의 경우 C

1. 새우칠리소스 (p.74)
2. 수프가 든 고기만두 (p.117)
3. 게살샥스핀수프 (p.95)
4. 닭고기캐슈너트볶음 (p.68)

2 人の場合 C

1. えびのチリソース (p.74)
2. スープ入り肉まんじゅう (p.117)
3. かに入りふかひれスープ (p.95)
4. 鶏とカシューナッツの炒めもの (p.68)

لشخصين (ج)

١. جمبري (روبيان) بصلصة الطماطم الحريفة (ص ٧٤)
٢. محشو اللحم المطهو على البخار (ص ١١٧)
٣. حساء زعانف القرش مع لحم الكابوريا (ص ٩٥)
٤. دجاج محمر مع الكاشوناتا (ص ٩٥)

Menü für 2 Personen C

1. Garnelen mit scharfer Tomatensoße (S. 74)
2. Gedünstete Teigtaschen mit saftigem Schweinefleisch (S. 117)
3. Haifischflossensuppe mit Krebsfleisch (S. 95)
4. Pfannengerührtes Hühnerfleisch mit Cashew-Nüssen (S. 68)

Pour 2 personnes C

1. Crevettes à la sauce tomate piquante (p.74)
2. Brioches de porc moelleux cuites à la vapeur (p.117)
3. Soupe aux ailerons de requin et au crabe (p.95)
4. Sauté de poulet et de noix de cajou (p.68)

Para 2 personas C

1. Langostinos con Salsa Picante de Tomate (p.74)
2. Relleno Jugosos de Cerdo al Vapor (p.117)
3. Sopa de Aleta de Tiburón con Carne de Cangrejo (p.95)
4. Salteado de Pollo y Nueces de Acajú (p.68)

Per 2 persone C

1. Gamberetti in salsa piccante di pomodoro (pag. 74)
2. Pagnottelle con ripieno di maiale al sugo (pag. 117)
3. Zuppa di pinne di pescecane e polpa di granchio (pag. 95)
4. Sauté di pollo e mandorle indiane (pag.68)

Para 2 pessoas C

1. Camarão com molho de tomate picante (pág. 74)
2. Bolinhos suculentos de porco, assados em vapor (pág. 117)
3. Sopa de barbatana de tubarão com carne de caranguejo (pág. 95)
4. Frango xadrez (pág. 68)

©S.T.

For 2 people D

1. Braised Bean Curd with Chili Sauce (p.88)
2. Egg Drop Soup (p.91)
3. Sauteed Vegetables (p.81)
4. Fried Dumplings (p.114)

2 個人時 D
1. 麻婆豆腐 (p.88)
2. 蛋花湯 (p.91)
3. 炒青菜 (p.81)
4. 鍋貼餃子 (p.114)

2 个人时 D
1. 麻婆豆腐 (p.88)
2. 蛋花汤 (p.91)
3. 炒青菜 (p.81)
4. 锅贴饺子 (p.114)

2 명의 경우 D
1. 마파두부 (p.88)
2. 달걀수프 (p.91)
3. 푸른채소볶음 (p.81)
4. 군만두 (p.114)

2 人の場合 D
1. マーボー豆腐 (p.88)
2. かき卵のスープ (p.91)
3. 青菜の炒めもの (p.81)
4. 焼き餃子 (p.114)

لشخصين (د)
١. توفو مطهو مع صلصة الفلفل الأحمر (ص ٨٨)
٢. حساء قطرات البيض (ص ٩١)
٣. خضر سوتيه (ص ٨١)
٤. محشوات محمرة (ص ١١٤)

Menü für 2 Personen D
1. Geschmorter Tofu mit Chili-Soße (S. 88)
2. Suppe mit Eieinlage (S. 91)
3. Sautiertes Gemüse (S. 81)
4. Gebratene Fleischklöße (S. 114)

Pour 2 personnes D
1. Pâte de soja braisée à la sauce pimentée (p.88)
2. Soupe aux œufs filés (p.91)
3. Sauté de légumes (p.81)
4. Raviolis frits (p.114)

Para 2 personas D
1. Salteado de Cuajada de Soja con Salsa Picante (p.88)
2. Sopa de Gotas de Huevo (p.91)
3. Verduras Salteadas (p.81)
4. Relleno Asado (p.114)

Per 2 persone D
1. Brasato di tofu con salsa piccante Doban Djan (pag. 88)
2. Stracciatella (pag. 91)
3. Sauté di verdure (pag. 81)
4. Ravioli fritti (pag. 114)

Para 2 pessoas D
1. Queijo de soja refogado com molho de pimenta (pág. 88)
2. Sopa com ovos escaldados (pág. 91)
3. Verduras ligeiramente refogadas (pág. 81)
4. Pasteizinhos recheados ao estilo chinês (pág. 114)

For 2 people with alcoholic beverage E
1. Deep-Fried Spring Rolls (p.111)
2. Stir-Fried Beef and Vegetables in Oyster Sauce (p.57)
3. Assorted Cold Plate Appetizer (p.72)

© S.T.

2 個人喝酒時 E
1. 春卷 (p.111)
2. 蠔油牛肉 (p.57)
3. 三色拼盆 (p.72)

Menü für 2 Personen mit alkoholischen Getränken E
1. Ausgebackene Frühlingsrollen (S. 111)
2. Pfannengerührtes Rindfleisch und Gemüse in Austernsoße (S. 57)
3. Appetitanregende gemischte kalte Platte (S. 72)

2 个人喝酒时 E
1. 春卷 (p.111)
2. 蚝油牛肉 (p.57)
3. 三色拼盆 (p.72)

Pour 2 personnes avec boissons alcoolisées E
1. Rouleaux de printemps frits (p.111)
2. Sauté de bœuf et de légumes à la sauce d'huîtres (p.57)
3. Hors-d'œuvre variés (p.72)

2 명이 술을 마실 경우 E
1. 춘권 (p.111)
2. 쇠고기와 야채의 굴소스볶음 (p.57)
3. 삼품전채 (삼품냉채) (p.72)

Para 2 personas con bebidas alcohólicas E
1. Rollos Fritos (p.111)
2. Salteado de Carne de Res y Verduras en Salsa de Ostras (p.57)
3. Entremés Combinado (p.72)

2 人でお酒を飲む場合 E
1. 春巻き (p.111)
2. 牛肉と野菜のオイスターソース炒め (p.57)
3. 三種前菜の盛り合わせ (p.72)

Per 2 persone (con bevande alcoliche) E
1. Involtini primavera (pag. 111)
2. Sauté di manzo e verdure in salsa di ostriche (pag. 57)
3. Misto di antipasti freddi (pag. 72)

لشخصين (مع مشروب كحولي) (هـ)
١. ملفوف الرقاق المحمر (ص ١١١)
٢. لحم بقري وخضر محمرة في صلصة المحار (ص ٥٧)
٣. تشكيلة من المشهيات الباردة (ص ٧٢)

Para 2 pessoas, com bebida alcoólica E
1. Rolinhos-primavera fritos (pág. 111)
2. Carne e vegetais refogados com molho de ostra (pág. 57)
3. Entrada sortida servida fria (pág. 72)

© S.T.

For 3-4 people F

1. Fried Rice (p.96)
2. Fried Bean Curd with Meat and Vegetables (p.89)
3. Sweet and Sour Pork (p.60)
4. Stir-Fried Combination (p.80)
5. Chinese-Style Corn Soup(p.92)

3〜4個人時 F
1. 什錦炒飯 (p.96)
2. 家常豆腐 (p.89)
3. 咕老肉 (p.60)
4. 八寶菜 (p.80)
5. 玉米羹 (p.92)

3〜4个人时 F
1. 什锦炒饭 (p.96)
2. 家常豆腐 (p.89)
3. 咕老肉 (p.60)
4. 八宝菜 (p.80)
5. 玉米羹 (p.92)

3〜4명의 경우 F
1. 볶음밥 (p.96)
2. 튀긴 두부졸임 (p.89)
3. 탕수육 (p.60)
4. 팔보채 (p.80)
5. 중국식 옥수수수프 (p.92)

3〜4人の場合 F
1. チャーハン (p.96)
2. 揚げ豆腐の炒め煮 (p.89)
3. 酢豚 (p.60)
4. 八宝菜 (p.80)
5. 中華風コーンスープ (p.92)

من ثلاثة إلى أربعة أشخاص (و)
١. أرز محمر (ص ٩٦)
٢. توفو محمر مع لحم وخضر (ص ٨٩)
٣. طبق حلو حامض من اللحم (ص ٦٠)
٤. طبق من خليط محمر (ص ٨٠)
٥. حساء كرية الذرة على الطريقة الصينية (ص٩٢)

Menü für 3 bis 4 Personen F
1. Gebratener Reis (S. 96)
2. Gebratener Tofu mit Fleisch und Gemüse (S. 89)
3. Süßsaures Schweinefleisch (S. 60)
4. Pfannengerührte Kombination (S. 80)
5. Maissuppe nach chinesischer Art (S. 92)

Pour 3-4 personnes F
1. Riz sauté (p.96)
2. Pâte de soja frite accompagnée de viande et de légumes (p.89)
3. Porc à l'aigre-doux (p.60)
4. Mélange sauté (p.80)
5. Soupe de maïs à la chinoise (p.92)

Para 3 ó 4 personas F
1. Arroz Frito (p.96)
2. Queso de Soja Frito con Carne y Verduras (p.89)
3. Cerdo Agridulce (p.60)
4. Combinación Salteada (p.80)
5. Crema de Maíz Estilo Chino (p.92)

Per 3-4 persone F
1. Riso fritto (pag. 96)
2. Tofu fritto con carne e verdure (pag. 89)
3. Maiale in agrodolce (pag. 60)
4. Sauté misto (pag. 80)
5. Minestra di mais alla cinese (pag. 92)

Para 3 ou 4 pessoas F
1. Arroz frito (pág. 96)
2. Queijo de soja frito com carne e vegetais (pág. 89)
3. Carne de porco agridoce (pág. 60)
4. Refogado de carne, frutos do mar e vegetais (pág. 80)
5. Sopa de milho ao estilo chinês (pág. 92)

© S.T.

For 3-4 people with alcoholic beverage G

1. Fried Dumplings (p.114)
2. Steamed Shrimp Dumplings (p.115)
3. Shrimp with Spicy Tomato Sauce (p.74)
4. Assorted Cold Plate Appetizer (p.72)
5. Deep-Fried Spring Rolls (p.111)

3〜4 個人喝酒時 G
1. 鍋貼餃子 (p.114)
2. 蝦餃 (p.115)
3. 幹燒蝦仁 (p.74)
4. 三色拼盆 (p.72)
5. 春卷 (p.111)

3〜4 个人喝酒时 G
1. 锅贴饺子 (p.114)
2. 虾饺 (p.115)
3. 干烧虾仁 (p.74)
4. 三色拼盆 (p.72)
5. 春卷 (p.111)

3〜4 명이 술을 마실 경우 G
1. 군만두 (p.114)
2. 새우만두 (p.115)
3. 새우칠리소스 (p.74)
4. 삼품전채 (삼품냉채) (p.72)
5. 춘권 (春卷) (p.111)

3〜4 人でお酒を飲む場合 G
1. 焼き餃子 (p.114)
2. えび入り蒸し餃子 (p.115)
3. えびのチリソース (p.74)
4. 三種前菜の盛り合わせ (p.72)
5. 春巻き (p.111)

من ثلاثة إلى أربعة أشخاص (مع مشروب كحولي)(ى)
١. محشوات محمرة (ص ١١٤)
٢. محشو الجمبري المطهر على البخار (ص ١١٥)
٣. جمبري (روبيان) بصلصة الطماطم الحريفة (ص ٧٤)
٤. تشكيلة من المشهيات الباردة (ص ٧٢)
٥. ملفوف الرقاق المحمر (ص ١١١)

Menü für 3 bis 4 Personen mit alkoholischen Getränken G
1. Gebratene Fleischklöße (S. 114)
2. Gedünstete Garnelenklöße in Teigtaschen (S. 115)
3. Garnelen mit scharfer Tomatensoße (S. 74)
4. Appetitanregende gemischte kalte Platte (S. 72)
5. Ausgebackene Frühlingsrollen (S. 111)

Pour 3-4 personnes avec boissons alcoolisées G
1. Raviolis frits (p.114)
2. Boulettes de crevettes à la vapeur (p.115)
3. Crevettes à la sauce tomate piquante (p.74)
4. Hors-d'œuvre variés (p.72)
5. Rouleaux de printemps frits (p.111)

Para 3 ó 4 personas con bebidas alcohólicas G
1. Relleno Asado (p.114)
2. Relleno de Langostino al Vapor (p.115)
3. Langostinos con Salsa Picante de Tomate (p.74)
4. Entremés Combinado (p.72)
5. Rollos Fritos (p.111)

Per 3-4 persone con bevande alcoliche G
1. Ravioli fritti (pag. 114)
2. Ravioli di gamberetti cotti a vapore (pag. 115)
3. Gamberetti in salsa piccante di pomodoro (pag. 74)
4. Misto di antipasti freddi (pag. 72)
5. Involtini primavera (pag. 111)

Para 3 ou 4 pessoas, com bebida alcoólica G
1. Pasteizinhos recheados ao estilo chinês (pág. 114)
2. Pasteizinhos de camarão assados em vapor (pág. 115)
3. Camarão com molho de tomate picante (pág. 74)
4. Entrada sortida servida fria (pág. 72)
5. Rolinhos-primavera fritos (pág. 111)

KOREAN
FOODS

韓國・朝鮮菜

韩国・朝鲜菜

한국・조선요리

韓国・朝鮮料理

أطباق كورية

Koreanische Gerichte

Cuisine Coréenne

Cocina Coreana

Piatti Coreani

Cozinha Coreana

불고기 (Bul-go-gi)

© S.T.

Stir-Fried Beef Slices

This typical Korean dish features thin slices of beef marinated in a richly flavored sauce and then stir-fried on a large skillet.

kcal ●●●●

炒牛肉片

這是將經過用風味醇甜的佐料浸漬，調味好的牛肉薄片，放在類似成吉思汗烤鍋上，輕輕翻烤烹制的一種朝鮮菜肴。

Pfannengerührte Rindfleisch-Scheiben

Dieses typisch koreanische Gericht besteht aus dünn geschnittenen Rindfleisch-Scheiben, die in einer üppig gewürzten Soße mariniert sind und dann auf einer großen Bratpfanne scharf angebraten werden.

炒牛肉片

这是将经过用风味醇甜的佐料浸渍，调味好的牛肉薄片，放在类似成吉思汗烤锅上，轻轻翻烤烹制的一种朝鲜菜肴。

Sauté d'émincé de bœuf

Ce plat typiquement coréen comprend de fines tranches de bœuf marinées dans une sauce sucrée richement aromatisée que l'on fait revenir dans un large poêlon.

불고기

달콤한 양념장에 재어두었던 얇게 저민 쇠고기를 징키스칸풍 남비에 구운 대표적인 한국·조선요리.

Salteado de Carne de Res

Este típico platillo coreano se caracteriza por sus delgadas rebanadas de carne de res escabechadas en una salsa muy condimentada y fritas en un sartén grande.

牛薄切り肉の炒め焼き

甘味のあるタレで味付けした薄切り牛肉を、ジンギスカン風の鍋で炒めるように焼いて食べる。

Fettine di carne bovina saltate

È un tipico piatto coreano di sottili fette di carne bovina macerate in un intingolo piuttosto dolce e poi saltate alla Gengis Khan.

شرائح اللحم المحمرة

هذا الطبق الكوري المعروف هو عبارة عن شرائح رفيعة السمك من لحم البقر تغمر في صلصة غنية بنكهتها ثم تحمر في مقلاة كبيرة.

Fatias de carne refogadas

Um prato típico coreano com carne de gado em finas fatias. Depois de marinadas em um molho ricamente aromático e levemente adoçado, as fatias de carne são refogadas na chapa de ferro mongol.

고기구이 (Ko-gi-Gu-i)

Grilled Beef

This popular meat dish allows virtually all cuts of beef to be enjoyed, including short rib, tenderloin, tongue and tripe. The meat is cut into bite-sized portions, flavored and grilled. The cooked meat is then dipped in a sauce as preferred.

© S.T.

kcal ●●●●

烤牛肉

這是一道能夠充分品嘗除了五花牛肉和里脊以外，還包括可以品嘗舌頭、內臟等各個部位美味的典型菜肴。將材料切成適合的大小，調味後進行烘烤。食用時，可根據各自的喜好選擇佐料。

烤牛肉

这是一道能够充分品尝除了五花牛肉和里脊以外、还包括可以品尝舌头、内脏等各个部位美味的典型菜肴。将材料切成适合的大小、调味后进行烘烤。食用时、可根据各自的喜好选择佐料。

고기구이

갈비, 로스에서 혀나 내장에 이르기까지 모든 부위를 맛있게 먹을 수 있는 대표적인 고기요리. 먹기 좋은 크기로 잘라 간을 하여 굽는다. 기호에 따라 양념장에 찍어 먹는다.

焼肉

カルビやロースからタン、内臓まで、牛肉のあらゆる部位をおいしく食べられる代表的な肉料理。食べやすい大きさに切って焼き、好みでタレをつける。

لحم البقر المشوي

هذا الطبق الشعبي يمكن إعداده باستخدام أي جزء تقريباً من لحم البقر، ويشمل ذلك الضلوع ولحم الخاصرة واللسان والكرش، ويقطع اللحم إلى أجزاء بحجم اللقمة تتبل وتشوى، ثم تغمر بعد ذلك قطع اللحم الناضجة في صلصة متبلة حسب الرغبة.

Gegrilltes Rindfleisch

Für dieses populäre Fleischgericht können dünne Fleisch-Scheiben von praktisch jedem Teil des Rindes verwendet werden, einschließlich kurzer Rippe, Lende, Zunge und Kutteln. Das Fleisch wird in mundgerechte Portionen geschnitten, gewürzt und dann gegrillt. Die fertigen Fleischstückchen kann man dann ganz nach Wunsch in eine Soße tauchen.

Bœuf grillé

Ce plat de viande populaire peut se préparer avec pratiquement tous les morceaux de bœuf, que ce soit les travers, le filet, la langue ou les tripes. Après avoir découpé la viande en petits carrés, on l'assaisonne et on la fait griller. On plonge ensuite la viande cuite dans une sauce, selon ses préférences.

Carne de Res Asada a la Parrilla

Este conocido platillo permite disfrutar prácticamente todos los cortes de res, incluyendo agujas, lomo, lengua o tripa. La carne se corta en trozos del tamaño de un bocado, se sazona y se asa a la parrilla. Cuando se ha dorado la carne, se remoja en una salsa al gusto.

Carne alla griglia

È un tipico piatto di carne, nel quale si possono usare tutti i tagli del manzo, dalla punta di petto al controfiletto, alla lingua, agli organi interni. I bocconcini preparati vengono cotti davanti ai commensali e si mangiano intingendoli a piacere in salsine varie.

Carne grelhada

Neste prato apreciado, pode-se desfrutar virtualmente todos os tipos de carne, entre as quais, falsa costela, filé, língua e dobradinha. A carne é cortada em pedaços do tamanho ideal para levar à boca, e então condimentada e assada na grelha. Uma vez assada, a carne é mergulhada num molho a gosto.

갈비구이 (Kal-bi-Gu-i)

Grilled Beef Short Ribs

Flavored beef short ribs are enjoyed while cooking on a grill. This is the most popular grilled meat dish in Korea, with the well-done sinew around the bone considered to be the most delicious.

kcal ●●●●

烤牛排

這是將經過調味的牛排放在烤網上邊烤邊喫的南朝鮮最普通的菜肴之一。烤熟後的排骨附近的筋蹄，富有彈性，味鮮色香。

烤牛排

这是将经过调味的牛排放在烤网上边烤边吃的南朝鲜最普通的菜肴之一。烤熟后的排骨附近的筋蹄，富有弹性，味鲜色香。

갈비구이

갈비뼈 채로 양념한 고기를 석쇠에 구워 먹는 한국에서 가장 인기있는 갈비구이. 잘 구워진 갈비뼈 주위의 힘줄이 맛있다.

牛骨付きカルビ焼き

味付けした牛骨付きあばら肉を網で焼きながら食べる、韓国・朝鮮でもっともポピュラーな焼肉。よく焼けた骨のまわりのスジがおいしい。

ريش البقر المشوية

يمكنك تناول ريش البقر المتبلة بينما تعدها بنفسك أمام الشواية، ويعد هذا هو الطبق المفضل من اللحم المشوي لدي الكوريين الذين يعتبرون الجزء المحيط بالعظم هو ألذ الأجزاء طعماً بعد شيه جيداً.

Gegrillte kurze Rippen vom Rind

Kurze Rippen vom Rind werden gewürzt und der köstliche Duft genossen, während das Fleisch auf dem Grill brät. Diese Art der Zubereitung ist das populärste gegrillte Fleischgericht in Korea. Die gut durchgebratenen Sehnen um die Knochen gelten als besondere Delikatesse.

Travers de bœuf grillés

Ce plat de viande est le plus populaire en Corée. Il se compose de travers de bœuf aromatisés que l'on déguste en les faisant griller directement. Le tendon, bien cuit autour de l'os, constituerait, dit-on, la partie la plus délicieuse.

Agujas de Res Asadas a la Parilla

Las agujas de res aderezadas se comen directamente desde la parrilla en que son asadas. Este es el platillo de carne de res asada más popular en Corea y el tendón bien asado alrededor del hueso se considera la parte más deliciosa.

Costicine con l'osso alla griglia

Queste costicine di carne bovina con l'osso macerate per insaporirle e poi cotte direttamente dai commensali, sono il piatto di carne più popolare in Corea. La parte intorno all'osso è la più gustosa.

Falsa costela de gado grelhada

Falsa costela de gado com condimentos, assada na grelha da mesa. Este é o prato de carne grelhada mais apreciado na Coréia. A parte considerada mais deliciosa é o tendão bem-passado, em torno dos ossos.

갈비찜 (Kal-bi-Chim)

Braised Beef Short Ribs

Beef short ribs and vegetables are simmered for a long time in a sweet and spicy sauce allowing the flavor of the sauce to penetrate throughout the tender meat.

kcal ●●

© S.T.

炖五花牛肉

這是一道將五花牛肉和蔬菜長時間炖煮而成的，具有鹹中帶甜風味的菜肴。肉質酥軟，香醇濃鬱。

Geschmorte Kurze Rippe vom Rind

Kurze Rippe vom Rind und Gemüse werden lange Zeit in einem süß-scharfen Sud geschmort, bis sich der Geschmack der Soße vollständig im zarten Fleisch verteilt hat.

炖五花牛肉

这是一道将五花牛肉和蔬菜长时间炖煮而成的，具有咸中带甜风味的菜肴。肉质酥软，香醇浓郁。

Poitrine de bœuf braisée

Poitrine de bœuf et légumes mijotés pendant longtemps dans une sauce sucrée et épicée permettent à la sauce de pénétrer dans toute la viande tendre.

갈비찜

쇠갈비와 야채를 달짝지근하게 장시간 조린 것. 고기 속까지 양념 맛이 배어 있어 부드럽다.

Guisado de Pecho de Res Dorado

El pecho de la res y las verduras son guisados durante un buen tiempo en una salsa dulce y aromática, permitiendo que el sabor de la salsa penetre a través de la suave carne.

牛バラ肉の煮もの

牛バラ肉と野菜を長時間煮込んだ甘辛味の煮もの。肉は柔らかく、中までよく味がしみ込んでいる。

Punta di petto in umido

Punta di petto di manzo e verdure vengono cotte a lungo con condimento dolce-piccante. La carne diventa morbida e si insaporisce fino all'interno.

ضلع البقر المطهو على نار هادئة

يتم طهي قطع من ضلع البقر مع الخضر على نار هادئة لمدة طويلة مع صلصة حلوة وحريفة حتى تتخلل نكهة الصلصة كل أجزاء اللحم اللين.

Falsa costela cozida

Falsa costela e vegetais são cozidos em fogo brando, num molho doce e apimentado, para permitir que o sabor do molho penetre bem na carne tenra.

육회 （Yuk-Hwe）

© S.T.

Seasoned Raw Beef

Fresh and tender raw beef is cut into thin slices and mixed with a sweet, soy-flavored sauce that is enjoyed with an egg yolk for a luxurious dish with a velvety flavor and texture. This dish is also served with pears which are believed to preserve the beef.

kcal ●●

生牛肉片

這是一道將松軟的生牛肉切絲，蘸上甜味醬油汁再拌上蛋黃後一起食用的菜肴。肉質滑潤細膩、美味可口。自古以來有與被稱之為具有去毒之功效的梨一起食用的習慣。

生牛肉片

这是一道将松软的生牛肉切丝，蘸上甜味酱油汁再拌上蛋黄后一起食用的菜肴。肉质滑润细膩、美味可口。自古以来有与被称之为具有去毒之功效的梨一起食用的习惯。

육회

곱게 다진 연한 쇠고기를 양념장에 버무려서 달걀 노른자를 섞어 날로 먹는다. 부드러운 육질이 먹기 좋고, 옛날부터 식중독을 예방하는 의미로 배와 같이 먹는다.

牛肉のさしみ

生の牛肉を細切りにして甘味のあるしょうゆダレであえ、卵黄と混ぜて食べる。なめらかな口当たりで食べやすく、昔から毒消しなどの意で添えられた梨も一緒に食べる。

لحم البقر المتبل النيئ

يقطع لحم البقر الطري الطازج إلى شرائح رفيعة السمك ويخلط بصلصة حلوة متبلة بالصويا، ثم يجمل بصفار بيضة نيئة لتحصل على طبق فاخر ناعم الطعم والقوام. يقدم هذا الطبق أحياناً مع الكمثرى التي يعتقد أنها تساعد على حفظ اللحم طازجاً.

Gewürztes rohes Rindfleisch

Frisches und zartes rohes Rindfleisch wird in dünne Scheiben geschnitten und mit einer süßlichen Sojasoße gemischt. Diese luxuriöse Speise wird mit Eigelb genossen und hat einen samtartigen Geschmack und Biß. Dieses Gericht wird ebenfalls mit Birnen serviert, die das Rindfleisch konservieren sollen.

Bœuf cru aromatisé

Ce mets somptueux à la saveur et à la texture veloutées se compose de bœuf cru frais et tendre que l'on a émincé et que l'on mélange à une sauce sucrée aromatisée au soja sur lequel on ajoute un jaune d'œuf. Ce plat peut également être servi avec des poires dont on dit qu'elles préservent toute la saveur du bœuf.

Carne Cruda de Res Sazonada

Para prepara este lujoso platillo de sabor y textura aterciopelada, la suave carne cruda de res se corta en pequeñas rebanadas y se mezcla con una salsa de soja azucarada para comer con una yema de huevo encima. Este platillo también se sirve con peras, pues se cree que preservan la carne de res.

Striscioline di carne cruda in salsa

Queste striscioline sottili di carne bovina cruda insaporite con salsa di soia dolce, si mangiano con tuorlo d'uovo che dà una sensazione di vellutato. Vengono anche servite con un contorno di pere, considerate dall'antichità come un antidoto.

Carne crua condimentada

Carne de gado fresca e tenra é cortada em finas fatias e misturada com um molho doce, condimentado com soja. Adiciona-se gema de ovo na hora de saborear esta deliciosa iguaria, de consistência aveludada. O prato também é servido com pêras, frutas a que se atribui a capacidade de preservar a carne.

김치볶음 (Kim-chi-Bok-eum)

Stir-Fried Pork with Kimchee

This stir-fried dish features the delicious combination of Kimchee and pork. The sour and spicy flavor of the Kimchee goes well with the pork, making it a favorite as an entree with rice or as a snack with drinks.

kcal ••

© S.T.

朝鮮腌菜炒豬肉

將朝鮮腌菜和豬肉放在一起煸炒。朝鮮腌菜的酸辣味滲透於豬肉、與其鮮味相輔相成， 是一道宜於喫飯和下酒的酸辣可口的菜肴。

朝鮮腌菜炒猪肉

将朝鮮腌菜和猪肉放在一起煸炒。朝鮮腌菜的酸辣味渗透于猪肉、与其鮮味相辅相成，是一道宜于吃饭和下酒的酸辣可口的菜肴。

김치볶음

김치와 잘 어울리는 돼지고기를 함께 볶은 것. 김치의 산미와 매운 맛이 돼지고기와 잘 어울리며 밥반찬이나 술안주로 좋다.

キムチと豚肉の炒めもの

キムチと相性のよい豚肉を一緒に炒めたもの。キムチの酸味と辛味が豚肉によく合い、ご飯のおかずにも酒の肴にもよい。

لحم مخمر مع الكيمنتشي

يجمع هذا الطبق بين لحم الخنزير ومخلل الكيمنتشي في مزيج محمر لذيذ الطعم. تمثل النكهة الحريفة والحمضية للكيمنتشي توليفة مناسبة للحم الخنزير مما يجعل هذا من الأطعمة المفضلة كطبق مشهيات مع الأرز أو "مزة" تؤكل مع الكحوليات.

Pfannengerührtes Schweinefleisch mit Kimchee

Dieses pfannengerührte Gericht ist eine köstliche Kombination aus Kimchee und Schweinefleisch. Der sauer-scharfe Geschmack des Kimchee paßt sehr gut zum Schweinefleisch. Mit Reis serviert ein beliebtes Gericht oder als Imbiß mit Getränken.

Sauté de porc avec du kimchee

Ce sauté est un délicieux mélange de porc et de kimchee dont la saveur aigre et piquante s'harmonise bien avec le porc. On le sert de préférence avec un accompagnement de riz ou en amuse-gueule.

Salteado de Cerdo con Kimchee

Este platillo salteado se caracteriza por la deliciosa combinación del Kimchee y el cerdo. El sabor agrio y picante del Kimchee se lleva bien con el cerdo y es favorito como plato fuerte con arroz o como entremés con bebidas.

Sauté di maiale con kimchi

È un piatto in cui il gusto agro e piccante del Kimchi ben si combina con la carne di maiale. Ottimo come pietanza o per accompagnare bevande alcoliche.

Porco refogado com kimchee

Esta iguaria refogada é uma deliciosa combinação de kimchee com carne de porco. O sabor acre e apimentado do kimchee harmoniza-se bem com a carne de porco. É o prato predileto para acompanhar arroz ou bebidas alcoólicas.

족발 (Jok-bal)

Boiled Pig's Feet

Boiled pig's feet are mixed with fermented soy bean paste flavored with vinegar and red pepper. This dish is known for the enjoyable crunchy texture of the cartilage, while the large amount of gelatinous meat when eaten is said to be a beauty aid.

豬蹄

將炖熟的豬蹄，蘸上醋味辣椒醬食用。蹄筋肉質堅實柔韌、久嚼不厭。由於含有豐富膠質，是美容的理想食品。

猪蹄

将炖熟的猪蹄，蘸上醋味辣椒酱食用。蹄筋肉质坚实柔韧、久嚼不厌。由于含有丰富胶质，是美容的理想食品。

족발

돼지발을 삶은 것으로 새우젓 또는 양념 초고추장에 찍어 먹는다. 연골의 쫄깃쫄깃한 부분이 맛있으며, 젤라틴이 풍부한 족발은 미용에도 좋다고 알려져 있다.

豚足

豚足をボイルしたもので、唐辛子酢みそ（チョジャン）をつけて食べる。軟骨のコリコリとした歯ごたえが楽しめ、ゼラチン質たっぷりなので美容によいといわれる。

الكوارع المسلوقة

تخلط كوارع الخنزير المسلوقة مع الميسو (مادة تتبيل من فول الصويا) المتبل بالخل والفلفل الأحمر، ويشتهر هذا الطبق بغضاريفه الهشة ويقال إن تناول كمية كبيرة من لحم الكوارع اللدنة له مفعول ممتاز بالنسبة للجمال.

Gekochte Schweinefüße

Gekochte Schweinefüße werden mit einer fermentierten Sojabohnenpaste gemischt, deren Grundgeschmack auf Essig und spanischem Pfeffer beruht. Dieses Gericht ist bekannt für die angenehme bißfeste Textur der Knorpel, während der große Anteil an gelatinehaltigem Fleisch der Schönheit förderlich sein soll.

Pieds de porc bouillis

On mélange des pieds de porc bouillis avec de la pâte de haricots de soja fermentés aromatisée au vinaigre et au piment rouge. Ce plat est apprécié pour l'agréable texture croustillante des cartilages, tandis que la consommation régulière de viande gélatineuse constituerait un vrai traitement de beauté.

Cocido de Pata de Cerdo

Se mezcla la pata de cerdo cocida con una pasta de soja fermentada aderezada con vinagre y chile. Este platillo es conocido por la apetitosa textura crujiente del cartílago. Según se dice, la gran proporción de carne gelatinosa que se come es un auxiliar cosmético para realzar la belleza.

Bollito di zampa di maiale

Questo bollito di zampa di maiale si mangia con un intingolo composto di peperoncino, aceto e miso coreano (Cio Djan). Piace per la consistenza delle cartilagini e si dice che l'abbondante gelatina faccia bene alla pelle.

Pés de porco fervidos

Pés de porco fervidos são misturados a uma pasta de soja fermentada já temperada com vinagre e pimenta-malagueta. Este prato é apreciado pela agradável consistência crocante da cartilagem. Dizem também que a ingestão substancial de carne gelatinosa tem ótimos efeitos estéticos.

삼계탕 (Sam-gye-Tang)

Whole Boiled Chicken with Ginseng Soup

A whole cleaned chicken is stuffed with glutinous rice, ginseng and other ingredients and then simmered to bring out the flavor for a truly invigorating dish.

kcal ●●

© S.T.

全雞參湯

這是在取出內臟的整雞肚內，塞入糯米和高麗參後一起炖煮而成的強身健體的補益菜肴。

Suppe mit einem ganzen gekochten Hühnchen und Ginseng

Ein ganzes gesäubertes Hühnchen wird mit klebrigem Reis gefüllt, der Ginseng und andere Zutaten hinzugegeben und dann ganz langsam geköchelt, um den Geschmack sorgfältig herauszuarbeiten. Ein wirklich kraftspendendes Gericht.

全鸡参汤

这是在取出内脏的整鸡肚内，塞入糯米和高丽参后一起炖煮而成的强身健体的补益菜肴。

Soupe de poulet entier bouilli avec du ginseng

Après avoir été nettoyé et farci de riz gluant, de ginseng et d'autres ingrédients, on fait mijoter un poulet entier afin d'en rehausser la saveur et d'obtenir un plat réellement tonifiant.

삼계탕

내장을 빼낸 통닭 뱃속에 찹쌀과 인삼 등을 넣어 푹 삶은 스태미너 요리.

Pollo Relleno en Sopa de Ginseng

Se rellena un pollo entero sin vísceras con arroz glutinoso, ginseng y otros ingredientes. Después se cuece a fuego lento para realzar el sabor y crear un platillo realmente energético.

丸鶏と朝鮮人参のスープ

内臓を取り出した丸鶏のおなかに、もち米や朝鮮人参などを詰め、スープで煮込んだスタミナ料理。

Pollo intero bollito con ginseng

Questo piatto rinvigorente viene preparato bollendo un pollo intero svuotato delle interiora e farcito con riso glutinoso, ginseng e altri ingredienti.

حساء دجاجة مسلوقة مع الأرالية

يتم حشو دجاجة نظيفة كاملة بالأرز اللدن ونبات الأرالية (الجنسن) وغيرهما ثم تطهى على نار هادئة حتى تبرز النكهة الطيبة لهذا الطعام الذي يعد بحق منشطاً قوياً للجسم.

Frango inteiro cozido com sopa de ginseng

Uma galinha limpa, inteira, é recheada com arroz glutinoso, ginseng e outros ingredientes. O cozimento em fogo brando enriquece o sabor deste prato revigorante.

생선조림 (Seng-seon-Jo-rim)

Spicy Boiled Fish

This typical Korean family dish is prepared by boiling a plump fish in a broth containing red pepper, soy sauce, sweet sake (mirin) and other ingredients. The radish that is boiled with the fish absorbs the flavor of the fish making it especially good.

kcal ●●

辣椒炖魚

這是一道將含有豐富脂肪的肥魚用辣椒、醬油、甜料酒烹飪做成的普通家常菜。與其一起烹飪的蘿蔔也因滲透著魚肉的鮮味，而美味可口。

辣椒炖鱼

这是一道将含有丰富脂肪的肥鱼用辣椒、酱油、甜料酒烹饪做成的普通家常菜。与其一起烹饪的萝卜也因渗透着鱼肉的鲜味，而美味可口。

생선조림

물이 오른 생선을 고추가루, 간장, 미림 등으로 조린 일반적인 가정요리. 같이 조린 무우에도 생선 맛이 배어 있어 맛있다.

魚の唐辛子煮

脂ののった魚を唐辛子、しょうゆ、みりんなどで煮た一般的な家庭料理。一緒に煮込む大根にも魚のうまみがしみておいしい。

سمك مسلوق حرّيف

يتم إعداد هذا الطبق الشعبي الكوري بسلق سمكة كاملة في بهريز يحتوي على الفلفل الأحمر وصلصة الصويا وخمر الأرز الحلو (الميرين) وغيرها من المكونات، ويلاحظ أنه إذا سلق الفجل أيضاً في هذا الحساء فإنه يمتص نكهة السمك ويكتسب طعماً لذيذاً رائعاً.

Scharfer gekochter Fisch

Dieses Gericht ist typische koreanische Hausmannskost. Fisch wird in einem Sud mit spanischem Pfeffer, Sojasoße, süßem Sake (Mirin) und anderen Zutaten gekocht. Der zusammen mit dem Fisch gekochte Rettich nimmt den Geschmack des Fisches auf und ist besonders wohlschmeckend.

Poisson bouilli aux épices

Ce plat familial typiquement coréen se prépare en faisant bouillir un poisson charnu dans un bouillon à base de piment rouge, de sauce de soja, de saké sucré (mirin) et d'autres ingrédients. Le radis bouilli avec le poisson absorbe l'arôme du poisson, ce qui le rend particulièrement savoureux.

Guisado de Pescado Aromático

Este típico platillo familiar coreano se prepara cociendo un pescado grande en un caldo que contiene chile, salsa de soja, sake dulce (mirin) y otros ingredientes. El rábano cocido con el pescado absorbe el olor desagradable haciéndolo especialmente sabroso.

Pesce in umido piccante

È un piatto di cucina casalinga preparato cuocendo in umido del pesce piuttosto grasso con peperoncino, salsa di soia e sakè dolce per cucina, unitamente a rapa asiatica che durante la cottura assorbe il sapore del pesce.

Peixe cozido picante

Este típico prato familiar coreano é feito com peixe adiposo, cozido em um caldo com pimenta-malagueta, molho de soja, vinho de arroz doce (mirin) e outros ingredientes. O nabo, que é cozido juntamente com o peixe, absorve o gosto do pescado e torna particularmente deliciosa esta iguaria.

오징어회 무침 (O-jing-eo-Hwe Mu-chim)

Vinegared Squid

Raw squid is flavored with fermented soy bean paste containing vinegar, hot red pepper, and then typically mixed with vegetables such as chrysanthemum leaves.

© S.T.

酸甜醬涼拌生烏賊

用芥末酸甜醬拌調的生烏賊，通常一起加拌有茼蒿等蔬菜。

Mit Essig gesäuerter Tintenfisch

Roher Tintenfisch wird mit einer fermentierten Sojabohnenpaste gewürzt, die Essig und scharfen spanischen Pfeffer enthält. Normalerweise wird er dann mit Gemüse gemischt, z.B. mit Chrysanthemenblättern.

酸甜酱凉拌生乌贼

用芥末酸甜酱拌调的生乌贼，通常一起加拌有茼蒿等蔬菜。

Calmars au vinaigre

Après avoir aromatisé les calmars crus d'une pâte de haricots de soja fermentés contenant du vinaigre et des piments rouges épicés, on les mélange généralement avec des légumes tels que des feuilles de chrysanthème.

오징어회 무침

생오징어를 초고추장으로 맛을 낸 것. 쑥갓 등의 야채와 함께 버무리는 경우가 많다.

Calamar Avinagrado

Se condimenta el calamar crudo con una pasta de soja fermentada que contiene vinagre y chile. Generalmente se mezcla con verduras tales como hojas de crisantemo.

いかのさしみの酢みそあえ

生のいかを唐辛子酢みそ（チョジャン）で調味したもの。春菊などの野菜を一緒にあえることが多い。

Seppia in salsa agra

Striscioline di seppia cruda vengono mescolate con una salsa di peperoncino rosso, aceto e miso coreano (Cio Djan), spesso con l'aggiunta di verdure, per esempio foglie di crisantemo commestibile.

سبيط بالخل

يتبل السبيط (الحبار) النيء بالميسو (مادة تتبيل من فول الصويا) المحتوي على الخل والفلفل الأحمر الحار ثم يخلط بنخبة من الخضر مثل أوراق الكريزنتيم.

Lula avinagrada

A lula crua é condimentada com pasta de soja fermentada, contendo vinagre e pimenta-malagueta. É comum servir-se este prato juntamente com uma mistura de vegetais, entre os quais as folhas de crisântemo.

kcal ●

전 (Jeon)

© S.T.

Fried Meat and Vegetables in Egg Batter

This dish formerly favored by members of Korean nobility is prepared by seasoning the ingredients such as meat, seafood, vegetables and bean curd prior to cooking, covering the ingredients with flour, dipping in beaten eggs and frying.

kcal ●

烤蛋拖

将已經調好味的肉、魚貝類、蔬菜、豆腐等蘸上面粉後，使其在打勻的雞蛋中拖過，再燒出的宮庭菜肴。

烤蛋拖

将已经调好味的肉、鱼贝类、蔬菜、豆腐等蘸上面粉后，使其在打勻的鸡蛋中拖过，再烧出的宫庭菜肴。

전

소금과 후추로 간을 한 고기, 생선류, 야채, 두부 등에 밀가루를 입히고 푼 달걀을 둘러 부친 것. 궁중요리의 일종.

卵のつけ焼き

下味をつけた肉、魚介類、野菜、豆腐などに小麦粉をまぶし、溶き卵をからめて焼いたもの。宮廷料理の一種。

لحم وخضر محمرة بالبيض والدقيق

في الماضي كان هذا هو الطبق المفضل لدي الكوريين من الأسر النبيلة ويتم إعداده بتتبيل المقادير مثل اللحم والأطعمة البحرية والخضر والتوفر ثم تغطي بالدقيق كل على حدة وتغمر في البيض المخفوق وتقلى في الزيت.

Gebratenes Fleisch und Gemüse in Eierpanade

Dieses Gericht war früher insbesondere beim koreanischen Adel beliebt. Die Zutaten, etwa Fleisch, Meeresfrüchte, Gemüse und Tofu (Sojabohnenquark) werden vor der Zubereitung gewürzt. Anschließend werden die Zutaten in Mehl gewendet, in Eierschnee eingetaucht und dann fritiert.

Viande et légumes à l'œuf grillé

Ce plat, autrefois apprécié par la noblesse coréenne, se prépare en assaisonnant les ingrédients (viande, fruits de mer, légumes et pâte de soja) avant de les faire cuire, en les enrobant de farine puis en les plongeant dans des œufs battus et en faisant frire le tout.

Carne y Verduras con Huevo a la Plancha

En la antigüedad, este era un platillo favorito de los miembros de la nobleza coreana. Se prepara sazonando primero ingredientes tales como carne, mariscos, verduras y cuajada de soja. Después se asan en sartén cubriendolos con harina y mojándolos en huevo batido.

Fritto misto all'uovo

È uno dei piatti della cucina di corte, in cui gli ingredienti, quali carne, crostacei e molluschi, verdure e tofu, vengono prima fatti insaporire, poi infarinati, passati nell'uovo e fritti.

Fritura de carne e vegetais com massa mole de ovo

Este prato era um dos favoritos da antiga nobreza coreana. Os vários ingredientes, como carne, frutos do mar, vegetais e queijo de soja, são condimentados previamente. Depois de passados na farinha e mergulhados em ovos batidos, são fritos.

아구찜 （A-gu-Chim）

Braised Angler with Hot Red Pepper

Steamed angler, bean sprouts and other vegetables are braised with fermented soy bean paste flavored with hot red pepper. This dish is popular as a snack with drinks and is particularly popular among people who like spicy foods.

kcal ●●

© S.T.

辣椒炖老頭魚

這是將蒸過的老頭魚及豆芽菜等蔬菜與醋味辣椒醬放在一起煸炒制成的，深受歡迎的下酒菜之一，也是偏愛辣味顧客的美味菜肴。

辣椒炖老头鱼

这是将蒸过的老头鱼及豆芽菜等蔬菜与醋味辣椒酱放在一起煸炒制成的，深受欢迎的下酒菜之一，也是偏爱辣味顾客的美味菜肴。

아구찜

찐 아구와 콩나물 등의 야채를 고추장에 볶아 조린 요리. 술안주로 인기가 있다. 매운 것을 좋아하는 사람에게 적격.

あんこうの唐辛子煮

蒸したあんこうともやしなどの野菜を、唐辛子みそで炒め煮にした料理。酒のつまみとして人気がある。辛いものが好きな人向き。

سمك مطهو مع الفلفل الأحمر الحار

يطهى سمك أبو الشص المسلوق مع براعم الفول وغيرها من الخضر على البخار ثم يحمر مع الميسو (مادة تتبيل من فول الصويا) والفلفل الأحمر الحار. هذا الطبق محبوب جدا كمزة مع الشراب وخاصة بين هواة الأطعمة الحريفة.

Geschmorter Seeteufel mit scharfem spanischen Pfeffer

Gedünsteter Seeteufel, Sojabohnensprossen und anderes Gemüse werden mit fermentierter Sojabohnenpaste geschmort, die mit scharfem spanischen Pfeffer gewürzt ist. Dieses Gericht ist als Imbiß zu Getränken beliebt und wird insbesondere von Leuten bevorzugt, die scharfe Gerichte lieben.

Lotte de mer braisée au piment rouge piquant

Ce plat, populaire comme en-cas accompagné de boissons et particulièrement apprécié par les amateurs de cuisine épicée, contient de la lotte cuite à la vapeur, des choux de Bruxelles et d'autres légumes braisés avec de la pâte de haricots de soja aromatisée au piment rouge piquant.

Cocido de Pejesapo Dorado en Salsa Chile

Una combinación de pejesapo, germen de soja y verduras salteadas y cocidas a fuego lento con pasta de frijol de soja fermentada y chile. Este es uno de los entremeses favoritos para acompañar bebidas y es especialmente popular entre la gente que gusta de la comida picante.

Coda di rospo in umido con peperoncino rosso

È un piatto di coda di rospo, precedentemente cotta a vapore, germogli di soia e altre verdure cotti in umido con miso coreano e peperoncino. È molto richiesto per accompagnare le bevande alcoliche. Adatto a chi ama i cibi piccanti.

Cozido de xarroco-maior com pimenta-malagueta

Xarroco-maior assado em vapor, brotos de feijão e outros vegetais são cozidos com pasta de soja fermentada contendo pimenta-malagueta. É uma ótima iguaria para acompanhar bebidas alcoólicas. Faz sucesso principalmente entre pessoas que apreciam pratos picantes.

김치 (Kim-chi)

Kimchee

Kimchee consists of salted vegetables pickled with various seasonings, spices and salted fish. Kimchee is the generic name for all pickled vegetables, and common examples of its ingredients include Chinese cabbage, cucumbers and white radishes.

kcal ●

朝鮮腌菜

這是在腌鹹的蔬菜中，加入香辣調味料及佐料、鹹魚或貝類而腌出的菜肴。朝鮮腌菜是"腌菜"的總稱。一般主要是以白菜、黃瓜、蘿蔔等為原料。

Kimchee

Kimchee besteht aus gesalzenem Gemüse, das mit verschiedenen Gewürzen und gesalzenem Fisch eingelegt wird. Kimchee ist ein Sammelbegriff für alle eingelegten Gemüse. Zu den normalerweise verwendeten Zutaten gehören Chinakohl, Gurken und weißer Riesenrettich.

朝鲜腌菜

这是在腌咸的蔬菜中，加入香辣调味料及佐料、咸鱼或贝类而腌出的菜肴。朝鲜腌菜是"腌菜"的总称。一般主要是以白菜、黄瓜、萝卜等为原料。

Kimchee

Le kimchee se compose de légumes salés macérés dans divers condiments, des épices et du poisson salé. Le kimchee est le nom générique de tous les légumes marinés, incluant fréquemment par exemple du chou chinois, des concombres et des radis blancs.

김치

소금에 절인 야채에 매운 향신료나 양념, 젓갈 등을 섞어 담근 음식. 김치란 "절임"의 총칭. 배추, 오이, 무우 등이 많이 사용된다.

Kimchee

Kimchee son legumbres en sal adobadas con distintos condimentos, especias y pescado en salmuera. Kimchee es el nombre común con el que se conocen todas las legumbres adobadas, y entre los ingredientes más conocidos se pueden citar la col china, el pepino y el rábano blanco.

キムチ

塩漬けにした野菜に辛い香辛料や薬味、塩辛などを混ぜて漬け込んだもの。キムチとは「漬けもの」の総称。白菜、きゅうり、大根などがよく使われる。

Kimchi

È il nome generico per tutte le verdure in salamoia, quali per esempio cavolo cinese, cetrioli, rapa asiatica. Le verdure vengono mescolate con una salamoia alla quale sono aggiunti vari condimenti, spezie e pesce salato.

الكيمتشي

يتكون مخلل الكيمتشي من خضر مملحة ومخللة في توابل ونكهات مختلفة مع السمك المملح، ويطلق اسم الكيمتشي على كافة الخضر المخللة، ومن بين الخضر الشائعة التخليل لمجد الكرنب الصيني والخيار والفجل الأبيض.

Kimchee

Os kimchees são vegetais salgados, preparados em conserva com vários condimentos, temperos e frutos do mar. Kimchee é o nome genérico dado a todos os vegetais em conserva. Entre os ingredientes mais usados estão: repolho-chinês, pepinos e nabos.

나물 (Na-mul)

Assorted Sesame-Flavored Vegetables

Lightly cooked vegetables are mixed with sesame oil, garlic, sesame seeds and other seasonings for a dish that is particularly beneficial for health, even among the many other healthy Korean foods.

kcal ●

© S.T.

拌蔬菜

這是在加工熟的蔬菜中拌入香油、蒜、芝麻等而做成的菜肴。即使被稱為"健康食品"的韓國、朝鮮菜中，這道菜也是尤為強身補益的。

拌蔬菜

这是在加工熟的蔬菜中拌入香油、蒜、芝麻等而做成的菜肴。即使被称为"健康食品"的韩国、朝鲜菜中，这道菜也是尤为强身补益的。

나물

데친 야채에 참기름, 마늘, 깨소금 등을 넣고 무친 것. 한국·조선요리는 몸에 좋다고 알려져 있는데 나물은 그 중에서도 훌륭한 건강식이라 할 수 있다.

野菜のあえもの（ナムル）

ゆでた野菜をごま油、にんにく、ごまなどであえたもの。「体によい」といわれる韓国・朝鮮料理のなかでも特にヘルシー。

خضر مشكلة بنكهة السمسم

تسلق الخضر قليلا ثم تخلط بزيت السمسم والثوم والسمسم وغير ذلك من التوابل لإعداد طبق يبرز كطعام صحي حتى بالمقارنة بأطباق كورية أخرى مفيدة أيضاً للصحة.

Gemischtes, mit Sesam gewürztes Gemüse

Leicht gekochtes Gemüse wird mit Sesamöl, Knoblauch, Sesamkörnern und anderen Gewürzen gemischt. Dieses Gericht ist selbst unter den vielen anderen gesunden koreanischen Speisen besonders gut für die Gesundheit.

Légumes mixtes agrémentés de sésame

Parmi les autres plats sains de la cuisine coréenne, ce mets est tout particulièrement bon pour la santé ; il contient des légumes légèrement cuits mélangés à de l'huile de sésame, de l'ail, des graines de sésame et d'autres condiments.

Verduras Mixtas en Sésamo

Varias verduras ligeramente cocidas se mezclan con aceite de sésamo, ajo, semillas de sésamo (ajonjolí) y otros condimentos en un platillo particularmente bueno para la salud, aun entre muchos otros platos coreanos saludables.

Verdure in salsa al sesamo

Verdure sbollentate e condite con olio e semi di sesamo, aglio e altri ingredienti, per un piatto particolarmente sano fra tutti i cibi coreani che si dice "facciano bene alla salute".

Vegetais sortidos condimentados com gergelim

Vegetais levemente cozidos são misturados com óleo de gergelim, alho, sementes de gergelim e outros condimentos. Particularmente saudável, destaca-se até mesmo entre os muitos outros pratos coreanos benéficos à saúde.

상추 생채 (Sang-chu-Seng-che)

Korean Lettuce Salad

Crisp and tender lettuce leaves are mixed with a soy sauce dressing flavored with spices and vinegar for a light and refreshing salad.

kcal ●

萵筍沙拉

這是以細膩柔軟的生萵筍葉或生菜為原料，用調味醋醬油拌成的口感清淡的沙拉。

Koreanischer Eisbergsalat

Knackige und weiche Blätter von Eisbergsalat oder Kopfsalat werden mit einer Sojasoße gemischt, die mit Gewürzen und Essig abgeschmeckt ist. Ein leichter und erfrischender Salat.

莴笋沙拉

这是以细腻柔软的生莴笋叶或生菜为原料，用调味醋酱油拌成的口感清淡的沙拉。

Salade de laitue coréenne

Cette salade légère et rafraîchissante est composée de feuilles de laitue tendres et croquantes agrémentées d'une sauce au soja relevée avec des épices et du vinaigre.

상추 생채

부드러워 먹기 좋은 상추 또는 양상추를 양념 초간장에 버무린 깨끗한 맛의 샐러드.

Ensalada de Lechuga Coreana

Para preparar esta ligera y refrescante ensalada se mezclan las hojas de lechuga crujientes y suaves con un aderezo de salsa de soja condimentado con especias y vinagre.

サンチュのサラダ

柔らかくて歯ざわりのよい生のサンチュの葉、あるいはレタスを、薬味酢じょうゆであえたさっぱりしたサラダ。

Insalata coreana

Insalata leggera di tenere foglie di sanchu o di lattuga, condite con salsa di soia mista ad aceto e a vari gusti.

سلطة الخس الكورية

تخلط أوراق الخس النضرة الهشة بسائل تتبيل من صلصة الصويا المضاف إليها التوابل والخل كي تحصل على سلطة خفيفة منعشة.

Salada de alface coreana

Folhas de alface frescas e tenras, misturadas com molho de soja condimentado com temperos e vinagre, formam uma salada de sabor leve e agradável.

잡채 (Jab-che)

Gelatin Noodles with Stir-Fried Meat and Vegetables

Thin strips of beef and vegetables are first stir-fried separately and flavored, followed by the addition of gelatin noodles after which all the ingredients are combined and flavored. The light soy sauce flavor makes this dish an easy one in which to indulge.

kcal ●

© S.T.

粉絲拌菜

將切成細絲的牛肉、蔬菜分別煸炒、調味後再拌入粉絲。這種菜肴略帶醬油味，令人開胃。

Glasnudeln mit pfannengerührtem Fleisch und Gemüse

Dünne Streifen von Rindfleisch und Gemüse werden zunächst getrennt voneinander pfannengerührt und gewürzt und dann Glasnudeln hinzugegeben. Danach werden alle Zutaten miteinander gemischt und gewürzt. Der milde Sojasoßen-Geschmack macht dieses Gericht besonders wohlschmeckend, so daß es wirklich jedermann genießen kann.

粉丝拌菜

将切成细丝的牛肉、蔬菜分别煸炒、调味后再拌入粉丝。这种菜肴略带酱油味，令人开胃。

Nouilles collantes accompagnées d'un sauté de viande et de légumes

Après avoir fait revenir séparément puis assaisonné du bœuf et des légumes émincés, on y ajoute des nouilles collantes et l'on mélange le tout puis on assaisonne. Le goût léger de la sauce de soja fait de ce plat un mets délicieux par lequel on se laisse facilement tenter.

잡채

채썬 쇠고기, 야채를 각각 볶으면서 간을 맞추고 당면을 섞어 조미한 요리. 담백한 간장 맛.

Salteado de Fideos Gelatinosos de Soja con Carne y Verduras

Primero se fríen y se condimentan por separado delgadas tiras de res y verduras. Después se les agregan fideos gelatinosos y se combinan todos los ingredientes mientras se van aderezando. El ligero sabor de la salsa de soja hace que este platillo sea uno de los más apetecibles.

春雨と野菜の炒めあえ

せん切りにした牛肉、野菜をそれぞれ炒めて下味をつけ、春雨を混ぜ合わせた料理。あっさりしたしょうゆ味。

Vermicelli di fecola e verdure

Carne bovina tagliata a sottili strisce e verdure separatamente saltate e condite vengono mescolate con vermicelli di fecola. È un piatto leggero al gusto di soia.

شعرية جيلاتينية مع اللحم والخضر المحمرة

يتم أولاً تحمير شرائح طولية رفيعة من اللحم والخضر تحميراً خفيفاً كل على حدة ثم تتبيلها ، ثم تضاف الشعرية الجيلاتينية وتخلط المقادير كلها معاً وتتبل. هنا نجد أن النكهة الخفيفة لصلصة الصويا تجعل الطبق مرضياً لكل الأذواق.

Fios gelatinosos com carne e vegetais refogados

Carne de gado e vegetais cortados em finas tiras são refogados separadamente e condimentados. Em seguida, os fios gelatinosos são adicionados. O suave sabor do molho de soja faz com que logo se aprecie este prato.

파전 (Pa-Jeon)

©S.T.

Leek Pancakes

Leeks are mixed into a batter prepared with flour and other ingredients. The mixture is then spread out into a thin layer on a griddle and both sides are fried to a golden brown. This dish is perfect as a snack or as an appetizer served with drinks, and is said to have originated in a region famous for its leeks.

kcal ●●

蔥烤餅

這種餅是將面粉和勻後再放入蔥、然後將其拉薄烘烤，使其兩面呈金黃色。最適合作為小喫和下酒菜食用。據說這道菜起源於蔥的著名產地。

Schnittlauch-Omelett

Koreanischer Schnittlauch wird mit einem dünnflüssigen Teig aus Weizenmehl und anderen Zutaten gemischt. Diese Mischung wird dann in einer dünnen Schicht auf einem Backblech ausgebreitet und auf beiden Seiten goldbraun gebraten. Dieses Gericht eignet sich hervorragend als Imbiß oder als Appetitshäppchen, die mit Getränken serviert werden. Dieses Gericht soll in einer Gegend entstanden sein, wo der beste Schnittlauch wächst.

葱烤饼

这种饼是将面粉和勻后再放入葱、然后将其拉薄烘烤，使其两面呈金黄色。最适合作为小吃和下酒菜食用。据说这道菜起源于葱的著名产地。

Crêpes de poireaux

Après avoir mélangé des poireaux à une pâte à crêpes à base de farine et d'autres ingrédients, on étale le tout en couches fines sur une plaque chauffante que l'on fait revenir jusqu'à ce que les deux côtés soient bien dorés. Ce plat est parfait comme en-cas ou comme amuse-gueule servi avec des boissons ; on dit qu'il provient d'une région célèbre pour ses poireaux.

파전

파를 넣은 밀가루 반죽을 프라이팬에 얇게 펴서 양면을 잘 구운 것. 간식이나 술안주로 최적. 파의 명산지에서 시작된 음식이라고 한다.

Panqueques de Puerro

Se mojan los puerros en una masa de rebozar hecha de harina y otros ingredientes. Después se esparce la mezcla en una delgada capa sobre una parrilla y se fríe por ambos lados hasta que queda dorada. Este platillo es perfecto como entremés o como aperitivo servido con bebidas. Según se dice, tuvo su origen en una región famosa por sus puerros.

ねぎのお好み焼き

小麦粉などを混ぜた生地にねぎを入れ、薄くのばして両面をこんがりと焼いたもの。軽食や酒の肴に最適。ねぎの名産地で生まれた料理といわれている。

Tortini di porri

Preparata una pasta di farina, vi si incorporano dei porri e la si spiana in sottili tortini che vengono cotti fino a dorarli da entrambe le parti. Ottimi come spuntino o per accompagnare bevande alcoliche. Si dice che la ricetta provenga da una regione famosa per la produzione di porri.

فطيرة البصل الأخضر

يمزج البصل الأخضر مع مزيج مخفوق من دقيق ومقادير أخرى ثم تُفرد العجينة على صينية تصبح رقيعة تشوى السمك ويحمر الجانبان حتى يكتسبا لوناً ذهبياً. يعد هذا طبقاً مثالياً كنوع من المشهيات أو المزة مع الشراب. ويقال إنه جاء أصلاً من إقليم يشتهر بزراعة البصل الأخضر.

Panquecas de cebolinha

Adiciona-se cebolinha a uma massa mole preparada com farinha e outros ingredientes. Uma fina camada da mistura é entao espalhada sobre a chapa de ferro e ambos os lados são fritos até dourar. É um prato perfeito como refeição leve ou como petisco para acompanhar bebidas alcoólicas. Dizem que se originou de uma região famosa pelo cultivo de cebolinha.

감자지짐 (Gam-ja-Ji-jim)

Fried Potato

Grated potatoes, which are formed into circles, are fried and then enjoyed by dipping in seasoned soy sauce.

kcal ●

©S.T.

燒馬鈴薯

將磋碎的馬鈴薯攢成團子烤成的東西。食用時蘸上調味醬油。

Gebratene Kartoffeln

Geriebene Kartoffeln werden zu kreisrunden Fladen geformt. Nach dem Braten taucht man sie vor dem Verzehr in gewürzte Sojasoße.

烧马铃薯

将磋碎的马铃薯攢成团子烤成的东西。食用时蘸上调味酱油。

Pommes de terre frites

On fait revenir des pommes de terre râpées en rondelles, que l'on déguste en les faisant tremper dans une sauce de soja relevée.

감자지짐

간 감자를 둥근 모양으로 부친 것. 양념장에 찍어 먹는다.

Patatas Fritas

Se hacen porciones de patatas ralladas en forma de panqueques y se fríen. Una vez preparadas, se comen remojándolas en una salsa de soja sanzonada.

じゃがいものおやき

すりおろしたじゃがいもを丸い形にまとめて焼いたもの。薬味じょうゆをつけて食べる。

Frittelle di patate

Si tratta di medaglioni di patate grattugiate, che vengono fritti e si mangiano intingendoli in salsa di soia mista a vari gusti.

بطاطس محمرة

تبشر البطاطس وتشكل على هيئة كرات ثم تحمر، وتؤكل بعد غمرها في صلصة الصويا المتبلة.

Batata frita

Rala-se batata e formam-se com ela círculos, que são então fritos e servidos após mergulho em molho de soja condimentado.

김 구이 (Kim-Gu-i)

© S.T.

Toasted Nori

Seaweed (nori) is coated with sesame oil and salt and gently heated over an open flame for a deep, aromatic flavor. This dish can be enjoyed simply as a snack eaten as is, or rolled up around piping hot rice.

kcal ●

烤紫菜

這是在紫菜上塗上麻油和鹽後、用明火微烤出鮮香味美的、風味濃鬱的一道菜。它既可作為小喫，也可用它卷米飯而食用。

烤紫菜

这是在紫菜上涂上麻油和盐后、用明火微烤出鮮香味美的、风味浓郁的一道菜。它既可作为小吃，也可用它卷米饭而食用。

김 구이

김에 참기름과 소금을 발라 불에 살짝 구운 것. 술안주나 밥을 싸서 먹어도 맛있다.

焼きのり

のりにごま油と塩をぬり、直火で軽くあぶった風味豊かな焼きのり。つまみにしたり、ご飯に巻いて食べてもおいしい。

نوري محمص

يغطى النوري (عشب بحري) بالملح وزيت السمسم ويحمص بخفة على لهب مكشوف للحصول على مذاق غني طيب . يمكن تناول هذا الطبق مباشرة كنوع من المزة أو بلفه حول الأرز الساخن جداً.

Gerösteter Nori-Seetang

Dünne Plättchen aus getrocknetem Seetang (Nori) werden mit Sesamöl bestrichen und gesalzen und anschließend über offenem Feuer vorsichtig geröstet. Sie haben einen vollen und aromatischen Geschmack. Dieses Gericht kann als Imbiß genossen oder heißer Reis darin eingewickelt werden.

Nori grillé

On fait chauffer à petit feu des algues (nori) arrosées d'huile de sésame et de sel afin d'obtenir une saveur aromatique et forte. Ce plat peut se consommer simplement tel quel comme snack ou enroulé autour de riz bouillant.

Nori Tostado

Se cubre al alga marina (nori) con aceite de sésamo (ajonjolí) y sal y se calienta con cuidado directamente sobre una llama, obteniendo un intenso y aromático sabor. Este manjar puede ser disfrutado simplemente como aperitivo tal como es o enrollándolo alrededor del arroz bien caliente.

Alghe nori tostate

Le alghe nori vengono spennellate di sale e olio di sesamo e poi leggermente tostate alla fiamma diretta, in modo che ne sprigioni il profumo. Ottime da mangiare così come sono, accompagnate da bevande alcooliche o avvolgendovi del riso cotto in bianco.

Alga nori tostada

A alga marinha (nori) recebe uma camada de óleo de gergelim e sal e é tostada levemente sobre a chama direta, produzindo-se uma iguaria muito aromática. Pode ser saboreada desta forma como petisco ou enrolada em arroz bem quente.

미역국 (Mi-yeok-Guk)

Wakame Soup

This soup is filled with delicious wakame, a seaweed known for its high calcium content, for a dish that is not only flavorful but nutritious as well. As evidence of this, this soup is enjoyed daily by women in North and South Korea for the 3 weeks following childbirth.

kcal ●

© S.T.

裙帶菜什錦湯

這是一種放有大量裙帶菜的湯。由於含有大量鈣質的裙帶菜營養豐富，在韓國和朝鮮有產後 3 周內每天都飲用此湯的習慣。

裙带菜什锦汤

这是一种放有大量裙带菜的汤。由于含有大量钙质的裙带菜营养丰富，在韩国和朝鲜有产后 3 周内每天都饮用此汤的习惯。

미역국

미역이 많이 들어 있는 국. 칼슘 등이 많이 포함된 미역은 영양이 풍부하므로 한국・조선에서는 산후 3주일 정도는 매일 먹는 습관이 있다.

わかめスープ

わかめがたっぷり入ったスープ。カルシウムなどを多く含むわかめは栄養価が高いので、韓国・朝鮮では産後 3 週間は毎日飲む習慣があるという。

حساء الواكامي

هو حساء، يمتلئ، بالواكامي اللذيذ وهو عشب بحري يشتهر باحتوائه على نسبة عالية من الكالسيوم ، وهذا الحساء طيب المذاق ومغذي جداً أيضاً، والدليل على ذلك هو أن النساء في كوريا الشمالية والجنوبية يتناولنه يومياً لمدة ثلاثة أسابيع عقب الولادة.

Wakame-Suppe

Diese Suppe ist reich an köstlichem Wakame, einem Seetang der für seinen hohen Kalziumgehalt bekannt ist. Ein Gericht, das nicht nur gut schmeckt, sondern auch besonders nahrhaft ist. Ein Beweis dafür ist die Tatsache, daß Frauen in Nord- und Süd Korea bis zu drei Wochen nach der Geburt eines Kindes diese Suppe täglich genießen.

Soupe de wakame

Cette soupe à base de délicieux wakame (algues à haute teneur en calcium) constitue un mets non seulement parfumé mais aussi nourrissant. Pour preuve, les femmes nord- et sud-coréennes consomment cette soupe tous les jours pendant les trois semaines qui suivent l'accouchement.

Sopa de Wakame

Esta sopa contiene una gran proporción de wakame, una deliciosa alga marina conocida por su alto contenido de calcio. Esta sopa no solo es sabrosa sino también nutritiva y la prueba está en que las mujeres de Corea del Norte y Corea del Sur la comen diariamente durante los tres semanas posteriores al parto.

Minestra di alghe wakame

È una minestra preparata con uso abbondante di alghe wakame, ricche di calcio e di altre sostanze nutrienti, tanto che le donne coreane hanno l'usanza di includerla nella dieta giornaliera per tre settimane dopo il parto.

Sopa de alga wakame

Esta sopa contém em abundância a deliciosa wakame, alga marinha conhecida por seu elevado teor de cálcio. É não apenas cheia de sabor, como também muito nutritiva. Prova disto, é o fato de ser saboreada diariamente por mulheres nas Coréias do Norte e do Sul, durante os três semanas que se sucedem ao parto.

갈비탕 (Kal-bi-Tang)

© S.T.

Beef Short Rib Soup

This soup contains tender, boiled beef short rib flavored in a rich, salt-flavored broth. This dish may also be served with rice added to the soup.

kcal ●●●

五花牛肉湯

這是用帶骨的五花牛肉煮熬成的味鮮濃厚的鹹味湯。有時湯中也加入米飯。

Suppe aus kurzer Rinderrippe

Diese Suppe enthält weichgekochte kurze Rippen vom Rind. Die Suppe hat einen vollen Geschmack und ist mit Salz gewürzt. Zur Variation kann auch Reis in die Suppe gegeben werden.

五花牛肉汤

这是用带骨的五花牛肉煮熬成的味鲜浓厚的咸味汤。有时汤中也加入米饭。

Soupe de travers de bœuf

Cette soupe contient de tendres travers de bœuf bouillis parfumés dans un riche bouillon au goût salé. Ce plat peut également être servi avec du riz que l'on ajoute à la soupe.

갈비탕

쇠갈비를 삶은 수프로 감칠 맛이 나는 소금 간. 수프에 밥을 넣은 국밥도 있다.

Sopa de Agujas de Res

Esta sopa contiene suaves agujas de res cocidas y adobadas en un rico caldo salado. Este platillo también se puede servir añadiendo arroz a la sopa.

牛バラ肉のスープ

牛骨付きあばら肉を煮込んだ、コクのある塩味のスープ。スープの中にご飯が入っている場合もある。

Minestra di costolette di manzo

È una minestra molto sapida ottenuta bollendo costolette di manzo con l'osso. In qualche caso al brodo viene anche aggiunto del riso.

حساء ريش البقر

يحتوي هذا الحساء، على ريش مسلوقة طرية من لحم البقر تتبل في بهريز ثخين مملح، ويمكن أيضاً تقديم هذا الحساء مضافاً إليه الأرز.

Sopa de falsa costela

Esta sopa contém falsa costela de gado tenra, que é cozida e condimentada com um suculento caldo salgado. Também pode-se adicionar arroz à sopa para serví-la.

곰탕 (Gom-Tang)

Oxtail Soup

This soup features a deep flavor produced by boiling the meat of an oxtail for a long time. The extract from the bone marrow gives this soup its characteristic white color. It is enjoyed by adding salt, hot red pepper or leeks as desired.

kcal ●●●

牛尾湯

這是將牛尾充分炖熟後而做成的香醇濃鬱的湯。其特點是由於骨中的髓汁溢出使湯色乳白、香醇味濃。可根據個人的喜好，放進鹽、辣椒、蔥等再飲喝。

牛尾汤

这是将牛尾充分炖熟后而做成的香醇浓郁的汤。其特点是由于骨中的髓汁溢出使汤色乳白、香醇味浓。可根据个人的喜好，放进盐、辣椒、葱等再饮喝。

곰탕

쇠꼬리를 장시간 삶은 것으로 맛이 진한 수프. 뼈속에서 나온 엑기스로 인하여 하얀 색깔이 나는 것이 특징. 기호에 따라 소금, 고춧가루, 파 등을 넣어 먹는다.

牛テールスープ

牛の尾を長時間煮込んだ味わい深いスープ。骨髄から出たエキスによって白く濁っているのが特徴。好みで塩、唐辛子、ねぎなどを入れて食べる。

حساء ذيل الثور

يتميز هذا الحساء بنكهة عميقة تنبع من سلق لحم بقري من ذيل الثور لفترة طويلة. ويكتسب الحساء لونه الأبيض المعروف من خلاصة النخاع الموجود في العظم، ويضاف إليه الملح والفلفل الأحمر الحار أو البصل الأخضر حسب الرغبة.

Ochsenschwanzsuppe

Diese Suppe hat einen besonders vollen Geschmack. Dies ist darauf zurückzuführen, daß Fleisch vom Ochsenschwanz lange Zeit gekocht wird. Der Extrakt vom Knochenmark gibt dieser Suppe seine charakteristische weiße Farbe. Nach Wunsch und Geschmack werden Salz, scharfer spanischer Pfeffer oder Schnittlauch hinzugegeben.

Queue de bœuf en soupe

Cette soupe au goût fort se prépare en faisant longuement bouillir une queue de bœuf. L'extrait de moelle osseuse confère à cette soupe une couleur blanche caractéristique. On peut la déguster en y ajoutant du sel, du piment rouge ou des poireaux, selon les goûts de chacun.

Sopa de Rabo de Buey

Esta sopa se caracteriza por el intenso sabor que adquiere al cocer la carne de rabo de buey durante muchas horas. El extracto del tuétano le da a la sopa su distintivo color blanco. Se come agregándole sal, chile o puerros al gusto.

Minestra di coda di bue

È una minestra di gusto intenso dato dalla coda di bue fatta bollire a lungo e di caratteristico colore biancastro dovuto al midollo. Si mangia aggiungendovi a piacere sale, peperoncino rosso, porri o altro.

Sopa de rabada

Sopa de sabor consistente feita com carne de rabo de boi cozida por longo tempo. O extrato de tutano dá a coloração branca característica à sopa. Para saboreá-la, adicionam-se, a gosto, sal, pimenta-malagueta e cebolinha.

육계장 (Yuk-ke-jang)

Spicy Beef and Vegetable Soup

This spicy soup contains beef and vegetables which are effective in restoring energy and stimulating the appetite.

kcal ●

辣味牛肉菜湯

是一道湯內放有大量牛肉、蔬菜，帶有適量辣味的湯。具有恢復疲勞和增進食欲之功效。

Scharfe Suppe mit Rindfleisch und Gemüse

Diese sehr scharfe Suppe, die Kraft gibt und den Appetit anregt, enthält Rindfleisch und Gemüse.

辣味牛肉菜汤

是一道汤内放有大量牛肉、蔬菜，带有适量辣味的汤。具有恢复疲劳和增进食欲之功效。

Soupe épicée aux légumes et au bœuf

Cette soupe épicée contenant du bœuf et des légumes stimule l'appétit et redonne efficacement de l'énergie.

육계장

쇠고기와 야채가 많이 들어 있는 매운맛의 수프. 피로회복이나 식욕증진에 효과적이다.

Sopa Aromática de Res y Verduras

Esta aromática sopa contiene res y verduras que son efectivas para restaurar la energía y estimular el apetito.

牛肉と野菜の辛味スープ

牛肉と野菜がたっぷり入った辛味のきいたスープ。疲労回復や食欲増進に効果的。

Minestra piccante di manzo e verdure

Questa piccante minestra preparata con abbondanza di manzo e verdure è efficace per ritemprare le energie e stimolare l'appetito.

حساء حريف من لحم البقر والخضر

يحتوي هذا الحساء الحريف على لحم بقري وخضر، وله فعالية كبيرة في استرداد الطاقة وفتح الشهية.

Sopa picante com carne e vegetais

Esta sopa picante contém carne de gado e vegetais, ingredientes eficazes para restaurar a energia e estimular o apetite.

떡국 (Teok-Guk)

Korean Rice Cake Soup

Rice cakes made of non-glutinous rice are added to a soy-based soup that is garnished with flavored meat, egg and seaweed.

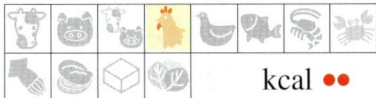

©S.T.

kcal ●●

韓國朝鮮特色燴年糕

這是一道在含有醬油味的湯內、加入用粳米做成的餅，並配上調過味的肉和蛋黃絲、紫菜等制成的燴年糕。

Koreanische Reiskuchensuppe

Aus trockenem Reis wird Reiskuchen hergestellt und in eine Suppe gegeben, die mit gewürztem Fleisch, Ei und Matten aus getrocknetem Seetang (Nori) garniert ist.

韩国朝鲜特色烩年糕

这是一道在含有酱油味的汤内、加入用粳米做成的饼，并配上调过味的肉和蛋黄丝、紫菜等制成的烩年糕。

Soupe de petits gâteaux de riz coréens

Des gâteaux de riz préparés avec du riz non collant sont ajoutés à une soupe à base de soja garnie de viande parfumée, d'œufs et d'algues.

떡국

간장으로 간을 한 국물에 멥쌀로 만든 떡을 넣고 볶은 고기와 달걀지단, 김 등을 얹은 요리.

Sopa de Pastel de Arroz Coreano

Se hacen pasteles de arroz glutinoso y se agregan a una sopa hecha a base de soja. Después son adornados con carne, huevo y algas sazonados.

韓国・朝鮮風雑煮

しょうゆ味のスープにうるち米で作った餅を加え、味付けした肉や錦糸卵、のりなどをあしらった料理。

Minestra con gnocchi di riso alla coreana

Ad un brodo al gusto di salsa di soia vengono uniti gnocchi tondi fatti di riso comune cotto a vapore e pestato in un mortaio, carne precedentemente insaporita, striscioline di sottile omelette, alghe nori e altri ingredienti.

حساء كعك الأرز الكوري

تضاف كعكات الأرز المصنوعة من الأرز العادي غير اللدن إلى حساء، بطعم صلصة الصويا يحتوي على اللحم والبيض وأعشاب البحر.

Sopa de bolinhos de arroz ao estilo coreano

Sopa à base de soja com bolinhos de arroz não-glutinoso. É guarnecida com carne condimentada, ovos e algas.

만두국 (Man-du-Guk)

© S.T.

Dumpling Soup

This light-tasting soup contains dumplings filled with beef, bean curd, Kimchee, mushrooms and other ingredients, making it a good partner with rice or as a snack.

kcal ●●

餃子湯

是一種內有牛肉、豆腐、朝鮮醃菜、香菇作餡包成的餃子湯。味鮮爽口、是理想的下飯菜或小喫菜肴。

Suppe mit Teigtaschen

Diese Suppe hat einen milden Geschmack und enthält Teigtaschen, die mit Rindfleisch, Tofu (Sojabohnenquark), Kimchee, Pilzen (Shiitake) und anderen Zutaten gefüllt sind. Diese Suppe paßt gut zu Reis oder kann als Imbiß genossen werden.

饺子汤

是一种内有牛肉、豆腐、朝鲜腌菜、香菇作馅包成的饺子汤。味鲜爽口、是理想的下饭菜或小吃菜肴。

Soupe de boulettes

Cette soupe au goût léger contient des boulettes farcies avec de la viande de bœuf, de la pâte de soja, du kimchee, des champignons et d'autres ingrédients, le tout constituant un bon accompagnement pour le riz ou comme en-cas.

만두국

쇠고기, 두부, 김치, 표고버섯 등의 소를 넣은 만두를 넣고 끓인 담백한 맛의 수프. 밥반찬이나 간식으로 권하기 좋다.

Sopa de Relleno de Carne

Esta sopa de sabor ligero contiene bolas de masa rellenas de res, cuajada de soja, Kimchee, champiñones y otros ingredientes, haciéndola la compañera ideal del arroz o como entremés.

餃子スープ

牛肉、豆腐、キムチ、しいたけなどの具が入った餃子入りのスープで、あっさりした味。ご飯のおかず、軽食におすすめ。

Minestra con ravioli cinesi

Questa minestra dal gusto leggero contiene ravioli ripieni di carne di manzo, tofu, Kimchi, funghi shiitake e altri ingredienti. Va bene come pietanza con il riso in bianco, ma anche da sola per un pasto leggero.

حساء المحشوات

هذا حساء، خفيف الطعم يحتوي على وحدات محشوة بلحم البقر والتوفو والكيمتشي وعش الغراب وغير ذلك، وهو يصلح للتناول مع الأرز أو كوجبة خفيفة.

Sopa de pasteizinhos recheados

Esta sopa de sabor leve contém pasteizinhos recheados com carne de gado, queijo de soja, kimchee, cogumelos e outros ingredientes. É ótima para acompanhar o arroz ou como refeição leve.

비빔밥 (Bi-bim-Bap)

Mixed Vegetables over Rice

This dish features excellent nutritional balance by mixing various vegetables and serving over rice. This dish may also be enjoyed by adding fermented soy bean paste flavored with red pepper, and mixing it with all the ingredients.

kcal ●●●

©S.T.

什錦蓋飯

在米飯上放上各種涼拌菜，營養全面，可根據愛好加入辣椒醬，食用時必須將各種菜充分拌勻。

什锦盖饭

在米饭上放上各种凉拌菜，营养全面，可根据爱好加入辣椒酱，食用时必须将各种菜充分拌勻。

비빔밥

밥 위에 여러 가지 나물을 얹은 건강요리. 기호에 따라 고추장을 넣기도 하며, 밥과 나물을 잘 비벼서 먹는다.

ビビンバ

ご飯の上に数種類の野菜のあえもの（ナムル）をのせた、ヘルシーな料理。好みで唐辛子みそを加え、全体をよく混ぜて食べる。

خضر متنوعة فوق الأرز

يحتوي هذا الطبق على مجموعة متازة من العناصر الغذائية المتوازنة حيث يتكون من مزيج من الخضر يقدم فوق الأرز، ويكن أيضاً إضافة الميسو (مادة تتبيل من فول الصويا) المتبل بالفلفل الأحمر وخلطه بباقي المقادير.

Gemischtes Gemüse auf Reis

Für dieses Gericht werden verschiedene Gemüsesorten gemischt und auf Reis serviert. Die Balance der Nährstoffe ist hierbei besonders gut. Zur Abwandlung kann man fermentierte Sojabohnenpaste hinzugeben, die mit spanischem Pfeffer gewürzt ist, und diese mit allen Zutaten mischen.

Légumes mixtes servis sur du riz

Ce mets contenant divers légumes servis sur du riz constitue un excellent plat équilibré. On peut également y ajouter de la pâte de haricots de soja fermentés aromatisée de piment rouge que l'on incorpore à tous les ingrédients.

Verduras Surtidas sobre Arroz

Este platillo se caracteriza por el excelente equilibrio nutritivo de la combinación de distintas verduras servidas sobre arroz. También se puede disfrutar aderezándolo bien con una pasta fermentada de soja y chiles.

Riso con copertura di verdure miste

È un sano piatto di riso con copertura di vari tipi di verdure mescolate con un particolare condimento (namur). A piacere, si può aggiungere miso coreano piccante. Si mangia mescolando bene il tutto.

Misto de vegetais sobre arroz

Este prato oferece um excelente equilíbrio nutritivo através de uma mistura de vários vegetais, servida sobre o arroz. Pode-se acrescentar pasta de soja fermentada contendo pimenta-malagueta. É essencial misturar bem todos os ingredientes.

돌솥비빔밥 (Dol-sot-Bi-bim-Bap)

©S.T.

Stone-Baked Mixed Vegetables over Rice

Rice, several kinds of flavored vegetables and beef are heaped into a vessel made of stone after which the entire vessel is baked. After baking, fermented soy bean paste flavored with red pepper is added and mixed well. The best part of this dish is said to be the scorched rice that forms in the bottom of the vessel after baking.

kcal ●●●

石烤什錦蓋飯

這是在用石頭做成的容器中，盛上米飯及用各種調好味的蔬菜及牛肉後，以各個容器分別燒烤作成的菜。食用時拌入辣椒醬後必須充分拌勻。這道菜的味道關鍵取決於容器底部形成的鍋巴。

石烤什锦盖饭

这是在用石头做成的容器中，盛上米饭及用各种调好味的蔬菜及牛肉后，以各个容器分别烧烤作成的菜。食用时拌入辣椒酱后必须充分拌勻。这道菜的味道关键取决于容器底部形成的锅巴。

돌솥비빔밥

돌솥에 밥과 여러 가지 나물이나 쇠고기를 넣고 돌솥 그 자체를 구운 요리. 고추장을 넣고 비벼서 먹는다. 돌솥 바닥에 눌어붙은 누룽지가 맛있다.

石焼きビビンバ

石の器にご飯と数種類の味付けした野菜(ナムル)や牛肉を盛り、器ごと焼いた料理。唐辛子みそを入れ、よく混ぜて食べる。器の底にできる、おこげがおいしい。

طاجن من الخضر المختلفة فوق الأرز

يوضع الأرز وفوقه مجموعة متنوعة من الخضر المتبلة مع لحم البقر في طاجن حجري ثم يوضع الطاجن على النار، وبعد أن ينضج الطعام يضاف إليه الميسو (مادة تتبيل من فول الصويا) المتبل بالفلفل الأحمر مع مزجه جيداً بباقي المقادير، يقال إن أفضل جزء في هذا الطبق هو الأرز المحمص الذي يتكون في قاع الطاجن بعد نضجه.

Im Steintopf gebackenes Mischgemüse auf Reis

Reis, verschiedene Sorten gewürzten Gemüses und Rindfleisch werden in einen Steintopf gegeben und dann in diesem Topf gebacken. Nach dem Backen wird fermentierte Sojabohnenpaste, die mit spanischem Pfeffer gewürzt ist, hinzugegeben und gut untergemischt. Als bester Teil dieses Gerichtes gilt der angebrannte Reis, der sich am Boden des Topfes nach dem Backen festsetzt.

Légumes mixtes cuits à la pierre et servis sur du riz

Dans un récipient en pierre, on mélange du riz, plusieurs sortes de légumes aromatisés et du bœuf que l'on passe ensuite au four. Après la cuisson, on y ajoute de la pâte de haricots de soja fermentés parfumée au piment rouge en mélangeant bien le tout. Le riz légèrement brûlé qui se forme au fond du récipient après la cuisson constitue, dit-on, la meilleure partie de ce plat.

Verduras Cocinadas sobre Arroz en una Vasija de Piedra

En una vasija de piedra se ponen arroz, verduras surtidas y carne de res y se cocina todo el conjunto. Cuando está en su punto, se le agrega pasta de soja fermentada sazonada con chile y se mezcla bien. Se dice que la parte más deliciosa del platillo es el arroz quemado que se forma en el fondo de la vasija después de cocinarla.

Riso e verdure miste cotti in tegame di pietra

Riso, vari tipi di verdure condite in modo particolare (namur) e manzo vengono sistemati in un tegame di pietra e fatti cuocere. Si mangia aggiungendo del miso coreano piccante e mescolando il tutto. Buono il riso bruciacchiato che si forma sul fondo.

Misto de vegetais sobre arroz, cozidos em tigela de pedra

Arroz, vários tipos de vegetais condimentados e carne de gado são dispostos num recipiente de pedra, que é levado ao fogo. Após o cozimento, acrescenta-se pasta de soja fermentada contendo pimenta-malagueta e mistura-se bem. Dizem que o melhor deste prato é a rapa de arroz que se forma no fundo da tigela após o cozimento.

김치볶음밥 (Kim-chi-Bok-eum-Bap)

© S.T.

Fried Rice with Kimchee

This fried rice dish contains Kimchee made from Chinese cabbage, meat and vegetables. The pleasant spicy and sour flavor of the Kimchee enhances the flavor of the rice and other ingredients.

kcal ●●●●

朝鮮腌菜炒飯

這是一種將朝鮮腌白菜、肉、蔬菜一起煸炒而成的炒飯。朝鮮腌菜酸辣味適中、使飯菜鮮味倍增。

Gebratener Reis mit Kimchee

Dieses Gericht aus gebratenem Reis enthält Chinakohl-Kimchee, Fleisch und Gemüse. Der angenehme würzige und saure Geschmack des Kimchee hebt das Aroma des Reis und der anderen Zutaten hervor.

朝鲜腌菜炒饭

这是一种将朝鲜腌白菜、肉、蔬菜一起煸炒而成的炒饭。朝鲜腌菜酸辣味适中、使饭菜鲜味倍增。

Riz sauté accompagné de kimchee

Ce plat de riz sauté contient du kimchee composé de chou chinois, de la viande et des légumes. L'agréable saveur aigre et épicée du kimchee relève la saveur du riz et des autres ingrédients.

김치볶음밥

배추김치, 고기, 야채 등을 넣고 볶은 밥. 김치의 적당한 산미와 매운 맛이 밥과 소재의 맛을 더욱 살려준다.

Arroz Frito con Kimchee

Este platillo de arroz frito contiene carne, verduras y Kimchee de col china. El delicioso sabor aromático del Kimchee realza el sabor del arroz y otros ingredientes.

キムチ入り炒めご飯

白菜キムチ、肉、野菜などが入った炒めご飯。キムチのほどよい酸味と辛味で、具やご飯のおいしさが増す。

Riso fritto con kimchi

Il riso viene fritto con Kimchi di cavolo cinese, carne, verdure e altri ingredienti. Il gusto agro e piccante al punto giusto del Kimchi esalta il sapore del riso e degli altri ingredienti.

أرز محمر مع الكيمتشي

هذا طبق من الأرز المحمر يحتوي على مخلل كيمتشي من الكرنب الصيني واللحم والخضر، هنا نجد أن النكهة الحريفة والحمضية للكيمتشي تبرز طعم الأرز والمقادير الأخرى.

Arroz refogado com kimchee

Este prato de arroz refogado contém kimchee, repolho-chinês, carne e vegetais. O acre e apimentado kimchee realça o sabor do arroz e dos demais ingredientes.

전복죽 (Jeon-bok-Juk)

© S.T.

Abalone Gruel

Abalone is stir-fried in sesame oil and then cooked until tender following the addition of soup and rice. The flavor of the abalone combines with the aroma of the sesame oil for a mouth-watering taste.

kcal ●●●

鮑魚粥

將鮑魚用香油炒過後，加入湯和米熬至孺軟。
其特點是油香濃鬱，鮑魚鮮美可口。

Sämige Reissuppe mit Abalone

Eine Abalone wird in Sesamöl scharf angebraten. Dann werden Suppe und Reis hinzugegeben und bei schwacher Hitze weitergekocht, bis die Abalone weich ist. Der Geschmack der Abalone mischt sich mit dem Aroma des Sesamöls zu einem Geschmack, der einem das Wasser im Munde zusammenlaufen läßt.

鲍鱼粥

将鲍鱼用香油炒过后，加入汤和米熬至孺软。
其特点是油香浓郁，鲍鱼鲜美可口。

Gruau d'ormeaux

Dans de l'huile de sésame, on fait revenir des ormeaux auxquels on ajoute de la soupe et du riz que l'on fait cuire jusqu'à ce que les ormeaux deviennent tendres. La saveur des ormeaux se mélange avec l'arôme de l'huile de sésame, conférant à ce plat un goût très appétissant.

전복죽

전복을 참기름에 볶다가 수프와 쌀을 넣고 부드러워질 때까지 끓인 것. 참기름향과 전복의 특유한 맛이 가득하다.

Puches de Oreja Marina

Se saltea la oreja marina en aceite de sésamo (ajonjolí) y se cocina en una sopa de arroz hasta que se suaviza. El sabor de la oreja marina hace una buena combinación con el aroma del aceite de sésamo (ajonjolí) en un platillo que excita el apetito.

あわびがゆ

あわびをごま油で炒め、スープ、米を加えて柔らかくなるまで炊き上げたもの。ごま油の風味が生き、あわびのうまみがたっぷり。

Minestra di riso con orecchia di mare

Rosolata l'orecchia di mare con olio di sesamo, si aggiungono brodo e riso, cuocendo finché il riso diventa tenero. Le note dominanti sono il profumo dell'olio di sesamo e il sapore dell'orecchia di mare.

ثريد اذن البحر

يحمر أذن البحر في زيت السمسم ثم يضاف إليه الحساء والأرز ويطهى حتى يصير ليناً، هنا يتحد طعم أذن البحر مع نكهة زيت السمسم لإضفاء، مذاق يثير الشهية.

Haliotes em mingau de arroz

Moluscos haliotes são refogado em óleo de gergelim e, após o acréscimo de caldo e arroz, cozidos até ficar tenros. O sabor dos haliotes combina com o aroma do óleo de gergelim, criando uma iguaria apetitosa.

국밥 (Kuk-Bap)

Cooked Rice in Hot Broth

A soup brimming with vegetables, egg and other ingredients is poured over hot cooked rice to create a dish that features a mild, pleasing flavor that is gentle on the stomach.

© S.T.

kcal ●●

澆湯飯

這是將大量蔬菜和雞蛋做成的湯澆到熱米飯上而成的飯。松軟可口，易於消化。

Gekochter Reis in heißem Sud

Eine Suppe mit reichlich Gemüse, Ei und anderen Zutaten wird über heißen, gekochten Reis geschüttet und ergibt ein Gericht, das mild und angenehm schmeckt und besonders magenfreundlich ist.

浇汤饭

这是将大量蔬菜和鸡蛋做成的汤浇到热米饭上而成的饭。松软可口，易于消化。

Riz cuit dans un bouillon chaud

Ce plat au goût plaisant et léger, également doux pour l'estomac, se compose d'une soupe garnie de légumes, d'œufs et d'autres ingrédients que l'on verse sur du riz chaud.

국밥

야채나 달걀 등의 건더기가 많은 수프에 더운 밥을 넣어 먹는 요리. 위에 부담이 없다.

Arroz Cocido en Caldo

Se baña al arroz caliente con una sopa repleta de verduras, huevos y otros ingredientes para crear un platillo que se caracteriza por un sabor suave y reconfortante que facilita la digestión.

スープかけご飯

野菜や卵などが入った具だくさんのスープを、温かいご飯にかけた料理。サラッとしておなかにやさしい。

Riso affogato

Una minestra con molti ingredienti, quali verdure, uova e altro, viene versata sul riso in bianco appena cotto. È un piatto leggero facilmente digeribile.

ارز مطبوخ في حساء ساخن

يسكب حساء مشبع بالخضر والبيض وغيرهما فوق صحن ساخن من الأرز المطبوخ للحصول على طبق ذي طعم لذيذ وخفيف لا يرهق المعدة.

Arroz cozido em sopa de verduras

Uma sopa repleta de vegetais, ovos e outros ingredientes é despejada sobre arroz cozido quente. Este prato tem um sabor agradável, de leve digestão.

비빔냉면 (Bi-bim-Neng-myeon)

Cold Noodles with Hot Sauce

Firmly cooked noodles are mixed with a hot sauce to create a noodle dish with only a small amount of broth. This noodle dish is served with chilled mild-tasting soup for a refreshing meal.

kcal ●●●

拌面

在富有彈性的面中拌入醋味辣椒醬而做成汁較少的拌面。由於面是辣味，可用清淡的涼湯邊潤滑嗓子邊食用。

Kalte Nudeln mit scharfer Soße

Bißfest gekochte Nudeln werden mit einer scharfen Soße gemischt und ergeben ein Nudelgericht mit nur geringem Flüssigkeitsanteil. Dieses Nudelgericht wird mit einer gekühlten milden Suppe serviert und ist ein erfrischendes Mahl.

拌面

在富有弹性的面中拌入醋味辣椒酱而做成汁少的拌面。由于面是辣味，可用清淡的凉汤边润滑嗓子边食用。

Nouilles froides à la sauce piquante

Ce plat de nouilles, contenant très peu de bouillon, est composé de nouilles fermement cuites mélangées à une sauce piquante. Ce plat se sert avec une soupe froide au goût léger, le tout constituant un repas rafraîchissant.

비빔냉면

쫄깃한 면을 고추장에 비빈 국수 요리. 매우므로 담백한 맛의 찬 국물을 곁들여서 먹는다.

Fideos Fríos con Salsa Picante

Los fideos firmemente cocidos se mezclan con una salsa picante para crear un platillo con tan solo una pequeña proporción de caldo. Como los fideos son picantes, se produce una reconfortante sensación al comerse con la sopa helada suavemente aderezada.

混ぜ麺

コシのある麺を唐辛子酢みそ（チョジャン）であえた汁けの少ない麺料理。麺が辛いので薄味の冷たいスープでのどをうるおしながら食べる。

Spaghettini asciutti con sugo piccante

È un piatto di spaghettini coreani asciutti cotti al dente e conditi con miso mescolato ad aceto e peperoncino rosso (Cio Djan). Dato il gusto piccante, lo si accompagna con un brodino freddo che rinfresca la gola.

شعرية باردة في صلصة حريفة

هذا طبق من شعرية مطبوخة متماسكة تضاف إليها صلصة حريفة لإعداد طبق شعرية مع كمية طفيفة من المرق، وعند التقديم يضاف إلى الشعرية حساء بارد سعدل المذاق لتنسج بوجبة منعشة.

Macarrão frio com molho picante

Mistura-se a um molho picante macarrão cozido até o ponto de adquirir uma consistência firme, formando-se um prato de massa com pouco caldo. Serve-se juntamente com sopa gelada, de sabor leve, para suavizar o gosto picante do prato.

물냉면 (Mul-Neng-myeon)

Cold Noodle Dish

This cold noodle dish is prepared by placing meat, Kimchee, egg and a wide variety of other ingredients over noodles and pouring a broth prepared from meat over the entire combination. The characteristic texture and flavor of the noodles is particularly appealing.

kcal ●●●●

冷面

在面條上盛放上切碎的肉、朝鮮腌菜、雞蛋、梨等配料，再澆上用肉汁做成的湯。面條滑溜，獨具風味。

Kaltes Nudelgericht

Bei diesem kalten Nudelgericht werden Fleisch, Kimchee, Eier und zahlreiche andere Zutaten auf Nudeln gelegt und dann Fleischbrühe über die gesamte Kombination gegossen. Besonders attraktiv ist dieses Gericht durch den charakteristischen Biß und Geschmack der Nudeln.

冷面

在面条上盛放上切碎的肉、朝鲜腌菜、鸡蛋、梨等配料，再浇上用肉汁做成的汤。面条滑溜，独具风味。

Plat de nouilles froides

Ce plat de nouilles froides se prépare en disposant de la viande, du kimchee, un œuf et une poire et de nombreux autres ingrédients sur des nouilles, et en versant sur le tout un bouillon à base de viande. La texture et le goût caractéristiques des nouilles en font un plat particulièrement appétissant.

물냉면

면 위에 고기, 김치, 달걀, 배 등을 얹고, 찬 고깃국물을 부은 면요리. 매끈한 면맛이 특징.

Fideos Fríos

En este platillo frío se cubren los fideos con cerdo, Kimchee, huevo y muchos otros ingredientes cortados en tiras y se baña todo con un caldo de carne. El sabor y la textura característicos de los fideos los hacen especialmente apetitosos.

冷麵

麵の上に肉、キムチ、卵、梨などの具をのせ、肉でだしをとったスープを注いだ冷たい麺料理。ツルッとした食感の麺が独特。

Spaghettini freddi

Carne, Kimchi, uova, pera e altri ingredienti vengono disposti su spaghettini freddi. Sul tutto si versa poi un brodo di carne. La pasta risulta liscia e scivola in bocca.

طبق من الشعرية الباردة

يتم إعداد هذا الطبق بوضع قطع من اللحم والكيمتشي والبيض والعديد من المقادير الأخرى فوق الشعرية ثم يسكب فوق الجميع بهريز معد من اللحم. هنا تتميز الشعرية بقوام متع ونكهة طيبة.

Macarrão servido frio

Prepara-se este prato frio dispondo carne, kimchee, ovo e uma ampla variedade de outros ingredientes sobre macarrão. Em seguida, adiciona-se um caldo preparado com carne. A textura característica e o aroma do macarrão são particularmente apetitosos.

온면 （On-Myeon）

Hot Noodle Dish

This noodle dish contains meat and vegetables over noodles and is served piping hot. The soy sauce broth prepared with dried fish and meat brings out the flavor of the noodles.

kcal ●●●●

溫面

這是一種在其上面盛放肉和蔬菜，再注入用小魚幹和肉做成的湯汁的、帶醬油味的溫湯面。

温面

这是一种在其上面盛放肉和蔬菜，再注入用小鱼干和肉做成的汤汁的、带酱油味的温汤面。

온면

고기와 야채 등을 국수 위에 얹고 뜨거운 국물을 부은 면요리. 멸칫국물이나 고깃국물에 간장으로 간을 한 국물이 면과 잘 어울린다.

温麺

肉や野菜などを麺の上にのせた温かい麺料理。煮干しや肉でだしをとったしょうゆ味のスープが麺によく合う。

طبق من الشعرية الساخنة

هذا الطبق هو عبارة عن لحم وخضر فوق صحن من الشعرية وهو يقدم ساخناً للغاية، وهنا نجد أن البهرج المعد من صلصة الصويا مع السمك المجفف واللحم يقري طعم الشعرية.

Heißes Nudelgericht

Dieses Nudelgericht enthält Fleisch und Gemüse auf Nudeln und wird glühendheiß serviert. Die Suppe auf Sojasoßenbasis wird mit getrocknetem Fisch und Fleisch hergestellt und hebt den Geschmack der Nudeln besonders gut hervor.

Plat de nouilles chaudes

Ce plat de nouilles, servi chaud, contient de la viande et des légumes disposés sur des nouilles. Le bouillon de sauce de soja, préparé à base de poisson séché et de viande rehausse la saveur des nouilles.

Fideos Calientes

Sobre los fideos calientes se ponen carne, verduras y otros ingredientes. El caldo preparado con salsa de soja, pescado seco y carne realza el sabor de los fideos.

Pasta in brodo caldo

È un piatto caldo di pasta con carne, verdure e altri ingredienti. Il brodo che vi si versa sopra, di pesciolini essiccati o di carne e dal gusto di soia, si combina bene con la pasta.

Macarrão quente

Este prato, que contém carne e vegetais sobre macarrão, é servido bem quente. O caldo de molho de soja preparado com peixe seco e carne ressalta o sabor do macarrão.

김치찌개 （Kim-chi-Chi-ge）

Pork and Kimchee Casserole

This spicy and richly flavored casserole features Chinese cabbage Kimchee, pork and tofu blended with fermented soy bean paste, making it the perfect accompaniment to a bowl of hot rice.

© S.T.

kcal ●●

朝鮮腌菜火鍋

這種火鍋內放有腌白菜、豬肉、豆腐 其特色是帶辣味的濃面醬味火鍋，最適合作為米飯的下飯菜。

Schweinefleisch- und Kimchee Kasserolle

Diese scharfe und reichlich gewürzte Kasserolle besteht aus Chinakohl-Kimchee, Schweinefleisch und Tofu (Sojabohnenquark), und ist mit fermentierter Sojabohnenpaste vermischt. Ein Gericht, das zusammen mit einer Schale heißem Reis serviert wird.

朝鲜腌菜火锅

这种火锅内放有腌白菜、猪肉、豆腐 其特色是带辣味的浓面酱味火锅，最适合作为米饭的下饭菜。

Cocotte de porc et de kimchee

Cette cocotte épicée et richement parfumée contient du kimchee de chou chinois, du porc et du tofu mélangés à une pâte de haricots de soja fermentés et constitue l'accompagnement parfait d'un bol de riz chaud.

김치찌개

배추김치, 돼지고기, 두부 등을 넣은 매운 맛이 나는 찌개. 밥반찬으로 최적.

Cacerola de Cerdo y Kimchee

Esta aromática y bien condimentada cacerola se caracteriza por la mezcla de Kimchee de col china, cerdo y queso de soja. Se acompaña a la perfección con un tazón de arroz caliente.

キムチ鍋

白菜キムチ、豚肉、豆腐などが入った辛味とコクのあるみそ味の鍋料理。ご飯のおかずに最適。

Pignatta con kimchi

È un piatto dal gusto corposo e piccante a base di miso. Nella pignatta di terracotta si mettono Kimchi di cavolo cinese, carne di maiale, tofu e altri ingredienti. È una pietanza ottima per accompagnare il riso in bianco.

طاجن اللحم مع الكيمتشي

هذا الطاجن بطعمه الحار اللذيذ يتكون من مخلل كيمتشي من الكرنب الصيني مع لحم خنزير وتوفو في مزيج من الميسو (مادة تتبيل من فول الصويا)، وهو يصلح كطبق مثالي مع صحن من الأرز الساخن.

Caçarola de porco e kimchee

Picante e muito saborosa, esta iguaria servida em caçarola contém kimchee de repolho-chinês, porco e tofu, numa mistura com pasta de soja fermentada. É ótima, acompanhada de uma tigela de arroz quente.

생선찌개 (Seng-seon-Chi-ge)

Hot and Spicy Fish Stew

Various types of seafood, vegetables and tofu are combined in a spicy broth to create an appetizing dish that warms the body. This dish is highly recommended for people who like seafood.

kcal ●●

魚類火鍋

這是一種放有各種魚貝類、豆腐及蔬菜並可溫暖身體的辣味火鍋。它是喜歡海味客人的最佳菜肴。

鱼类火锅

这是一种放有各种鱼贝类、豆腐及蔬菜并可温暖身体的辣味火锅。它是喜欢海味客人的最佳菜肴。

생선찌개

여러 가지 어패류와 두부, 야채를 넣은 매운 맛의 찌개로 몸을 따뜻하게 해 준다. 어패류를 좋아하는 사람에게 권장한다.

魚の鍋

さまざまな魚介類と豆腐、野菜が入った体の温まる辛口の鍋料理。シーフードが好きな人におすすめ。

ياخني ساخن من السمك الحريف

تمزج أنواع عديدة من المأكولات البحرية مع الخضر والتوفو في بهريز متبل حريف للحصول على طبق فاتح للشهية يبعث على الدفء. هذا طبق ننصح بتناوله لكل من يهوى الأطعمة البحرية .

Scharfer und würziger Fischeintopf

Verschiedene Sorten Meeresfrüchte, Gemüse und Tofu (Sojabohnenquark) werden mit einem würzigen Sud kombiniert und ergeben ein appetitanregendes Gericht, das den ganzen Körper erwärmt. Dieses Gericht eignet sich besonders für Liebhaber von Meeresfrüchten.

Ragoût de poisson chaud épicé

Ce plat appétissant qui réchauffe le corps de la tête aux pieds est composé de diverses sortes de fruits de mer et de légumes ainsi que de tofu mélangés à un bouillon épicé. Ce plat est tout particulièrement recommandé aux amateurs de fruits de mer.

Cacerola de Pescado Aromático

Este platillo combina varias clases de mariscos y verduras con queso de soja en un aromático caldo que hace entrar en calor todo el cuerpo. Se recomienda especialmente a los amantes de los mariscos.

Pignatta di pesce

Per questo piatto piccante che riscalda vengono usati vari tipi di pesci, crostacei e molluschi, tofu e verdure. Raccomandato a chi ama i frutti di mare.

Ensopado de peixe apimentado e condimentado

Vários tipos de frutos do mar e vegetais, e tofu, são preparados em um caldo apimentado, criando uma iguaria apetitosa que aquece o corpo. É uma recomendação obrigatória para quem aprecia frutos do mar.

곱창전골 (Kop-chang-Jeon-gol)

Beef Entrails Stew

Beef entrails and an abundance of vegetables are boiled in a soup flavored with fermented soy bean paste with red peppers to produce a hearty flavor.

kcal ●●

©S.T.

雜燴火鍋

這是將牛的內臟及各種蔬菜放入用辣椒醬調成的湯中炖煮成的一種火鍋菜肴。

Eintopf aus Rinderinnereien

Rinderinnereien und zahlreiche Gemüsesorten werden in einer Suppe gekocht, die mit fermentierter Sojabohnenpaste und spanischem Pfeffer gewürzt ist. Ein Gericht mit herzhaftem Geschmack.

杂烩火锅

这是将牛的内脏及各种蔬菜放入用辣椒酱调成的汤中炖煮成的一种火锅菜肴。

Ragoût de tripes de bœuf

C'est un plat au goût fort qui contient des tripes de bœuf et divers légumes bouillis dans une soupe agrémentée à la pâte de haricots de soja fermentés et aux piments rouges.

곱창전골

쇠고기의 내장과 각종 야채를 고추장 국물에 끓인 찌개.

Cacerola de Vísceras

En este apetitosa cacerola se cuecen las vísceras de res con verduras en abundancia en una sopa condimentada con pasta de soja fermentada y chiles.

もつ鍋

牛の内臓とたっぷりの野菜を、唐辛子みそのスープで煮込んだ鍋料理。

Pignatta di interiora di manzo

Interiora di manzo e abbondante quantità di verdure vengono fatte bollire in un brodo con miso coreano piccante.

ياخني احشاء البقر

تسلق أحشاء البقر مع مجموعة وفيرة من الخضر في حساء متبل بالميسو (مادة تتبيل من فول الصويا) مع الفلفل الأحمر لإعداد طبق شهي الطعم.

Ensopado de miúdos

Miúdos de boi e vegetais em abundância são fervidos numa sopa condimentada com pasta de soja fermentada e pimenta-malagueta. É um prato com sabor apetitoso.

약식 （Yak-sik）

© S.T.

Steamed Sweet Rice

Glutinous rice, Chinese dates, chestnuts and other treats are steamed and flavored with brown sugar and honey. The many nourishing fruits and nuts used in this dish make it quite healthy.

kcal ●●

藥膳

這是將糯米, 樹木的果實蒸熟後, 再用紅糖和蜂蜜調味而做成的甜米飯。其中使用了大量強身補益的樹木的果實, 如棗、白果、栗子等。

药膳

这是将糯米, 树木的果实蒸熟后, 再用红糖和蜂蜜调味而做成的甜米饭。其中使用了大量强身补益的树木的果实, 如枣、白果、栗子等。

약식

찹쌀과 나무열매를 쪄서 검은 설탕과 꿀로 맛을 낸 달콤한 밥. 대추, 은행, 밤 등 몸에 좋은 나무 열매가 많이 사용된다.

藥食

もち米と木の実を蒸し, 黒砂糖やはちみつで味付けした甘いご飯。なつめ、ぎんなん、栗など, 滋養のある木の実がたくさん使われている。

ارز حلو مطهو على البخار

يطهى الأرز من النوع اللدن على البخار مع البلح الصيني والكستناء وغيرها من الفواكه ويضاف إليه العسل والسكر غير المكرر، ويحتوي هذا الصنف على العديد من الفواكه والمكسرات مما يجعله طبقاً صحياً للغاية.

Gedämpfter süßer Reis

Klebriger Reis, chinesische Datteln, Eßkastanien und andere Leckereien werden gedämpft und mit braunem Zucker und Honig gewürzt. Die zahlreichen nahrhaften Früchte und Nüsse, die bei dieser Nachspeise verwendet werden, machen sie zu einem gesunden Genuß.

Riz sucré cuit à la vapeur

Riz collant, dattes chinoises, marrons et autres friandises sont cuits à la vapeur et parfumés au sucre brun et au miel. La grande quantité de noix et de fruits nourrissants qu'il contient en fait un plat particulièrement sain.

Arroz Dulce

Se cuecen al vapor arroz glutinoso, dátiles chinos, nues de ginko, castañas y otras delicias aderezadas con azúcar morena y miel. Este platillo es bastante saludable por la gran cantidad de nutritivas frutas y semillas oleaginosas que contiene.

Dolce di riso con frutta secca

È un dolce assai nutriente, che contiene molta frutta secca, per esempio datteri cinesi, semi di ginko e di altri alberi, castagne. Viene preparato mescolando la frutta secca con riso glutinoso, miele e zucchero di canna e cuocendo a vapore.

Bolinhos de arroz doce cozidos em vapor

Arroz glutinoso, tâmaras, nozes de gingko, castanhas e outras delícias são cozidos em vapor e temperados com açúcar mascavo e mel. As várias frutas e castanhas nutritivas que este prato contém são muito saudáveis.

떡 (Teok)

Rice Cake Sweets

This desert is prepared for celebrations and special events. These rice cakes come in various shapes, including those in the shape of balls and pine cones sprinkled with soybean flour and sweet bean jam.

© S.T.

kcal ●

糕餅

這種點心通常用於慶祝活動或儀式典禮。將黃豆面和小豆餡拌在一起後可做成類似米粉團子或松果等各種形狀的糕餅。

Süßigkeiten aus Reiskuchen

Dieser Nachtisch wird für Feierlichkeiten und besondere Veranstaltungen zubereitet. Die Reiskuchen werden in verschiedenen Formen hergestellt, etwa kugelförmig oder wie Tannenzapfen, und werden mit Sojabohnenmehl und süßem Bohnenmuß besprenkelt.

糕饼

这种点心通常用于庆祝活动或仪式典礼。将黄豆面和小豆馅拌在一起后可做成类似米粉团子或松果等各种形状的糕饼。

Dessert de gâteaux de riz

Ce dessert se prépare pour les fêtes et les événements spéciaux. Ces gâteaux de riz présentent des formes variées, telles que des boules et des pommes de pin, que l'on saupoudre de farine de haricots de soja ou de confiture de haricots rouges sucrés.

떡

축하할 일이나 행사가 있을 때에 만드는 음식. 콩가루, 팥가루를 묻힌 경단과 갓모양 등 여러 가지 종류가 있다.

Golosinas de Arroz Glutinoso

Se preparan para celebrar acontecimientos y eventos especiales. Estos ricos dulces se moldean en distintas figuras tales como bolas, rombos, etc. sobre las cuales se espolvorea harina de soja y pasta de judías azucaradas.

餅菓子

祝い事や行事の時に作られる菓子。きな粉や小豆あんをまぶした団子や松笠の形をしたものなど、さまざまな種類がある。

Dolcetti di mochi

L'ingrediente principale di questi dolcetti è riso glutinoso cotto a vapore e pestato in un mortaio fino a che diventa morbido e plastico (mochi). Di forma rotonda o oblunga, sono ricoperti di farina dolce di semi di soia o marmellata di fagioli azuki. Ne esistono numerose varietà e vengono preparati in occasione di celebrazioni e festività.

كعكات الأرز الحلوة

يعد هذا الصنف من الحلوى في الأعياد والمناسبات الخاصة، وتأتي الكعكات في أشكال متعددة مثل الكرة أو المخروط وينشر فوقها دقيق الصويا أو مربى حلوة من الفول.

Doces de bolinhos de arroz glutinoso

Sobremesa preparada para celebrações e eventos especiais. São bolinhos de arroz glutinoso de várias formas, entre as quais bolas e cones de pinheiro, recobertos com farinha de soja e geléia de feijão doce.

강정 (Gang-jeong)

©S.T.

Confections

These cakes come in a diverse range of types, including those containing roasted sesame seeds solidified in thick malt syrup, and those prepared by deep-frying rice flour dough into fluffy delicacies and then sprinkling with pine seeds or rice flour. They also use healthy ingredients that make them not only delicious, but also good for you.

kcal ●

各色點心

品種豐富多彩、代表性的有:將煎炒過的芝麻用糖稀凝固制成的芝麻塊、蓬松脆酥的油炸米粉圈,或在米粉中拌入松子等各種天然健康素材制成的點心。

各色点心

品种丰富多彩、代表性的有:將煎炒过的芝麻用糖稀凝固制成的芝麻块、蓬松脆酥的油炸米粉团,或在米粉中拌入松子等各种天然健康素材制成的点心。

강정

볶은 깨를 조청으로 굳힌 것이나 쌀가루 반죽을 튀겨 부풀린 것에 잣가루나 쌀가루를 묻힌 것 등 헬시한 재료를 이용한 과자가 많다.

菓子

煎ったごまを水あめで固めたものや、米粉の生地を揚げてふくらませ、松の実や米の粉をまぶしたものなど、ヘルシーな素材を生かしたお菓子がいろいろ。

حلوى مشكلة

هذه تشكيلة متنوعة من الكعك يحتوي بعضها على السمسم المحمص في شراب سيك من الشعير، بينما يصنع البعض الآخر بقلي عجينة من دقيق الأرز للحصول على كعكة هشة يرش فرقها البعض الصنوبر أو دقيق الأرز، ويلاحظ أن المواد المكونة لهذه الحلوى لاتتميز فقط بطعمها اللذيذ بل هي أيضاً صحية للجسم.

Konfekt

Diese kleinen Kuchen werden ebenfalls auf verschiedene Art und Weise zubereitet. Einige enthalten geröstete Sesamkörner, die mit einem dicken Malzsirup verfestigt sind, andere bestehen aus in Öl ausgebackenem Reisteig, der zu einer luftigen Delikatesse gebacken und dann mit Pinienkernen oder Reismehl umhüllt wird. Hierzu werden ebenfalls wieder nur gesunde Zutaten verwendet, die nicht nur eine köstliche Nachspeise liefern sondern auch gut für die Gesundheit sind.

Sucreries

Ces gâteaux très variés sont composés notamment de graines de sésame grillées solidifiées dans un sirop de malt épais ou préparés en faisant frire de la pâte à base de farine de riz que l'on façonne en légères pâtisseries et que l'on saupoudre de pignons ou de farine de riz. On utilise également des ingrédients sains qui font de ces gâteaux de délicieuses douceurs bonnes pour la santé.

Confituras

Estas golosinas se preparan en diversas formas, incluyendo aquellas que contienen semillas de sésamo (ajonjolí) tostadas adheridas con un espeso jarabe de malta. Otra forma de preparar es friendo donas de harina de arroz hasta que quedan esponjosas y cubriéndolas con piñones o harina de arroz. Además de ser deliciosas son magníficas para la salud, pues en su confección también se utilizan ingredientes saludables.

Dolcetti vari

Ve ne sono di molti tipi e tutti valorizzano i sani ingredienti usati. Alcuni, ad esempio, sono fatti di semi di sesamo tostati tenuti insieme ad un denso sciroppo di miglio. Altri, che si presentano rigonfi e cosparsi di pinoli o farina di riso, sono preparati con pasta di farina di riso e poi fritti.

Confeitos

Vários tipos de doces, entre os quais: sementes de gergelim tostadas e solidificadas em um xarope grosso de malte, e fofos confeitos de massa de farinha de arroz fritos por mergulho em óleo e salpicados com sementes de pinheiro ou farinha de arroz. Utilizam-se ótimos ingredientes que os tornam não apenas deliciosos como também saudáveis.

차 (Cha)

Tea

Although barley tea and corn tea are frequently served in restaurants, teas which contain medicinal plants having their own characteristic aroma are also enjoyed.

kcal

茶

餐廳一般供應麥茶或玉米茶，此外人們還經常飲用具有獨特芳香的藥用植物茶。

Tee

Obwohl in Restaurants häufig Roggentee und Maistee serviert werden, kann man auch Tees erhalten, die medizinische Pflanzen enthalten und ein charakteristisches Aroma besitzen.

茶

餐厅一般供应麦茶或玉米茶，此外人们还经常饮用具有独特芳香的药用植物茶。

Thé

Bien que le thé à l'orge et le thé au maïs soient fréquemment servis dans les restaurants, on consomme également des thés à base de plantes médicinales possédant leur propre arôme caractéristique.

차

레스토랑에서 흔히 주는 보리차나 옥수수차. 그 밖에 독특한 향기가 나는 약용식물로 만든 차가 많이 이용된다.

Té

En los restaurantes se sirven con frecuencia tés de cebada tostada y maíz. También pueden ser disfrutados los tés que contienen plantas medicinales con sus aromas característicos.

茶

レストランでよく出されるのは麦茶やコーン茶。ほかに独特の香りを持つ薬用植物を使った茶類もよく飲まれる。

Tè

Nei ristoranti vengono spesso serviti tè di orzo e mais. Si possono però gustare altre qualità di tè dal particolare aroma e tisane preparate con piante medicinali.

الشاي

رغم أن المطاعم تقدم في أغلب الأحيان الشاي المصنوع من الشعير أو الذرة فهناك أيضاً أنواع من الشاي تحتوي على أعشاب طبية ولكل منها نكهتها المميزة.

Chá

Embora o chá de cevada e o de milho sejam freqüentemente servidos em restaurantes, outros chás que contêm plantas medicinais com características próprias também são bastante apreciados.

술 (Sul)

© S.T.

Liquor

The various types of liquor that are enjoyed in Korea are primarily made from grain in one of two ways, namely by brewing or distilling. Some of the more popular brands include spirits such as Jinro, Bidan and Green, and rice wines´ such as Mackgulri.

kcal ●

酒

韓國及朝鮮酒以穀物為原料，可分為釀造酒和蒸流酒。其中有代表性的燒酒是：Jinro 、Bidan 、Green 等，釀造酒是 Mackgulri 等。

Alkoholische Getränke

Die verschiedenen Arten von alkoholischen Getränken, die man in Korea genießt, werden in erster Linie aus Getreide hergestellt. Die Produktion erfolgt auf zwei Arten, d.h. die Getränke werden entweder gebraut oder destilliert. Zu den populären Marken gehören Spirituosen wie z.B. Jinro, Bidan und Green, und Reiswein, etwa Mackgulri.

酒

韩国及朝鲜酒以谷物为原料，可分为酿造酒和蒸流酒。其中有代表性的烧酒是：Jinro、Bidan、Green 等，酿造酒是 Mackgulri 等。

Boissons alcoolisées

Les différentes variétés d'alcool consommées en Corée sont produites à partir de grains soit brassée soit distillés. Les marques les plus populaires sont Jinro comme eau-de-vie, et Bidan, Green et Mackgulri comme vin de riz.

술

한국・조선 술은 곡류를 주원료로 한 양조주와 증류주로 나뉘며, 대표적인 것으로는 진로, 비단, 그린 등의 소주와 막걸리 등이 있다.

Licor

Los diversos tipos de licor que se disfrutan en Corea se hacen básicamente a base de grano en una o dos maneras, principalmente la infusión o la destilación. Entre las marcas de destiladas más populares se encuentran Jinro, Bidan, Green y del arroz fermentado, el Mackgulri.

酒

韓国・朝鮮の酒には穀類を主原料とした蒸留酒と醸造酒があり、焼酎ではJINRO, BIDAN, GREENなど、酒ではマッコルリなどが代表的。

Bevande alcoliche

Le bevande alcoliche della Corea sono prodotte mediante distillazione o fermentazione di cereali. Le marche più conosciute sono Jinro, Bidan e Green come acquavite e Mackgulri come sakè.

المشروبات الروحية

هناك أنواع عديدة من المشروبات الكحولية في كوريا ويصنع معظمها من الحبوب إما بالتخمير أو بالتقطير. من بين الماركات المفضلة نجد "جينرو" و"بيدان" و"جرين" وكذلك أنواع من نبيذ الأرز مثل "ماكجولري".

Bebidas alcoólicas

Os vários tipos de bebidas alcoólicas, apreciados na Coréia, são feitos de cereais por dois métodos básicos: fermentação ou destilação. Entre os destilados estão: Jinro, Bidan, Green e de arroz fermentado, e Mackgulri.

맥주 (Mek-ju)

Beer

Korean beer is known to go well with grilled beef. Some typical examples of Korean beers are, from left to right, Cafri, OB Lager, Hite, Cass, and Red Rock.

© S.T.

kcal ●

啤酒

韓國啤酒最適合配著烤肉飲用。從左到右依次為：Cafri、OB Lager、Hite、Cass、Red Rock。

Bier

Koreanisches Bier ist bekannt dafür, daß es gut zu gegrilltem Rindfleisch paßt. Einige typische Beispiele für koreanisches Bier sind von links nach rechts Cafri, OB Lager, Hite, Cass, Red Rock.

啤酒

韩国啤酒最适合配着烤肉饮用。从左到右依次为：Cafri、OB Lager、Hite、Cass、Red Rock。

Bières

La bière coréenne se marie bien avec le bœuf grillé. Quelques exemples typiques de bières coréennes sont, de gauche à droite, Cafri, OB Lager, Hite, Cass, et Red Rock.

맥주

불고기와 잘 어울리는 한국 맥주. 왼쪽부터 카프리, 오비 라거, 하이트, 카스, 레드락.

Cerveza

La cerveza coreana se lleva bastante bien con la carne asada a la parrilla. Algunas de las cervezas coreanas más conocidas son, de izquierda a derecha; Cafri, OB Lager, Hite, Cass, Red Rock.

ビール

焼肉によく合う韓国のビール。左からCafri, OB Lager, Hite, Cass, Red Rock。

Birra

La birra coreana si accompagna bene con la carne alla griglia. Le birre coreane più conosciute sono: Cafri, OB Lager, Hite, Cass, Red Rock.

البيرة

تشتهر البيرة الكورية بملائمتها مع اللحم المشوي. هنا نعرض بعض الماركات المعروفة، من اليسار لليمين: "كافري"، "أو بي لاجر"، "هايت"، "كاس"، "رد روك".

Cerveja

A cerveja coreana é famosa por fazer boa companhia à carne grelhada. Alguns exemplos típicos de cervejas coreanas são (da esquerda para a direita): Cafri, OB Lager, Hite, Cass, Red Rock.

Korean Set Menu

The following provides an introduction to some convenient dinner menus that add to the pleasure of enjoying typical Korean dishes.

© S.T.

Grilled Beef Dinner

1. Grilled Beef (p.143)
2. Kimchee (p.154)

烤肉套餐
1. 烤牛肉 (p.143)
2. 朝鲜腌菜 (p.154)

Menü mit gegrilltem Rindfleisch
1. Gegrilltes Rindfleisch (S. 143)
2. Kimchee (S. 154)

烤肉套餐
1. 烤牛肉 (p.143)
2. 朝鲜腌菜 (p.154)

Dîner à base de bœuf grillé
1. Bœuf grillé (p.143)
2. Kimchee (p.154)

불고기 정식
1. 불고기 (p.143)
2. 김치 (p.154)

Plato Combinado de Res Asada a la Parrilla
1. Carne de Res Asada a la Parrilla (p.143)
2. Kimchee (p.154)

焼肉定食
1. 焼肉 (p.143)
2. キムチ (p.154)

Menu di carne alla griglia
1. Carne alla griglia (pag. 143)
2. Kimchi (pag. 154)

عشاء من اللحم المشوي
١. لحم البقر المشوي (ص ١٤٣)
٢. الكيمتشي (ص ١٥٤)

Refeição com carne grelhada
1. Carne grelhada (pág. 143)
2. Kimchee (pág. 154)

Mixed Vegetables over Rice Dinner

1. Mixed Vegetables over Rice (p.167)
2. Kimchee (p.154)

拌飯套菜
1. 什錦盖飯 (p.167)
2. 朝鮮腌菜 (p.154)

拌饭套菜
1. 什锦盖饭 (p.167)
2. 朝鲜腌菜 (p.154)

비빔밥 정식
1. 비빔밥 (p.167)
2. 김치 (p.154)

ビビンバ定食
1. ビビンバ (p.167)
2. キムチ (p.154)

عشاء من الخضر المتنوعة فوق الأرز
١. خضر متنوعة فوق الأرز (ص ١٦٧)
٢. الكيمتشي (ص ١٥٤)

Menü mit gemischtem Gemüse über Reis
1. Gemischtes Gemüse auf Reis (S. 167)
2. Kimchee (S. 154)

Dîner à base de légumes et de riz
1. Légumes mixtes servis sur du riz (p.167)
2. Kimchee (p.154)

Plato Combinado de Verduras Surtidas sobre Arroz
1. Verduras Surtidas sobre Arroz (p.167)
2. Kimchee (p.154)

Menu di verdure miste con riso
1. Riso con copertura di verdure miste (pag. 167)
2. Kimchi (pag. 154)

Refeição com misto de vegetais sobre arroz
1. Misto de vegetais sobre arroz (pág. 167)
2. Kimchee (pág. 154)

JAPANESE
FOODS

日本菜

日本菜

일본요리 메뉴

日本料理

أطباق يابانية

Japanische Gerichte

Cuisine Japonaise

Cocina Japonesa

Piatti Giapponesi

Cozinha Japonesa

牛たたき (Gyūtataki)

© S.T.

Rare-Broiled Beef Sashimi

This healthy meat dish is prepared by lightly browning the outside of the beef and then serving in thin slices with fragrant vegetables and a refreshing lemon soy sauce.

kcal ●

拍牛肉

這是一道把整塊牛肉放在火上略烤一下後切成薄牛肉片，拌上清香的蔬菜，澆上爽口的橙子汁食用的、健康性肉類菜肴。

Sashimi aus rohem leicht angebratenem Rindfleisch

Dieses gesunde Fleischgericht besteht aus Rindfleisch, das außen leicht angebräunt ist und dann in dünne Scheiben geschnitten mit duftendem Gemüse und einer erfrischenden Zitronen-Sojasoße serviert wird.

拍牛肉

这是一道把整块牛肉放在火上略烤一下后切成薄牛肉片，拌上清香的蔬菜，浇上爽口的橙子汁食用的、健康性肉类菜肴。

Sashimi de bœuf grillé saignant

Ce plat sain à base de viande se prépare en faisant légèrement dorer l'extérieur du bœuf et en le servant en fines tranches accompagné de légumes agrémentés d'une sauce rafraîchissante au soja et au citron.

쇠고기다짐

쇠고기 표면을 살짝 불에 익혀서 얇게 썬 다음, 향미 야채를 곁들인 헬시한 고기요리. 단백한 맛으로 초간장에 찍어 먹는다.

Sashimi de Res Ligeramente Asada a la Parrilla

Este saludable platillo de carne se prepara asando ligeramente el exterior para servirla en finas rebanadas con fragantes vegetales y una refrescante salsa de limón y soja.

牛たたき

牛肉の表面をさっと焼いて薄切りにし、香味野菜を添えたヘルシーな肉料理。さっぱり味のポン酢で食べる。

Manzo leggermente arrostito

È un piatto sano, in cui la carne viene velocemente e leggermente arrostita a fuoco vivo da entrambi i lati. Tagliata a fette sottili, viene presentata con verdure aromatiche e la si mangia con intingolo leggero di salsa di soia e aceto di riso.

لحم بقري نيء بلمسة من الشواء

هذا الطبق الصحي من اللحم يتم إعداده بشي السطح الخارجي فقط للحم بخفة شديدة، ثم يقدم بعد تقطيعه في شرائح رفيعة السمك مع بعض الخضر ذات الرائحة الطيبة وصلصة منعشة من الصويا والليمون.

Sashimi de carne levemente grelhada

Prepara-se este saudável prato de carne de gado, grelhando levemente somente o exterior da carne e servindo-a em fatias finas, com vegetais aromáticos e molho de soja de leve sabor, com um pouco de vinagre.

豚肉のしょうが焼き (Butaniku no Shōga-yaki)

Stir-Fried Pork with Ginger

After flavoring the pork with ground ginger, soy sauce, sweetened rice wine and sake, the pork is stir-fried over high heat to create an aromatic dish that really brings out the appetite.

kcal ●●

© S.T.

姜汁烤肉

這是把切好的豬肉薄片用姜末、醬油、甜料酒、酒先腌一下，然後用強火燒烤出香味。這道菜由於烤肉和調味汁香味共存，使人食欲倍增。

姜汁烤肉

这是把切好的猪肉薄片用姜末、酱油、甜料酒、酒先腌一下，然后用强火烧烤出香味。这道菜由于烤肉和调味汁香味共存，使人食欲倍增。

돼지고기 생강볶음

얇게 썬 돼지고기를 간 생강과 간장, 미림, 요리술로 양념하여 센불에서 노릇노릇하게 볶은 식욕을 돋구는 요리.

豚肉のしょうが焼き

おろししょうがとしょうゆ、みりん、酒で薄切りの豚肉に下味をつけ、強火で香ばしく焼いた食欲を誘う料理。

لحم محمر مع الزنجبيل

يتبل لحم الخنزير بالزنجبيل المفري وصلصة الصويا والساكي ونبيذ الأرز الحلو (الميرين) ثم يحمر فوق لهب قوي لتحصل علي طبق ذكي الرائحة يفتح شهيتك للطعام.

Pfannengerührtes Schweinefleisch mit Ingwer

Nachdem das Schweinefleisch mit geriebenem Ingwer, Sojasoße, süßem Reiswein (Mirin) und Sake gewürzt wurde, wird es bei großer Hitze in der Pfanne gebraten. Ein aromatisches Gericht, das wirklich Appetit macht.

Sauté de porc au gingembre

C'est un mets aromatique qui éveille réellement l'appétit et qui contient du porc que l'on fait sauter à feu vif après l'avoir agrémenté de gingembre haché, d'une sauce de soja, d'alcool de riz sucré et de saké.

Cerdo Salteado con Jengibre

Después de sazonar al cerdo con jengibre, salsa de soja, vino dulce de arroz y sake, se saltea a fuego vivo para crear un platillo aromático que realmente excita el apetito.

Maiale in padella allo zenzero

Fette sottili di carne di maiale vengono prima insaporite con zenzero grattugiato, sakè dolce per cucina, salsa di soia e sakè e in seguito saltate in padella a fuoco vivo. È un piatto dal buon aroma, che stimola l'appetito.

Porco refogado com gengibre

Refoga-se, em fogo alto, carne de porco condimentada com gengibre ralado, molho de soja, vinho doce de arroz e saquê. É um prato aromático que realmente desperta o apetite.

トンカツ (Tonkatsu)

Breaded Pork Cutlet

A thick slice of pork is coated with bread crumbs and deep-fried for a truly satisfying dish. The delightful juices of the pork are enhanced by the crispy texture of the coating.

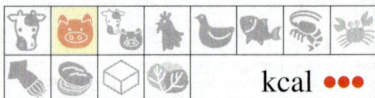

© S.T.

kcal ●●●

炸豬排

這是把切成厚塊豬排裹上面包粉放在熱油里炸熟的一道菜肴。其特點是容量豐盛、香脆的面包粉外殼內包裹著豬肉的鮮美，原味無損。

Paniertes Schweinekotelett

Eine dicke Scheibe Schweinekotelett wird mit Semmelbröseln paniert und dann fritiert. Ein wirklich leckeres, duftendes Gericht. Das köstlich saftige Schweinefleisch wird durch den krossen Biß der Panade noch akzentuiert.

炸猪排

这是把切成厚块猪排裹上面包粉放在热油里炸熟的一道菜肴。其特点是容量丰盛、香脆的面包粉外壳内包裹着猪肉的鲜美，原味无损。

Escalope de porc panée

Ce plat vraiment nourrissant est composé d'une épaisse tranche de porc enrobée de chapelure que l'on fait frire. La texture croustillante de la chapelure relève la saveur exquise du jus de porc.

포크 커틀렛

두텁게 썬 돼지고기에 빵가루를 묻혀 기름에 튀긴 볼륨이 있는 요리. 바삭한 껍데기 속으로 씹히는 돼지고기의 맛이 일품이다.

Chuleta de Cerdo Rebozada

Para preparar este apetitoso platillo se cubre con pan molido una gruesa chuleta de cerdo y se fríe en aceite abundante. La crujiente textura del empanado realza el delicioso jugo de la carne de cerdo.

トンカツ

厚めに切った豚肉にパン粉をつけて揚げたボリュームたっぷりの料理。サクッとした衣の中に豚肉のうまみが詰まっている。

Cotolette di maiale impanate

È un piatto che sazia molto, costituito da fette alquanto spesse di maiale impanate e fritte in abbondante olio. La croccante impanatura imprigiona tutto il buon sapore della carne di maiale.

ريش اللحم البانيه

تغطي الريش السميكة من لحم الخنزير بطبقة من البقسماط ثم تقلى للحصول على طبق شهي يتمتع بعصارة اللحم اللذيذة مع الطبقة الخارجية الهشة.

Milanesa de carne de porco ao estilo japonês

Uma grossa fatia de carne de porco é passada em farinha de rosca e frita por mergulho em óleo no preparo deste prato delicioso. A carne de porco suculenta é enriquecida com a textura crocante da cobertura.

串カツ (Kushikatsu)

Deep-Fried Pork on Skewers

Bite-sized pieces of pork and vegetables are alternately arranged on skewers, coated with bread crumbs and deep-fried. This informal dish can be enjoyed by eating directly from the skewers.

kcal ●●●

© S.T.

炸肉菜串

把切成一口大小的豬肉和蔬菜交替串在一起，然後蘸上面包粉放在熱油中炸熟。因為是拿著竹扦喫，所以食用很方便。

炸肉菜串

把切成一口大小的猪肉和蔬菜交替串在一起，然后蘸上面包粉放在热油中炸熟。因为是拿着竹扦吃，所以食用很方便。

꼬치 포크커틀렛

한입 크기로 자른 돼지고기와 야채를 꼬치에 끼워서 빵가루를 묻혀 튀긴 것. 꼬치가 있어 먹기에 편하다.

串カツ

ひと口大に切った豚肉と野菜を串に交互に刺し、パン粉をつけて揚げたもの。串を持って食べられるので、食べやすい。

لحم محمر بالأسياخ

توضع في السيخ قطع صغيرة من لحم الخنزير والخضر بالتناوب وتغطى بالبقساط ثم تحمر في زيت غزير، ويمكنك الاستمتاع بتناول هذا الطعام من السيخ مباشرة.

Fritierte Schweinefleisch-Spießchen

In mundgerechte Stücke geschnittenes Schweinefleisch und Gemüse werden abwechselnd auf Spieße gesteckt, dann paniert und in Öl ausgebacken. Dieses Gericht für formlose Gelegenheiten kann direkt von den Spießen gegessen werden.

Brochettes de porc frit

Des morceaux de porc et de légumes sont successivement placés sur des brochettes, enrobés de chapelure et frits. C'est un plat simple dont on peut déguster la viande directement à partir des brochettes.

Brochetas de Cerdo Fritas en Aceite

En una brocheta se alternan trozos de cerdo y verduras. Se cubren con pan molido y se fríen en bastante aceite. Este sencillo plato se puede disfrutar comiéndolo directamente de la brocheta.

Spiedini fritti di maiale

Bocconcini di carne di maiale e tronchetti di porro infilzati alternati su spiedini vengono impanati e fritti in abbondante olio. Si mangiano direttamente dallo spiedino.

Porco frito em espetinhos

Carne de porco, cortada em pedaços do tamanho ideal para levar à boca, e vegetais são dispostos alternadamente em espetinhos, passados em farinha de rosca e fritos por mergulho em óleo. É um prato informal, que pode ser saboreado diretamente dos espetinhos.

豚の角煮 (Buta no Kaku-ni)

Simmered Pork

This dish is prepared by simmering pork flank or shoulder roast in soy sauce, sake and sugar to produce a rich, deep flavor. The flavor of the broth penetrates the meat making it so tender that it practically melts in your mouth.

kcal ●●●●

炖豬肉塊

這道菜是把五花豬肉用醬油、酒、白糖等佐料一起炖數小時後而烹成。其特點是味鮮色濃、十分入味，具有酥嫩、入口即化的口感。

Gedünstetes Schweinefleisch

Für dieses Gericht wird kurze Rippe vom Schwein in Sojasoße, Sake und Zucker geköchelt und zu einem Gericht mit reichem und vollem Geschmack verarbeitet. Das Aroma des Suds durchdringt das Fleisch vollständing und mache es so zart, daß es praktisch im Munde zergeht.

炖猪肉块

这道菜是把五花猪肉用酱油、酒、白糖等佐料一起炖数小时后而烹成。其特点是味鲜色浓、十分入味，具有酥嫩、入口即化的口感。

Porc mijoté

Ce plat se prépare en faisant mijoter du flanchet de porc ou du rôti d'épaule dans une sauce de soja, du saké et du sucre afin d'obtenir un goût riche et fort. La saveur du bouillon pénètre dans la viande, la rendant si tendre qu'elle fond littéralement dans la bouche.

돼지고기찜

사각으로 큼직하게 썬 돼지고기의 삼겹살을 간장, 술, 설탕 등으로 조린 음식. 농후한 맛이 고깃속까지 배어있어 녹는 듯이 부드럽다.

Carne de Cerdo Cocida a Fuego Lento

Este platillo se prepara cociendo a fuego lento espaldilla o lomo de cerdo en salsa de soja, sake y azúcar, impregnando a la carne de un delicioso e intenso sabor. El gusto del cocido penetra en la carne, haciéndola tan suave que prácticamente se deshace en la boca.

豚の角煮

豚バラ肉をしょうゆ、酒、砂糖などで煮込んだもの。濃厚な味が肉の中までしみ、とろけるように柔らかい。

Bollito di maiale

Un pezzo della pancia viene sobbollito in un brodo di salsa di soia, sakè, zucchero e altri ingredienti. L'intenso sapore penetra fin dentro la carne, così tenera che sembra fondere in bocca.

لحم مطهو على نار هادئة

يعد هذا الطبق بطهي لحم الخنزير من الخاصرة أو الكتف على نار هادئة في صلصة الصويا مع الخمر الياباني (الساكي) وقليل من السكر للحصول على مذاق شهي. هنا تتخلل الصلصة اللحم بطعمها اللذيذ ويكون اللحم ليناً حتى يكاد يذوب في فمك.

Carne de porco cozida

Este prato é preparado pelo cozimento em fogo brando de carne de lombo ou paleta de porco em molho de soja, saquê e açúcar, criando-se um sabor rico e intenso. O sabor do caldo penetra na carne, tornando-a tão macia que praticamente derrete na boca.

焼きとり (Yakitori)

Japanese Broiled Chicken

Tender chunks of chicken are placed on skewers and broiled for a delicious aroma, making them the perfect accompaniment to beer or cocktails. They are then dipped in a sweetened soy sauce or simply salted.

kcal ●●

© S.T.

烤雞肉串

是一種色香味俱全的烤雞肉串，最適合作為下酒菜。其調味佐料有2種：一是灑上鹽、另一種是帶甜味的汁。

Japanisches Brathühnchen

Zarte Hühnchenteile werden auf Spieße gesteckt und dann gegrillt. Das köstliche Aroma machen sie zu einem perfekten Imbiß zum Bier oder Cocktail. Nach dem Grillen werden sie in gesüßte Sojasoße getaucht oder einfach gesalzen.

烤鸡肉串

是一种色香味俱全的烤鸡肉串，最适合作为下酒菜。其调味佐料有2种：一是洒上盐、另一种是带甜味的汁。

Brochette de poulet

Ce plat à l'arôme délicieux constitue l'accompagnement parfait d'une bière ou d'un cocktail. Il se compose de tendres morceaux de poulet disposés sur des brochettes puis grillés. Ceux-ci sont ensuite trempés dans une sauce de soja sucrée ou simplement salés.

닭꼬치구이

꼬치에 꽂은 닭고기를 불에 구어 낸 음식으로 안주로 알맞다. 달짝지근한 양념장맛과 소금맛구이의 두 종류가 있다.

Brochetas de Pollo Japonés Asado

Se ensartan trozos de pollo tierno en las brochetas y se asan hasta que despiden un delicioso aroma. Son la combinación perfecta con la cerveza o los cócteles. Se sumergen en una salsa dulce de soja o simplemente se salan.

焼きとり

串に刺した鶏肉を香ばしく焼いたおつまみにピッタリの一品。甘辛いタレをつけたものと塩焼きがある。

Spiedini di pollo

Questi spiedini di pollo arrostito dall'invitante profumo sono degli ottimi stuzzichini. Si mangiano con un intingolo dolce-salato oppure arrostiti semplicemente con sale.

دجاج مشوي على الطريقة اليابانية

توضع قطع الدجاج اللينة في الأسياخ وتشوى للحصول على مذاق طيب يجعلها مثالية للأكل مع البيرة أو الكوكتيل، ويغمس الدجاج بعد شيه في صلصة الصويا المحلاة أو يتبل بالملح فحسب.

Frango em espetinhos

Pedaços tenros de frango são colocados em espetinhos e assados até adquirir um delicioso aroma, num acompanhamento perfeito para cerveja e coquetéis. São mergulhados em molho de soja adocicado ou simplesmente condimentados com sal.

とりの唐揚げ (Tori no Kara-age)

©S.T.

Deep-Fried Chicken

Chicken pieces that have been marinated in soy sauce and various spices are deep-fried to a golden brown, making this the Japanese version of fried chicken. This popular dish can be enjoyed as an entree with rice or simply as a snack with drinks.

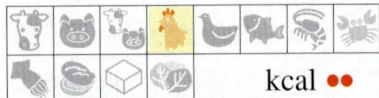

kcal ●●

日式炸子雞

先把雞肉在醬油中浸漬使其入味，然後放在熱油裏炸熟呈金黃色。這是一道典型的日本風味炸雞，無論作為下酒菜還是下飯菜肴都很受歡迎。

Fritiertes Hühnchen

Mundgerechte Stücken Hühnerfleisch werden in Sojasoße und mit verschiedenen Gewürzen mariniert und dann goldbraun in Öl ausgebacken. Dies ist sozusagen die japanische Version von Brathähnchen. Dieses populäre Gericht eignet sich als Hauptgericht mit Reis oder kann als Imbiß zu Getränken gereicht werden.

日式炸子鸡

先把鸡肉在酱油中浸漬使其入味，然后放在热油里炸熟呈金黄色。这是一道典型的日本风味炸鸡，无论作为下酒菜还是下饭菜肴都很受欢迎。

Poulet frit

Ce plat qui est la version japonaise du poulet grillé est un mets populaire qui peut être consommé avec du riz ou simplement comme en-cas avec des boissons. Il est composé de morceaux de poulet marinés dans une sauce de soja et diverses épices que l'on fait ensuite sauter jusqu'à ce qu'ils deviennent parfaitement dorés.

닭튀김

간장 등으로 맛을 낸 닭고기를 노릇노릇하게 튀긴 일본식 프라이드 치킨. 술안주나 밥반찬으로도 인기있는 요리.

Pollo Frito en Aceite

Primero se escabechan las piezas de pollo en salsa de soja y varios condimentos para después freírlas en aceite abundante hasta que quedan doradas, creando la versión japonesa del pollo frito. Este popular platillo puede ser disfrutado como plato principal con arroz o simplemente como acompañante de las bebidas.

とりの唐揚げ

しょうゆなどで下味をつけた鶏肉を、こんがりと揚げた日本風フライドチキン。おつまみ、おかずにいい人気の一品。

Pollo fritto alla giapponese

Bocconcini di carne di pollo fatta macerare in salsa di soia e altri ingredienti vengono fritti in abbondante olio fino a che diventano dorati. Questa versione giapponese del pollo fritto è molto popolare sia come pietanza che come stuzzichino.

دجاج مقلي

تغمر قطع الدجاج في صلصة الصويا مع التوابل المختلفة ثم تقلى حتى يصير لونها ذهبياً غامقاً لتتحصل على دجاج مقلي على الطريقة اليابانية، ويقدم هذا الصنف كنوع من المشهيات مع الأرز أو كطعام خفيف مع الشراب.

Frango frito

Pedaços de frango marinados em molho de soja e vários temperos são fritos por mergulho em óleo até dourar. É a versão japonesa do frango a passarinho ocidental. Este prato popular pode ser apreciado como entrada, acompanhado de arroz, ou simplesmente como petisco juntamente com bebidas alcoólicas.

とりの照り焼き (Tori no Teriyaki)

Chicken Teriyaki

Chicken is broiled until the surface appears almost glossy while bathing in a sweet sauce flavored with soy sauce to create a dish that goes perfectly with rice.

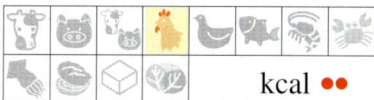

kcal ●●

© S.T.

日式醬烤雞

其烹飪方法是一邊往雞肉上抹帶醬油味的甜佐料汁，一邊烘烤。 這是一道非常適合於下飯的可口菜肴。

Hühnchen-Teriyaki

Hühnchen wird gebraten, bis die Oberfläche fast wie lackiert aussieht. Hierbei wird das Hühnerfleisch immer wieder mit einer süßen Soße bestrichen, die mit Sojasoße gewürzt ist. Ein Gericht, das hervorragend zu Reis paßt.

日式酱烤鸡

其烹饪方法是一边往鸡肉上抹带酱油味的甜佐料汁，一边烘烤。这是一道非常适合于下饭的可口菜肴。

Teriyaki de poulet

Ce plat qui se marie parfaitement avec du riz se compose de poulet que l'on fait griller jusqu'à ce que la surface arbore une apparence luisante, puis que l'on trempe dans une sauce sucrée aromatisée à la sauce de soja.

닭고기양념구이

닭고기에 달콤한 간장 양념을 바르면서 윤이 나도록 구운 것으로 밥반찬으로 좋다.

Pollo Teriyaki

Se asa al pollo hasta que la superficie se torna casi brillante mientras se va bañando en una salsa dulce sazonada con salsa de soja para lograr un platillo que se lleva a la perfección con el arroz.

とりの照り焼き

鶏肉にしょうゆ風味の甘いタレをつけながら、照りよく焼き上げたご飯によく合うおかず。

Pollo "laccato" (teriyaki)

Questi pezzi di pollo rosolati bagnandoli continuamente con una salsa dolce al gusto di soia, cosicché assumono un aspetto "laccato", sono una pietanza che si accompagna benissimo con il riso in bianco.

ترياكي الدجاج المشوى

يشوي الدجاج مع تغطيته باستمرار بصلصة حلوة لها نكهة الصويا إلى أن يلمع سطحه، ويعد هذا طبقا ممتازاً للتناول مع الأرز.

Frango teriyaki

A carne de frango é grelhada até ficar com a superfície quase lustrosa, regando-se constantemente com um molho doce à base de molho de soja. É um ótimo acompanhamento para o arroz.

さしみの盛り合わせ (Sashimi no Moriawase)

Assorted Sashimi

This traditional Japanese dish consists of slicing fresh, raw fish and shellfish into attractive portions and then dipping them in soy sauce flavored with Japanese horseradish.

kcal ●

生魚片拼盆

這是一道把新鮮的生魚貝類切成薄片，蘸上芥茉和醬油而食用的最具代表性的日本菜肴。

Gemischtes Sashimi

Bei diesem traditionellen japanischen Gericht werden frischer roher Fisch und Muscheln in attraktive Portionen geschnitten und dann in Sojasoße getaucht, die mit japanischem Meerrettich gewürzt ist.

生鱼片拼盆

这是一道把新鲜的生鱼贝类切成薄片，蘸上芥茉和酱油而食用的最具代表性的日本菜肴。

Assortiment de sashimi

Ce plat japonais traditionnel se prépare en découpant en portions attrayantes du poisson et des fruits de mer crus et frais, puis en les plongeant dans une sauce de soja agrémentée de raifort japonais.

모듬회

신선한 생선류를 얇게 저며 와사비, 간장 등을 찍어 먹는 대표적인 일본요리.

Sashimi Surtido

Este tradicional platillo japonés consiste en rebanadas de pescado y mariscos crudos y frescos dispuestos en atractivas porciones que se impregnan en una salsa de soja condimentada con mostaza verde japonés.

さしみの盛り合わせ

新鮮な生の魚介類を切り、わさび、しょうゆなどをつけて食べる代表的な日本料理。

Misto di fettine di pesce crudo (sashimi)

Piatto tipico della cucina giapponese, consiste di pesce e frutti di mare freschissimi e crudi, tagliati a fettine e mangiati intingendoli in salsa di soia e rafano giapponese grattugiato.

تشكيلة من السمك النيء

هذا الطبق الياباني التقليدي يتكون من شرائح نيئة طازجة من السمك والمحار مرتبة في شكل جميل وتغمس قبل الأكل في صلصة الصويا المتبلة بالفجل الحار.

Sashimi sortido

Neste prato tradicional japonês, fatias de peixes e de mariscos frescos e crus, são dispostas em atraentes porções. Para comer, molham-se levemente as fatias em molho de soja condimentado com raiz-forte-do-japão.

天ぷらの盛り合わせ (Tempura no Moriawase)

Assorted Tempura

Various vegetables, fish and shellfish are dipped in a water, egg and flour batter and then deep-fried. This typical Japanese dish is enjoyed by dipping the crispy deep-fried treats in a special soy-based sauce.

kcal ●●●

© S.T.

天婦羅拼盆(酥炸拼盆)

這是將蔬菜或魚貝類裹上用水、雞蛋和面粉調成的稠漿，用油炸成金黃、酥脆，然後蘸上特製調料食用的一種日本傳統菜肴。

天妇罗拼盆(酥炸拼盆)

这是将蔬菜或鱼贝类裹上用水、鸡蛋和面粉调成的稠浆，用油炸成金黄、酥脆，然后蘸上特制调料食用的一种日本传统菜肴。

모듬튀김

야채나 어패류에 물과 달걀로 반죽한 밀가루를 묻혀서 기름에 튀긴 대표적인 일본요리. 바삭바삭한 튀김옷을 묽은 간장에 찍어 먹는 요리.

天ぷらの盛り合わせ

野菜や魚介類に水と卵で溶いた小麦粉をつけ、油で揚げた代表的な日本料理。カラッと揚がった衣に天つゆをつけて食べる。

منوعات من التميورا

عبارة عن تشكيلة من الخضر والأسماك والمحار يغمس كل منها في مزيج مخفوق من الدقيق والبيض والماء ، ثم يقلى في الزيت، وهذا الطبق الياباني الشعبي يؤكل بغمس الوحدات المقلية الهشة في صلصة خاصة تحمل نكهة الصويا.

Gemischtes Tempura

Verschiedene Gemüsesorten, Fisch und Muscheln werden in einen Teig aus Wasser, Ei und Mehl getaucht und anschließend in Öl ausgebacken. Beim Essen dieses typischen japanischen Gerichts werden die knusprigen, ausgebackenen Stücke in eine spezielle Soße auf Sojabasis getaucht.

Assortiment de tempura

Divers légumes, du poisson et des fruits de mer sont mélangés à une pâte composée d'eau, d'œufs et de farine puis frits. Ce plat typiquement japonais se déguste en plongeant les délicieuses fritures croustillantes dans une sauce spéciale à base de soja.

Tempura Surtido

Diversas verduras, pescado y mariscos son rebozados con una pasta de agua, huevo y harina para freírse en aceite abundante. Este típico platillo japonés se disfruta humedeciendo estas delicias fritas y crujientes en una salsa especial hecha a base de soja.

Fritto misto alla giapponese (tempura)

È un piatto tipico della cucina giapponese, costituito da verdure, pesci e frutti di mare passati in una pastella di farina, uova e acqua e poi fritti croccanti in abbondante olio. Si mangia con intingolo di salsa di soia, sakè dolce da cucina e brodo.

Tempura sortido

Vários vegetais, peixes e mariscos são passados numa massa de água, ovo e farinha e fritos por mergulho em óleo. Saboreia-se este tradicional prato japonês mergulhando as frituras crocantes em um molho especial à base de soja.

えびフライ (Ebi Furai)

Deep-Fried Breaded Shrimp

Fresh shrimps are breaded and lightly deep-fried so that they retain an appetizing texture while wrapped in a fragrant coating that stimulates the appetite. This dish is served with tartar sauce that accents the flavor of the shrimp.

kcal ●●●

炸蝦

把新鮮的大蝦裹上面包粉後放在油里炸熟。蝦肉質地柔韌、摻和著香脆的面衣誘發人們的食欲，蘸上調味醬食用更是風味倍增。

Panierte fritierte Garnelen

Frische Garnelen werden paniert und leicht in Öl ausgebacken, so daß sie ihren appetitlichen Biß behalten. Die duftende Panade, in die sie gehüllt sind, regen den Appetit an. Dieses Gericht wird mit Tartar-Soße serviert, die den Geschmack der Garnelen akzentuiert.

炸虾

把新鲜的大虾裹上面包粉后放在油里炸熟。虾肉质地柔韧、掺和着香脆的面衣诱发人们的食欲，蘸上调味酱食用更是风味倍增。

Crevettes panées frites

Ce plat servi en hors-d'œuvre se compose de crevettes fraîches panées et légèrement frites afin qu'elles conservent une texture appétissante, que l'on enrobe ensuite d'une chapelure aromatisée. Ce plat est servi avec une sauce tartare qui rehausse la saveur des crevettes.

새우튀김

신선한 새우에 빵가루를 묻혀서 튀긴 요리. 바삭바삭하고 고소한 튀김옷과 새우 맛이 식욕을 돋구어 주며, 타르타르 소스를 곁들이면 한층 더 맛있다.

Langostinos Rebosados

Para preparar este apetitoso platillo que estimula el apetito se empanan los langostinos frescos y se fríen ligeramente para que retengan su apetitosa textura al ser envueltos en una fragante cubierta. Este platillo se sirve con salsa tártara, que acentúa el sabor de los langostinos.

えびフライ

新鮮なえびにパン粉をつけて揚げたもの。えびの歯ごたえと香ばしい衣が食欲をそそり、タルタルソースがうまみを引き立てる。

Gamberi impanati

Gamberi freschissimi vengono impanati e fritti in abbondante olio. La croccante impanatura e la consistenza "al dente" dei gamberi solleticano l'appetito. Si mangiano con salsa tartara, che ne esalta il sapore.

جمبري بانيه مقلي

يغلف الجمبري الطازج (الروبيان) بالبقسماط ويقلي بخفة بحيث يحتفظ بنسيجه الممتع مع غطاء لذيذ يثير الشهية، ويقدم هذا الطبق مع صلصة التارتار التي تبرز النكهة الذكية للجمبري.

Camarões empanados

Camarões frescos são empanados com farinha de rosca e fritos ligeiramente por mergulho em óleo. Os camarões mantêm uma textura apetitosa, envoltos numa cobertura aromática. Saboreia-se com molho tártaro, para realçar o sabor dos camarões.

魚の塩焼き (Sakana no Shioyaki)

Broiled Salted Fish

Fresh fish are lightly salted and then broiled to a golden brown for a simple dish that brings out the unique flavors of each type of fish.

kcal ●●

© S.T.

鹽烤魚

在新鮮的魚表面塗上鹽後，用火烘烤至恰到好處，使原料保持其自然風味。這是一道簡單易做的菜。

Gegrillter gesalzener Fisch

Frischer Fisch wird leicht gesalzen und dann goldbraun gegrillt. Ein einfaches Gericht, das jeweils den charakteristischen Geschmack der einzelnen Fischsorten herausarbeitet.

盐烤鱼

在新鲜的鱼表面涂上盐后，用火烘烤至恰到好处，使原料保持其自然风味。这是一道简单易做的菜。

Grillade de poissons salés

Ce plat simple qui relève la saveur unique de chaque poisson est préparé avec des poissons frais légèrement salés que l'on fait griller jusqu'à ce qu'ils deviennent dorés.

생선소금구이

신선한 생선에 소금을 뿌리고 노릇노릇하게 구워낸 것. 소재가 지닌 맛을 살린 심플한 요리.

Pescado Salado a las Brasas

Se sala ligeramente el pescado fresco y se asa a las brasas hasta que adquiere un tono dorado. Este sencillo platillo realza el peculiar sabor de cada clase de pescado.

魚の塩焼き

新鮮な魚に塩をふり、こんがりと焼き上げる。素材の持ち味を味わうシンプルな料理。

Pesce grigliato con sale

Pesce fresco spruzzato di sale viene grigliato fino a che assume un colore dorato. È un piatto semplice che permette di gustare il sapore particolare di ogni pesce.

سمك مشوي بالملح

يملح السمك الطازج تمليحاً خفيفاً ثم يشوى حتى يصير لونه ذهبياً غامقاً فنحصل على طبق بسيط يحمل الطعم المميز لكل نوع من الأسماك.

Peixe grelhado com sal

O peixe fresco é ligeiramente salgado e assado na grelha até dourar. Este prato simples realça o sabor particular de cada tipo de peixe.

魚の照り焼き (Sakana no Teriyaki)

Grilled Teriyaki-Style Fish

Slices of fish are grilled by applying a flavorful sauce, and repeatedly grilled two or three times to create a dish characterized by the glossy surface of the fish.

kcal ●●

醬烤魚

將不經任何調味、烤熟的魚,抹上調料汁烘烤,然後再抹上調料汁烘烤,反復兩到三次,直到魚烤得色香俱全。

Gegrillter Fisch nach Teriyaki-Art

Fischscheiben werden mit einer wohlschmeckenden Soße bestrichen und dann gegrillt. Dieser Vorgang wird dann zwei- bis dreimal wiederholt und ergibt ein Gericht, das durch die glänzende Oberfläche des Fischs eine besondere Note erhält.

酱烤鱼

将不经任何调味、烤熟的鱼,抹上调料汁烘烤,然后再抹上调料汁烘烤,反复两到三次,直到鱼烤得色香俱全。

Teriyaki de poisson

On fait revenir à la poêle des deux côtés et à plusieurs reprises des tranches de poisson sur lesquelles on applique régulièrement une sauce parfumée afin d'obtenir une surface luisante sur le poisson.

생선양념구이

살짝 구운 생선에 양념장을 바르면서 2~3회 반복하여 윤이 나도록 구운 생선 요리.

Pescado a la Brasa al Estilo Teriyaki

Se asa aplicándoles una gustosa salsa a la carne de pescado cortada en filete. La labor de aplicar la salsa y retornar a las brasas se repite dos o tres veces hasta que se obtiene un platillo caracterizado por la brillante superficie del pescado.

魚の照り焼き

素焼きした魚にタレをつけては焼き、つけては焼きを2、3回繰り返し、照りよく焼き上げた魚料理。

Pesce grigliato laccato (teriyaki)

Il pesce viene grigliato, bagnato con una particolare salsa e nuovamente grigliato varie volte, in modo che la superficie risulti come laccata.

ترياكي السمك المشوى

تشوى شرائح السمك مع إضافة صلصة الصويا وتكرار الشى مرتين أو ثلاث مرات حتى تحصل على طبق يتميز بالسطح اللامع للسمك.

Peixe assado ao estilo teriyaki

Postas de peixe são assadas, aplicando-se um molho delicioso. Volta-se a assá-las duas ou três vezes, sempre passando o molho. As postas de peixe adquirem uma superfície brilhante.

さばのみそ煮 (Saba no Miso-ni)

Simmered Mackerel in Miso Sauce

This dish consists of simmering mackerel in a sauce flavored with miso, sugar, sake and other ingredients to create a rich and aromatic taste. The miso serves to remove the fishy taste, making it more enjoyable.

kcal ●●

炖面酱鲐鱼

這是將鲐魚中加入日本面酱、白糖、酒等調料炖煨而成的一道道濃鬱的魚菜肴。日本醬具有解除魚腥味之功效，因而魚肉可口入味。

炖面酱鲐鱼

这是将鲐鱼中加入日本面酱、白糖、酒等调料炖煨而成的一道味道浓郁的鱼菜肴。日本酱具有解除鱼腥味之功效，因而鱼肉可口入味。

고등어 된장조림

고등어를 된장, 설탕, 술 등으로 조린 진한 맛의 생선 요리. 된장이 생선의 비린내를 제거하여 먹기좋다.

さばのみそ煮

さばを、みそ、砂糖、酒などの調味料で煮た、こってり味の魚料理。みそが魚の臭みを消すので、食べやすい。

سمك مطهو في صلصة الميسو

يتكون هذا الطبق من سمك الماكريل (الإسقمري) المطهي على نار هادئة في صلصة من الميسو والخمر الياباني (الساكي) وبعض السكر والمقادير الأخرى للحصول على طبق غني طيب الرائحة، ويساهم الميسو (مادة تتبيل من فول الصويا) في إزالة النكهة القوية للسمك فيصبح له طعماً ألذ.

Gedünstete Makrele in Miso-Soße

Für dieses Gericht wird eine Makrele in einer Soße gedünstet, die mit Miso (fermentierter Sojabohnenpaste), Zucker, Sake und anderen Zutaten gewürzt ist und einen abgrundeten und aromatischen Geschmack ergibt. Das Miso hat die Aufgabe, den Fischgeschmack zu mildern und das Gericht noch appetitlicher zu machen.

Maquereau mijoté dans une sauce de miso

Ce plat consiste à faire mijoter du maquereau dans une sauce parfumée avec du miso, du sucre, du saké et d'autres ingrédients afin d'obtenir un goût riche et aromatique. Le miso sert à atténuer le goût du poisson, le rendant ainsi encore plus savoureux.

Caballa Cocida a Fuego Lento en Salsa de Miso

Se cuece la caballa a fuego lento en una salsa aderezada con miso, azúcar, sake y otros ingredientes hasta que adquiere un delicioso y aromático sabor. El miso sirve para eliminar el olor a pescado, haciéndolo más apetecible.

Sgombro in umido con miso

È un piatto molto sapido, preparato cuocendo dello sgombro in umido con condimento di miso, zucchero, sakè e altri ingredienti. Il pesce perde così l'odore e risulta più appetibile.

Cavala cozida em fogo brando com molho de miso

Prepara-se este prato cozinhando em fogo brando o peixe cavala em um molho condimentado com pasta miso, açúcar, saquê e outros ingredientes, para criar um sabor rico e aromático. A pasta condimentícia miso serve para suavizar o gosto forte do peixe, tornando-o mais agradável ao paladar.

Raw Tuna Topped with Ground Yam

まぐろの山かけ (Maguro no Yamakake)

Raw Tuna Topped with Ground Yam

Ground yam is poured over appetizing chunks of raw tuna, which are then enjoyed with soy sauce flavored with Japanese horseradish. This dish is known for the sticky texture of the ground yams.

kcal ●

山芋澆蓋金槍魚

在切成小塊的生金槍魚內拌入磨成糊狀的山芋，再澆上芥茉醬油調勻食用。由於山芋中會流出很黏的汁，使得這道菜具有特殊風味。

Roher Thunfisch mit geriebener Jamswurzel

Geriebene Jamswurzel wird über rohen Thunfisch gegeben, der in appetitliche Stücke geschnitten ist. Diese Mischung wird dann mit Sojasoße genossen, die mit japanischem Meerrettich gewürzt ist. Dieses Gericht ist für die etwas schaumig-schleimige Textur der geriebenen Jamswurzel bekannt.

山芋浇盖金枪鱼

在切成小块的生金枪鱼内拌入磨成糊状的山芋，再浇上芥茉酱油调匀食用。由于山芋中会流出很黏的汁，使得这道菜具有特殊风味。

Thon cru parsemé d'ignames râpées

Ce plat contient d'appétissants morceaux de thon cru recouverts d'ignames râpées que l'on déguste avec une sauce de soja parfumée au raifort japonais. Ce mets est célèbre pour la texture collante des ignames râpées.

참치와 참마 무침

사각으로 먹기 좋게 썬 참치와 간 참마를 버무려서 와사비 간장을 끼얹어 먹는다. 참마의 끈끈함이 특징.

Atún Crudo Cubierto con Ñame Molido

Deliciosa carne de atún crudo cortada en trozos, se cubre con una pasta de ñame molido y se disfrutan con una salsa de soja condimentada con mostaza verde japonesa. Este platillo es conocido por la viscosa textura del ñame rallado.

まぐろの山かけ

角切りにした生のまぐろにすりおろした山いもをからめ、わさびじょうゆをかけて食べる。山いもから出る粘りけが特徴。

Tonno crudo con copertura di patata yam grattugiata

Bocconcini di tonno crudo vengono presentati coperti di patata yam grattugiata e mangiati con salsa di soia mista a rafano giapponese. La caratteristica di questo piatto è la consistenza vischiosa della patata.

سمك التونة النيء مع اليام المغري

يسكب اليام المغري (نبات يشبه البطاطا) فوق قطع شهية من سمك التونة النيء ، ويؤكل المزيج مع صلصة الصويا المتبلة بالفجل الياباني الحار ، ويعرف هذا الطبق بالقوام اللزج لليام المغري.

Atum cru coberto com inhame-da-china ralado

Dispõe-se o inhame ralado sobre apetitosas postas de atum cru, que são saboreadas com molho de soja contendo raiz-forte-do-japão. Este prato é conhecido pela textura viscosa do inhame ralado.

ししゃも (Shishamo)

Broiled Smelt with Roe

These broiled fish are served full of surprisingly delicious roe. Their small 10~15 centimeter size enables them to be enjoyed entirely, including bones, and the aromatic fragrance produced by broiling is outstanding.

© S.T.

kcal ●

鬍瓜魚

把肚里滿是魚子的、大約10~15厘米長的小魚用火燒烤後食用。連頭帶刺都可以喫，其香味美妙絕倫。

胡瓜鱼

把肚里满是鱼子的、大约10~15厘米长的小鱼用火烧烤后食用。连头带刺都可以吃，其香味美妙绝伦。

별빙어

알이 가득찬 크기 10~15cm 정도의 작은 생선을 구운 것. 뼈까지 전부 먹을 수 있고 고소한 맛이 일품이다.

ししゃも

おなかに卵がたっぷり詰まった、体長10～15cmほどの小魚を焼いたもの。骨までまるごと食べられ、香ばしさは抜群。

سمك مشوي بالبطارخ

يشوى سمك الحساس ببطارخه اللذيذة التي تتميز بكثافتها المدهشة، ونظراً لأن حجم السمكة صغير إذ يتراوح طولها بين ١٠-١٥ سم فيمكن تناولها كاملة بالعظام بينما تنبعث منها رائحة الشواء الرائعة.

Gegrillter Stint mit Rogen

Dieser gegrillte Fisch wird komplett mit dem Rogen serviert, der überraschend köstlich schmeckt. Die geringe Größe von 10 bis 15cm ermöglicht es, den Fisch ganz zu essen - einschließlich der Gräten. Der beim Grillen entstehende aromatische Duft ist einfach phantastisch.

Eperlans grillés accompagnés d'œufs de poisson

Ces poissons grillés se servent garnis d'œufs de poisson dont le goût surprenant est exquis. De par leur petite taille (environ 10 à 15 cm), on peut les savourer entiers avec leurs arêtes, alors que le parfum aromatique qu'ils dégagent quand on les fait griller est sans précédent.

Eperlano Seco con Huevas Asado

Este pescado asado se sirve lleno de huevas sorprendentemente deliciosas. Su tamañito de 10 a 15 centímetros permite que sean disfrutados en su totalidad, incluyendo las espinas. La aromática fragancia que despiden al ser asados es extraordinaria.

Sperlani alla griglia

Sono pesciolini di 10-15cm grigliati con tutte le loro uova. Si può mangiare anche la lisca e sprigionano un eccellente profumo.

Eperlano com ovas grelhado

Este peixe grelhado é servido repleto de ovas surpreendentemente deliciosas. O reduzido tamanho, entre 10 e 15 centímetros, permite saborear o peixe inteiramente, com espinhas. Destaca-se a fragrância aromática criada na grelha.

あさりの酒蒸し (Asari no Saka-mushi)

© S.T.

Steamed Short- Necked Clams in Sake

Sake is sprinkled over the clams before steaming after which they are seasoned with salt for a healthy snack. Steaming in sake produces a different flavor from that of steaming in wine.

kcal ●

酒蒸蛤蜊

在蛤蜊中倒入日本酒用火清蒸，這是道帶鹹味的健康性的下酒菜肴。如果改用葡萄酒則將是另具一種不同的風味。

Gedünstete kleine Miesmuscheln in Sake

Vor dem Dünsten wird Sake über die Muscheln gesprenkelt und dann mit Salz gewürzt. Dies ist ein herzhafter und gesunder Imbiß. Dünsten in Sake ergibt einen anderen Geschmack als das Dünsten in Wein.

酒蒸蛤蜊

在蛤蜊中倒入日本酒用火清蒸，这是道带咸味的健康性的下酒菜肴。如果改用葡萄酒则将是另具一种不同的风味。

Palourdes cuites à la vapeur dans du saké

Ce hors-d'œuvre est constitué de palourdes arrosées de saké avant d'être cuites à la vapeur, puis assaisonnées avec du sel. La cuisson des aliments à la vapeur de saké produit une saveur différente de la cuisson à la vapeur de vin.

모시조개찜

모시조개에 정종을 뿌린 다음 소금으로 간을 하여 살짝 끓여낸 술안주. 와인을 넣은 것과는 또 다른 맛이 난다.

Almejas Cocidas al Vapor en Sake

Antes de cocer al vapor, se impregna a las almejas con sake y se condimentan con sal. En este saludable platillo, el sake evaporado produce un sabor diferente al de la comida cocida en vino.

あさりの酒蒸し

あさりに日本酒をふりかけて蒸した、塩味のヘルシーなおつまみ。ワインで蒸したものとはひと味違ったおいしさ。

Vongole cotte a vapore con sakè

Queste vongole spruzzate di sakè e cotte a vapore costituiscono un sano stuzzichino dal sapore di sale, di una bontà diversa da quelle cotte al vino bianco.

قواقع مطهوة على البخار في الساكي

ينثر الساكي على القواقع قبل طهيها على البخار ثم تتبل بالملح للحصول على طبق صحي من المشهيات، ويلاحظ أن الطهي مع الخمر الياباني (الساكي) ﻫﻨﺎ؛ القواقع مذاقاً يخلف عما إذا طهيت مع النبيذ.

Mariscos ao vapor de saquê

Saquê é salpicado sobre um fruto do mar semelhante ao marisco vênus antes do seu cozimento a vapor. Em seguida, os mariscos são condimentados com sal para crIar uma saudável refeição. O cozimento ao vapor de saquê produz um sabor diferente do que se obtém ao utilizar vinho.

いくらおろし (Ikura Oroshi)

Salmon Roe with Grated Radish

This light-tasting dish combines salmon roe with grated radish and is enjoyed with a little soy sauce poured on top.

kcal ●

© S.T

鹽漬大馬哈魚子醬

這是把鹽漬馬哈魚子醬和蘿蔔泥拌和一起，蘸著醬油食用的清淡、爽口的菜肴。

Lachsrogen mit geriebenem Rettich

Dieses Gericht hat einen leichten Geschmack und kombiniert Lachsrogen mit geriebenem Riesenrettich. Vor dem Essen wird etwas Sojasoße darüber geträufelt.

盐渍大马哈鱼子酱

这是把盐渍马哈鱼鱼子酱和萝卜泥拌和一起，蘸着酱油食用的清淡、爽口的菜肴。

Œufs de saumon servis sur du radis râpé

Ce plat au goût léger est composé d'œufs de saumon et de radis râpé que l'on déguste avec un filet de sauce de soja versée sur le dessus.

연어알과 간 무우무침

연어알에 무우를 갈아 버무려서 간장을 끼얹어 먹는 담백한 요리.

Huevas de Salmón con Rábano Rallado

Este platillo de sabor ligero combina las huevas de salmón con rábano rallado y se disfruta rociando un poco de salsa de soja sobre la parte superior.

いくらおろし

さけの卵のいくらに大根おろしを混ぜ合わせ、しょうゆをかけて食べるさっぱりした一品。

Uova di salmone con rapa giapponese grattugiata

È un piatto leggero di uova di salmone salate e lavorate, miste a rapa giapponese grattugiata con una spruzzata di salsa di soia.

بيض السلمون مع الفجل المبشور

هذا طبق خفيف المذاق يجمع بين بيض السلمون والفجل المبشور وهو يؤكل مع سكب القليل من صلصة الصويا فوقه.

Ovas de salmão com nabo-japonês ralado

Este prato de sabor leve combina ovas de salmão com nabo-japonês ralado e é saboreado regando-se um pouco de molho de soja por cima.

肉じゃが (Niku-jaga)

Simmered Beef and Potatoes

This traditional family-style dish consists of simmering potatoes with beef and onions and then flavoring with slightly sweetened soy sauce.

kcal ●●

土豆燒牛肉

這是把土豆、牛肉和洋蔥一起炖煨，略帶甜味的醬油風味的、很具代表性的日本家常菜。

Gekochtes Rindfleisch und Kartoffeln

Für diese traditionelle Hausmannskost werden Kartoffeln mit Rindfleisch und Zwiebeln gekocht und dann mit leicht gesüßter Sojasoße gewürzt.

土豆烧牛肉

这是把土豆、牛肉和洋葱一起炖煨，略带甜味的酱油风味的、很具代表性的日本家常菜。

Bœuf mijoté avec des pommes de terre

Ce plat familial traditionnel consiste à faire mijoter des pommes de terre avec du bœuf et des oignons, dont le tout est agrémenté d'une sauce de soja légèrement sucrée.

쇠고기 감자조림

감자를 쇠고기나 양파와 함께 조린 대표적인 일본의 가정요리. 조금 단 간장 맛.

Carne de Res con Patatas Cocidas a Fuego Lento

Este tradicional platillo familiar consiste de un cocido de patatas con carne de res y cebollas, sazonado con una salsa de soja ligeramente dulce.

肉じゃが

じゃがいもを牛肉や玉ねぎと一緒に煮た、代表的な日本の家庭料理。少し甘めのしょうゆ味。

Stufato di manzo e patate

È un tipico piatto di cucina casalinga: manzo, patate e cipolle vengono insaporiti con salsa di soia leggermente dolce e stufati.

لحم البقر المطهو مع البطاطس

هذا طبق عائلي تقليدي يتكون من بطاطس تطهى على نار هادئة مع اللحم البقري والبصل ثم تتبل بصلصة الصويا المحلاة قليلاً.

Carne e batata cozidas

Este tradicional prato caseiro consiste em batatas cozidas em fogo brando com carne de gado e cebolas, condimentados com molho de soja levemente adoçado.

コロッケ (Korokke)

Potato Croquettes

Mashed potatoes and cooked ground beef are mixed together into patties, coated with bread crumbs and deep-fried to create a hearty, filling dish.

kcal ●●●

© S.T.

酥炸土豆肉餅

這是把煮熟的土豆搗碎，和肉餡兒拌在一起，然後裹上面包粉用油油炸的菜肴。

Kartoffelkroketten

Kartoffelpüree und gebratenes Hackfleisch werden miteinander vermischt und dann zu flachen Klößen geformt. Diese werden anschließen paniert und in Öl ausgebacken. Ein herzhaftes und sättigendes Gericht.

酥炸土豆肉饼

这是把煮熟的土豆搗碎，和肉馅儿拌在一起，然后裹上面包粉用油油炸的菜肴。

Croquettes de pommes de terre

Ce plat copieux et nourrissant se compose d'une purée de pommes de terre et de bœuf haché cuit que l'on façonne en petits pâtés et que l'on enrobe de chapelure avant de les faire frire.

크로켓

다진 고기를 볶아서 삶아 으깬 감자와 섞어 모양을 빚은 것에 빵가루를 묻혀 기름에 튀긴 요리.

Croquetas de Patata

En este delicioso platillo que satisface al estómago se mezcla el puré de patatas con la carne molida para hacer pastelillos cubiertos de pan molido y freírlos en aceite abundante.

コロッケ

ゆでてつぶしたじゃがいもと炒めたひき肉を混ぜてまとめ、パン粉をつけて揚げたもの。

Crocchette

Sono polpettine di patate bollite e schiacciate miste a carne tritata già cotta che poi vengono impanate e fritte.

بطاطس باللحم المفري والبقسماط

تُمزج البطاطس المهروسة مع لحم البقر المفري وتشكل على هيئة وحدات شبه مستديرة تغطى بالبقسماط وتقلى في الزيت للحصول على طبق شهي مشبع.

Croquetes de batata

Purê de batatas e carne de gado moída, previamente cozida, são misturados em bolinhos. Estes, depois de passados em farinha de rosca, são fritos por mergulho em óleo. É um quitute apetitoso, que satisfaz plenamente o paladar.

筑前煮 (Chikuzen-ni)

© S.T.

Braised Vegetables with Chicken

Chicken and root vegetables such as burdock, carrots and lotus root are braised and then simmered to produce a dish rich in natural fiber flavored with just the right amount of soy sauce.

kcal ●●

築前炖

這道菜把雞肉和牛蒡、鬍蘿蔔、藕等根菜放在一起煸炒後炖煮。其特點是略帶醬油味並含有豐富的食物纖維。

筑前炖

这道菜把鸡肉和牛蒡、胡萝卜、藕等根菜放在一起煸炒后炖煮。其特点是略带酱油味并含有丰富的食物纤维。

닭고기 야채조림

닭고기와 우엉, 당근, 연근 등의 근채류를 볶아서 조린 요리. 적당한 간장맛으로 식물성 섬유질이 풍부하다.

筑前煮

鶏肉とごぼう、にんじん、れんこんなどの根菜類を炒め煮にしたもの。ほどよいしょうゆ味で食物繊維が豊富。

خضر مطهوة مع الدجاج

يحمر الدجاج قليلاً مع بعض الجذور من الخضر مثل الجزر والجوبو والزنكون ثم يطهى المزيج على نار هادئة لإعداد طبق غني بالألياف الطبيعية وستبل بكمية مناسبة تماماً من صلصة الصويا.

Geschmortes Gemüse mit Huhn

Huhn und Wurzelgemüse, z.B. Schwarzwurzeln, Karotten und Lotuswurzeln, werden zunächst geschmort, dann geköchelt, und ergeben ein Gericht, das reich an natürlichen Ballaststoffen mit gerade der richtigen Menge Sojasoße gewürzt ist.

Légumes braisés accompagnés de poulet

Ce plat, riche en fibres naturelles et parfumé avec la quantité nécessaire de sauce de soja, contient du poulet, des racines telles que de la bardane, des carottes et des racines de lotus que l'on fait braiser puis mijoter.

Pollo y Verduras Dorados a Fuego Lento

Se dora a fuego lento y se cuece también a fuego lento el pollo junto con tubérculos tales como lampazo, zanahoria y raíz de loto. Este platillo rico en fibra se sazona con una cantidad exacta de salsa de soja.

Verdure e pollo in umido

Pollo e radici varie, fra le quali carote, radici di bardana e di loto, vengono soffritte e poi cotte in umido. È un piatto ricco di fibre e dal sapore di soia al punto giusto.

Vegetais com frango cozidos

Frango e raízes comestíveis, como bardana, cenoura e raiz de lótus, são refogados e em seguida cozidos em fogo brando no preparo deste prato rico em fibras naturais. O molho de soja, na medida certa, é adicionado como tempero.

野菜の煮もの (Yasai no Nimono)

Boiled Vegetables

Vegetables in season are boiled in a soy sauce-based broth for a healthy dish that brings out the flavor of the ingredients without using a drop of oil.

kcal ●

© S.T.

炖煨蔬菜

把時鮮蔬菜放在以醬油味為主的湯汁內炖煮。這道菜的特點是不用油，充分體現材料的自然風味，有益於健康的菜肴。

Gekochtes Gemüse

Gemüse der Jahreszeit wird in einem Sud auf Sojasoßen-Basis gekocht und ergibt ein gesundes Gericht, das den Eigengeschmack der Zutaten ohne einen Tropfen Öl hervorhebt.

炖煨蔬菜

把时鲜蔬菜放在以酱油味为主的汤汁内炖煮。这道菜的特点是不用油，充分体现材料的自然风味，有益于健康的菜肴。

Légumes bouillis

Ce plat sans graisse est composé de légumes assaisonnés bouillis dans un bouillon à base de sauce de soja qui relève la saveur des ingrédients sans que l'on ait besoin d'ajouter une goutte d'huile.

야채조림

계절의 야채를 간장 풍미로 조린 것. 기름을 사용하지 않으며 소재의 맛을 살린 헬시한 요리.

Verduras Cocidas

En este saludable platillo, las verduras de la temporada son cocidas en un caldo a base de salsa de soja destacando el sabor de los ingredientes sin usar una gota de aceite.

野菜の煮もの

季節の野菜をしょうゆ風味の煮汁で煮たもの。油を使わず、素材のうまみを生かしたヘルシーな料理。

Verdure in umido

Verdure di stagione cotte in umido con brodo insaporito di salsa di soia. È un piatto sano, senza uso di olio, in cui risalta il gusto degli ingredienti.

خضر مسلوقة

تسلق خضر الموسم في حساء بنكهة صلصة الصويا للحصول على طبق صحي تستمتع بمذاق مكوناته دون إضافة قطرة واحدة من الزيت.

Vegetais cozidos

Vegetais da estação são cozidos num caldo à base de molho de soja. É um prato saudável em que se realça o sabor dos ingredientes, sem utilizar uma gota de óleo.

きんぴらごぼう (Kimpira Gobō)

Stir-Fried Burdock

Julienne strips of burdock are combined with thinly sliced carrot strips after which they are stir-fried in oil and given a pungent, sweet and spicy flavor to create a dish that goes well with rice.

kcal ●

牛蒡絲

這是把牛蒡絲和鬍蘿蔔用油煸炒而成的，鹹中帶甜、清爽脆香的適合下飯的家常菜。

Pfannengerührte Schwarzwurzeln

Gestiftelte Schwarzwurzeln werden mit dünn geschnittenen Karotten gemischt und anschließend in Öl pfannengerührt. Dieses Gericht hat einen pikanten, süßen und würzigen Geschmack, der gut zu Reis paßt.

牛蒡丝

这是把牛蒡丝和胡萝卜用油煸炒而成的,咸中带甜、清爽脆香的适合下饭的家常菜。

Sauté de bardane

Après avoir mélangé de la bardane émincée en julienne avec des carottes coupées en fines lamelles, on les fait revenir dans l'huile et on les agrémente d'une saveur sucrée et piquante, ce qui en fait un plat qui se marie bien avec le riz.

우엉조림

채썬 우엉과 당근을 기름에 볶아서 달짝지근하게 맛을 낸 밥반찬.

Lampazo Salteado

Se cortan y se combinan tiras delgadas de lampazo y zanahoria para ser salteadas en aceite y darles un picante, dulce y aromático sabor, creando un platillo que se lleva bien con el arroz.

きんぴらごぼう

細切りにしたごぼうとにんじんを油で炒め、甘辛くシャキッと仕上げたお惣菜。ご飯によく合う。

Bardana saltata in padella

Bardana e carote tagliate a fiammifero vengono saltate in olio e condite in modo dolce-piccante. Si accompagnano bene al riso in bianco.

الجوبو المحمر

يقطع الجوبو (نوع من الجذور) في شرائح طولية رفيعة ويمزج مع شرائح مماثلة من الجزر، ويحمران معاً في الزيت للحصول على مذاق قوي حلو وحريف يكون لذيذاً جداً مع الأرز.

Bardana refogada

Finíssimas tiras de bardana são misturadas a fatias finas de cenoura e refogadas em óleo. Cria-se um sabor característico, doce o picante. É um ótimo acompanhamento para o arroz.

ひじきの煮もの (Hijiki no Nimono)

Simmered Hijiki

Hijiki, a type of seaweed known for its high calcium and iron content, is simmered in a sweetened soy sauce broth that produces the rich aroma of the ocean.

kcal ●

© S.T.

炖羊棲菜

這是一道用海菜類的羊棲菜烹飪而成鹹中帶甜風味的家常菜。由於其含有豐富的鈣和鐵質，您可以盡情享受來自大海的美味。

Gekochter Hijiki

Hijiki, eine Art Seetang, der für seinen hohen Kalzium- und Eisengehalt bekannt ist, wird in einem Sud aus leicht gesüßter Sojasoße gekocht und ergibt ein Gericht, das so richtig nach Meer schmeckt.

炖羊栖菜

这是一道用海菜类的羊栖菜烹饪而成咸中带甜风味的家常菜。由于其含有丰富的钙和铁质，您可以尽情享受来自大海的美味。

Hijiki mijoté

Ce plat contient de l'hijiki, un type d'algues à haute teneur en calcium et en fer, que l'on fait mijoter dans un bouillon à base de sauce de soja sucrée qui dégage un riche arôme marin.

녹미채(해초)조림

해산물의 일종인 녹미채를 달짝지근하게 조린 반찬. 칼슘과 철분이 많이 들어 있으며 바다내음을 맛볼 수 있는 요리.

Hijiki Cocido a Fuego Lento

La variedad de alga Hijiki, conocida por su alto contenido de hierro y calcio, se cuece a fuego lento en un caldo de soja azucarada para recrear el delicioso aroma del mar.

ひじきの煮もの

海草の一種のひじきを甘辛く煮たお惣菜。カルシウムと鉄分たっぷりで、豊かな海の香りを楽しめる。

Alghe hijiki in umido

Le nere alghe hijiki, ricche di calcio e di ferro, vengono cotte in umido con un condimento dolce-salato. Hanno un gradevole profumo di mare.

هيجيكي مطهو على نار هادئة

الهيجيكي هو نوع من الأعشاب البحرية يمتاز بنسبة عالية من الكالسيوم والحديد ويطهى في بهريز من صلصة الصويا المحلاة لإعداد طبق له نكهة بحرية غنية.

Hijiki cozida em fogo brando

Hijiki, um espécie de alga marinha conhecida por seu elevado teor de cálcio e ferro, é cozida em fogo brando em um molho de soja adocicado. Destaca-se o aroma de mar.

おひたし (Ohitashi)

©S.T.

Boiled Spinach with Bonito Shavings

Spinach boiled to an appetizing color is sprinkled with soy sauce flavored with soup stock and covered with a sprinkling of bonito shavings.

kcal ●

涼拌菠菜

這是一道把菠菜放入開水中燙焯後澆上佐料醬油汁，再撒上木魚片屑的簡單家常菜。

涼拌菠菜

这是一道把菠菜放入开水中烫焯后浇上佐料酱油汁，再撒上木鱼片屑的简单家常菜。

일식 시금치나물

살짝 데친 시금치에 간장 풍미의 국물을 끼얹고 얇은 가다랭이포를 얹어 먹는 심플한 반찬.

おひたし

色よくゆでたほうれん草にだしじょうゆをかけ、かつおぶしをふりかけたシンプルなお惣菜。

سبانخ مسلوقة مع مبشور السمك

تسلق السبانخ حتى تكتسب لوناً جميلاً ثم ينثر فوقها قطرات من صلصة الصويا المتبلة بالبهريز وتغطى بمبشور سمك البينيت المجفف.

Gekochter Spinat mit Bonitfisch-Flocken

Spinat wird gekocht, bis er eine appetitliche Farbe angenommen hat, und dann mit Sojasoße beträufelt, die mit Brühe gewürzt ist. Anschließend werden dünne Flocken von geraspeltem getrockneten Bonitfisch darübergestreut.

Epinards bouillis accompagnés de bonite séchée râpée

Ce plat contient des épinards, bouillis jusqu'à ce que leur couleur soit appétissante, que l'on parfume avec de la sauce de soja mélangée à un bouillon de volaille; on saupoudre ensuite le tout de bonite séchée râpée.

Espinacas Cocidas con Hojuelas de Bonito Seco

Se cuecen las espinacas hasta que adquieren un color apetitoso y se bañan con salsa de soja aderezada con caldo de extracto para después cubrirse con una pizca de hojuelas de bonito seco.

Spinaci con fiocchi di bonito essiccato

È un semplice piatto di verdura costituito da spinaci sbollentati in modo che mantengano un bel colore, conditi con un brodino al gusto di salsa di soia e cosparsi di fiocchi di bonito essiccato.

Espinafre fervido com flocos de bonito seco

Espinafre, fervido até adquirir uma coloração apetitosa, é regado a molho de soja condimentado com caldo concentrado. Salpicam-se flocos de peixe bonito seco.

ごまあえ (Goma-ae)

Vegetables in Sesame Dressing

Spinach, green beans and other vegetables lightly boiled to maintain their appealing color are mixed with a sweet dressing of ground sesame seeds for a light-tasting yet fragrant dish.

kcal ●

芝麻拌涼菜

將菠菜、四季豆等蔬菜放入開水中燙焯後，拌上磨碎的芝麻和調料而成。這道菜以清甜醇香為特色。

芝麻拌凉菜

将菠菜、四季豆等蔬菜放入开水中烫焯后，拌上磨碎的芝麻和调料而成。这道菜以清甜醇香为特色。

깨소금무침

시금치, 강낭콩 등의 야채를 살짝 데쳐서 간깨소금으로 달게 양념하여 버무린 고소한 요리.

ごまあえ

ほうれん草、いんげんなどの野菜を色よくゆで、すりつぶしたごまの甘いあえ衣をからめた香ばしい一品。

Gemüse mit Sesamsoße

Spinat, grüne Bohnen und andere Gemüsesorten werden leicht gekocht, damit sie eine ansprechende Farbe behalten und dann mit einer süßen Soße aus gemahlener Sesamsaat gemischt. Ein Gericht mit mildem aber doch würzigem Geschmack.

Légumes servis avec un assaisonnement au sésame

Ce plat au goût léger mais très parfumé se compose d'épinards, de haricots verts et d'autres légumes légèrement bouillis afin d'en conserver une couleur attirante, que l'on mélange ensuite à une sauce sucrée à base de graines de sésame.

Verduras en Salsa de Sésamo (ajonjolí)

En este platillo de sabor ligero pero fragante se cuecen ligeramente espinacas, judías verdes y otras verduras para que conserven su apetitoso color y se mezclan en una dulce salsa de semillas de sésamo (ajonjolí) molidas.

Verdura al sesamo

È un piatto dall'aroma invitante di spinaci o fagiolini sbollentati in modo che conservino un bel colore e mescolati con un condimento di semi di sesamo pestati nel mortaio e addolciti.

خضر متبلة بمحلول السمسم

تسلق السبانخ أوالفاصوليا أوغيرهما من الخضر سلقاً خفيفاً للحفاظ على لونها الجميل ثم تمزج بمحلول تتبيل حلو من السمسم لتتحصل على طبق طيب الرائحة خفيف المذاق.

Vegetais em molho de gergelim

Espinafre, vagem e outros vegetais, fervidos ligeiramente para conservar a sua coloração apetitosa, são misturados com um molho de sementes de gergelim moídas. É um prato de sabor suave, ainda que aromático.

酢のもの (Sunomono)

© S.T.

Seaweed and Cucumber Salad

This refreshing salad combines seaweed and thinly sliced cucumbers in a dressing of vinegar, sugar and soy sauce for a refreshing flavor featuring a superb balance of sweet and sour tastes.

kcal ●

醋拌涼菜

在黃瓜和裙帶菜中加入三合一的調味醋(醋、白糖、醬油各為一杯)後調味而成的，酸中帶甜、清爽可口的涼菜。

Salat aus Seetang und Gurken

Für diesen erfrischenden Salat werden Seetang (Wakame) und dünn geschnittene Gurken in einem Dressing aus Essig, Zucker und Sojasoße kombiniert. Der erfrischende Geschmack hat eine hervorragende Balance zwischen Süße und Säure.

醋拌涼菜

在黄瓜和裙带菜中加入三合一的调味醋（醋、白糖、酱油各为一杯）后调味而成的，酸中带甜、清爽可口的凉菜。

Salade d'algues et de concombres

Cette salade rafraîchissante contient des algues et des concombres coupés en fines rondelles arrosés d'un mélange de vinaigre, de sucre et de sauce de soja, ce qui lui confère un goût rafraîchissant tout en conservant un excellent équilibre entre la saveur sucrée et aigre.

초무침

오이와 미역을 식초, 설탕, 간장으로 조미하여 새콤달콤하게 무친 깔끔한 맛의 요리.

Ensalada de Algas y Pepinos

Esta refrescante ensalada combina las algas con finas rebanadas de pepino en un aderezo de vinagre, azúcar y salsa de soja que se caracteriza por una magnífico equilibrio entre el sabor avinagrado y el sabor dulce.

酢のもの

きゅうりとわかめを三杯酢（酢、砂糖、しょうゆ）で調味し、酸味と甘味をきかせたあえもの。さっぱりした味わい。

Insalata di alghe e cetrioli

Si tratta di una fresca insalata di alghe e cetrioli conditi in agrodolce con aceto, zucchero e salsa di soia.

سلطة الخيار والأعشاب البحرية

هذه السلطة المنعشة تجمع بين الأعشاب البحرية والخيار المقطع في شرائح طولية رفيعة، وتتبل بمزيج من الخل والسكر وصلصة الصويا لإعداد طبق له مذاق منعش هو خليط ممتاز من الطعم الحلو والحمضي.

Salada de algas e pepinos

Esta salada de sabor leve combina algas e pepinos em finas fatias num tempero com vinagre, açúcar e molho de soja. Apresenta um excelente equilíbrio de sabores doces e avinagrados.

漬けもの (Tsukemono)

Salt-Pickled Vegetables

Various types of vegetables are pickled in salted rice bran paste or salt. The mildly salty flavor and the crunchy texture of the vegetables make this a perfect partner for rice.

kcal ●

© S.T.

腌菜

這是把蔬菜放入米糠醬或加入鹽後腌浸而成的腌菜。其特點是鹹淡適中、爽口脆香，適合作為下飯菜。

腌菜

这是把蔬菜放入米糠酱或加入盐后腌浸而成的腌菜。其特点是咸淡适中、爽口脆香，适合作为下饭菜。

야채절임

야채 등을 쌀겨나 소금으로 절인 것. 적당한 짠맛과 깨끗한 맛이 밥반찬으로 적격이다.

漬けもの

野菜などをぬかみそや塩などで漬けたもの。ほどよい塩加減とパリッとした歯ごたえで、ご飯のおともにぴったり。

In Salz eingelegtes Gemüse

Verschiedene Gemüsesorten werden in gesalzener Reiskleie oder Salz eingelegt. Der mild salzige Geschmack und der knackige Biß machen das so zubereitete Gemüse ideal als Beilage für Reis.

Légumes marinés dans du sel

De par sa texture croustillante et son goût légèrement salé, cet assortiment de légumes constitue le partenaire idéal du riz. Il est préparé avec divers légumes marinés dans une pâte de son de riz salé ou dans du sel.

Verduras en Salmuera

Se adoban distintos tipos de verduras en sal o en una pasta de salvado salado. Su sabor ligeramente salado y su textura crujiente hacen a este platillo el acompañante ideal del arroz.

Verdure in salamoia

Verdure varie vengono messe in salamoia con sale o pasta di crusca di riso polverizzata. Per il loro gusto salato e la consistenza un po' dura si accompagnano bene con il riso in bianco.

خضر مخللة في الملح

تخلل أنواع عديدة من الخضر في الملح أو في معجون من نخالة الأرز المملحة، وتتميز الخضر هنا بقوام هش ومذاق مملح معتدل مما يجعلها مناسبة للأكل مع الأرز.

Vegetais em conserva de sal

Vários tipos de vegetais preparados em conserva, com pasta condimentícia de farelo de arroz salgada ou sal. O sabor levemente salgado e a textura crocante dos vegetais tornam este prato uma ótima companhia para o arroz.

枝豆 (Edamame)

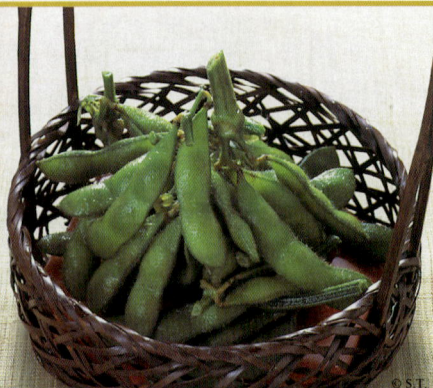

Salted Green Soybeans Boiled in the Pod

Green soybeans are boiled in saltwater while still in the pod for a snack that goes well with beer. The beans, which are rich in protein and vitamins, are enjoyed straight from the pod.

kcal ●

煮毛豆

將帶殼的毛豆煮熟灑上鹽後，是深受歡迎的啤酒下酒菜。它不僅含有豐富的蛋白質和維生素，且能使您感受從殼中擠出豆來食用的樂趣。

煮毛豆

将带壳的毛豆煮熟洒上盐后，是深受欢迎的啤酒下酒菜。它不仅含有丰富的蛋白质和维生素，且能使您感受从壳中挤出豆来食用的乐趣。

삶은 콩

풋콩을 콩깍지 채로 삶아서 소금을 뿌린 것으로 맥주 안주로 좋다. 단백질이나 비타민이 풍부한 콩의 일종으로 껍질을 까면서 먹는다.

枝豆

さや付きの豆を塩ゆでにした、ビールによく合うおつまみ。タンパク質やビタミンを多く含む豆の一種で、さやから出しながら食べる。

فول الصويا المملح المسلوق

يسلق فول الصويا الأخضر دون تقشيره في ماء مملح لإعداد طبق مناسب كمزة مع البيرة حيث تؤكل حبات الفول الغنية بالبروتين والفيتامينات بنزعها مباشرة من القشرة.

Gesalzene grüne Sojabohnenschoten

Grüne Sojabohnen, die noch in der Schote sind, werden in Salzwasser gekocht und ergeben einen Imbiß, der gut zum Bier paßt. Die Bohnen sind reich an Protein und Vitaminen und werden direkt aus der Schote in den Mund gedrückt und gegessen.

Haricots de soja vert salés bouillis avec leurs cosses

Cet en-cas qui s'harmonise bien avec la bière est composé de haricots de soja vert non écossés bouillis dans de l'eau salée. Les haricots de soja, riches en protéines et en vitamines, se dégustent directement à partir des cosses.

Frijoles de Soja Verdes en Vaina Cocidos en Agua Salada

Este entremés, que se lleva bien con la cerveza, se prepara cociendo en agua salada los frijoles de soja verdes dentro de su vaina. Estos frijoles, ricos en vitaminas y proteínas, se comen directamente de la vaina.

Fagioli verdi di soia

I fagioli di soia verdi, bolliti in acqua salata ancora nei loro baccelli, si accompagnano bene con la birra. Sono ricchi di proteine e vitamine e si mangiano estraendoli dal baccello.

Feijão-soja verde fervido, na vagem

Grãos de feijão-soja verdes ainda na vagem são fervidos com sal. É um excelente petisco para acompanhar a cerveja. Ricos em proteínas e vitaminas, os feijões são saboreados apertando-se as vagens com os dedos.

冷や奴 (Hiyayakko)

Chilled Tofu

This simple summer favorite consists of chilling a block of tofu and seasoning with soy sauce on top along with ginger, green onions and other favorite toppings.

© S.T.

kcal ●

涼拌豆腐

在經過冷卻的豆腐上，撒上姜、蔥等佐料並澆上醬油後做出的一道簡單的菜肴。它已成了日本夏天必喫的菜。

Gekühlter Tofu

Dieses einfache Gericht ist insbesondere im Sommer beliebt. Es besteht aus einem gut gekühlten Tofu-Block (Sojabohnenquark), der mit Sojasoße und Ingwer, grünen Zwiebeln und anderen Zutaten gewürzt wird.

涼拌豆腐

在经过冷却的豆腐上，撒上姜、葱等佐料并浇上酱油后做出的一道简单的菜肴。它已成了日本夏天必吃的菜。

Tofu froid

Ce plat, très apprécié en été, se prépare en faisant refroidir un bloc de tofu puis en l'aromatisant d'une sauce de soja, de gingembre, de poireau et d'autres aromates favoris.

냉두부

차게 해 둔 두부에 생강, 파 등을 얹고 간장을 끼얹어 먹는 심플한 요리. 일본의 대표적인 여름 반찬.

Tofu Helado (Queso de Soja)

Este sencillo plato del verano consiste de un bloque de tofu cortado en forma de cubo rodeado de hielo. Se remoja la parte superior con la salsa de soja al colocar un poco de jengibre rallado, cebollas verdes y otros ingredientes al gusto personal. Es un plato de acompañamiento popular de Japón, principalmente en verano.

冷や奴

よく冷やした豆腐にしょうが、ねぎなどの薬味をのせ、しょうゆをかけて食べるシンプルな一品。日本の夏のおかずの定番。

Tofu freddo

È un semplice piatto prettamente estivo di tofu freddo insaporito con salsa di soia, zenzero e porro.

التوفو البارد

هذا الطبق المفضل في الصيف يتكون من قطعة باردة من التوفو تتبل بصلصة الصويا التي تنثر فوقها مع الزنجبيل والبصل الأخضر وغيرهما من المتبلات المحببة.

Queijo de soja gelado

Esta simples iguaria de verão é um bloco de tofu gelado, regado com molho de soja e salpicado com gengibre, cebolinha e outros condimentos preferidos.

揚げだし豆腐 (Agedashi-dōfu)

©S.T

Deep-Fried Tofu

This popular tofu dish is prepared by deep-frying tofu to a golden brown, sprinkling on various condiments and then pouring a warm sauce over the tofu.

kcal ●

油炸豆腐

在炸成色澤金黃的豆腐上放上許多佐料並澆上熱湯。這是一道受人歡迎的菜肴。

Fritierter Tofu

Für dieses populäre Tofu-Gericht wird Tofu (Sojabohnenquark) goldbraun in Öl ausgebacken, mit verschiedenen Zutaten gewürzt und dann mit einer warmen Soße übergossen.

油炸豆腐

在炸成色泽金黄的豆腐上放上许多佐料并浇上热汤。这是一道受人欢迎的菜肴。

Tofu frit

Ce plat populaire à base de tofu se prépare en faisant frire du tofu, en l'assaisonnant de divers condiments et en l'arrosant d'une sauce chaude.

튀김두부

노릇노릇하게 튀긴 두부에 양념을 얹고 뜨거운 국물을 끼얹은 인기있는 두부요리.

Tofu Frito en Aceite

Este popular platillo de tofu se prepara friendo el tofu en bastante aceite hasta que alcanza un color dorado. Una vez frito, se adereza con varios condimentos y se reboza con una salsa caliente.

揚げだし豆腐

きつね色に揚げた豆腐に薬味をたっぷりのせ、熱いつゆをかけた人気の豆腐料理。

Tofu fritto

Per questo piatto popolare il tofu viene fritto in abbondante olio fino a farlo diventare dorato, quindi cosparso di vari gusti e irrorato di un apposito brodino.

التوفو المقلي

هذا الطبق المحبوب من التوفو يصنع بقلي قطع التوفو حتى تكتسب لونا ذهبيا غامقا ثم تنثر فوقها التوابل المختلفة وبعد ذلك تسكب عليها الصلصة الدافئة.

Queijo de soja frito por mergulho em óleo

Prepara-se este prato popular fritando o queijo de soja por mergulho em óleo até dourar. Salpicam-se vários condimentos e em seguida rega-se com um molho aquecido.

豆腐ステーキ (Tōfu Sutēki)

Pan-Fried Tofu

This dish features tofu- known to be rich in high-quality protein- fried in oil in the same manner as steak for a healthy dish which is low in calories while featuring the aromatic fragrance of soy sauce.

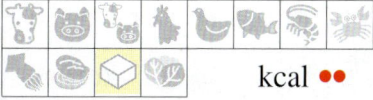

© S.T.

kcal ●●

油煎豆腐

這是一道用油將富含優良蛋白質的豆腐,以烤牛肉的方式煎烤而成的菜肴。它具有醬油香味,熱量低,是一種健康性食品。

In der Pfanne gebratener Tofu

Bei diesem Gericht wird Tofu (Sojabohnenquark), der für seinen hohen Proteingehalt bekannt ist, wie ein Steak in Öl gebraten. Dieses gesunde Gericht hat wenig Kalorien und wird durch den aromatischen Geschmack der Sojasoße charakterisiert.

油煎豆腐

这是一道用油将富含优良蛋白质的豆腐,以烤牛肉的方式煎烤而成的菜肴。它具有酱油香味,热量低,是一种健康性食品。

Steak de tofu

Ce plat sain, pauvre en calories, est constitué de tofu (connu pour sa haute teneur en protéines essentielles), que l'on fait frire dans l'huile de la même manière qu'un steak et que l'on agrémente d'une sauce de soja aromatique.

두부스테이크

양질의 단백질을 많이 포함하고 있는 두부를 스테이크처럼 기름에 구운 요리. 간장 향기가 구수하며 헬시한 저칼로리 요리.

Tofu Frito en Sartén

Este saludable platillo de fragante aroma a salsa de soja se caracteriza por el tofu frito en aceite al igual que un bistec. El tofu es famoso por ser rico en proteínas de gran calidad y bajo en calorías.

豆腐ステーキ

良質のタンパク質を多く含む豆腐を、ステーキ風に油で焼いたもの。しょうゆの香りが香ばしく、低カロリーでヘルシー。

Bistecca di tofu

Il tofu, cibo ricco di proteine nobili e povero di calorie, viene cotto come una bistecca. È un piatto sano dal profumo di salsa di soia.

توفو محمر في المقلاة

يحتوي هذا الطبق على التوفو-المعروف بغناه بالبروتينات- وهنا يحمر في الزيت تماماً مثل البفتيك لإعداد طبق صحي منخفض السعرات يتميز بالرائحة الطيبة لصلصة الصويا.

Queijo de soja frito

Este prato consiste em queijo de soja - conhecido por ser rico em proteína de alta qualidade - frito em óleo, como um bife. É uma iguaria saudável com baixo nível de calorias, que apresenta a fragrância aromática do molho de soja.

だし巻き卵 (Dashi-maki Tamago)

Japanese Style Omelet

This delicate dish is prepared by first combining eggs with a small amount of soup stock, dividing the mixture into several portions, and then frying thin layers one at a time, gradually rolling them up to form a kind of rolled omelet, which is served sliced up.

kcal ●

湯汁蛋卷

將拌入調味料的雞蛋打勻，分幾次倒入煎鍋，鋪展，卷起。卷成的層層相疊的蛋卷，柔然蓬松，口感鮮美。

Japanisches Omelett

Für dieses delikate Gericht werden zunächst Eier mit etwas Brühe vermischt, dann das Gemisch in mehrere Portionen geteilt und anschließend in dünnen Lagen einzeln gebraten. Diese werden dann vorsichtig aufgerollt und ergeben eine Art Omelettrolle, die in Scheiben geschnitten serviert wird.

汤汁蛋卷

将拌入调味料的鸡蛋打勻，分几次倒入煎锅，铺展，卷起。卷成的层层相叠的蛋卷，柔然蓬松，口感鲜美。

Omelette à la japonaise

Ce mets délicat se prépare en incorporant d'abord des œufs dans un peu de bouillon de volaille et en séparant le mélange en petites portions que l'on fait revenir en fines couches une par une. On les enroule ensuite petit à petit afin de constituer une omelette roulée que l'on sert coupée en tranches.

달걀부침

달걀에 맛국물을 넣고 풀어 여러 차례에 나누어 프라이팬에 부어가면서 모양좋게 말아 놓은 요리. 부드러운 맛.

Tortilla de Huevo al Estilo Japonés

Este delicado platillo se prepara combinando huevos batidos con una pequeña cantidad de caldo de extracto; se vierte la mezcla de huevos batidos dividiendo en varias porciones y se fríe en capas delgadas una tras otra, enrollándolas gradualmente hasta formar una especie de tortilla enrollada que se sirve cortada en rebanadas.

だし巻き卵

だし汁入りの卵液を数回に分けてフライパンに流し入れ、くるくる巻いて形よく焼き上げる。フワッとした食感。

Omelette alla giapponese

Un composto di uova e brodino viene versato in padella a più riprese e cotto avvolgendolo in modo da formare un soffice rotolo che si serve affettato.

اومليت على الطريقة اليابانية

لإعداد هذا الطبق الشهي يمزج البيض أولاً مع كمية صغيرة من الهبرة وبقسم المزيج إلى عدة كميات، ثم تقلى الواحدة وراء الأخرى مع لفها تدريجياً لتكوين نوع من الأومليت الملفوف، ويقدم بعد تقطيعه إلى شرائح اسطوانية.

Omelete ao estilo japonês

Para o preparo desta refinada iguaria, juntam-se primeiramente ovos a uma pequena quantidade de caldo concentrado. Divide-se a mistura em várias porções à medida em que são fritas em finas camadas, uma de cada vez, enrolando-as gradualmente para dar forma à omelete, que é servida fatiada.

茶碗蒸し (Chawan-mushi)

Savory Egg Custard

Various ingredients are mixed into eggs thinned with soup stock followed by steaming. The smooth texture of the savory custard blends perfectly with the flavor of the ingredients.

© S.T

kcal ●

蒸雞蛋羹

這是用調味湯汁打勻的雞蛋中放入多種配料後蒸熟的一種菜肴。配料的各色鮮味充分溶於細膩滑溜的蛋羹中，使其風味無窮。

蒸鸡蛋羹

这是在用调味汤汁打勻的鸡蛋中放入多种配料后蒸熟的一种菜肴。配料的各色鲜味充分溶于细腻滑溜的蛋羹中，使其风味无穷。

달걀찜

맛국물로 푼 달걀에 여러 가지 재료를 넣고 찐 요리. 부드러운 달걀 속에 재료의 맛이 살아있다.

茶碗蒸し

だし汁で溶いた卵液の中に、さまざまな具を入れて蒸したもの。なめらかな舌ざわりの卵液の中に、具のうまみが溶け込んでいる。

بودنج البيض المملح

تمزج المقادير المختلفة مع البيض المخفف بالبهريز ثم تطهى على البخار، هنا نجد الملمس الناعم للبودنج يتجانس تماماً مع نكهة المكونات الأخرى بتعدد أنواعها.

Pikanter Eierstich mit Einlage

Verschiedene Zutaten werden mit Ei verrührt, das mit Brühe verdünnt ist. Anschließend wird die Mischung im Dampfbad gestockt. Der weiche Biß des Eierstichs paßt perfekt zum Geschmack der einzelnen Zutaten.

Crème onctueuse aux œufs

Après avoir mélangé divers ingrédients à des œufs délayés dans un bouillon de bonite, on fait cuire le tout à la vapeur. La texture lisse de cette savoureuse crème se mélange parfaitement à la saveur de tous les ingrédients.

Flan de Huevo Aderezado

El huevo adelgazado con caldo de extracto se mezcla con diversos ingredientes y se cuece al vapor. La suave textura del apetitoso flan hace una perfecta combinación con el sabor de los ingredientes.

Budino salato in tazza

È un composto di uova, brodino e ingredienti vari versato in tazza e cotto a bagnomaria. Ha la consistenza di un budino, ma non è dolce e il sapore degli ingredienti si fonde con l'uovo.

Creme de ovos suculento

Vários ingredientes são misturados com ovos diluídos em sopa de concentrado e em seguida cozidos em vapor. A consistência leve do creme suculento mescla-se perfeitamente com o sabor dos ingredientes.

みそ汁 (Miso-shiru)

Miso Soup

This soup is prepared by dissolving miso, Japan's original seasoning, in soup stock, then adding tofu, seaweed and other ingredients. Make sure to enjoy it with rice.

kcal ●

日本式醬湯

這是將日本特有的調味醬溶入湯汁中，並加放豆腐和裙帶菜等做成的一種適合與米飯一起食用的湯。

Miso-Suppe

Zur Zubereitung dieser Suppe löst man Miso, das typische japanische Gewürz aus fermentierten Sojabohnen, in Brühe auf, und fügt dann Tofu (Sojabohnenquark), Seetang (Wakame) und andere Zutaten hinzu. Genießen Sie diese Suppe unbedingt mit Reis.

日本式酱汤

这是将日本特有的调味酱溶入汤汁中，并加放豆腐和裙带菜等做成的一种适合与米饭一起食用的汤。

Soupe de miso

Cette soupe se prépare en délayant du miso - un condiment originaire du Japon - dans un bouillon de volaille, auquel on ajoute du tofu, des algues et d'autres ingrédients. Elle se déguste de préférence avec du riz.

된장국

일본된장을 맛국물에 풀어서 두부나 미역 등을 넣어 끓인 국. 밥과 함께 먹는다.

Sopa de Miso

Esta sopa se prepara disolviendo la masa de soja (miso), un condimento original de Japón, en caldo de extracto y agregando tofu, algas y otros ingredientes. Le recomendamos que lo saboree con arroz.

みそ汁

日本独特の調味料のみそをだし汁に溶かし、豆腐やわかめなどを加えた汁もの。ご飯と一緒に。

Minestra di miso

Il miso, un particolare ingrediente della cucina giapponese, viene fatto fondere in un brodino e, con l'aggiunta di tofu, alghe wakame e altri ingredienti, costituisce una minestra che viene servita con il riso in bianco.

حساء الميسو

يعد هذا الحساء بإذابة الميسو-وهي مادة تتبيبل من فول الصويا-في خلاصة الحساء ثم يضاف إليه التوفو والأعشاب البحرية وغيرها. إحرص على تناول هذا الحساء مع الأرز.

Sopa de miso

Prepara-se esta sopa dissolvendo a pasta miso, condimento típico japonês, em caldo concentrado. Adicionam-se então tofu, algas e outros ingredientes. Serve-se acompanhada de arroz.

すまし汁 (Sumashi-jiru)

Clear Soup

This is a light-tasting soup flavored with soy sauce and a small amount of salt in a soup stock made from bonito and kelp, and is known for its transparent appearance.

© S.T.

kcal ●

清湯

這是在用木魚和海帶熬成的湯汁中放進醬油、鹽等制成的湯汁。其特點是湯液清徹，透明碧純。

Klare Suppe

Dies ist eine leichte Suppe, die mit einer Brühe aus Bonitfisch und Seetang gekocht und mit Sojasoße und etwas Salz abgeschmeckt wird. Diese Suppe ist für ihr durchsichtiges Aussehen bekannt.

清汤

这是在用木鱼和海带熬成的汤汁中放进酱油、盐等制成的汤汁。其特点是汤液清彻，透明碧纯。

Soupe claire

Cette soupe au goût léger, célèbre pour sa transparence, parfumée à la sauce de soja et contenant un peu de sel, est préparée à partir d'un bouillon à base de bonite et de varech.

맑은 국

얇은 가다랭이포와 다시마로 맛을 낸 국물에 간장이나 소금 등으로 담백하게 간을 한 국. 맑은 국물이 특징.

Sopa Clara

Es una sopa de sabor ligero que se condimenta con salsa de soja y una pizca de sal en caldo de extracto de bonito y algas marinas. Es famosa por su apariencia transparente.

すまし汁

かつおぶしと昆布からとっただし汁を、しょうゆ、塩などであっさりと調味した汁もの。汁ににごりがなく、透き通っているのが特徴。

Consommé alla giapponese

È un brodino preparato con fiocchi di bonito essiccato e alghe kombu, insaporito con salsa di soia, sale e altro. Una sua caratteristica è la limpidezza.

الحساء الشفاف

هذا حساء ، خفيف المذاق يتبل بإضافة صلصة الصويا وقليل من الملح إلى بهريز من سمك البينيت والعشب البحري ويعرف بلونه الشفاف.

Sopa clara

Esta é uma sopa de sabor leve, condimentada com molho de soja e uma pitada de sal em um caldo preparado com peixe bonito e alga. É conhecida por sua aparência transparente.

豚汁 (Ton-jiru)

Pork and Vegetable Miso Soup

Ample amounts of pork and other ingredients such as root vegetables are contained in this miso soup in which the flavor of the pork blends in perfectly with the soup.

kcal ●●

豬肉醬湯

這是一道用豬肉和許多根菜類等配料烹飪而成的醬味湯。湯內豬肉的香味四溢，鮮美可口。

Miso-Suppe mit Schweinefleisch und Gemüse

Diese Miso-Suppe enthält reichlich Schweinefleisch und andere Zutaten, wie z.B. Wurzelgemüse. Der volle Geschmack des Schweinefleischs paßt perfekt zu dieser Suppe.

猪肉酱汤

这是一道用猪肉和许多根菜类等配料烹饪而成的酱味汤。汤内猪肉的香味四溢，鲜美可口。

Soupe de miso au porc et aux légumes

Cette soupe de miso contient de grandes quantités de porc, dont l'arôme se confond parfaitement à la soupe, et d'autres ingrédients tels que des racines.

돼지고기국

돼지고기와 근채류 등의 재료가 푸짐하게 들어있는 볼륨있는 된장국. 돼지고기 맛이 국물에 우러나와 맛있다.

Sopa de Miso con Carne de Cerdo y Verduras

Esta sopa de miso contiene generosas porciones de carne de cerdo y otros ingredientes entre los que se encuentran los tubérculos. El sabor del cerdo combina a la perfección con la sopa.

豚汁

豚肉と根菜などの具がたっぷり入った、ボリュームのあるみそ味の汁もの。豚肉のうまみが汁に溶け込んでおいしい。

Minestra di miso e maiale

È una minestra al gusto di miso che riempie lo stomaco per il suo contenuto di carne di maiale, radici varie e altri ingredienti. Il brodo è particolarmente insaporito dalla carne di maiale.

حساء ميسو مع اللحم والخضر

يحتوي هذا الحساء من الميسو (مادة تتبيل من فول الصويا) على كمية وفيرة من لحم الخنزير والمقادير الأخرى مثل الجذور من الخضر، وفيه يندمج طعم اللحم في انسجام تام مع مذاق الحساء.

Sopa de miso com porco e vegetais

Esta rica sopa de miso contém, em quantidade generosa, carne de porco e outros ingredientes, entre os quais raízes comestíveis. O sabor da carne de porco forma uma combinação perfeita com a própria sopa.

けんちん汁 (Kenchin-jiru)

Vegetable Chowder

This soy sauce-flavored soup is brimming with root vegetables, tofu and numerous other ingredients. The ingredients are stir-fried in sesame oil before being placed in the soup for a rich and aromatic taste that accents the flavor of the soup.

kcal ●●

© S.T.

（日式）雜燴湯

這是以醬油為主要調味、湯內含有大量根菜類和豆腐配料的菜肴。由於配料是經過麻油煸炒後放入的，因而香氣撲鼻，誘人食欲。

Dicke Gemüsesuppe

Diese mit Sojasoße gewürzte Suppe ist vollgepackt mit Wurzelgemüse, Tofu (Sojabohnenquark) und zahlreichen anderen Zutaten. Ehe die Zutaten in die Suppe gegeben werden, werden sie in Sesamöl angebraten, und der volle und aromatische Geschmackt akzentuiert das Aroma der Suppe.

（日式）杂烩汤

这是以酱油为主要调味、汤内含有大量根菜类和豆腐配料的菜肴。由于配料是经过麻油煸炒后放入的，因而香气扑鼻，诱人食欲。

Potée de légumes

Cette soupe parfumée à la sauce de soja est garnie de racines, de tofu et de nombreux autres ingrédients que l'on fait revenir dans de l'huile de sésame avant de les incorporer à la soupe afin d'obtenir un goût riche et aromatique qui relève la saveur de la soupe.

일식 두부국

근채류와 두부를 넣고 간장으로 간을 한 국. 재료를 참기름에 볶아서 끓이므로 국물이 고소하다.

Guisado de Verduras

Esta sopa con sabor a soja tiene abundantes tubérculos, tofu y otros ingredientes. Antes de guisarlos en el caldo, los ingredientes son salteados en aceite de sésamo (ajonjolí) hasta que adquieren un sabor aromático que acentúa el sabor de la sopa.

けんちん汁

根菜類と豆腐が入った、具だくさんのしょうゆ味の汁もの。材料をごま油で炒めるので、コクと香りが豊か。

Minestra di verdura

Questa minestra dal gusto di salsa di soia viene preparata con vari tipi di radici, tofu e numerosi altri ingredienti precedentemente saltati in padella con olio di sesamo. Ha un ricco sapore e un buon profumo.

حساء الخضر

هذا الحساء، بنكهة صلصة الصويا يمتلي، بالخضروات والتوفو والعديد من المكونات الأخرى، وتحمر جميع المقادير أولاً في زيت السمسم ثم توضع في الحساء، لتكسبه طعماً مميزاً بنكهتها القوية اللذيذة.

Ensopado de vegetais

Esta sopa, condimentada com molho de soja, é repleta de raízes comestíveis, queijo de soja e vários outros ingredientes. Antes de sua adição, os ingredientes são refogados ligeiramente com óleo de gergelim, para adquirir um aroma suculento e aromático que realça o sabor da sopa.

ちらし寿司 (Chirashi-zushi)

©S.T.

Mixed Sushi

This famous dish is prepared by attractively arranging fresh pieces of raw fish, shellfish and flavored vegetables on a bed of vinegared rice to create a dish that is pleasing to both the eye and palate.

kcal ●●●

拼盆壽司

在壽司飯上排上各種調好味的蔬菜及生魚貝類，即美觀又豐盛味鮮。

Gemischtes Sushi

Bei diesem berühmten Gericht werden frische rohe, Fischstücke, Muscheln und zum Teilgewürztes Gemüse attraktiv auf einem Bett aus gesäuertem Reis angeordnet und ergeben ein Gericht, das nicht nur den Gaumen sondern auch das Auge erfreut.

拼盆寿司

在寿司饭上排上各种调好味的蔬菜及生鱼贝类，即美观又丰盛味鲜。

Sushi décoré

Ce plat célèbre se prépare en disposant de façon attrayante des morceaux frais de poisson cru, des crustacés et des légumes aromatisés sur un lit de riz vinaigré, afin d'obtenir un mets qui enchante à la fois les yeux et le palais.

일식 회덮밥

초밥 위에 각각 맛을 낸 야채와 생선회를 보기좋게 덮어 놓은 보기에도 먹음직스런 요리.

Sushi mixto

Este famoso platillo apetitoso para la vista y el paladar se prepara colocando en forma atractiva frescos cortes de pescado crudo, mariscos y verduras sobre raciones de arroz avinagrado.

ちらし寿司

すし飯の上にそれぞれ味付けした野菜や生の魚介類をきれいに盛り付けた、見た目に美しく味わい豊かな寿司。

Insalata di riso alla giapponese

La base è il "riso per sushi" di gusto agrodolce, al quale sono aggiunti, con bella decorazione, vari ingredienti, quali verdure cotte e condite a parte e frutti di mare crudi. È un piatto gustoso che soddisfa sia la vista che il palato.

تشكيلة متبلة فوق ارز السوشي

يتم إعداد هذا الطبق الشهير بوضع قطع طازجة من السمك النيّ، والمحار والخضر المتبلة في تنسيق جميل فوق قاعدة من الأرز بالخل للحصول على صنف شهي جميل الشكل.

Sushi misto

Prepara-se este prato famoso dispondo-se de modo atraente fatias de peixe e frutos do mar crus ou frescos, e vegetais condimentados sobre uma porção de arroz avinagrado. É um prato que agrada tanto aos olhos quanto ao paladar.

にぎり寿司 (Nigiri-zushi)

Sushi

Fresh fish and seafood are placed on vinegared rice which is carefully shaped by hand into bite-sized pieces. This Japanese delicacy skillfully combines the flavor of the ingredients with the appeal of flavored rice.

kcal ●●

© S.T.

壽司

在捏成一口大的飯團上放上新鮮的生魚貝類。這是即充分突出生魚貝類的鮮美味、又不失米飯獨特風味的、唯日本獨有的一道菜肴。

Sushi

Frischer Fisch und Seefrüchte werden auf gesäuerten Reis gelegt, der sorgfältig mit der Hand zu mundgerechte Stücke geformt wurde. Diese berühmte japanische Delikatesse kombiniert aufs Feinste den Eigengeschmack der Zutaten mit dem Aroma des gesäuerten Reis.

寿司

在捏成一口大的饭团上放上新鲜的生鱼贝类。这是即充分突出生鱼贝类的鲜美味、又不失米饭独特风味的、唯日本独有的一道菜肴。

Sushi

On dispose du poisson frais et des fruits de mer sur du riz vinaigré que l'on façonne en bouchées avec la main. Ce mets japonais raffiné combine harmonieusement la délicieuse saveur des ingrédients avec le goût attrayant du riz aromatisé.

초밥

한입 크기의 초밥 위에 신선한 어패류를 얹은 것. 어패류와 초밥의 맛이 잘 어울리는 일본만의 요리.

Sushi

Se coloca pescado fresco y mariscos sobre arroz avinagrado cuidadosamente moldeado a mano en raciones del tamaño de un bocado. Este manjar japonés combina a la perfección el sabor de los ingredientes y la atractiva apariencia del arroz aderezado.

にぎり寿司

ひと口大に握ったすし飯の上に、新鮮な生の魚介類をのせたもの。魚介の味とご飯のうまみを生かした日本ならではの料理。

Sushi

Su gnocchetti di "riso per sushi", preparati comprimendo il riso nella mano, si appoggiano fettine di pesce crudo e frutti di mare freschissimi o altri ingredienti. Sono una prelibatezza unica della cucina giapponese, che valorizza al massimo i sapori dei frutti di mare e del riso.

السوشي

توضع وحدات طازجة نيئة من السمك والكائنات البحرية فوق أرز متبل بالخل ومشكل يدوياً في حجم القضمة الواحدة. هذا الطبق الياباني يجمع في مهارة بين مذاق الأرز بالخل ونكهة الطعام الموضوع فوقه.

Sushi

Peixe fresco e frutos do mar são dispostos sobre bolinhos de arroz avinagrado, cuidadosamente preparados à mão, no tamanho ideal para levar à boca. Esta iguaria japonesa combina de maneira habilidosa o sabor dos ingredientes com o aroma do arroz condimentado.

Akami

赤身

- **Red tuna**
- 紅色生魚片
- 红色生鱼片
- 참치
- 赤身
- لحم تونة غامق
- Mageres rotes Thunfischfleisch
- Thon rouge
- Carne de atún rojo
- Tonno magro
- Atum vermelho

Chūtoro

中トロ

- **Fatty tuna**
- 金槍魚中段
- 金枪鱼中段
- 중도로(참치의 지방이 적당히 있는 부분)
- 中トロ
- لحم تونة فاتح قليلاً
- Fettes Thunfischfleisch
- Thon gras
- Carne de atún grasoso
- Tonno semimagro
- Atum gordo

Ōtoro

大トロ

- **Very fatty tuna**
- 金槍魚大段
- 金枪鱼大段
- 대도로(참치의 지방이 많은 부분)
- 大トロ
- لحم تونة فاتح
- Sehr fettes Thunfischfleisch
- Thon très gras
- Carne de atún super grasoso
- Tonno grasso
- Atum muito gordo

Tai

たい

- **Sea bream**
- 加級魚
- 加级鱼
- 도미
- たい
- أسبور
- Seebrasse
- Brème de mer
- Besugo
- Dentice
- Pargo

Kampachi

かんぱち

- **Yellowtail**
- 間八魚(鱸魚目)
- 间八鱼(鲈鱼目)
- 방어
- かんぱち
- أصفر الذيل
- Gelbschwanz
- Sériole
- Casabe
- Seriola
- Olho-de-boi

Hirame

ひらめ

- **Flounder**
- 比目魚
- 比目鱼
- 넙치
- ひらめ
- مقلطم
- Flunder
- Flet
- Lenguado
- Rombo
- Linguado

Sake

さけ

• **Salmon**

大馬哈魚	• Lachs
大马哈鱼	• Saumon
연어	• Salmón
さけ	• Salmone
سلمون	• Salmão

Saba

さば

• **Mackerel**

鲐魚	• Makrele
鲐鱼	• Maquereau
고등어	• Caballa
さば	• Sgombro
أسقمري	• Cavala

Kohada

こはだ

• **Gizzard shad**

斑鰶魚	• Junger Maifisch
斑鰶鱼	• Gésier d'alose
전어	• Sábalo
こはだ	• Alosa
شابل	• Espécie de savelha

Aji

あじ

• **Horse mackerel**

鯵科魚	• Roßmakrele
鯵科鱼	• Chinechard
전갱이	• Jurel
あじ	• Sorello
تن	• Cavala-do-japão

Anago

穴子

• **Sea eel**

星鰻	• Seeaal
星鳗	• Anguille de mer
아나고 (붕장어)	• Anguila marina
穴子	• Grongo
ثعبان البحر	• Congro

Tamago

卵

• **Egg omelet**

煎雞蛋	• Omelett
煎鸡蛋	• Omelette aux œufs
달갈	• Tortilla de huevo
卵	• Omelette
بيض الدجاج	• Omelete

Ika　いか

- **Squid**
- 烏賊　　　　・ Tintenfisch
- 乌贼　　　　・ Calmar
- 오징어　　　・ Calamar
- いか　　　　・ Seppia
- سيط　　　　・ Lula

Tako　たこ

- **Octopus**
- 章魚　　　　・ Oktopus
- 章鱼　　　　・ Pieuvre
- 문어　　　　・ Pulpo
- たこ　　　　・ Polipo
- أخطبوط　　　・ Polvo

Ebi　えび

- **Boiled shrimp**
- 蝦　　　　　・ Gekochte Garnelen
- 虾　　　　　・ Crevette bouillie
- 새우　　　　・ Langostino cocido
- えび　　　　・ Gamberetti lessati
- جمبري مسلوق　・ Camarão fervido

Amaebi　甘えび

- **Raw shrimp**
- 紅蝦　　　　・ Rohe junge Garnelen
- 红虾　　　　・ Crevette crue
- 생새우　　　・ Langostino crudo
- 甘えび　　　・ Gamberetti crudi
- جمبري نيء　　・ Camarão cru

Kani　かに

- **Crab**
- 螃蟹　　　　・ Krebsfleisch
- 螃蟹　　　　・ Crabe
- 게　　　　　・ Cangrejo
- かに　　　　・ Granchio
- كابوريا　　　・ Caranguejo

Shako　しゃこ

- **Mantis shrimp**
- 蝦蛄　　　　・ Heuschreckenkrebs
- 虾蛄　　　　・ Crevette mante
- 가재　　　　・ Esquila
- しゃこ　　　・ Canocchie
- جمبري قريدس　・ Tamaru

Hokki-gai

ほっき貝

- **Surf clam**
- 姥蛤
- 姥蛤
- 함박조개
- ほっき貝
- محار الشاطيء

- Hocki-Muschel
- Palourde
- Almeja marina
- Spisula di Sakhalin
- Espécie de marisco

Hotate-gai

ほたて貝

- **Scallop**
- 扇貝
- 扇贝
- 가리비
- ほたて貝
- محار أسقلوب

- Jakobsmuschel
- Coquille Saint Jacques
- Escalope
- Capesante
- Concha de vieira

Aka-gai

赤貝

- **Red clam**
- 魁蛤
- 魁蛤
- 새고막조개
- 赤貝
- محار أحمر

- Archenmuschel
- Palourde rouge
- Berberecho
- Cuore di mare
- Amêijoa

Aoyagi

あおやぎ

- **Round clam**
- 馬珂肉
- 马珂肉
- 개량조개
- あおやぎ
- محار مستدير

- Aojagi-Muscheln
- Palourde ronde
- Carne de almeja marina
- Aoyaghi
- Concha aoyagi

Ikura

いくら

- **Salmon roe**
- 大馬哈魚子
- 大马哈鱼子
- 연어알
- いくら
- بيض السلمون

- Lachsrogen
- Œufs de saumon
- Huevas de salmón
- Uova di salmone lavorate
- Ovas de salmão

Uni

うに

- **Sea urchin**
- 海膽
- 海胆
- 성게알
- うに
- محار الرتسة

- Seeigel
- Oursin de mer
- Erizo marino
- Riccio di mare
- Ouriço-do-mar

太巻き寿司 (Futo-maki-zushi)

Thick Sushi Rolls

Various ingredients, including sliced omelet and flavored vegetables, are rolled together with vinegared rice in seaweed for a voluminous treat.

kcal ●●

粗卷壽司

將拌好糖、醋、酒的米飯攤在紫菜上，中間放上煎雞蛋、調好味道的蔬菜等各種配料作芯、卷成的一種壽司飯。

Dicke Sushi-Rollen

Gesäuerter Reis wird auf einer Matte aus getrocknetem Seetang (Nori) verteilt, verschiedene Zutaten, einschließlich kleingeschnittenem Omelett und gewürztem Gemüse, auf den Reis gelegt und dann zu einer Rolle aufgewickelt. Etwas zum satt essen.

粗卷寿司

将拌好糖、醋、酒的米饭摊在紫菜上，中间放上煎鸡蛋、调好味道的蔬菜等各种配料作芯、卷成的一种寿司饭。

Sushi en rouleaux épais

Divers ingrédients tels que de l'omelette coupée en lamelles et des légumes aromatisés sont enroulés ensemble dans du riz vinaigré puis enrobés d'une algue séchée, le tout formant une volumineuse friandise.

굵은 김초밥

김에 초밥을 얇게 편 후 달걀 부침이나 간을 한 야채 등의 재료를 얹어 말은 것.

Rollos de Sushi Gruesos

Para preparar este rico y voluminoso manjar se utilizan hojas de alga marina en las que se envuelve arroz avinagrado junto con diversos ingredientes, tales como rebanadas de tortilla y verduras condimentadas.

太巻き寿司

のりの上にすし飯をのせ、卵焼きや味付けした野菜など、数種類の具を芯にして巻いた寿司。

Sushi in rotolo grosso

Questo piatto viene preparato stendendo del riso su un foglio di alghe essiccate nori, mettendovi al centro strisce di omelette, di verdure e di altri ingredienti conditi e arrotolando il tutto.

ملفوف السوشي السميك

يوضع الأرز بالخل مع مقادير أخرى من بينها الأومليت وبعض الخضر المتبلة فوق ورقة من عشب البحر، ويلف بها ليكون أسطوانة كبيرة لذيذة الطعم.

Rolos grossos de sushi

Vários ingredientes, incluindo fatias de omelete e vegetais condimentados sobre arroz avinagrado, são enrolados em alga marinha, formando uma volumosa delícia.

細巻き寿司 (Hoso-maki-zushi)

Thin Sushi Rolls

These smaller versions of the larger sushi rolls contain only one or two of your favorite ingredients such as cucumber and dried gourd shavings. They are prepared in the same way by rolling up vinegared rice in seaweed.

© S.T.

kcal ●

細巻壽司

將拌好糖、醋、酒的米飯攤在紫菜上，中間放上黃瓜或葫蘆條等作芯，卷成細型的另一種壽司飯。它與粗卷壽司不同，做芯的材料只有一種或兩種。

细巻寿司

将拌好糖、醋、酒的米饭摊在紫菜上，中间放上黄瓜或葫芦条等作芯，卷成细型的另一种寿司饭。它与粗卷寿司不同，做芯的材料只有一种或两种。

가는 김초밥

김에 초밥을 얇게 펴고 오이, 박고지 등의 재료를 넣고 가늘게 말은 것. 굵은 김초밥과의 차이는 재료를 1종류 또는 2종류만을 사용한다는 것.

細巻き寿司

のりの上にすし飯をのせ、きゅうり、かんぴょうなどを芯にして巻いた細めの寿司。太巻き寿司と違い、具は1種類か2種類だけ。

ملفوف السوشي الرفيع

هو صورة مصغرة من ملفوف السوشي السميك لكنه يحتوي على صنف واحد أو صنفين فقط من اختيارك مثل الخيار أو الكامبيو (نوع من القرع)، ويتم إعداده أيضا بلف هذه المقادير مع الأرز المتبل بالخل في ورقة من عشب البحر.

Dünne Sushi-Rollen

Diese kleinere Version der großen Sushi-Rollen enthält lediglich eine oder zwei ihrer Lieblingszutaten, etwa Gurken und getrocknete Kürbisstreifen. Sie werden auf dieselbe Weise zubereitet, indem die Zutaten mit gesäuerten Reis in einer Matte aus getrocknetem Seetang (Nori) eingewickelt werden.

Sushi en rouleaux fins

C'est la version plus petite des grands rouleaux de sushi. Ils contiennent seulement une ou deux sortes d'ingrédients tels que du concombre ou de la calebasse séchée. Ils sont préparés de la même façon, en enroulant les ingrédients dans du riz vinaigré que l'on enrobe d'une algue séchée.

Rollos de Sushi Delgados

Esta versión pequeña de los rollos gruesos contiene solo uno o dos de sus ingredientes favoritos tales como pepino u hojuelas de calabaza seca. Se preparan en la misma forma que los grandes, enrollando arroz avinagrado y envolviéndolo en una hoja de alga marina.

Sushi in rotolo sottile

Viene preparato stendendo del riso su un foglio di alghe essiccate nori, mettendovi al centro un ingrediente o due, come strisce di cetrioli o strisce di una cucurbitacea (essiccate, fatte rinvenire e condite) e arrotolando il tutto.

Rolos finos de sushi

Estas versões reduzidas dos rolos de sushi maiores contêm somente um ou dois ingredientes selecionados, como pepino ou flocos de cabaça ressequida. São preparadas da mesma maneira, enrolando-se arroz avinagrado, com o recheio, em alga marinha.

手巻き寿司 (Temaki-zushi)

© S.T.

Hand-Rolled Sushi

Your choice of ingredients, including fish, shellfish and vegetables, are placed on a bed of vinegared rice on a small piece of seaweed, and then rolled up by hand. Some new varieties that have become popular in the U.S. in particular include the California Roll and Salmon Skin Roll.

kcal ●●

手卷壽司

將壽司飯和魚貝類等自己喜歡的食物切碎後放在紫菜上，卷好後食用的一種壽司。 在美國其主要新品種有加利福尼亞手卷壽司和帶皮鮭魚手卷壽司。

手卷寿司

将寿司饭和鱼贝类等自己喜欢的食物切碎后放在紫菜上，卷好后食用的一种寿司。在美国其主要新品种有加利福尼亚手卷寿司和带皮鲑鱼手卷寿司。

즉석김초밥

상추쌈을 먹듯, 즉석에서 손수 손바닥 크기만한 김 위에 초밥을 얇게 펴서 어패류나 야채 등 각자가 먹고 싶은 재료를 얹어서 삼각형으로 말아 먹는 김밥. 미국에는 주로 캘리포니아롤이나 새먼스킨롤 등의 새로운 타입이 있다.

手巻き寿司

のりの上にすし飯と魚介類や野菜などの好みの具をのせ、くるくると巻いて食べる料理。主としてアメリカでは、カリフォルニアロールやサーモンスキンロールなどの新しいタイプが好評。

السوشي الملفوف يدويا

توضع المقادير التي تختارها بنفسك من أسماك أو محار أو خضر أو غيرها فوق طبقة من الأرز المتبل بالخل ثم تلف، يدوياً في ورقة صغيرة من عشب البحر. من بين الأصناف الجديدة ذات الشعبية في الولايات المتحدة بصفة خاصة نجد "ملفوف كليفورنيا" و"ملفوف جلد السلمون"

Handgerolltes Sushi

Ihre Lieblingszutaten zu denen Fisch, Muscheln und Gemüse gehören können, werden auf ein kleines Stück Matte aus getrocknetem Seetang (Nori) gelegt, auf der vorher gesäuerter Reis verteilt wurde, und dann mit der Hand aufgerollt. Einige neue, vor allem in den USA beliebte Varianten sind die California-Rolle und die Lachshautrolle.

Sushi roulés à la main

Les ingrédients que vous choisissez (poisson, crustacés ou légumes) sont disposés sur un lit de riz vinaigré puis enroulés à la main dans une petite algue séchée. Aux Etats-Unis, le California Roll (Rouleau de Californie) et le Salmon Skin Roll (Rouleau de peau de saumon) sont deux nouveaux types de sushi très populaires.

Sushi Enrollado a Mano

Se colocan ingredientes al gusto, tales como pescado, mariscos y verduras en una ración de arroz avinagrado colocada sobre una pequeña hoja de alga marina que después es enrollada a mano. Entre las nuevas variedades de sushi, especialmente en los Estados Unidos, se encuentran el Rollo de California y el Rollo de Piel de Salmón.

Sushi avvolti a piacere

Su un quadrato di alga essiccata nori il commensale adagia del riso per sushi, su questo dispone pesce, molluschi, crostacei o verdure a piacere e infine avvolge il tutto. In America in particolare sono nati nuovi tipi, quali, per esempio, i California rolls e i Salmon skin rolls.

Sushi enrolado à mão

Ingredientes de sua preferência, incluindo peixe, marisco e vegetais, são dispostos numa porção de arroz avinagrado, sobre um pedaço de alga marinha, e enrolados à mão. Algumas novas variedades - como Rolo à Califórnia e Rolo de Pele de Salmão - são muito apreciadas nos Estados Unidos, em particular.

いなり寿司 (Inari-zushi)

Stuffed Deep-Fried Tofu Pouches

Deep-fried tofu pouches boiled in sugar and soy sauce are stuffed with vinegared rice that enhances the mildly sweet taste of the deep-fried tofu.

kcal ●●

油豆腐壽司

在用醬油、白糖作調料浸成的油豆腐中，裝入壽司米飯。油豆腐本身微甜又入味，所以喫口很香。

Gefüllte fritierte Tofu-Taschen

In Öl ausgebackene Tofu-Taschen (Sojabohnenquark), die in Zucker und Sojasoße gekocht sind, werden mit gesäuertem Reis gefüllt, der den milden süßlichen Geschmack des ausgebackenen Tofus verstärkt.

油豆腐寿司

在用酱油、白糖作调料浸成的油豆腐中，装入寿司米饭。油豆腐本身微甜又入味，所以吃口很香。

Petites poches de tofu frit farcies

Après avoir fait bouillir des poches de tofu frit dans du sucre et de la sauce de soja, on les garnit de riz vinaigré qui relève le goût légèrement sucré du tofu frit.

유부초밥

간장, 설탕 등으로 찐 유부에 초밥을 넣은 것. 달콤한 맛이 밴 유부가 맛있다.

Bolsitas de Tofu Fritas en Aceite y Rellenas

Se trata de bolsitas de tofu fritas y cocidas en azúcar y salsa de soja. Se rellenan con arroz avinagrado, que realza el suave y dulce sabor del tofu asado en aceite.

いなり寿司

しょうゆ、砂糖などで煮た油揚げに、すし飯を詰めたもの。ほんのり甘く、よく味がしみ込んだ油揚げがおいしい。

Fagottini ripieni di sushi

Con del riso per sushi vengono riempiti dei quadrati sottili, incisi a tasca, di tofu fritto e poi bollito in salsa di soia dolce. Ne risultano dei fagottini saporiti, leggermente dolci.

اكياس التوفو المحمرة المحشوة

تغلى أكياس التوفو المحمرة في صلصة الصويا مع السكر ثم يتم حشوها بالأرز المتبل بالخل الذي يقوي المذاق الحلو المعتدل لأكياس التوفو.

Bolsinhas de tofu frito com recheio

Bolsinhas de tofu frito por mergulho em óleo, e cozidas em molho de soja e açúcar, são recheadas com arroz avinagrado, ingrediente que realça o sabor levemente adocicado do tofu frito.

牛丼 (Gyū-don)

© S.T.

Beef over Rice

Beef and onions are boiled in sweetened soy sauce and then served over rice in a bowl.

kcal ●●●

牛肉蓋飯

這是一種在米飯上盛放煮成甜鹹適中的牛肉和洋蔥的蓋飯。洋蔥的香甜和牛肉的鮮味交織相融，美味可口。

Rindfleisch über Reis

Rindfleisch und Zwiebeln werden in gesüßter Sojasoße gekocht und dann auf Reis in einer Schale serviert.

牛肉盖饭

这是一种在米饭上盛放煮成甜咸适中的牛肉和洋葱的盖饭。洋葱的香甜和牛肉的鲜味交织相融，美味可口。

Bœuf servi sur du riz

Bœuf et oignons bouillis dans une sauce de soja sucrée sont servis sur un bol de riz.

쇠고기덮밥

달짝지근하게 조린 쇠고기와 양파로 밥을 덮어 놓은 것. 양파의 단맛과 쇠고기 맛이 잘 어울린다.

Tazón de Arroz con Carne de Res

La carne de res se cuece con cebollas en una salsa dulce de soja y se sirve sobre un tazón de arroz.

牛丼

甘辛く煮た牛肉と玉ねぎをご飯にのせた丼。玉ねぎの甘みと牛肉のうまみがマッチ。

Scodella di riso con manzo

Sul riso in bianco viene versato un composto di cipolle e manzo cotti in umido dal gusto dolce-salato. Il dolce delle cipolle ben si sposa con il sapore della carne.

لحم بقري فوق الأرز

يغلى اللحم البقري مع البصل في صلصة صويا محلاة ثم يقدم فوق الأرز في وعاء عميق.

Carne sobre arroz

Carne de gado e cebolas são cozidas em molho de soja adocicado e servidas sobre arroz numa tigela.

カツ丼 (Katsu-don)

Deep-Fried Pork Cutlet over Rice

This satisfying dish is prepared by simmering deep-fried pork cutlet in a sweetened soy sauce broth thickened with beaten eggs and then serving in a bowl over rice.

© S.T.

kcal ●●●

豬排蓋飯

這是將炸豬排（裏上面包粉油炸的豬肉）放入甜鹹調料炖煨並用雞蛋勾芡盛放在米飯上，給人一種味美量足的感覺。

猪排盖饭

这是将炸猪排（裏上面包粉油炸的猪肉）放入甜咸调料炖煨并用鸡蛋勾芡盛放在米饭上，给人一种味美量足的感觉。

포크커틀렛덮밥

돈가스(포크커틀렛, 빵가루를 묻혀 튀긴 돼지고기)를 푼 달걀에 달짝지근하게 조린 다음 밥에 덮은 것. 볼륨감 있는 요리.

カツ丼

トンカツ（パン粉をつけて揚げた豚肉）を甘辛く煮て卵でとじ、ご飯にのせたもの。ボリュームたっぷり。

ضلع اللحم المدمر فوق الأرز

يتم إعداد هذا الطبق الشهي بطهي ضلع الخنزير المحمر في بهريز من صلصة الصويا مع البيض المخفوق ثم تقديمه فوق الأرز في وعاء عميق الشكل.

Fritiertes Schweinekotelett auf Reis

Für dieses wohlschmeckende Gericht wird fritiertes Schweinekotelett in einem Sud aus gesüßter Sojasoße geköchelt, mit geschlagenem Ei angedickt und dann auf Reis in einer Schale serviert.

Côtelette de porc frite servie sur du riz

Ce plat nourrissant se prépare en faisant mijoter une côtelette de porc frite dans un bouillon à base de sauce de soja sucrée épaissie avec des œufs battus que l'on sert sur un bol de riz.

Tazón de Arroz con Chuleta de Cerdo Rebozada

Este delicioso platillo se prepara poniendo a cocer la chuleta de cerdo rebozado en un jugo dulce con salsa de soja y huevos revueltos para servir sobre un tazón de arroz.

Scodella di riso con maiale impanato

È un piatto che riempie lo stomaco: sul riso viene messa della carne di maiale impanata, fritta e poi ancora cotta in umido con condimento dolce-salato insieme a uovo sbattuto.

Porco empanado sobre arroz

Prepara-se este prato apetitoso cozinhando carne de porco empanada, frita previamente por mergulho em óleo e cortada em fatias, em um caldo com molho de soja adocicado e engrossado com ovos batidos. É servido numa tigela sobre o arroz.

親子丼 (Oyako-don)

©S.T.

Chicken and Eggs over Rice

This dish is served in a bowl containing rice, on top of which is placed chicken and onions cooked with eggs to seal in the flavor.

kcal ●●●

母子蓋飯

這種蓋飯的特點是雞肉和洋蔥的固有鮮味通過澆蓋在其上面的半生不熟的雞蛋而得到完好地保留。這道菜由於雞肉和雞蛋同時使用而故得其名。

Huhn und Eier auf Reis

Dieses Gericht wird in einer Schale mit Reis serviert. Huhn und Zwiebeln werden mit Eiern gekocht, um das Aroma zu versiegeln, und dann auf den Reis gelegt.

母子盖饭

这种盖饭的特点是鸡肉和洋葱的固有鲜味通过浇盖在其上面的半生不熟的鸡蛋而得到完好地保留，这道菜由于鸡肉和鸡蛋同时使用而故得其名。

Poulet et œufs servis sur du riz

Ce plat est servi dans un bol contenant du riz sur lequel on dispose du poulet et des oignons cuits avec des œufs afin d'en imprégner la saveur.

닭고기 달걀덮밥

달짝지근하게 조린 닭고기와 양파에 푼 달걀을 넣고 반숙으로 익혀 밥에 덮어 놓은 것.

Tazón de Arroz con Pollo y Huevos

En un tazón con arroz se colocan pollo y cebollas cocinados con huevos para impregnar su sabor a este platillo.

親子丼

甘辛く煮た鶏肉と玉ねぎに卵を流して半熟状にし、ご飯にのせた丼。鶏肉と鶏卵を使うことからこの名前がある。

Scodella di pollo e uova

Sul riso viene versato un composto di carne di pollo e porri cotti in umido con condimento dolce-salato e amalgamati con uovo sbattuto. Questo piatto viene chiamato "madre e figlio" per via degli ingredienti di gallina e uovo.

دجاج وبيض فوق الأرز

يوضع الأرز في وعاء عميق ثم يرص فوقه الدجاج والبصل المطهو مع البيض للحصول على نكهة لذيذة.

Frango e ovos sobre arroz

A carne de frango, cortada em pequenos pedaços e cozida com ovos e cebola, é servida numa tigela com arroz.

天丼 (Ten-don)

Tempura Rice Bowl

This delicacy is prepared by batter-frying fresh vegetables, fish and shellfish into tempura, mixing with a special tempura sauce and serving in a bowl over rice.

© S.T.

kcal ●●●●

炸蝦蓋飯

這是將新鮮的蝦類及蔬菜天婦羅(酥炸蔬菜)澆上湯汁後盛放在米飯上的一種蓋飯。

Tempura-Reisschale

Für diese Delikatesse werden frisches Gemüse, Fisch und Muscheln mit einem Teig zu Tempura verarbeitet, dann mit einer speziellen Tempura-Soße gemischt und auf einer Schale mit Reis serviert.

炸虾盖饭

这是将新鲜的虾类及蔬菜天妇罗(酥炸蔬菜)澆上汤汁后盛放在米饭上的一种盖饭。

Tempura servis sur du riz

Ce mets fin se prépare en faisant frire des légumes frais, du poisson et des crustacés dans une pâte à tempura que l'on arrose d'une sauce spéciale tempura et que l'on sert sur un bol de riz.

튀김덮밥

신선한 어패류나 야채 튀김에 튀김 간장을 묻혀 밥에 덮어 놓은 것.

Tazón de Arroz con Tempura

Este manjar se prepara friendo verduras frescas, pescado y mariscos rebozados en tempura, los cuales son mezclados con una salsa especial para tempura y se sirven sobre un tazón de arroz.

天丼

新鮮な魚介類や野菜の天ぷらにつゆをからめ、ご飯にのせたぜいたくな丼。

Scodella di riso con tempura

È un ricco e gustoso piatto di riso su cui è adagiato un fritto misto alla giapponese (tempura) di pesce, frutti mare e verdure.

وعاء الأرز بالتمبورا

تصنع التمبورا بغمس أنواع من الخضر الطازجة والأسماك والقواقع البحرية في الدقيق والبيض المخفوق ثم تحميرها، بعد ذلك تمزج التمبورا مع صلصة خاصة وتقدم فوق الأرز في وعاء عميق الشكل.

Tempura em tigela de arroz

Prepara-se esta iguaria empanando vegetais, pescados e mariscos frescos ao estilo tempura. Serve-se numa tigela sobre arroz, depois de regar o prato com um molho especial.

うな重 (Unajū)

Broiled Eel over Rice

Broiled eel basted with a richly flavored sauce is served on rice, covered in more sauce and then sprinkled with Japanese pepper as desired.

kcal ●●●●

鰻魚盒飯

在米飯上放上烤鰻魚片，再澆上汁。各人可根據自己的喜好撒上花椒粉。

Gegrillter Aal auf Reis

Aal wird gegrillt und dabei mit einer gewürzten Soße übergossen. Er wird dann auf Reis serviert, mit noch mehr Soße übergossen und nach Geschmack mit japanischem Pfeffer bestreut.

鳗鱼盒饭

在米饭上放上烤鳗鱼片，再浇上汁。各人可根据自己的喜好撒上花椒粉。

Anguilles grillées servies sur du riz

Après avoir fait griller les anguilles, on les arrose d'une sauce richement aromatisée et on les dispose sur du riz, le tout étant encore arrosé de sauce et saupoudré de piments japonais, selon ses goûts.

장어덮밥

밥 위에 잘 구운 장어를 얹은 다음 양념장을 끼얹은 것. 기호에 따라 산초 등을 뿌려 먹는다.

Anguila de Mar Asada sobre Arroz

Se impregna a la anguila de mar asada en una salsa bien condimentada y se sirve sobre arroz. Después se cubre con más salsa y se sazona con pimienta japonesa al gusto.

うな重

ご飯の上にかば焼きにしたうなぎをのせ、タレをかけたもの。好みで粉山椒をふって食べる。

Riso con anguilla

Sul riso vengono deposti tranci di anguilla cotta alla griglia spennellandola con una apposita salsa. A piacere si spolvera di pepe giapponese.

سمك الثعبان المشوي فوق الأرز

يشوى الثعبان مع تتبيله باستمرار بصلصة لذيذة الطعم ويقدم فوق الأرز ثم يغطى بمزيد من الصلصة وينثر فوقه مسحوق الفلفل الياباني حسب الرغبة.

Enguia grelhada sobre arroz

A enguia, grelhada e regada com um molho ricamente aromático, é servida sobre o arroz, coberta com mais molho e depois salpicada com pimenta-japonesa em pó, a gosto.

鉄火丼 (Tekka-don)

Raw Tuna over Rice

This healthy dish consists of slices of raw tuna served on a bed of vinegared rice in a bowl and garnished with Japanese horseradish and soy sauce.

kcal ●●●●

生金槍魚片蓋飯

是一種將金槍魚做成的生魚片放在壽司飯上，蘸著芥茉醬油汁食用的健康菜肴。

Roher Thunfisch auf Reis

Bei diesem gesunden Gericht werden rohe Thunfischstücken in einer Schale auf gesäuerten Reis gelegt, und vor dem Verzehr mit japanischem Meerrettich und Sojasoße ergänzt.

生金枪鱼片盖饭

是一种将金枪鱼做成的生鱼片放在寿司饭上，蘸着芥茉酱油汁食用的健康菜肴。

Thon cru servi sur du riz

Ce plat sans graisse se compose de tranches de thon cru servies sur un bol de riz vinaigré agrémenté de raifort japonais et de sauce de soja.

참치덮밥

참치회를 초밥 위에 덮은 다음, 와사비를 푼 간장으로 먹는 헬시한 음식.

Atún Crudo sobre Arroz

Este saludable platillo consiste de rebanadas de atún crudo servidas sobre una ración de arroz avinagrado en un tazón. Se condimenta con mostaza verde japonés y salsa de soja.

鉄火丼

まぐろのさしみをすし飯の上にのせ、わさびじょうゆで食べるヘルシーな丼。

Scodella di riso con tonno crudo

È un sano piatto di riso per sushi con copertura di sashimi di tonno, che si mangia con salsa di soia mista a rafano giapponese.

سمك التونة النيء فوق الأرز

هذا الصنف الصحي يتكون من شرائح نيئة من التونة تقدم في الطبق فوق كمية من الأرز المتبل بالخل ويضاف إليها الفجل الياباني الحار وصلصة الصويا.

Atum cru sobre arroz

Este prato saudável consiste em fatias de atum cru servidas sobre arroz avinagrado numa tigela e guarnecidas com raiz-forte-do-japão e molho de soja.

カレーライス (Karē Raisu)

© S.T.

Curry with Rice

This family favorite is prepared by cooking meat, onions, potatoes, carrots and other ingredients in a thick curry-flavored roux and serving over rice.

kcal ●●●●

咖喱飯

這是用咖喱醬將肉、洋蔥、土豆、鬍蘿蔔等煮熟成黏稠狀，澆在米飯上的一種蓋飯。

Curry mit Reis

Für dieses populäre Gericht werden Fleisch, Zwiebeln, Kartoffeln, Karotten und andere Zutaten in einer dicken Einbrenne mit Curry-Geschmack gekocht und auf Reis serviert.

咖喱饭

这是用咖喱酱将肉、洋葱、土豆、胡萝卜等煮熟成黏稠状，浇在米饭上的一种盖饭。

Riz au curry

Ce plat familial populaire se prépare en faisant cuire de la viande, des oignons, des pommes de terre, des carottes et d'autres ingrédients dans un roux épais parfumé au curry que l'on sert sur du riz.

카레라이스

고기, 양파, 감자, 당근 등에 카레를 넣고 끓어 밥 위에 끼얹은 것.

Cari con Arroz

Este es uno de los platillos preferidos por las familias japonesas y se prepara cocinando carne, cebollas, patatas, zanahorias y otros ingredientes en una espesa pasta condimentada con cari que se esparce sobre arroz.

カレーライス

肉、玉ねぎ、じゃがいも、にんじんなどを煮てカレールウでとろみをつけ、ご飯にかけたもの。

Riso al curry

Con il riso in bianco viene servito un denso composto di carne, cipolle, carote e altri ingredienti cotti in umido con del curry.

ارز بالكاري

يعد هذا الصنف المفضل للعائلات بطهي اللحم والبصل والبطاطس والجزر والمقادير الأخرى في صلصة ثخينة متبلة بالكاري ثم يسكب المزيج فوق الأرز.

Curry com arroz

Prepara-se este apreciado prato caseiro cozinhando carne, cebolas, batatas, cenouras e outros ingredientes num denso ensopado à base de farinha de trigo tostada, temperado e aromatizado com curry. Serve-se sobre o arroz.

オムライス (Omu Raisu)

Seasoned Fried Rice Omelet

This unique dish is prepared by stir-frying rice, chicken, onions and peas, flavoring with tomato ketchup and wrapping in a thin egg omelet. It's a real favorite among children.

© S.T.

kcal ●●●●

蛋包飯

將米飯、雞肉、洋蔥、豌豆煸炒後用番茄醬等調味，然後再用薄蛋卷皮將其裹上。這種蛋包飯深受兒童的歡迎。

蛋包饭

将米饭、鸡肉、洋葱、豌豆煸炒后用番茄酱等调味，然后再用薄蛋卷皮将其裹上。这种蛋包饭深受儿童的欢迎。

오므라이스

밥, 닭고기, 양파, 그린피스 등을 볶아 토마토케첩으로 맛을 낸 것을 얇게 부친 달걀로 감싼 요리. 어린이에게 인기있는 메뉴.

オムライス

ご飯、鶏肉、玉ねぎ、グリンピースを炒めてトマトケチャップなどで調味し、それを薄焼き卵で包んだ料理。子供にも人気の味。

اومليت الأرز المحمر بالتوابل

يعد هذا الصنف الفريد بتحمير الأرز مع الدجاج والبصل والبسلة وتتبل بصلصة طماطم من نوع الكاتشوب ثم يغلف بطبقة رقيقة من أومليت البيض، وهو طبق مفضل لدي الأطفال.

Omelett mit gewürztem gebratenen Reis

Für dieses beliebte Gericht werden Reis, Huhn, Zwiebeln und Erbsen in der Pfanne scharf angebraten, dann mit Tomatenketchup gewürzt und in ein dünnes Omelett eingeschlagen. Dieses Gericht ist insbesondere bei Kindern beliebt.

Riz sauté enrobé d'omlette

Ce plat se prépare en faisant revenir du riz, du poulet, des oignons et des pois, en les aromatisant de ketchup et en les enveloppant dans une fine omelette aux œufs. Un des plats favoris des enfants.

Arroz Frito Condimentado

Este original platillo se prepara salteando arroz, pollo, cebollas y guisantes. Se condimenta con salsa catsup y se envuelve en una hoja de crepa de huevo. Es uno de los alimentos favoritos de los niños.

Omelette ripieno di riso

Un sottile strato di omelette incorpora del riso cotto e poi saltato con pollo, piselli, cipolle e insaporito con ketchup. È un piatto consigliato per i bambini.

Omelete recheada com arroz frito e temperado

Prepara-se este prato original refogando arroz, frango, cebolas e ervilhas, condimentando-os com ketchup e envolvendo-os numa omelete fina. É um dos pratos favoritos das crianças.

炊き込みご飯 (Takikomi Gohan)

Steamed Rice Flavored with Chicken and Vegetables

Rice, chicken and thinly sliced vegetables are steamed together in a rice cooker for a dish that allows you to enjoy the flavors of the particular season, including edible wild plants in spring and mushrooms or chestnuts in autumn.

kcal ●●●

十錦菜飯

這是將米飯、雞肉及切成絲的蔬菜放在一起煮熟並調好味的飯。春天是用野菜，秋天是用蘑菇或栗子為原料，您可盡情品嘗四季的時鮮美味。

十锦菜饭

这是将米饭、鸡肉及切成丝的蔬菜放在一起煮熟并调好味的饭。春天是用野菜，秋天是用蘑菇或栗子为原料，您可尽情品尝四季的时鲜美味。

닭고기야채밥

쌀에 닭고기나 채 썬 야채를 넣고 함께 지은 밥. 봄에는 산채, 가을에는 버섯이나 밤 등 계절의 맛을 즐길 수 있다.

炊き込みご飯

米に鶏肉やせん切りにした野菜を加え、一緒に炊き上げた味付けご飯。春は山菜、秋はきのこや栗など、季節の味を楽しめる。

ارز مطهو مع الدجاج والخضر

يخلط الأرز مع الدجاج والخضر المقطعة رفيعاً ويطهى على البخار في وعاء الأرز الكهربائي للحصول على طبق يمتعك بنكهة الموسم من الخضروات البرية في الربيع وعش الغراب أو الكستناء في الخريف.

Gedämpfter Reis mit Huhn und Gemüse

Reis, Huhn und dünn geschnittenes Gemüse werden zusammen in einem Reiskocher gedünstet. Der besondere Pfiff bei diesem Gericht ist, daß Sie den Geschmack der jeweiligen Jahreszeit genießen können, einschließlich eßbaren wilden Pflanzen im Frühling und Pilzen oder Kastanien im Herbst.

Riz à la vapeur accompagné de poulet et de légumes

Ce plat est composé de riz, de poulet et de légumes émincés cuits ensemble à la vapeur dans un auto-cuiseur pour le riz. Ce plat qui s'adapte à chaque saison peut être agrémenté de pousses sauvages comestibles au printemps et de champignons ou de châtaignes en automne.

Arroz con Pollo y Verduras

En una olla eléctrica para cocinar arroz se cuece el arroz junto con el pollo y verduras rebanadas en pequeños trozos. Este delicioso platillo permite disfrutar los sabores particulares de cada estación, incluyendo plantas silvestres comestibles en primavera y champiñones o castañas en otoño.

Risotto alla giapponese

Il riso viene cotto nel particolare modo giapponese unendovi però fin dall'inizio condimenti e pezzetti di pollo e verdure. Con questo piatto si possono gustare i sapori delle stagioni, per esempio erbe di montagna in primavera, funghi o castagne in autunno.

Arroz cozido com frango e verduras em vapor

Arroz, frango e verduras picados são cozidos a vapor, num aparelho para preparar arroz. É um prato que permite saborear as iguarias particulares da estação, como plantas silvestres comestíveis na primavera, e cogumelos ou castanhas no outono.

お茶漬け (Ocha-zuke)

Flavored Tea and Rice

This dish is enjoyed as a light snack by pouring hot green tea over rice with cooked salmon, seaweed and other favorites such as pickled plums and cod roe.

kcal ●

茶泡飯

這是在米飯上放上烤熟的大馬哈魚片、紫菜等並澆上熱茶食用的簡便餐。米飯上也可以放置梅子、鱈魚子等。

茶泡饭

这是在米饭上放上烤熟的大马哈鱼片、紫菜等并浇上热茶食用的简便餐。米饭上也可以放置梅子、鳕鱼子等。

차에 만 밥

밥 위에 구운 연어, 김 등을 얹고 그 위에 뜨거운 녹차를 부어 가볍게 먹는 음식. 밥 위에는 매실, 명란젓 등을 얹기도 한다.

お茶漬け

ご飯の上に、焼いたさけ、のりなどをのせ、熱いお茶をかけて食べる軽食。のせる具には梅干し、たらこなどもある。

مزيج الشاي والأرز المتبل

يؤكل هذا الصنف كنوع من المشهيات حيث يسكب الشاي الأخضر الساخن فوق الأرز مع السلمون المطهي وأعشاب البحر وغير ذلك من الأطعمة المحببة مثل البرقوق المخلل ويطارخ سمك القد.

Gewürzter Tee und Reis

Dieses Gericht ist eine beliebte leichte Zwischenmahlzeit. Heißer grüner Tee wird über Reis gegossen, der mit gebratenem Lachs, Schnipseln aus getrockneten Seetangmatten (Nori) und anderen beliebten Zutaten versehen ist, z.B. eingelegten Pflaumen und Kabeljaurogen.

Riz arrosé de thé vert

C'est un en-cas léger qui se prépare en arrosant de thé vert chaud du riz accompagné de saumon cuit, d'algues et d'autres ingrédients favoris tels que des prunes confites ou des œufs de morue.

Arroz con té aromático

Este platillo considerado como un entremés se disfruta sirviendo té verde caliente sobre arroz con salmón asado, algas marinas y otros ingredientes tales como ciruelas secas curtidas en sal y huevas de bacalao.

Riso al tè verde

È un piatto leggero che può servire da spuntino. Sul riso in bianco si mettono a piacere pezzetti di salmone cotto, alghe o altri ingredienti, per esempio susine in salamoia o uova di merluzzo salate, e poi si versa sul tutto del tè verde ben caldo.

Chá e arroz aromatizados

Este prato é saboreado como uma refeição leve, despejando-se chá verde quente sobre o arroz, com salmão assado, alga marinha e outros ingredientes selecionados, como ameixas japonesas em conserva e ovas de bacalhau.

おにぎり (Onigiri)

© S.T.

Rice Balls

Cooked salmon, pickled plums or any other of your favorite ingredients are packed inside rice which is then formed into the shape of balls or triangles. Wrapping the finished rice balls in seaweed gives them an appetizing aroma.

kcal ●

飯團子

這是將烤熟的大馬哈魚屑、梅子等放入米飯中後，捏成團來食用的一種飯團子。如果用紫菜卷包後食用，則更是清香芬芳，別有味道。

Reisklöße

Gekochter Lachs, fermentierte Salzpflaumen oder andere beliebte Zutaten werden mit Reis umhüllt und dann zu Kugeln oder Dreiecken geformt. Anschließend werden die fertiggestellten Reisklöße mit Matten aus getrocknetem Seetang (Nori) umhüllt, die ihnen das appetitliche Aroma verleihen.

饭团子

这是将烤熟的大马哈鱼屑、梅子等放入米饭中后，捏成团来食用的一种饭团子。如果用紫菜卷包后食用，则更是清香芬芳，别有味道。

Boulettes de riz

Ce plat est à base de riz que l'on garnit de saumon cuit, de prunes confites ou de tout autre ingrédient favori, que l'on façonne ensuite en boules ou en triangles. En enveloppant les boulettes prêtes dans une algue, on obtient un goût encore plus appétissant.

주먹밥

밥 안에 구운 연어나 매실 등을 넣고 손으로 꼭꼭 쥐어서 만든 것. 구운 김으로 싸면 구수하고 먹기도 좋다.

Bolas de Arroz

Se preparan bolas de arroz en forma triangular y se rellenan con salmón cocido, ciruelas secas curtidas en sal o cualquier otro ingrediente al gusto. Una vez que han sido moldeadas las bolas de arroz, se les envuelve en hojas de alga marina que les da un apetitoso sabor.

おにぎり

ご飯の中に焼いたさけ、梅干しなどを入れ、手でギュッと握ったもの。のりを巻くと香ばしく、食べやすい。

Palle di riso

Si preparano comprimendo il riso in forma sferica (o triangolare) attorno a un nucleo di salmone grigliato o susine in salamoia o altri ingredienti a piacere, e avvolgendo in un foglio di alghe essiccate nori. Vanno bene in svariate occasioni.

كرات الأرز المغلفة بعشب البحر

يوضع السلمون المطهو أو البرقوق المخلل أو أي من الأطعمة المحببة إليك داخل كتلة من الأرز تشكل على هيئة كرة أو مثلث ثم تغلف الكرة بورقة من عشب البحر تمنحها نكهة مثيرة للشهية.

Bolinhos de arroz

Arroz glutinoso, com recheio de salmão assado, ameixas japonesas em conserva e muitos outros ingredientes selecionados, é preparado em forma de bolas e triângulos. Enrolam-se os bolinhos de arroz em alga para dar a esta iguaria um aroma apetitoso.

ざるそば (Zaru Soba)

Chilled Buckwheat Noodles

This simple yet delightful dish is served cold and is prepared by placing buckwheat noodles, cooked to an appealing texture, on a bamboo mat and then dipping the noodles in a dipping sauce.

kcal ●●

蕎麥面條

將煮得軟硬適中的蕎麥面條冰鎮降溫後，蘸著佐料汁食用的一種冷面。烹飪簡單卻味道醇正。

荞麦面条

将煮得软硬适中的荞麦面条冰镇降温后，蘸着佐料汁食用的一种冷面。烹饪简单却味道醇正。

메밀국수

쫄깃쫄깃하게 삶아서 식힌 모밀을 맛간장에 찍어 먹는 면요리. 심플하지만 맛있다.

ざるそば

歯ごたえよくゆでて冷ましたそばを、つゆにつけながら食べる冷たい麺。シンプルだが、うまみは十分。

شعرية باردة من الحنطة السمراء

هذا صنف لذيذ مع بساطته ويؤكل بارداً، هنا تسلق الشعرية حتى درجة مناسبة ثم تقدم باردة فوق وسادة من البامبو، وتغمس قبل تناولها في نوع خاص من الصلصة.

Gekühlte Buchweizennudeln

Dies ist ein einfaches und dennoch sehr wohlschmeckendes Gericht, das kalt serviert wird. Zur Zubereitung werden Buchweizennudeln, die bißfest gekocht wurden, auf eine Bambusmatte gelegt und die Nudeln vor dem Verzehr in eine Soße getaucht.

Nouilles de sarrasin froides

Ce plat simple mais délicieux se sert froid et se prépare en disposant sur une natte en bambou des nouilles de sarrasin que l'on a fait cuire jusqu'à ce que la texture en soit appétissante et que l'on plonge ensuite dans une sauce spéciale.

Fideos de Alforfón Helados

Este sencillo pero delicioso platillo se sirve frío. Se prepara colocando sobre una esterilla de bambú los fideos de alforfón cocidos hasta que han alcanzado una textura atractiva. Este platillo se come impregnando los fideos en una salsa de soja y vinagre.

Soba al setaccio

Questi spaghettini di grano saraceno (soba) cotti al dente, raffreddati e presentati su un setaccio di bambù, si mangiano intingendoli in una apposita salsina. Piatto semplice, ma gustoso.

Macarrão de trigo-sarraceno servido gelado

Este prato simples mas muito delicioso é servido frio. Dispõe-se sobre uma esteira de bambu, macarrão de trigo-sarraceno que foi fervido até o ponto de adquirir uma consistência apetitosa. Para comer, mergulha-se o macarrão em um molho especial.

きつねそば・うどん (Kitsune Soba, Udon)

© S.T.

Buckwheat or Wheat Flour Noodles with Deep-Fried Tofu

Deep-fried tofu, seasoned to have a slightly sweet taste, is served with hot buckwheat or wheat flour noodles. Please specify buckwheat noodles (soba) or wheat flour noodles (udon) when ordering.

kcal ●●●

油渣豆腐湯蕎麥面・切面

這是一種在其上面盛放著用甜味調料長時間煮熟的油炸豆腐片的熱湯面。訂菜時，請指明是蕎麥面還是切面。

油渣豆腐汤乔麦面・切面

这是一种在其上面盛放着用甜味调料长时间煮熟的油炸豆腐片的热汤面。订菜时，请指明是荞麦面还是切面。

유부 메밀국수・우동

달콤하게 맛을 내 끓인 유부가 들어있는 따뜻한 국물의 면요리. 주문시에는 메밀국수이나 우동 중의 어느 쪽인가를 지정한다.

きつねそば・うどん

甘く味付けして煮た油揚げが入った温かい汁麺。注文の際には、そばかうどんを指定してください。

شعرية الحنطة البيضاء أو السمراء مع التوفو المقلي

يتبل التوفو المقلي ليكتسب مذاقاً سكرياً خفيفاً ويقدم ساخناً مع الشعرية الساخنة. رجاء تحديد نوع الشعرية عند الطلب: شعرية الحنطة السمراء (صويا)، أو شعرية الحنطة البيضاء (أودون).

Buchweizen- oder Weizenmehlnudeln mit fritiertem Tofu

In Öl ausgebackener Tofu (Sojabohnenquark), der leicht süßlich gewürzt ist, wird auf heißen Buchweizen- oder Weizenmehlnudeln in Suppe serviert. Bitte geben Sie bei der Bestellung an, ob Sie Buchweizennudeln (Soba) oder Weizenmehlnudeln (Udon) bevorzugen.

Nouilles de sarrasin ou de froment avec tofu frit

Le tofu frit, préparé pour donner un goût légèrement sucré, est servi avec des nouilles de sarrasin ou de froment chaudes. A la commande, préciser soba (nouilles de sarrasin) ou udon (nouilles de froment).

Sopa de Fideos de Alforfón o Fideos de Trigo con Tofu Frito

El tofu frito en bastante aceite se aderaza para que adquiera un ligero sabor dulce y se sirve dentro del caldo caliente los fideos de alforfón o trigo cocidos. Al ordenar, haga el favor de especificar si desea fideos de alforfón (soba) o fideos de trigo (udon).

Soba/udon in brodo con tofu fritto

È un piatto caldo di spaghettini di grano saraceno (soba) o di tagliolini di grano tenero (udon) in brodo con pezzi di sottile tofu fritto e poi cotto in umido con condimento dolce. Quando si ordina, precisare se si desidera "soba" o "udon".

Macarrão de trigo-sarraceno ou macarrão japonês com queijo de soja frito

O queijo de soja, frito por mergulho em óleo e condimentado para adquirir um sabor levemente adoçado, é servido com macarrão de trigo-sarraceno quente ou macarrão japonês. Ao fazer o pedido, indique se deseja macarrão de trigo-sarraceno (soba) ou macarrão japonês (udon).

たぬきそば・うどん (Tanuki Soba, Udon)

Buckwheat or Wheat Flour Noodles with Tempura Batter Pieces

This delicious noodle dish contains small pieces of tempura batter and leeks. Please specify buckwheat noodles (soba) or wheat flour noodles (udon) when ordering.

kcal ●●●

© S.T.

油渣湯蕎麥面・切面

這是一種湯內放入油渣及蔥花的熱湯面。訂菜時，請指明是蕎麥面還是切面。

Buchweizen- oder Weizenmehlnudeln mit ausgebackenen Tempura-Teigteilen

Dieses köstliche Nudelgericht enthält kleine Teile ausgebackenen Tempura-Teigs und grüne Zwiebeln. Bitte geben Sie bei der Bestellung an, ob Sie Buchweizennudeln (Soba) oder Weizenmehlnudeln (Udon) bevorzugen.

油渣汤乔麦面・切面

这是一种汤内放入油渣及葱花的热汤面。订菜时，请指明是荞麦面还是切面。

Nouilles de sarrasin ou de froment saupoudrées de pâte à frire de tempura

Ce plat délicieux est servi avec des petits morceaux de pâte à frire de tempura et des oignons verts émincés. A la commande, préciser soba (nouilles de sarrasin) ou udon (nouilles de froment).

메밀국수・우동

튀김 알갱이와 파를 넣은 따뜻한 국물의 면 요리. 주문시에는 메밀국수이나 우동 중의 어느 쪽인가를 지정한다.

Sopa de Fideos con hojuelas de tempura

Se sirve dentro de un caldo caliente los Fideos de Alforfón o Trigo cocidos con Fragmentos de Pasta de Tempura.Este delicioso plato de fideos contiene pequeños fragmentos de pasta de tempura, verduras y cebollas verdes. Al ordenar, haga el favor de especificar si desea fideos de alforfón (soba) o fideos de trigo (udon).

たぬきそば・うどん

揚げ玉とねぎが入った温かい汁麺。注文の際には、そばかうどんを指定してください。

Soba/udon in brodo con palline di pastella fritta

È un piatto caldo di pasta in brodo con pezzettini di pastella fritta e porri tagliuzzati. Quando si ordina, precisare se si desidera "soba" o "udon".

شعرية الحنطة البيضاء أو السمراء مع بيض التمبورا

يحتوي هذا الطبق اللذيذ من الشعرية على قطع صغيرة من البيض المخفوق المحمر مع الدقيق والبصل الأخضر. رجاءً، تحديد نوع الشعرية عند الطلب: شعرية الحنطة السمراء (صويا)، أو شعرية الحنطة البيضاء (أودون).

Macarrão de trigo-sarraceno ou macarrão japonês com floquinhos fritos de tempura

Este prato delicioso contém pequenos flocos fritos de massa de tempura misturados com cebolinha. Ao fazer o pedido, indique se deseja macarrão de trigo-sarraceno (soba) ou macarrão japonês (udon).

天ぷらそば・うどん (Tempura Soba, Udon)

©S.T.

Tempura and Noodles

This noodle dish is served piping hot with several pieces of tempura on top, usually batter fried shrimp. Please specify buckwheat noodles (soba) or wheat flour noodles (udon) when ordering.

kcal ●●●

天婦羅面(酥炸蝦仁面)

這是在面條上放上酥炸蝦仁的熱湯面。訂菜時，請指明是蕎麥面還是切面。

Tempura und Nudeln

Diese Nudelsuppe wird glühendheiß serviert und dann mit mehreren Stücken Tempura, normalerweise in Teig ausgebackene Garnelen, ergänzt. Bitte geben Sie bei der Bestellung an, ob Sie Buchweizennudeln (Soba) oder Weizenmehlnudeln (Udon) bevorzugen.

天妇罗面(酥炸虾仁面)

这是在面条上放上酥炸虾仁的热汤面。订菜时，请指明是荞麦面还是切面。

Nouilles à la tempura

Ce plat de nouilles est servi brûlant, garni de plusieurs morceaux de tempura, la plupart du temps des crevettes. A la commande, préciser soba (nouilles de sarrasin) ou udon (nouilles de froment).

튀김 메밀국수 · 우동

면 위에 튀김을 얹은 따뜻한 국물의 면요리. 주문시에는 메밀국수이나 우동 중의 어느 쪽인가를 지정한다.

Sopa de Fideos con Tempura

Este plato de fideos de Alforfón o Trigo, se sirve bien caliente colocando encima diversas frituras, generalmente langostinos rebozados. Al ordenar, haga el favor de especificar si desea fideos de alforfón (soba) o fideos de trigo (udon).

天ぷらそば・うどん

麺の上に天ぷらをのせた温かい汁麺。注文の際には、そばかうどんを指定してください。

Soba/udon in brodo con tempura

È un piatto caldo di pasta in brodo con copertura di tempura. Quando si ordina, precisare se si desidera "soba" o "udon".

تمبورا مع الشعرية

يقدم هذا الطبق من الشعرية ساخنا جدا وفوقه عدة قطع من التمبورا (ص ١٩٧) وتكون في الأغلب س الجمبري (الروبيان). رجاء تحديد نوع الشعرية عند الطلب: شعرية الحنطة السمراء (صويا) ، أو شعرية الحنطة البيضاء (أودون).

Tempura e macarrão de trigo-sarraceno ou macarrão japonês

Esta sopa de massa é servida bem quente, com várias frituras tempura por cima, em geral camarão empanado. Ao fazer o pedido, indique se deseja macarrão de trigo-sarraceno (soba) ou macarrão japonês (udon).

鍋焼きうどん (Nabe-yaki Udon)

Wheat Flour Noodle Casserole

Thick, wheat flour noodles, tempura, boiled fish paste and various vegetables are placed in an earthen casserole dish and boiled up for a dish that warms you from head to toe.

kcal ●●●

砂鍋面條

這道菜肴的特色是將面條、天婦羅(酥炸蝦仁)、魚糕、蔬菜放在砂鍋中熱氣騰騰地邊煮邊喫。

Kasserole mit Weizenmehlnudeln

Dicke Weizenmehlnudeln (Udon), Tempura, gekochte Fischpastete und verschiedene Gemüse werden in eine Steingut-Kasserole gegeben und aufgekocht. Ein Gericht, das den Körper von Kopf bis Fuß erwärmt.

砂锅面条

这道菜肴的特色是将面条、天妇罗(酥炸虾仁)、鱼糕、蔬菜放在砂锅中热气腾腾地边煮边吃。

Cocotte de nouilles de farine de blé

Ce plat qui réchauffe le corps de la tête aux pieds se compose d'épaisses nouilles de farine de blé, de tempura, de pâte de poisson bouilli et de divers légumes que l'on plonge dans une cocotte en terre et que l'on fait bouillir.

남비우동

남비에 우동, 튀김, 어묵, 야채 등을 넣어 끓인 우동.

Cacerola de Fideos de Harina de Trigo

En una cacerola de barro se colocan fideos de trigo gruesos, tempura, pasta de pescado cocido y diversas verduras. Este platillo es tan caliente que hace que el comensal entre en calor de pies a cabeza.

鍋焼きうどん

土鍋にうどん、天ぷら、かまぼこ、野菜などを入れて煮込んだアツアツの麺料理。

Udon cotti in pignatta

Udon alquanto grossi vengono cotti in brodo in una pignatta di terracotta con Tempura, impasto bollito di farina di pesce, verdure e altro. Si mangiano ben caldi dalla pignatta.

طاجن شعرية الحنطة البيضاء

توضع الشعرية السميكة مع التمبورا (ص ١٩٧) والسمك المسلوق وأنواع من الخضر في طاجن فخاري ويسلق المزيج لإعداد صنف ساخن يبعث الدفء في دمائك.

Caçarola de macarrão japonês

Macarrão japonês grosso, tempura, pasta de peixe cozida e vários vegetais são cozidos na caçarola de barro. É um prato delicioso, que aquece todo o corpo.

ラーメン (Rāmen)

Ramen Noodles

This hot noodle dish contains Chinese noodles with various ingredients in a soy sauce, miso or salt-based soup, and is considered to be one of the more popular foods in Japan. The photo shows the most popular kind, ramen in soy sauce-based soup.

kcal ●●●

中國湯面

以醬油、日本醬、鹹味為代表的中國熱湯面，是一種深受歡迎的大眾面食。 照片中表示的是最普通的醬油湯面。

Ramen-Nudelsuppe

Diese heiße Nudelsuppe enthält chinesische Nudeln (in Japan: Ramen) mit verschiedenen Zutaten in einer Suppe auf Sojasoßen-, Miso- oder Salzgrundlage. Diese Suppe gilt als eine der beliebtesten Gerichte in Japan. Das Foto zeigt die populärsten Ramen-Sorten auf Sojasoßenbasis.

中国汤面

以酱油、日本酱、咸味为代表的中国热汤面，是一种深受欢迎的大众面食。照片中表示的是最普通的酱油汤面。

Nouilles ramen

Ce plat de nouilles chaudes est composé de nouilles chinoises et de divers ingrédients mélangés à une sauce de soja, une soupe à base de sel ou de miso. On le considère comme le plat le plus populaire au Japon. La photo illustre le type de ramen le plus populaire dans une soupe à base de soja.

라면

중국면을 간장, 된장, 소금 등으로 맛을 낸 따뜻한 국물의 면요리. 서민적인 맛. 사진은 가장 일반적인 간장맛 라면.

Sopa de Fideos Chinos (Ramen)

Este platillo de fideos calientes contiene fideos chinos con diversos ingredientes en una sopa hecha a base de salsa de soja, miso o sal y es considerado uno de los alimentos más populares de Japón. La foto muestra la sopa de ramen más común hecha a base de salsa de soja.

ラーメン

中華麺をしょうゆ味、みそ味、塩味などのスープで食べる温かい麺料理。庶民的な味。写真は、最も一般的なしょうゆラーメン。

Ramen

Piatto caldo di spaghettini cinesi (ramen) in brodo di vario genere: alla salsa di soia, al miso, al sale. È uno dei cibi più popolari in Giappone. Nella foto, il più comune tipo di ramen, quello in brodo al gusto di salsa di soia.

شعرية الرامن

يحتوي هذا الطبق الساخن على شعرية صينية تقدم مع مقادير أخرى في حساء من صلصة الصويا مع الميسو (مادة تتبيل من فول الصويا) أو حساء مضاف إليه الملح، وهو يعد من أهم الأطعمة لدي اليابانيين. في الصورة نرى أكثر أنواع الرامن شعبية وهو حساء الرامن بالميسو.

Sopa de macarrão chinês (Ramen)

Este prato contém macarrão chinês e vários ingredientes em uma sopa à base de molho de soja, pasta condimentícia miso ou sal. É uma das refeições mais populares no Japão. A foto mostra o tipo mais apreciado: sopa de macarrão chinês à base de molho de soja.

ラーメン各種 (Rāmen Kakushu)

Miso Ramen
- 醬湯面
- 酱汤面
- 된장맛 라면
- みそラーメン
- رامى بالميسو
- Miso Ramen
- Ramen au Miso
- Ramen de Miso
- Ramen al miso
- Sopa de macarrão chinês com miso

Salt-Based Ramen
- 鹹味面
- 咸味面
- 소금맛 라면
- 塩ラーメン
- رامى متبل بالملح
- Ramen auf Salzgrundlage
- Ramen au sel
- Ramen a base de Sal
- Ramen in brodo salato
- Sopa de macarrão chinês à base de sal

Ramen with Vegetables
- 熱湯面
- 热汤面
- 탄면
- タンメン
- رامى بالخضر
- Ramen mit Gemüse
- Ramen aux légumes
- Ramen con Verduras
- Ramen con verdure
- Sopa de macarrão chinês com vegetais

Ramen with Bean Sprouts
- 豆芽面
- 豆芽面
- 숙주나물 라면
- もやしラーメン
- رامى ببراعم الفول
- Ramen mit Sojabohnensprossen
- Ramen aux pousses de haricots
- Ramen con Brotes de Soja
- Ramen con germogli di semi di soia
- Sopa de macarrão chinês com brotos de feijão

Ramen with Shrimp
- 蝦仁面
- 虾仁面
- 새우 라면
- えびラーメン
- رامى بالجمبري
- Ramen mit Krabben
- Ramen aux crevettes
- Ramen con Langostinos
- Ramen con gamberetti
- Sopa de macarrão chinês com camarão

Ramen with Spicy Tofu Sauce
- 麻婆面
- 麻婆面
- 마파 라면
- マーボーラーメン
- رامى بالتوفر مع الصلصة الحريفة
- Ramen mit scharf gewˌrzter Tofu-Soße
- Ramen avec sauce de tofu épicée
- Ramen con Salsa Aromática de Cuajada de Soja
- Ramen con salsa piccante
- Sopa de macarrão chinês com molho de queijo de soja picante

Assorted Meat and Vegetable Stew with Noodles
(See p.99)
- 什錦湯面
- 什锦汤面
- 잡탕면
- 五目汁そば
- ياخني اللحم والخضر مع حساء الشعرية
- Fleisch-und Gemüseeintopf mit Nudeln
- Ragoût de viande et de légumes mixtes accompagnés de nouilles
- Caldo de Fideos con Carne y Verduras
- Spaghettini in brodo con carn e veroure
- Sopa de macarrão chinês com molho de carne e vegetais cozidos

Roasted Pork and Noodles
(See p.100)
- 叉燒湯面
- 叉烧汤面
- 구운 돼지고기면
- チャーシュー麺
- روستو اللحم مع الشعرية
- Schweinerostbraten und Nudeln
- Porc rôti et nouilles
- Caldo de Fideos con Cerdo Asado
- Spaghettini con maiale arrosto
- Sopa de porco assado e macarrão chinês

Wonton Noodle Soup
(See p.105)
- 餛飩面
- 馄饨面
- 완탕면
- ワンタン麺
- حساء الشعرية بالوانتان
- Wan-Tan-Nudelsuppe
- Soupe de nouilles au wonton
- Sopa de Fideos y Ravioles Chinos
- Spaghettini con won ton
- Sopa de macarrão chinês com wonton

すき焼き (Sukiyaki)

© S.T.

Sukiyaki

This nutritional stew-like favorite contains thin slices of beef, tofu and a wide assortment of vegetables flavored with a broth of soy sauce and sugar. The quality of the beef used is considered to make or break this dish. Some people prefer to dip the cooked treat in a beaten egg for extra flavor.

kcal ●●

日本式牛肉火鍋

這是將牛肉片、豆腐、蔬菜等放在用湯汁、醬油、白糖調味的火鍋內煮燒的一種營養豐富的火鍋，其味道取決於牛肉的質量。根據喜好，可沾著生雞蛋喫。

日本式牛肉火锅

这是将牛肉片、豆腐、蔬菜等放在用汤汁、酱油、白糖调味的火锅内煮烧的一种营养丰富的火锅，其味道取决于牛肉的质量。根据喜好，可沾着生鸡蛋吃。

스키야키

얇게 저민 쇠고기, 두부, 야채 등을 달짝지근한 양념 국물로 끓인 영양 풍부한 냄비요리. 쇠고기가 요리 맛을 좌우하며 기호에 따라 풀어 놓은 날달걀에 찍어서 먹는다.

すき焼き

薄切り牛肉、豆腐、野菜などを甘辛いタレで煮た栄養たっぷりの鍋もの。牛肉のよしあしが味の決め手。好みで生卵をつけて食べる。

سوكياكي

هو طبق شعبي غني بالفيتامينات يشبه الياخني ويحتوي على شرائح رفيعة من لحم البقر مع التوفو وتشكيلة من الخضر تطهى جميعاً في بهريز من صلصة الصويا وبعض السكر، ويتوقف نجاح هذا الطبق على جودة اللحم المستخدم في اعداده، ويفضل البعض تناوله مع بيضة مخفوقة يغمسون فيها القطع المطبوخة فتكتسب مذاقا لذيذا.

Sukiyaki

Dieses beliebte und nahrhafte, einem Stew ähnliche Gericht enthält dünne Rindfleisch-Scheiben, Tofu (Sojabohnenquark) und zahlreiche Gemüsesorten, die mit einem Sud aus Sojasoße und Zucker gewürzt werden. Häufig wird rohes Ei gereicht, in das die einzelnen Bissen nach Geschmack vor dem Verzehr getaucht werden können. Die Qualität des verwendeten Rindfleischs bestimmt nach allgemeiner Auffassung, ob dieses Gericht gelungen ist oder nicht.

Sukiyaki

Ce mets nourrissant qui s'apparente à un ragoût contient de fines tranches de bœuf, du tofu et un large assortiment de légumes agrémentés d'un bouillon à la sauce de soja et de sucre. C'est la qualité du bœuf utilisé qui en détermine la saveur. Trempez la viande dans un œuf battu avant de déguster.

Sukiyaki

Este nutritivo platillo estofado contiene finas rebanadas de carne de res, tofu y un amplio surtido de verduras condimentadas con un caldo hecho a base de salsa de soja y azúcar. Según se dice, este platillo puede ser una delicia o un fracaso, dependiendo de la calidad de la carne de res que se emplee.

Sukiyaki

Piatto molto nutriente preparato in casseruola con sottilissime fette di carne bovina, tofu, verdure e altri ingredienti insaporiti in modo dolce-salato. La buona riuscita del piatto dipende dalla qualità della carne. A piacere, si mangia intingendo in uovo crudo sbattuto.

Sukiyaki

Esta iguaria nutritiva ao estilo cozido contém finas fatias de carne de gado, queijo de soja e uma grande variedade de vegetais dispostos num caldo com molho de soja e açúcar. A qualidade da carne de gado utilizada é considerada decisiva para o sucesso deste prato. Há quem prefira mergulhar a iguaria em ovos batidos para obter um sabor extra ao comer.

しゃぶしゃぶ (Shabu-shabu)

© S.T.

Shabu-Shabu

This dish uses the finest thinly sliced beef as well as other popular ingredients that are cooked rapidly by dipping into a steaming hot broth and then dipped in several varieties of sauces.

kcal ●●

涮牛肉

這是將質地上等的牛肉片和各自挑選的新鮮蔬菜在煮沸的火鍋中稍稍涮過後，蘸上佐料食用的一種菜肴。

涮牛肉

这是将质地上等的牛肉片和各自挑选的新鲜蔬菜在煮沸的火锅中稍稍涮过后，蘸上佐料食用的一种菜肴。

샤브샤브

얇게 저민 양질의 쇠고기나 야채 등을 냄비에 맛국물을 끓이면서 살짝 데쳐 양념장에 찍어 먹는 냄비요리.

しゃぶしゃぶ

上質の薄切り牛肉や好みの野菜などをアツアツの煮汁でサッとゆがき、タレにつけて食べる鍋料理。

شابو شابو

يستخدم لإعداد هذا الطبق أفضل أنواع اللحم البقري مقطعاً إلى شرائح رقيقة مع عدد من المقادير المفضلة الأخرى وتطهى بغمسها سريعاً في البهريز المغلي ثم تتبل في إحدى الصلصات المقدمة معها.

Shabu-Shabu

Für dieses Gericht werden hauchdünn geschnittene Rindfleisch-Scheiben und andere beliebte Zutaten verwendet, die rasch gekocht werden, indem man sie mit den Stäbchen in eine glühendheiße Brühe taucht und anschließend mit verschiedenen Arten von Soßen würzt.

Shabu-shabu

Dans ce plat, on utilise des tranches de bœuf extrêmement fines ainsi que d'autres ingrédients populaires que l'on fait cuire rapidement en les plongeant dans un bouillon fumant puis en les trempant dans différentes variétés de sauces.

Shabu-Shabu

Este platillo emplea carne de res cortada en finísimas rebanadas y otros ingredientes populares que se hierven rápidamente remojándolos en un caldo humeante y sazonándolos en varias clases de salsa.

Shabu-shabu

Si prepara sbollentando velocemente in un brodo sottilissime fette di carne bovina della migliore qualità, verdure e altri ingredienti. Ci si serve direttamente dalla pentola e si mangia intingendo in salse di vario tipo.

Shabu-shabu

Neste prato, utiliza-se a carne de gado da mais alta qualidade, em fatias finíssimas, bem como outros ingredientes apreciados, que são fervidos ligeiramente em um caldo fumegante e saboreados após seu mergulho em vários tipos de molhos.

寄せ鍋 (Yose-nabe)

© S.T.

Seafood & Vegetable Casserole

Flavored soup stock is poured into an earthenware dish followed by the addition of various seafood and vegetables which are then eaten as they simmer together.

kcal ●●

什錦火鍋

這種火鍋是先在鍋中加入調好味的湯汁，然後放入魚貝類及蔬菜等各種材料，邊煮邊喫。

Kasserole mit Meeresfrüchten und Gemüse

Eine würzige Brühe wird in eine Steingutschale geschüttet und dann verschiedene Meeresfrüchte und Gemüse hinzugegeben, die gegessen werden, während sie gemeinsam köcheln.

什锦火锅

这种火锅是先在锅中加入调好味的汤汁，然后放入鱼贝类及蔬菜等各种材料，边煮边吃。

Cocotte de légumes et de fruits de mer

Dans un plat en terre, on verse un bouillon de varech parfumé auquel on ajoute divers fruits de mer et des légumes et que l'on déguste au fur et à mesure qu'ils mijotent.

잡탕남비

남비에 맛국물을 넣고, 어패류, 야채 등 여러 가지 재료를 넣고 끓여가면서 먹는 요리.

Cacerola de Mariscos y Verduras

Se pone a calentar extracto de sopa a fuego lento en una cacerola de barro y se van agregando mariscos y verduras hasta que se cuecen juntos.

寄せ鍋

鍋に味付けしただし汁をはり、魚介類や野菜などのさまざまな材料を入れ、煮ながら食べる料理。

Pesce e verdure in pignatta

In una pignatta di terracotta contenente del brodo si fanno cuocere via via pesce, molluschi e crostacei, verdure e altro. Ci si serve direttamente dalla pignatta man mano che gli ingredienti arrivano al punto giusto di cottura.

طاجن الخضر والقواقع البحرية

يوضع حساء، متبل في الطاجن الفخاري ويضاف إليه تشكيلة من الخضر والقواقع البحرية ويقدم على المائدة ليؤكل بينما يطهى على نار هادئة.

Caçarola de frutos do mar e vegetais

O caldo de sopa é despejado na caçarola de barro. Em seguida, adicionam-se vários frutos do mar e vegetais. Saboreia-se esta iguaria à medida que os ingredientes são fervidos em fogo brando.

水炊き (Mizutaki)

Boiled Chicken Casserole

Chicken, tofu and vegetables are boiled in soup stock and enjoyed by dipping in a sauce flavored with vinegar and soy sauce for a dish that is both light and satisfying.

kcal ●●

雞肉氽鍋

這是用湯汁將雞肉、豆腐、蔬菜煮熟後，蘸著橙子汁和醬油食用的清淡爽口的火鍋菜肴。

Kasserole mit gekochtem Huhn

Huhn, Tofu (Sojabohnenquark) und Gemüse werden in Brühe gekocht. Vor dem Verzehr werden sie mit einer Soße gewürzt, die Essig aus Zitrusfrüchten (Ponzu) und Sojasoße enthält. Ein leichtes und doch sättigendes Gericht.

鸡肉氽锅

这是用汤汁将鸡肉、豆腐、蔬菜煮熟后，蘸着橙子汁和酱油食用的清淡爽口的火锅菜肴。

Cocotte de poulet bouilli

Ce plat à la fois léger et nourrissant se compose de poulet, de tofu et de légumes que l'on a fait bouillir dans un bouillon de volaille et que l'on trempe dans une sauce aromatisée au vinaigre et au soja.

일식 영계백숙

맛국물에 닭고기, 두부, 야채를 끓여서 초간장에 찍어먹는 담백한 냄비요리.

Cacerola de Pollo Cocido

Para preparar este platillo ligero y provechoso se cuecen pollo, tofu y verduras en extracto de sopa y se comen remojándolos en una salsa preparada con vinagre y salsa de soja.

水炊き

だし汁で鶏肉、豆腐、野菜を煮て、ポン酢しょうゆで食べるさっぱりとした鍋料理。

Pollo e verdure in pignatta

In una pignatta di terracotta contenente del brodo si fanno cuocere pollo, tofu e verdure varie. È un piatto leggero che si mangia direttamente dalla pignatta intingendo in soia mista ad aceto di riso.

طاجن الدجاج المسلوق

يسلق أمامك الدجاج والتوفو والخضر في حساء، متبل ويؤكل كل منها بعد غمسه في صلصة متبلة بالخل وصلصة الصويا لتحصل على وجبة خفيفة ومشبعة.

Caçarola de frango

Frango, queijo de soja e vegetais são fervidos em caldo de sopa e saboreados após mergulho num molho especialmente preparado com vinagre e molho de soja. É um prato ao mesmo tempo leve e delicioso.

おでん (Oden)

© S.T.

Fish Cake and Vegetable Casserole

Japanese radishes, potatoes, hard-boiled eggs and numerous types of fish cakes are cut into large chunks and simmered slowly in a special broth that allows the flavor to permeate the ingredients for a dish that is perfect on a cold night.

kcal ●●●

炖雜燴

這是將切成大塊的蘿蔔、土豆、雞蛋及魚肉加工品用帶有醬油的湯汁炖熟而成的菜肴。趁著熱喫，味道鮮美是其特色。

炖杂烩

这是将切成大块的萝卜、土豆、鸡蛋及鱼肉加工品用带有酱油的汤汁炖熟而成的菜肴。趁着热吃，味道鲜美是其特色。

오뎅

큼직하게 썬 무우, 감자, 달걀, 어묵 등을 간장 풍미의 국물에 푹 끓여 먹는 요리. 뜨거울 때 먹는 것이 맛있다.

おでん

大きく切った大根、じゃがいも、卵、魚の練り製品などをしょうゆ風味の煮汁でじっくり煮込んだもの。アツアツがおいしい。

طاجن الخضر مع كرات السمك

يقطع الفجل الياباني والبطاطس والبيض المسلوق وكرات السمك من أنواع مختلفة إلى قطع كبيرة ويطهى الجميع ببطء، في بمرير تخلل نكهته المكونات المختلفة لتحصل على طبق مثالي في الليالي الباردة.

Kasserole aus Fischpastete und Gemüse

Japanischer Riesenrettich, Kartoffeln, hart gekochte Eier und verschiedene Arten von Fischpasteten werden in große Stücke geschnitten und dann langsam in einem speziellen Sud geköchelt. Diese Art der Zubereitung ermöglicht es, daß der Geschmack aller Zutaten durchdringt. Dieses Gericht eignet sich perfekt für kalte Winterabende.

Cocotte de légumes et de pain de poisson

Ce plat qui convient parfaitement pour les nuits froides comprend du radis japonais, des pommes de terre, des œufs durs et diverses sortes de pains de poisson coupés en gros morceaux que l'on fait mijoter doucement dans un bouillon spécial dont la saveur imprègne tous les ingrédients.

Cacerola de Pastas de Pescado y Verduras

Se cortan en grandes trozos los rábanos japoneses, patatas, huevos cocidos y una gran variedad de pastas de pescado para cocer a fuego lento en un caldo especial que permite impregnar de sabor a los ingredientes y crear un platillo perfecto para una noche fría.

Bollito misto alla giapponese (oden)

In un particolare brodo al gusto di soia vengono bolliti lentamente pezzi di rapa giapponese, patate, uova semisode, vari tipi di impasti di farina di pesce o altro fino a che il sapore penetra all'interno degli ingredienti. Ottimo se mangiato molto caldo.

Caçarola de bolinhos de massa de peixe e vegetais

Pedaços grandes de nabo-japonês, batatas, ovos cozidos e vários tipos de massas de peixe são fervidos em fogo brando, em um caldo especial cujo sabor penetra nos ingredientes. É o prato perfeito para uma noite fria.

湯豆腐 (Yu-dōfu)

Simmered Tofu

This simple yet delicious dish involves placing blocks of tofu in a soup stock made from kelp, gently boiling, and adding various condiments and flavored soy sauce that enhance the true flavor of the tofu.

kcal ●

© O.S.T.

豆腐火鍋

用海帶絲熬出的湯汁將豆腐稍燉一下後加入佐料，蘸汁食用使您可充分品嘗材料本身的自然美味。

Gekochter Tofu

Für dieses einfache aber köstliche Gericht werden Tofu-Würfel (Sojabohnenquark) in eine Brühe gegeben, die aus Seetang hergestellt wurde und vorsichtig gekocht. Die verschiedenen Zutaten und die gewürzte Sojasoße heben den Geschmack des Tofu noch hervor.

豆腐火锅

用海带丝熬出的汤汁将豆腐稍炖一下后加入佐料，蘸汁食用使您可充分品尝材料本身的自然美味。

Tofu mijoté

Ce plat simple mais délicieux consiste à plonger des blocs de tofu dans un bouillon de varech et en faisant bouillir doucement le tout avec divers condiments et de la sauce de soja qui relèvent la vraie saveur du tofu.

두부탕

다시마 국물에 두부를 살짝 끓여 양념장에 찍어 먹는다. 두부 자체의 맛을 즐기는 심플한 요리.

Tofu Cocido a Fuego Lento

Este sencillo pero delicioso platillo se prepara colocando cubos de tofu en extracto de sopa de alga marina e hirviéndo con cuidado mientras se agregan distintos condimentos que realzan el verdadero sabor del tofu.

湯豆腐

昆布のだし汁で豆腐を軽く煮、薬味を入れたタレで味わう。豆腐の持ち味を楽しむ、シンプルな鍋料理。

Tofu bollito

È un piatto semplice di tofu bollito in un brodo di alghe kombu. Ci si serve dalla pignatta di terracotta e si intinge il tofu in un'apposita salsina con l'aggiunta di gusti. Si può così apprezzare appieno il sapore del tofu.

التوفو المطهو على نار هادئة

هذا طبق لذيذ الطعم رغم بساطته ويصنع بسلق قطع التوفو ببطء في حساء معد من أعشاب البحر مع إضافة صلصة الصويا المتبلة وبعض التوابل الأخرى لتقوية النكهة الطبيعية للتوفو.

Queijo de soja fervido

Este prato simples mas delicioso contém blocos de queijo de soja em um delicado caldo preparado com alga marinha. Ferve-se lentamente, com vários temperos e molho de soja condimentado, que realçam o sabor autêntico do queijo de soja.

鉄板焼き（Teppan-yaki）

©S.T.

Mixed Grill

This hearty dish is enjoyed by cooking meat, seafood and vegetables on an iron skillet and eating them piping hot by taking them directly from the skillet and dipping in a flavorful sauce.

kcal ●●

鐵板烤

這是將肉、魚貝類、蔬菜用鐵板烤熟後，趁熱蘸佐料食用的一道菜肴。

Gemischte Grillplatte

Bei diesem herzhaften Gericht werden Fleisch, Meeresfrüchte und Gemüse auf einer heißen Eisenpfanne bei Tisch gebraten. Man ißt dann jeweils ein Stück glühendheiß direkt aus der Pfanne und taucht es vor dem Verzehr in eine würzige Soße ein.

铁板烤

这是将肉、鱼贝类、蔬菜用铁板烤熟后，趁热蘸佐料食用的一道菜肴。

Grillades mixtes

Ce plat copieux se déguste après avoir fait cuire de la viande, des fruits de mer et des légumes dans un poêlon en métal, que l'on savoure directement dans le poêlon après les avoir fait tremper dans une sauce aromatisée.

철판구이

고기나 어패류, 야채를 철판에 구어 양념장에 찍어 먹는 요리.

Surtido a la Plancha

Este sabroso platillo se disfruta asando carne, mariscos y verduras en una plancha de acero. Se comen bien calientes tomándolos directamente del lugar en que se están cocinando y se mojan en una salsa bien condimentada.

鉄板焼き

肉や魚介類、野菜を鉄板でこんがりと焼き、アツアツのところをタレにつけて食べる料理。

Misto alla piastra (teppanyaki)

Sulla piastra rovente si cuociono carne, pesce, frutti di mare e verdure, che si mangiano ben caldi intingendoli in apposite salsine.

تشكيلة من المشويات

هذا طبق شهي يتكون من تشكيلة من اللحم والقواقع البحرية والخضر تطهى أمامك في مقلاة الشي وتؤكل ساخنه من المقلاة مباشرة بعد غمسها في صلصة لذيذة الطعم.

Misto na chapa

Prepara-se este prato apetitoso assando carne, frutos do mar e vegetais na chapa de ferro. Saboreia-se bem quente, servindo-se diretamente da chapa e mergulhando os ingredientes num molho aromático.

お好み焼き (Okonomi-yaki)

Grilled Japanese-Style Pancakes

This popular snack contains cabbage, eggs, meat and seafood in a flour batter which is spread out onto a grill and cooked on both sides to an appealing golden brown.

kcal ●●

© S.T.

十錦煎菜餅

　這是一種在面粉中摻入圓白菜、雞蛋、肉、魚貝類等，然後平攤在鐵板上將其煎成兩面黃的菜餅。

十锦煎菜饼

这是一种在面粉中掺入圆白菜、鸡蛋、肉、鱼贝类等，然后平摊在铁板上将其煎成两面黄的菜饼。

일식 부침개

묽은 밀가루 반죽에 잘게 썬 양배추, 달걀, 고기, 어패류 등을 섞어 철판에 둥글게 펴서 양면을 노릇노릇하게 부친 요리.

お好み焼き

小麦粉をだし汁で溶いた生地にキャベツや卵、肉、魚介類などを混ぜ、鉄板に丸く広げて両面をこんがりと焼いたもの。

قطيرة مشوية على الطريقة اليابانية

هي صنف شعبي من المشهيات يحتوي على كرنب وبيض ولحم وقواقع بحرية تغمر معاً في عجينة سائلة من الدقيق، ثم تسكب العجينة على صاج الشي وتطهى على الجانبين حتى تكتسب لوناً ذهبياً جميلاً.

Gegrillte japanische Pfannkuchen

Dieses beliebte Gericht enthält Kohl, Eier, Fleisch und Meeresfrüchte, die mit einem dünnen Weizenmehlteig gemischt und dann auf einer heißen Pfanne ausgebreitet werden. Sie sind zum Verzehr bereit, wenn sie auf beiden Seiten goldbraun angebraten sind.

Crêpes épaisses grillées à la japonaise

Cet en-cas populaire contient du chou, des œufs, de la viande et des fruits de mer mélangés à une pâte à crêpes que l'on verse sur un grill et que l'on fait griller des deux côtés jusqu'à obtenir une dorure appétissante.

Panqueques Asados al Estilo Japonés

Este popular entremés contiene col, huevos carne y mariscos en una pasta de harina que se esparce sobre una parrilla y se cocina por ambos lados hasta que alcanza un atractivo color dorado.

Tortine alla piastra

Ad una pastella di farina e brodo si uniscono cavolo finemente tritato, uova, carne, gamberetti o altri ingredienti; il composto viene appiattito in forma di tortine sulla piastra rovente e cotto da entrambi i lati fino a che prende colore.

Panquecas ao estilo japonês

Esta refeição leve e muito apreciada contém repolho, ovos, carne e frutos do mar misturados a uma massa mole de farinha de trigo. A mistura é espalhada na chapa de ferro e assada nos dois lados até adquirir um dourado apetitoso.

みつ豆 (Mitsumame)

© S.T.

Gelatin (Agar-agar) and Fruit Dessert

Gelatin (Agar-agar), assorted fruits and sweet beans are covered with a sweet syrup and then chilled before serving.

kcal ●

什錦甜涼粉

是用洋粉、水果及豆混和均匀，然後澆上果子露而做成的一道涼甜點。

Dessert aus Gelatine (Agar-Agar) und Früchten

Gelatine (Agar-Agar), gemischte Früchte und süße Bohnen werden mit einem süßen Sirup übergossen und eiskalt serviert.

什锦甜凉粉

是用洋粉、水果及豆混和均匀, 然后浇上果子露而做成的一道凉甜点。

Agar-agar accompagné de fruits et de haricots rouges

Ce plat est un mélange de gelée d'agar-agar, de fruits et de haricots rouges sucrés dans un sirop sucré, on laisse refroidir le tout avant de servir.

콩시럽 디저트

한천이나 과일, 콩을 섞어서 시럽을 끼얹어 차게 먹는 디저트.

Postre de Gelatina con Fruta

Este popular postre, es una combinación de ingredientes tales como gelatina, frutas surtidas y judías azucaradas cubiertas con un jarabe dulce que se sirve bien helado.

みつ豆

寒天やくだもの、豆をミックスし、甘いシロップをかけた冷たいデザート。

Dessert di gelatina e frutta

È un dessert freddo di gelatina di agar-agar, frutta e fagioli azuki dolci irrorati di sciroppo dolce.

حلوى الفاكهة والجيلي

مكعبات من الجيلي مع الفول المحلي بالسكر وتشكيلة منوعة من الفاكهة، يسكب فوقها جميعاً شراب حلو وتوضع في الثلاجة لتقدم باردة.

Sobremesa de gelatina(ágar-ágar) e frutas

Gelatina(ágar-ágar), frutas sortidas e feijão doce são cobertos com um xarope doce e levados ao refrigerador antes de serem servidos.

抹茶アイスクリーム (Maccha Aisu-kurīmu)

Green Tea Ice Cream

This attractive ice cream gets its appearance from the green tea from which it is made. The creamy sweet flavor of the ice cream is a perfect match for the astringency of the tea resulting in a refreshing taste.

kcal ●

© S.T.

末茶冰淇淋

這是一種放入鮮綠色末茶的冰淇淋。奶油的甜味巧妙地中和了末茶的澀味，口感清爽。

Eiscreme aus grünem Tee

Diese attraktive Eiscreme erhält ihr Aussehen vom zur Verarbeitung verwendeten grünen Tee. Der cremig süße Geschmack der Eiscreme paßt perfekt zum herben Geschmack des Tees und ergibt eine erfrischende Geschmackskombination.

末茶冰淇淋

这是一种放入鲜绿色末茶的冰淇淋.奶油的甜味巧妙地中和了末茶的涩味，口感清爽。

Glace au thé vert

Cette glace appétissante tire son apparence du thé vert utilisé pour la préparer. L'onctueuse saveur sucrée de la glace se combine parfaitement avec l'astringence du thé, ce qui lui confère un goût rafraîchissant.

녹차 아이스크림

녹차잎을 갈아 만든 깔끔한 녹색 아이스크림. 크림의 단맛과 녹차의 떫은 맛이 잘 어울리는 깨끗한 맛.

Helado de Té Verde

Este atractivo helado que está hecho a partir del té verde presenta un precioso color verde. El cremoso y dulce sabor del helado es la perfecta combinación para la sobriedad del té, lo cual da como resultado un sabor refrescante.

抹茶アイスクリーム

抹茶を混ぜ込んだきれいな緑色のアイスクリーム。クリームの甘味と抹茶の渋みがマッチし、さっぱりした味わい。

Gelato di tè verde

Il bel colore verde è dovuto al finissimo tè in polvere mescolato alla crema. Il dolce della crema e l'aspro del tè ben si combinano in un sapore leggero.

آيس كريم من الشاي الأخضر

هذا الآيس كريم جميل الشكل يكتسب لونه من الشاي الأخضر المستخدم في إعداده. وهنا نجد النكهة الحلوة الدسمة للآيس كريم تتناسب تماماً مع الطعم القابض للشاي مما يحقق في النهاية مذاقاً منعشاً.

Sorvete de chá verde

Este sorvete atraente tem a cor do chá verde com o qual é preparado. O sabor cremoso e doce do sorvete é a companhia perfeita para a adstringência do chá, resultando em uma sobremesa muito refrescante.

小豆アイスクリーム (Azuki Aisu-kurīmu)

© S.T.

Sweet Bean Ice Cream

This ice cream contains sweet beans which are frequently used in Japanese confections for a simple, truly Japanese flavor.

kcal ●●

小豆冰淇淋

這是將日式點心所用的甜豆餡放入冰淇淋中而制成的，味覺中帶有獨特的日本式清醇。

Eiscreme aus süßen Bohnen

Diese Eiscreme enthält süße Bohnen, die häufig für japanisches Konfekt verwendet werden. Ein einfacher aber typisch japanischer Geschmack.

小豆冰淇淋

这是将日式点心所用的甜豆馅放入冰淇淋中而制成的，味觉中带有独特的日本式清醇。

Glace aux haricots rouges sucrés

Cette glace contient des haricots rouges sucrés que l'on emploie fréquemment dans les desserts japonais et qui procurent une saveur simple et typiquement japonaise.

단팥 아이스크림

일본 과자에 사용하는 단팥이 들어 있는 아이스크림. 소박한 일본 고유의 맛.

Helado de Judías Azucaradas

Este helado con el sencillo y auténtico sabor japonés, es una combinación de judías y pasta de judías azucaradas, que se usa con frecuencia en confituras japonesas.

小豆アイスクリーム

和菓子に使う甘いつぶあんの入ったアイスクリーム。和風の素朴な味。

Gelato con fagioli azuki dolci

È un gelato con i fagioli azuki spesso usati nella pasticceria giapponese. Gusto semplice e tipicamente giapponese.

آيس كريم من الفول الحلو

يتميز هذا الآيس كريم بطعم ياباني بسيط وحقيقي حيث يحتوي على الفول المحلى بالسكر الذي يستخدم كثيراً في الحلوى اليابانية.

Sorvete de feijão doce

Este sorvete contém feijão doce, ingrediente muito utilizado em confeitos japoneses. Tem um sabor simples e autêntico.

ようかん (Yōkan)

Sweet Bean Jelly

Strained bean paste is added to liquid gelatin (agar-agar) and then chilled to solidify for the perfect dessert with Japanese tea.

kcal ●

© S.T.

羊羹

是在洋粉汁中加入豆沙餡，使其冷卻凝固後做成的日式甜點，很適合飲日本茶時食用。

Gelee aus süßen Bohnen

Eine Paste aus passierten Bohnen wird mit flüssiger Gelatine (Agar-Agar) versetzt und dann zum Festwerden gekühlt. Das perfekte Dessert für den Genuß mit japanischem Tee.

羊羹

是在洋粉汁中加入豆沙馅，使其冷却凝固后做成的日式甜点，很适合饮日本茶时食用。

Gelée de haricots rouges sucrés

Ce dessert qui se marie parfaitement avec le thé japonais se prépare en mélangeant de la pâte de haricots rouges broyés à de l'agar-agar liquide que l'on fait ensuite refroidir pour solidifier le tout.

양갱

한천액에 단팥을 넣고 차게 굳힌 것으로 녹차와 잘 어울리는 일본과자.

Pasta de Judías Azucaradas

Para lograr este postre, que combina a la perfección con el té japonés, se agrega una consistente pasta de judías azucaradas a la gelatina líquida y se pone a enfriar hasta que solidifica.

ようかん

寒天液にこしあんを加えて冷やし固めた、日本茶によく合う和菓子。

Gelatina di fagioli azuki dolci

Viene preparata unendo marmellata di azuki passati al setaccio con agar-agar liquido. Raffreddando, il composto solidifica e viene servito a fette. È un dolce che ben si accompagna con il tè verde.

جيلي الفول الحلو

يضاف معجون الفول المصفى إلى الجيلاتين السائل ويثلج حتى يتماسك فتتحصل على صنف حلو مثالي مع الشاي الياباني.

Gelatina de feijão doce

Adiciona-se pasta de feijão coado ao ágar-ágar líquido e solidificado no refrigerador. É a sobremesa perfeita para ser saboreada com chá japonês.

みたらし団子 (Mitarashi Dango)

© S.T.

Dessert Dumplings

Dumplings made from glutinous rice are placed on skewers, grilled to a golden brown and covered with a thick, sweet soy-based sauce.

kcal ●

丸子串

是一種將用竹扦串起來的丸子放在烤網上適當燒烤，然後蘸上帶醬油味的甜味佐料食用的日式點心。

Dessert-Kugeln

Aus klebrigem Reis hergestellte Kugeln werden auf Spieße gesteckt, goldbraun gegrillt und dann mit einer dicken, süßen Sojasoße übergossen.

丸子串

是一种将用竹扦串起来的丸子放在烤网上适当烧烤，然后蘸上带酱油味的甜味佐料食用的日式点心。

Brochettes de boulettes sucrées

On dispose des boulettes confectionnées à partir de riz gluant sur des brochettes que l'on fait griller jusqu'à ce qu'elles deviennent dorées et que l'on enrobe d'une épaisse sauce sucrée à base de soja.

떡꼬치

꼬치에 경단을 여러개 끼워서 석쇠에 노릇노릇하게 구워 달콤한 간장 소스를 바른 일본과자.

Postre de Bolas de Masa

Se hace bolas de masa de arroz glutinoso y se ensartan en brochetas para asarse hasta que logran un color dorado oscuro. Acto seguido, se cubren con un jarabe espeso hecho a base de la salsa de soja.

みたらし団子

竹串に刺した団子をこんがり焼き、しょうゆ風味の甘いタレをかけた和菓子。

Palline dolci di farina di riso

Palline fatte con farina di riso glutinoso vengono infilzate in spiedini e abbrustolite su una rete. Si mangiano ricoperte di una densa e dolce salsa a base di soia.

كرات الأرز الحلوة

تصنع كرات من عجينة الأرز اللدن وتوضع في سيخ وتشوى حتى تكتسب لوناً ذهبياً ثم تغطى بشراب حلو مكثف بطعم صلصة الصويا.

Sobremesa de bolinhos

Bolinhos de arroz glutinoso semelhantes a nhoques são dispostos em espetinhos, grelhados até dourar e cobertos com um molho doce espesso, à base de soja.

茶 (Cha)

Tea

Japanese tea, best known for its attractive green color, is also extremely healthy, containing vitamin C and an abundance of other natural ingredients.

kcal

© S.T.

茶

鮮嫩綠色的日本茶含有豐富的維生素Ｃ等天然成分，是一種理想的健康飲料。

Tee

Japanischer Tee ist weithin wegen seiner attraktiven grünen Farbe bekannt. Außerdem ist er besonders gesund, enthält Vitamin C und zahlreiche andere natürliche Bestandteile.

茶

鲜嫩绿色的日本茶含有丰富的维生素C等天然成分，是一种理想的健康饮料。

Thé

Le thé japonais, connu pour son attrayante couleur verte est également excellent pour la santé car il contient de la vitamine C ainsi que toute une palette d'autres ingrédients naturels.

차

초록색을 띤 일본차는 비타민C 등의 천연 성분을 풍부하게 포함한 건강에 좋은 음료수.

Té

El té japonés, mejor conocido por su atractivo color verde, es también extremadamente saludable, pues contiene vitamina C en abundancia y otros ingredientes naturales.

茶

きれいな緑色をした日本茶は、ビタミンＣなどの天然成分が豊富に含まれた健康的な飲みもの。

Tè

Il tè giapponese ha un bel colore verde ed è una salutare bevanda ricca di vitamina C e di altri componenti naturali.

الشاي

يشتهر الشاي الياباني بلونه الأخضر الجميل وهو صحي للغاية حيث يحتوي على فيتامين ج إلى جانب وفرة من المواد الطبيعية الأخرى.

Chá

O chá japonês, bastante conhecido por sua atraente coloração verde, é extremamente saudável, contendo vitamina C e muitos outros ingredientes naturais.

日本酒 (Nihon-shu)

© S.T.

Sake

Sake is brewed from rice and rice malt. There are numerous types of sake depending on the production method and ingredients. Each type is prepared while taking into consideration the proper balance of sweetness, sourness, astringency, harshness and bitterness.

kcal ●●

日本酒

是以米和米曲為主要原料醸造制成的一種酒。根據原料和醸造方法的不同，可分為許多種類。甜酸味、澀味、辣味、苦味全面得以中和平衡是其擁有的特色。

Sake

Sake wird aus Reis und Reismalz gebraut. Es gibt zahllose Arten von Sake, deren Geschmack vom Produktionsverfahren und den Zutaten abhängt. Bei der Herstellung jedes einzelnen Typs wird auf die gewünschte Balance zwischen Süße, Säure, Herbheit, harschem Geschmack und Bitterstoffen geachtet.

日本酒

是以米和米曲为主要原料酿造制成的一种酒。根据原料和酿造方法的不同，可分为许多种类。甜酸味、涩味、辣味、苦味全面得以中和平衡是其拥有的特色。

Saké

Le saké est brassé à partir de riz ou de malt de riz. Il existe de nombreuses sortes de saké qui varient suivant la méthode de production et les ingrédients utilisés. Chaque sorte est préparée de façon à ce que l'équilibre entre les saveurs sucrée, acide, astringente, âpre et amère soit harmonieusement respecté.

일본술(정종)

쌀이나 누룩을 주원료로 한 양조주. 원료와 만드는 방법에 따라 여러 종류의 맛이 있으며, 단맛, 신맛, 떫은 맛, 쓴맛, 자극적인 맛 등이 잘 조화되어 있다.

Sake

El sake se destila del arroz y la malta del arroz. Hay numerosos tipos de sake, dependiendo del método de producción y los ingredientes. Cada variedad se prepara teniendo en cuenta el justo equilibrio de dulzura, acidez, astringencia, aspereza y amargor.

日本酒

米と米麹を主原料にした醸造酒。原料、製法の違いによってさまざまな種類があり、甘味、酸味、苦みなどがバランスよく調和されている。

Sakè

È una bevanda alcolico prodotta dalla fermentazione del riso. A seconda delle materie prime e dei metodi di produzione usati, si hanno tipi di sakè diversi, ma tutti con un armonico equilibrio di dolce, agro e amaro.

الساكي

يصنع هذا المشروب الكحولي من حبوب وملت الأرز، وهناك أنواع عديدة من الساكي طبقاً لطريقة الإنتاج ونوعية المكونات، ويصنع كل نوع منه مع مراعاة شديدة للتوازن المناسب في مذاقه بين الحلو والحامض والقابض والحاد والمر.

Saquê

O saquê é feito através da fermentação de arroz e malte de arroz. Os tipos de saquê variam conforme o método de produção e seus ingredientes. Cada tipo é preparado levando-se em consideração o equilíbrio adequado entre doçura, acidez, adstringência, acidez e amargor.

ビール (Bīru)

Beer

There are many varieties of Japanese beer. Some major brands are, from left to right, Asahi, Kirin, Orion, Sapporo and Suntory. Beers brewed by smaller, regional breweries have gained in popularity recently.

kcal ●

© S.T.

啤酒

日本啤酒種類豐富，從左到右依次為：朝日、麒麟、獵戶、札幌、三得利。最近，地方產啤酒也深受消費者歡迎。

Bier

Es gibt zahlreiche japanische Biersorten. Zu den wichtigsten Marken gehören von links nach rechts Asahi, Kirin, Orion, Sapporo und Suntory. In jüngster Zeit haben Biere, die von kleinen, regionalen Brauereien produziert werden ("ji-biru"), an Beliebtheit gewonnen.

啤酒

日本啤酒种类丰富，从左到右依次为：朝日、麒麟、猎户、札幌、三得利。最近，地方产啤酒也深受消费者欢迎。

Bières

Il existe plusieurs variétés de bière japonaise. Les principales marques sont de gauche à droite : Asahi, Kirin, Orion, Sapporo et Suntory. Les bières fabriquées dans des brasseries régionales plus petites sont récemment devenues populaires.

맥주

종류가 풍부한 일본 맥주. 왼쪽부터 아사히, 기린, 오리온, 삿포로, 산토리. 최근에는 지역 맥주도 인기가 높다.

Cerveza

Hay muchas variedades de cerveza japonesa. Entre las principales marcas se pueden citar, de izquierda a derecha: Asahi, Kirin, Orion, Sapporo y Suntory. Recientemente están cobrando gran popularidad las cervezas fabricadas por cervecerías regionales más pequeñas.

ビール

種類が豊富な日本のビール。左からアサヒ、キリン、オリオン、サッポロ、サントリー。最近では地ビールの人気も高い。

Birra

Il Giappone ha molti tipi di birre: le marche più conosciute sono: Asahi, Kirin, Orion, Sapporo e Suntory. Recentemente sono in voga le birre di produzione locale.

البيرة

هناك أنواع كثيرة من البيرة اليابانية نقدم هنا بعضاً من أشهرها. من اليسار لليمين: أساهي، كيرين، أوريون، سابورو، سانتوري، ويلاحظ في الآونة الأخيرة ارتفاع شعبية بعض أنواع البيرة المحلية من إنتاج مصانع أصغر.

Cerveja

Produz-se no Japão uma grande variedade de cervejas. Entre as principais estão (da esquerda para a direita): Asahi, Kirin, Orion, Sapporo e Suntory. Ultimamente, cervejas produzidas por pequenos fabricantes, de atuação regional, têm sido cada vez mais consumidas pelo público.

The following provides an introduction to some convenient dinner menus for added enjoyment when dining in a Japanese restaurant.

© S.T.

Tempura Dinner

1. Assorted Tempura (p.197)
2. Boiled Vegetables (p.209)
3. Boiled Spinach with Bonito Shavings (p.212)
4. Savory Egg Custard (p.221)
5. Clear Soup (p.223)

天婦羅套餐(酥炸套菜)

1. 天婦羅拼盆(酥炸拼盆)(p.197)
2. 炖煨蔬菜 (p.209)
3. 涼拌菠菜 (p.212)
4. 蒸雞蛋羹 (p.221)
5. 清　湯 (p.223)

天妇罗套餐(酥炸套菜)

1. 天妇罗拼盆(酥炸拼盆)(p.197)
2. 炖煨蔬菜 (p.209)
3. 涼拌菠菜 (p.212)
4. 蒸鸡蛋羹 (p.221)
5. 清　汤 (p.223)

튀김 정식

1. 모듬튀김 (p.197)
2. 야채조림 (p.209)
3. 일식 시금치나물 (p.212)
4. 달걀찜 (p.221)
5. 맑은 국 (p.223)

天ぷら定食

1. 天ぷらの盛り合わせ (p.197)
2. 野菜の煮もの (p.209)
3. おひたし (p.212)
4. 茶碗蒸し (p.221)
5. すまし汁 (p.223)

عشاء التمبورا

١. منوعات من التمبورا (ص ١٩٧)
٢. خضر مسلوقة (ص ٢٠٩)
٣. سبانخ مسلوقة مع ميشور السمك (ص ٢١٢)
٤. بودنج البيض المملح (ص ٢٢١)
٥. الحساء الشفاف (ص ٢٢٣)

Menü mit Tempura

1. Gemischtes Tempura (S. 197)
2. Gekochtes Gemüse (S. 209)
3. Gekochter Spinat mit Bonitfisch-Flocken (S. 212)
4. Pikanter Eierstich mit Einlage (S. 221)
5. Klare Suppe (S. 223)

Dîner à base de tempura

1. Assortiment de tempura (p.197)
2. Légumes bouillis (p.209)
3. Epinards bouillis accompagnés de bonite séchée râpée (p.212)
4. Crème onctueuse aux œufs (p.221)
5. Soupe claire (p.223)

Plato Combinado de Tempura

1. Tempura Surtido (p.197)
2. Verduras Cocidas (p.209)
3. Espinacas Cocidas con Hojuelas de Bonito Seco (p.212)
4. Flan de Huevo Aderezado (p.221)
5. Sopa Clara (p.223)

Menu di tempura

1. Fritto misto alla giapponese (tempura) (pag.197)
2. Verdure in umido (pag.209)
3. Spinaci con fiocchi di bonito essiccato(pag.212)
4. Budino salato in tazza (pag.221)
5. Consommé alla giapponese (pag.223)

Refeição com tempura

1. Tempura sortido (pág. 197)
2. Vegetais cozidos (pág. 209)
3. Espinafre fervido com flocos de bonito seco (pág. 212)
4. Creme de ovos suculento (pág. 221)
5. Sopa clara (pág. 223)

Sashimi Dinner

1. Assorted Sashimi (p.196)
2. Boiled Vegetables (p.209)
3. Savory Egg Custard (p.221)
4. Salt-Pickled Vegetables (p.215)
5. Miso Soup (p.222)

© S.T.

生魚片套餐

1. 生魚片拼盆 (p.196)
2. 炖煨蔬菜 (p.209)
3. 蒸雞蛋羹 (p.221)
4. 腌菜 (p.215)
5. 日本式醬湯 (p.222)

生鱼片套餐

1. 生鱼片拼盆 (p.196)
2. 炖煨蔬菜 (p.209)
3. 蒸鸡蛋羹 (p.221)
4. 腌菜 (p.215)
5. 日本式酱汤 (p.222)

생선회 정식

1. 모듬회 (p.196)
2. 야채조림 (p.209)
3. 달걀찜 (p.221)
4. 야채절임 (p.215)
5. 된장국 (p.222)

さしみ定食

1. さしみの盛り合わせ (p.196)
2. 野菜の煮もの (p.209)
3. 茶碗蒸し (p.221)
4. 漬けもの (p.215)
5. みそ汁 (p.222)

عشاء السمك النيء

١. تشكيلة من السمك النيء (ص ١٩٦)
٢. خضر مسلوقة (ص ٢٠٩)
٣. بودنج البيض الملح (ص ٢٢١)
٤. خضر مخللة في الملح (ص ٢١٥)
٥. حساء الميسو (ص ٢٢٢)

Menü mit Sashimi

1. Gemischtes Sashimi (S. 196)
2. Gekochtes Gemüse (S. 209)
3. Pikanter Eierstich mit Einlage (S. 221)
4. In Salz eingelegtes Gemüse (S. 215)
5. Miso-Suppe (S. 222)

Dîner à base de sashimi

1. Assortiment de sashimi (p.196)
2. Légumes bouillis (p.209)
3. Crème onctueuse aux œufs (p.221)
4. Légumes marinés dans du sel (p.215)
5. Soupe de miso (p.222)

Plato Combinado de Sashimi

1. Sashimi Surtido (p.196)
2. Verduras Cocidas (p.209)
3. Flan de Huevo Aderezado (p.221)
4. Verduras en Salmuera (p.215)
5. Sopa de Miso (p.222)

Menu di sashimi

1. Misto di fettine di pesce crudo (sashimi) (pag.196)
2. Verdure in umido (pag.209)
3. Budino salato in tazza (pag.221)
4. Verdure in salamoia (pag.215)
5. Minestra di miso (pag.222)

Refeição com peixe cru

1. Sashimi sortido (pág. 196)
2. Vegetais cozidos (pág. 209)
3. Creme de ovos suculento (pág. 221)
4. Vegetais em conserva de sal (pág. 215)
5. Sopa de miso (pág. 222)

©S.T.

Grilled Fish Dinner

1. Broiled Salted Fish (p.199)
2. Savory Egg Custard (p.221)
3. Boiled Vegetables (p.209)
4. Salt-Pickled Vegetables (p.215)
5. Boiled Spinach with Bonito Shavings (p.212)
6. Miso Soup (p.222)

烤魚套餐
1. 鹽烤魚 (p.199)
2. 蒸雞蛋羹 (p.221)
3. 炖煨蔬菜 (p.209)
4. 腌菜 (p.215)
5. 涼拌菠菜 (p.212)
6. 日本式醬湯 (p.222)

烤鱼套餐
1. 盐烤鱼 (p.199)
2. 蒸鸡蛋羹 (p.221)
3. 炖煨蔬菜 (p.209)
4. 腌菜 (p.215)
5. 凉拌菠菜 (p.212)
6. 日本式酱汤 (p.222)

생선구이 정식
1. 생선소금구이 (p.199)
2. 달걀찜 (p.221)
3. 야채조림 (p.209)
4. 야채절임 (p.215)
5. 일식 시금치나물 (p.212)
6. 된장국 (p.222)

焼き魚定食
1. 魚の塩焼き (p.199)
2. 茶碗蒸し (p.221)
3. 野菜の煮もの (p.209)
4. 漬けもの (p.215)
5. おひたし (p.212)
6. みそ汁 (p.222)

عشاء السمك المشوي
١. سمك مشوي بالملح (ص ١٩٩)
٢. بودنج البيض الملح (ص ٢٢١)
٣. خضر مسلوقة (ص ٢٠٩)
٤. خضر مخللة في الملح (ص ٢١٥)
٥. سبانخ مسلوقة مع مبشور السمك (ص ٢١٢)
٦. حساء الميسو (ص ٢٢٢)

Menü mit gegrilltem Fisch
1. Gegrillter gesalzener Fisch (S. 199)
2. Pikanter Eierstich mit Einlage (S. 221)
3. Gekochtes Gemüse (S. 209)
4. In Salz eingelegtes Gemüse (S. 215)
5. Gekochter Spinat mit Bonitfisch-Flocken (S. 212)
6. Miso-Suppe (S. 222)

Dîner à base de poisson grillé
1. Grillade de poissons salés (p.199)
2. Crème onctueuse aux œufs (p.221)
3. Légumes bouillis (p.209)
4. Légumes marinés dans du sel (p.215)
5. Epinards bouillis accompagnés de bonite séchée râpée(p.212)
6. Soupe de miso (p.222)

Plato Combinado de Pescado Frito
1. Pescado Salado a las Brasas (p.199)
2. Flan de Huevo Aderezado (p.221)
3. Verduras Cocidas (p.209)
4. Verduras en Salmuera (p.215)
5. Espinacas Cocidas con Hojuelas de Bonito Seco (p.212)
6. Sopa de Miso (p.222)

Menu di pesce
1. Pesce grigliato con sale (pag.199)
2. Budino salato in tazza (pag.221)
3. Verdure in umido (pag.209)
4. Verdure in salamoia (pag.215)
5. Spinaci con fiocchi di bonito essiccato (pag.212)
6. Minestra di miso (pag.222)

Refeição com peixe grelhado
1. Peixe grelhado com sal (pág. 199)
2. Creme de ovos suculento (pág. 221)
3. Vegetais cozidos (pág. 209)
4. Vegetais em conserva de sal (pág. 215)
5. Espinafre fervido com flocos de bonito seco (pág. 212)
6. Sopa de miso (pág. 222)

Stir-Fried Pork with Ginger and Onion Dinner

1. Stir-Fried Pork with Ginger (p.189)
2. Salt-Pickled Vegetables (p.215)
3. Boiled Spinach with Bonito Shavings (p.212)
4. Miso Soup (p.222)

© S.T.

姜汁烤肉套餐

1. 姜汁烤肉 (p.189)
2. 腌菜 (p.215)
3. 凉拌菠菜 (p.212)
4. 日本式醬湯 (p.222)

姜汁烤肉套餐

1. 姜汁烤肉 (p.189)
2. 腌菜 (p.215)
3. 凉拌菠菜 (p.212)
4. 日本式酱汤 (p.222)

돼지고기생강볶음 정식

1. 돼지고기 생강볶음 (p.189)
2. 야채절임 (p.215)
3. 일식 시금치나물 (p.212)
4. 된장국 (p.222)

しょうが焼き定食

1. 豚肉のしょうが焼き (p.189)
2. 漬けもの (p.215)
3. おひたし (p.212)
4. みそ汁 (p.222)

عشاء اللحم المحمر مع الزنجبيل والبصل

١. لحم محمر مع الزنجبيل (ص ١٨٩)
٢. خضر مخللة في الملح (ص ٢١٥)
٣. سبانخ مسلوقة مع مبشور السمك (ص ٢١٢)
٤. حساء الميسو (ص ٢٢٢)

Menü mit pfannengerührtem Schweinefleisch und Ingwer

1. Pfannengerührtes Schweinefleisch mit Ingwer (S. 189)
2. In Salz eingelegtes Gemüse (S. 215)
3. Gekochter Spinat mit Bonitfisch-Flocken (S. 212)
4. Miso-Suppe (S. 222)

Dîner à base de sauté de porc au gingembre et aux oignons

1. Sauté de porc au gingembre (p.189)
2. Légumes marinés dans du sel (p.215)
3. Epinards bouillis accompagnés de bonite séchée râpée (p.212)
4. Soupe de miso (p.222)

Plato Combinado de Cerdo Salteado con Jengibre

1. Cerdo Salteado con Jengibre (p.189)
2. Verduras en Salmuera (p.215)
3. Espinacas Cocidas con Hojuelas de Bonito Seco (p.212)
4. Sopa de Miso (p.222)

Menu di maiale allo zenzero

1. Maiale in padella allo zenzero (pag.189)
2. Verdure in salamoia (pag.215)
3. Spinaci con fiocchi di bonito essiccato (pag.212)
4. Minestra di miso (pag.222)

Refeição com carne de porco refogada com gengibre e cebola

1. Porco refogado com gengibre (pág. 189)
2. Vegetais em conserva de sal (pág. 215)
3. Espinafre fervido com flocos de bonito seco(pág. 212)
4. Sopa de miso (pág. 222)

Breaded Pork Cutlet Dinner

1. Breaded Pork Cutlet (p.190)
2. Salt-Pickled Vegetables (p.215)
3. Boiled Spinach with Bonito Shavings (p.212)
4. Miso Soup (p.222)

炸豬排套餐

1. 炸豬排 (p.190)
2. 醃菜 (p.215)
3. 涼拌菠菜 (p.212)
4. 日本式醬湯 (p.222)

炸猪排套餐

1. 炸猪排 (p.190)
2. 腌菜 (p.215)
3. 凉拌菠菜 (p.212)
4. 日本式酱汤 (p.222)

포크 커틀렛 정식

1. 포크 커틀렛 (p.190)
2. 야채절임 (p.215)
3. 일식 시금치나물 (p.212)
4. 된장국 (p.222)

トンカツ定食

1. トンカツ (p.190)
2. 漬けもの (p.215)
3. おひたし (p.212)
4. みそ汁 (p.222)

Menü mit paniertem Schweinekotelett

1. Paniertes Schweinekotelett (S. 190)
2. In Salz eingelegtes Gemüse (S. 215)
3. Gekochter Spinat mit Bonitfisch-Flocken (S. 212)
4. Miso-Suppe (S. 222)

Dîner à base d'escalope de porc panée

1. Escalope de porc panée (p.190)
2. Légumes marinés dans du sel (p.215)
3. Epinards bouillis accompagnés de bonite séchée râpée (p.212)
4. Soupe de miso (p.222)

Cena de Chuleta de Cerdo Rebozada

1. Chuleta de Cerdo Rebozada (p.190)
2. Verduras en Salmuera (p.215)
3. Espinacas Cocidas con Hojuelas de Bonito Seco(p.212)
4. Sopa de Miso (p.222)

Menu di maiale impanato

1. Cotolette di maiale impanate (pag.190)
2. Verdure in salamoia (pag.215)
3. Spinaci con fiocchi di bonito essiccato (pag.212)
4. Minestra di miso (pag.222)

عشاء ريش اللحم البانيه

١. ريش اللحم البانيه (ص ١٩٠)
٢. خضر مخللة في الملح (ص ٢١٥)
٣. سبانخ مسلوقة مع ميشور السمك (ص. ٢١٢)
٤. حساء الميسو (ص ٢٢٢)

Refeição com carne de porco empanada

1. Milanesa de carne de porco ao estilo japonês (pág. 190)
2. Vegetais em conserva de sal (pág. 215)
3. Espinafre fervido com flocos de bonito seco (pág. 212)
4. Sopa de miso (pág. 222)

Traditional Japanese Dinner

1. Assorted Tempura (p.197)
2. Assorted Sashimi (p.196)
3. Boiled Vegetables (p.209)
4. Savory Egg Custard (p.221)
5. Salt-Pickled Vegetables (p.215)
6. Clear Soup (p.223)

©S.T.

日式套餐
1. 天婦羅拼盆 (p.197)
2. 生魚片拼盆 (p.196)
3. 炖煨蔬菜 (p.209)
4. 蒸雞蛋羹 (p.221)
5. 腌菜 (p.215)
6. 清湯 (p.223)

日式套餐
1. 天妇罗拼盆 (p.197)
2. 生鱼片拼盆 (p.196)
3. 炖煨蔬菜 (p.209)
4. 蒸鸡蛋羹 (p.221)
5. 腌菜 (p.215)
6. 清汤 (p.223)

일식 정식
1. 모듬튀김 (p.197)
2. 모듬회 (p.196)
3. 야채조림 (p.209)
4. 달걀찜 (p.221)
5. 야채절임 (p.215)
6. 맑은 국 (p.223)

和定食
1. 天ぷらの盛り合わせ (p.197)
2. さしみの盛り合わせ (p.196)
3. 野菜の煮もの (p.209)
4. 茶碗蒸し (p.221)
5. 漬けもの (p.215)
6. すまし汁 (p.223)

Traditionelles japanisches Menü
1. Gemischtes Tempura (S. 197)
2. Gemischtes Sashimi (S. 196)
3. Gekochtes Gemüse (S. 209)
4. Pikanter Eierstich mit Einlage (S. 221)
5. In Salz eingelegtes Gemüse (S. 215)
6. Klare Suppe (S. 223)

Dîner japonais traditionnel
1. Assortiment de tempura (p.197)
2. Assortiment de sashimi (p.196)
3. Légumes bouillis (p.209)
4. Crème onctueuse aux œufs (p.221)
5. Légumes marinés dans du sel (p.215)
6. Soupe claire (p.223)

Plato Combinado a la Japonesa Tradicional
1. Tempura Surtido (p.197)
2. Sashimi Surtido (p.196)
3. Verduras Cocidas (p.209)
4. Flan de Huevo Aderezado (p.221)
5. Verduras en Salmuera (p.215)
6. Sopa Clara (p.223)

Menu tradizionale giapponese
1. Fritto misto alla giapponese (tempura) (pag.197)
2. Misto di fettine di pesce crudo (sashimi) (pag.196)
3. Verdure in umido (pag.209)
4. Budino salato in tazza (pag.221)
5. Verdure in salamoia (pag.215)
6. Consommé alla giapponese (pag.223)

عشاء ياباني تقليدي
١. منوعات من التمبورا (ص ١٩٧)
٢. تشكيلة من السمك النيء (ص ١٩٦)
٣. خضر مسلوقة (ص ٢٠٩)
٤. بودنج البيض المملح (ص ٢٢١)
٥. خضر مخللة في الملح (ص ٢١٥)
٦. الحساء الشفاف (ص ٢٢٣)

Refeição japonesa tradicional
1. Tempura sortido (pág. 197)
2. Sashimi sortido (pág. 196)
3. Vegetais cozidos (pág. 209)
4. Creme de ovos suculento (pág. 221)
5. Vegetais em conserva de sal (pág. 215)
6. Sopa clara (pág. 223)

List of Helpful Cookbooks

烹調菜譜書一覧表

烹调菜谱书一览表

요리책 일람표

クッキングブックリスト

قائمة كتب مفيدة للطبخ

Liste mit nützlichen Kochbüchern

Liste de livres de cuisine utiles

Lista de libros de cocina útiles

Elenco di libri di cucina

Lista de livros de receitas úteis

This list provides an introduction to cookbooks that can be referred to when preparing Chinese, Korean and Japanese dishes. Please inquire directly at your nearest bookstore or the respective publisher for further information on how to obtain these books. (Note: The abbreviation "cph" indicates the number of color photographs.)

INTERNATIONAL MAGAZINE AND BOOK

- **ICR THE INTERNATIONAL COOKBOOK REVEW (bi-monthly) (English)**
  SPA S.L., Spain
  ISSN: 1136-2073 (English)

- **THE BOOK OF COOKBOOKS**
  SPA S.L., Spain, Published 1994
  p336 ISBN: 84-89131-00-7 (English)

CHINESE FOOD

- **TYPICAL RECIPES OF CHINA**
  Wan Li Book Co., Ltd., Hong Kong, Published 1992
  p96 cph138 ISBN: 962-14-0064-3 (English & Chinese)

- **CHINESE COOKING FOR BEGINNERS**
  Huang Su-Huei, Wei-Chuan Publishing, Taiwan, Published 1994
  p96 cph169 ISBN: 0-941676-30-7 (English & Chinese)

- **CHINESE CUISINE**
  Huang Su-Huei, Wei-Chuan Publishing, Taiwan, Published 1983
  p206 cph254 ISBN: 0-941676-44-7 (English & Chinese)

- **HIGHLIGHT CHINESE CUISINE**
  Madame Chin Hau, Hilit Publishing Co., Ltd., Taiwan, Published 1981
  p223 cph350 ISBN: 0-914929-02-H (English)

- **HOME ENTERTAINMENT**
  Li Mei Xien, Culture & Life Publishing Company, Taiwan, Published 1992
  p152 cph457 ISBN: 957-630-188-2 (English & Chinese)

- **CHINESE APPETIZERS & SIDE DISHES**
  Culture & Life Publishing Company, Taiwan, Published 1996
  p112 cph357 ISBN: 957-630-401-6 (English & Chinese)

- **THE BEST OF CHINESE COOKING**
  Culture & Life Publishing Company, Taiwan, Published 1992
  p140 cph150 ISBN: 957-630-200-5 (English & Chinese)

- **CHINESE LIGHT MEALS & SNACKS**
  Sumi Hatano, Shufunotomo Co., Ltd., Japan, Published 1991
  p112 cph224 ISBN: 4-07-975368-3 (English)

List of Helpful Cookbooks
クッキングブックリスト

- **THE ESSENTIALS OF CHINESE COOKING**
  Sumi Hatano, Shufunotomo Co., Ltd., Japan, Published 1987
  p122 cph261 ISBN: 4-07-974570-2 (English)

- **EASY CHINESE APPETIZERS AND FAMILY DISHES**
  Tomiteru Shu, Joie, Inc., Japan, Published 1997
  p100 cph478 ISBN: 4-915831-78-7 (English)

- **ENJOY CHINESE CUISINE**
  Judy Lew, Joie, Inc., Japan, Published 1984
  p120 cph476 ISBN: 4-915249-01-8 (English)

- **CHINESE COOKING FAMILY STYLE**
  Lily Ger, Heian International, Inc., U.S.A., Published 1994
  p96 cph197 ISBN: 0-89346-796-0 (English)

- **COOKERY AROUND THE WORLD CHINA**
  Xiao Hui Wang / Cornelia Schinharl, Time-Life, U.S.A., Published 1993
  p144 cph136 ISBN: 0-7054-1196-6 (English)

- **LES GRANDES TRADITIONS CULINAIRES CHINE**
  Xiao Hui Wang / Cornelia Schinharl, Time-Life, U.S.A., Published 1993
  p144 cph136 ISBN: 2-7344-0668-3 (French)

- **LES GRANDES TRADITIONS CULINAIRES CHINE DU SUD**
  Thomas Gwinner / Zhenhuan Zhang, Time-Life, U.S.A., Published 1996
  p144 cph118 ISBN: 2-7344-0765-5 (French)

- **LES GRANDES TRADITIONS CULINAIRES CHINE DU NORD**
  Thomas Gwinner / Zhenhuan Zhang, Time-Life, U.S.A., Published 1996
  p144 cph118 ISBN: 2-7344-0748-5 (French)

- **CHINESE COOKING CLASS COOKBOOK**
  ACP Publishing Pty. Limited, Australia, Published 1978
  p128 cph460 ISBN: 0-949128-73-2 (English)

- **CHINESE COOKBOOK No.2**
  ACP Publishing Pty. Limited, Australia, Published 1996
  p128 cph379 ISBN: 1-86396-050-3 (English)

- **COCINA TRADICIONAL CHINA**
  Deh-Ta Hsiung, Ediciones Librum, S.A., Spain, Published 1996
  p64 cph114 ISBN: 84-89064-03-2 (Spanish)

- **COCINAS DEL MUNDO CHINA**
  Xiao Hui Wang / Cornelia Schinharl, Editorial Everest, S.A.,
  Spain, Published 1993 p144 cph136 ISBN: 84-241-2181-3 (Spanish)

- **DELLA CUCINA CINESE**
  Piero Antolini / The Lian Tjo, Arnoldo Mondadori Editore S.p.A., Italy,
  Published 1990 p310 cph261 ISBN: 88-04-33877-6 (Italian)

- **CUCINA CINESE**
  Piero Antolini, Arnoldo Mondadori Editore S.p.A., Italy, Published 1992
  p194 cph194 ISBN: 88-04-33784-2 (Italian)

- **LA CINA IN TAVOLA**
  Stefano Scolari, Demetra s.r.l., Italy, Published 1994
  p80 cph20 ISBN: 88-7122-471-X (Italian)

- **LA CUCINA CINESE**
  "Il Mosaico" s.r.l., Italy, Published 1996
  p160 ISBN: 88-442-0057-0 (Italian)

- **FAVORITE CHINESE DISHES**
  Lee Hwa Lin, Chin Chin Publishing Co., Ltd., Taiwan, Published 1992
  p96 cph160 ISBN: 0-941676-27-2 (English & Chinese)

- **HOME STYLE CHINESE COOKING**
  Culture & Life Publishing Company, Taiwan, Published 1997
  p112 cph325 ISBN: 957-630-424-5 (English & Chinese)

- **THE FOOD AND COOKING OF CHINA**
  Francine Halvorsen, John Wiley & Sons, Inc., U.S.A., Published 1996
  p226 ISBN: 0-471-1105-8 (English)

- **CHINESE FAMILY FEAST DISHES**
  Zhang Lianming / Li Siusong / Xiong Sizhi / Qui Pangtong,
  Shandong Science and Technology Press, China, Published 1993
  p384 cph8 pages ISBN: 7-5331-1150-8 (English)

- **THE CHINESE WAY**
  Eileen Yin-Feilo, Macmillan, U.S.A., Published 1997
  p326 ISBN: 0-02-860381-8 (English)

- **HEARTSMART CHINESE COOKING**
  Stephen Wong, Douglas & McIntyre, Canada, Published 1996
  p140 ISBN: 1-55054-496-9 (English)

● **CANTONESE COOKING**
Hilit Publishing Co., Ltd., Taiwan, Published 1986
p119 cph378 ISBN: 0-914929-97-6 (English)

● **CHINESE CUISINE SZECHWAN STYLE**
Lee Hwa Lin, Chin Chin Publishing Co., Ltd., Taiwan, Published 1993
p96 cph273 ISBN: 0-941676-31-5 (English & Chinese)

● **SZECHUAN COOKING**
Hilit Publishing Co., Ltd., Taiwan, Published 1984
p78 cph167 ISBN: 0-914929-75-5 (English)

● **PEKING COOKING**
Hilit Publishing Co., Ltd., Taiwan, Published 1988
p120 300 color plates ISBN: 0-944-929-852 (English)

● **CHINESE CUISINE SHANGHAI STYLE**
Lee Hwa Lin, Chin Chin Publishing Co., Ltd., Taiwan, Published 1994
p96 cph217 ISBN: 0-941676-55-2 (English & Chinese)

● **SHANGHAI COOKING**
Hilit Publishing Co., Ltd., Taiwan, Published 1988
p120 300 color plates ISBN: 0-914929-87-9 (English)

● **HUNAN COOKING**
Hilit Publishing Co., Ltd., Taiwan, Published 1988
p120 300 color plates ISBN: 0-914929-87-9 (English)

● **CHINESE CUISINE TAIWANESE STYLE**
Wei-Chuan Cultural-Educational Foundation, Chin Chin Publishing Co., Ltd.
Taiwan, Published 1991 p120 cph267 ISBN: 0-941676-25-0 (English & Chinese)

● **TAIWANESE COOKING**
Hilit Publishing Co., Ltd., Taiwan, Published 1988
p120 cph406 ISBN: None (English)

● **CHINESE DIM SUM**
Wei-Chuan Cultural-Educational Foundation, Chin Chin Publishing Co., Ltd.,
Taiwan, Published 1990 p128 cph360 ISBN: 0-941676-24-2 (English & Chinese)

● **CHINESE DIMSUM RECIPES**
Tuan-hsi Shou, Hilit Publishing Co., Ltd., Taiwan, Published 1983
p120 cph423 ISBN: 0-914929-58-5 (English)

- **DUMPLINGS**
  Leo Lee, Seashire Publishing Co., Hong Kong, Published 1994
  p96 cph46 ISBN: 962-365-293-3 (English & Chinese)

- **DIM SUM APPETIZERS AND LIGHT MEALS**
  Judy Lew, Joie,Inc., Japan, Published 1990
  p104 cph393 ISBN: 4-915249-68-9 (English)

- **CHINESE SEAFOOD**
  Tuan-hsi Shou, Hilit Publishing Co., Ltd., Taiwan, Published 1983
  p119 cph287 ISBN: 0-914929-20-8 (English)

- **CHINESE HOME-COOKING NOODLES**
  Lee Hwa Lin, Chin Chin Publishing Co., Ltd., Taiwan, Published 1994
  p96 cph137 ISBN: 0-941676-35-8 (English & Chinese)

- **CONGEE, NOODLES AND RICE**
  Loo Kin Yip, Seashire Publishing Co., Hong Kong, Published 1991
  p96 cph46 ISBN: 962-365-137-6 (English & Chinese)

- **CHINESE PORRIDGE**
  Liang Chiung Pai, Culture & Life Publishing Company, Taiwan, Published 1994
  p112 cph129 ISBN: 957-630-325-7 (English & Chinese)

- **SIMPLY VEGETARIAN**
  Lee Hwa Lin, Chin Chin Publishing Co., Ltd., Taiwan, Published 1997
  p96 cph159 ISBN: 0-941676-71-4 (English & Chinese)

- **CHINESE VEGETARIAN COOKING**
  Y.D Cheng, Culture & Life Publishing Company, Taiwan, Published 1994
  p112 cph432 ISBN: 957-630-309-5 (Chinese)

- **CHINESE HEALTHY RECIPES**
  Tuan-hsi Shou, Hilit Publishing Co., Ltd., Taiwan, Published 1983
  p119 cph368 ISBN: 0-914929-39-9 (English)

- **SPICY NUTRITIOUS RECIPES**
  Loo Kin Yip, Seashire Publishing Co., Hong Kong, Published 1991
  p96 cph73 ISBN: 962-365-128-7 (English & Chinese)

- **APPETIZERS CHINESE STYLE**
  Lee Hwa Lin, Chin Chin Publishing Co., Ltd., Taiwan, Published 1996
  p96 cph120 ISBN: 0-941676-69-2 (English & Chinese)

KOREAN FOOD

● **KOREAN COOKERY**
Joan Rutt & Sandra Mattielli, Hollym International Corp., Korea,
Published 1974 p95 cph248 ISBN: 0-930878-45-0 (English)

● **PRACTICAL KOREAN COOKING**
Noh Chin-hwa, Hollym International Corp., Korea, Published 1985
p214 cph1066 ISBN: 0-930878-37-x (English)

● **TRADITIONAL KOREAN COOKING**
Noh Chin-hwa, Hollym International Corp., Korea, Published 1985
p78 cph339 ISBN: 0-930878-48-5 (English)

● **KOREAN COOKING FOR EVERYONE**
Ji Sook Choe & Yukiko Moriyama, Joie, Inc., Japan, Published 1986
p112 cph518 ISBN: 4-915249-36-0 (English)

● **FLAVOURS OF KOREA**
Marc and Kim Millon, André Deutsch Limited, England, Published 1991
p201 cph15 ISBN: 0-233-98635-9 (English)

● **THE KOREAN COOKBOOK**
Judy Hyun, Hollym International Corp., Korea, Published 1970
p294 cph18 ISBN: 1-56591-001-x(Hard), ISBN: 1-56591-002-8(Paper) (English)

● **HOMESTYLE KOREAN COOKING IN PICTURES**
Cho Joong Ok, Shufunotomo Co., Ltd., Japan, Published 1991
p96 cph66 ISBN: 0-87040-502-0 (English)

● **KIMCHI A KOREAN HEALTH FOOD**
Florence C. Lee & Helen C. Lee, Hollym International Corp., Korea,
Published 1988 p64 cph211 ISBN: 0-930878-59-0 (English)

● **LOW-FAT KOREAN COOKING FISH, SHELLFISH & VEGETABLES**
Noh Chin-hwa, Hollym International Corp., Korea, Published 1985
p76 cph382 ISBN: 0-930878-47-7 (English)

● **HEALTHFUL KOREAN COOKING MEATS & POULTRY**
Noh Chin-hwa, Hollym International Corp., Korea, Published 1985
p76 cph343 ISBN: 0-930878-46-9 (English)

JAPANESE FOOD

- **THE JOY OF JAPANESE COOKING**
  Kuwako Takahashi, Shufunotomo Co., Ltd., Japan, Published 1986
  p311 cph112 ISBN: 4-07-975150-8 (English)

- **TASTE OF JAPAN**
  Shufunotomo Co., Ltd., Japan, Published 1997
  p64 cph156 ISBN: 4-07-976391-3 (English)

- **THE JAPANESE MENU COOKBOOK**
  Constance D. Chang, Shufunotomo Co., Ltd., Japan, Published 1975
  p65 cph34 ISBN: 4-07-975300-4 (English)

- **JAPANESE HOME STYLE COOKING**
  Better Home Japan, Japan, Published 1986
  p96 cph212 ISBN: 4-938508-40-0 (English)

- **FAVORITE JAPANESE DISHES**
  Yukiko Moriyama, Joie, Inc., Japan, Published 1987
  p96 cph550 ISBN: 4-915249-37-9 (English)

- **JAPANESE CUISINE FOR EVERYONE**
  Yukiko Moriyama, Joie, Inc., Japan, Published 1985
  p120 cph513 ISBN: 4-915249-20-4 (English)

- **MODERN JAPANESE COOKING AT HOME**
  Toshiro Kandagawa, Joie, Inc., Japan, Published 1997
  p104 cph345 ISBN: 4-915831-82-5 (English)

- **JAPANESE SNACKS AND LIGHT MEALS**
  Yukiko Moriyama, Joie, Inc., Japan, Published 1991
  p104 cph293 ISBN: 4-915249-01-9 (English)

- **PRACTICAL JAPANESE COOKING**
  Shizuo Tsuji / Koichiro Hata, Kodansha International Ltd., Japan,
  Published 1986 p152 cph349 ISBN: 0-87011-762-9(US)
  ISBN: 4-7700-1262-4(Japan) (English)

- **JAPANESE FAMILY-STYLE RECIPES**
  Hiroko Urakami, Kodansha International Ltd., Japan, Published 1992
  p120 cph55 ISBN: 4-7700-1583-6 (English)

List of Helpful Cookbooks
クッキングブックリスト

- **JAPANESE COOKING FOR TWO**
  Kurumi Hayter, Chartwell Books, Inc., U.S.A., Published 1996
  p80 cph104 ISBN: 0-7858-0632-6 (English)

- **JAPANESE CUISINE**
  Chen Shiu-Lee, Wei-Chuan Publising, Taiwan, Published 1988
  p103 cph309 ISBN: 0-941676-19-6 (English & Chinese)

- **IL GIAPPONE IN CUCINA**
  Arnoldo Mondadori Editore, Italy, Published 1996
  p108 cph238 ISBN: 88-04-41225-9 (Italian)

- **GRAZIANA CANOVA TURA IL GIAPPONE IN CUCINA**
  Arnoldo Mondadori Editore, Italy, Published 1994
  p350 ISBN: 88-04-38018-7 (Italian)

- **100 RECIPES FROM JAPANESE COOKING**
  Hata Koichiro / Kondo Kazuki, Kodansha International Ltd., Japan, Published
  1997 p259 cph16 ISBN: 4-7700-2079-1 (English & Japanese)

- **SUSHI FOR PARTIES MAKI-ZUSHI AND NIGIRI-ZUSHI**
  Ken Kawasumi, Graph-sha Ltd., Japan, Published 1996
  p80 cph498 ISBN: 0-87040-956-5 (English)

- **SUSHI AT HOME**
  Kay Shimizu, Shufunotomo Co., Ltd., Japan, Published 1988
  p142 cph174 ISBN: 0-87040-930-1 (English)

- **SUSHI COOKBOOK**
  Heihachiro Tohyama / Yukiko Moriyama, Joie, Inc., Japan, Published 1983
  p108 cph819 ISBN: 4-915249-04-2 (English)

- **SUSHI THE DELICATE FLAVOR OF JAPAN**
  Masuo Yoshino, Gakken Co., Ltd., Japan, Published 1986
  p96 cph88 ISBN: 0-87040-742-2, ISBN: 4-05-151404-8(Japan) (English)

- **SUSHI**
  Masuo Yoshino, Gakken Co., Ltd., Germany, Published 1996
  p96 cph88 ISBN: 3-930614-01-4 (German)

- **JAPANESE VEGETARIAN COOKING FROM SIMPLE SOUPS TO SUSHI**
  Patricia Richfield, The Crossing Press, U.S.A., Published 1996
  p176 ISBN: 0-895948-05-2 (English)

- **THE CLASSIC RICE COOKBOOK**
  Junko Takagi, Shufunotomo Co., Ltd., Japan, Published 1996
  p132 cph262 ISBN: 4-07-976209-7 (English)

- **TOFU COOKING**
  Junko Lampert, Shufunotomo Co., Ltd., Japan, Published 1983
  p97 cph100 ISBN: 4-07-973850-1 (English)

- **JAPANESE FOODS FOR HEALTH**
  Kay Shimizu, Shufunotomo Co., Ltd., Japan, Published 1974
  p20 cph20 ISBN: 4-07-973547-2 (English)

- **HEALTHY VEGETABLE COOKING**
  Asako Tohata,M.D., Graph-Sha Ltd., Japan, Published 1995
  p64 cph174 ISBN: 0-87040-959-X (English)

- **JAPANESE COOKING FOR HEALTH AND FITNESS**
  Kiyoko Konishi, Gakken Co., Ltd., Japan, Published 1983
  p120 color photographs ISBN: 4-05-151330-0 (English)

- **A GUIDE TO FOOD BUYING IN JAPAN**
  Carolyn R. Krouse, Charles E. Tuttle Company, Japan, Published 1986
  p191 ISBN: 0-8048-1503-8 (English)

- **JAPANESE COOKING FOR EVERYONE**
  Miyoko Sakai / Motoko Abe, The Japan Times, Ltd., Japan, Published 1989
  p128 ISBN: 4-7890-0496-1 (English)

- **A DICTIONARY OF JAPANESE FOOD**
  Richard Hosking, Charles E. Tuttle Company, Japan, Published 1996
  p239 ISBN: 0-8048-2042-2 (English)

- **WHAT'S WHAT IN JAPANESE RESTAURANTS**
  Robb Satterwhite, Kodansha International Ltd., Japan, Published 1988
  p178 ISBN: 4-7700-2086-4 (English)

Eikō Setsu

Master chef at the "Mielparque Yokohama Yubin Chokin Hall", Managing Trustee of the Yokohama Chinatown Development Association, Proprietor of the Chinese Restaurant, "SETSUEN".

勢津 栄興（せつ えいこう）

「メルパルク横浜郵便貯金会館」総料理長、横浜中華街発展会協同組合常務理事、中国料理店「接筵」店主。
（神奈川県横浜市）

Kamyon Cho

Cooking researcher. Director of the Korean cooking school, "FARAN Cooking School".

曺甲連（チョ カムヨン）

料理研究家。韓国料理「花朗料理教室」主宰。
（東京都新宿区）

Kikuo Takada

Head chef in charge of Japanese cuisine at "Mielparque Yokohama Yubin Chokin Hall".

高田 喜久雄（たかだ きくお）

「メルパルク横浜郵便貯金会館」和食料理長。
（神奈川県横浜市）

Kiyotomi Ozawa

Managing Director and Head Chef of the Japanese Restaurant, "Irifune Jaya".

**小沢 清富
（おざわ きよとみ）**

すし・懐石「入船茶屋」常務。
（東京都立川市）

Nobuaki Ogawa

Manager and Head Chef of the Japanese noodle restaurant, "Soba Honjin".

**小川 信昭
（おがわ のぶあき）**

日本そば「蕎麦本陣」店主。
（東京都立川市）

Takayoshi Murano

Proprietor and Head Chef of the Chinese Restaurant, "Fukushinrō".

**村野 高義
（むらの たかよし）**

中国料理店「福心楼」店主。
（東京都立川市）

Special Thanks
協力者

JAPAN

(Chinese Foods)
Yokohama Chinatown Development Association
Asu Hanten, Tachikawa, Tokyo

(Korean Foods)
Hosenka, Minato-ku, Tokyo
Yakiniku Restaurant "DON", Shibuya-ku, Tokyo
Korai-en, Itabashi-ku, Tokyo

(Japanese Foods)
Akio Kizawa, Joetsu, Niigata
Takashi Kobayashi, Kawasaki, Kanagawa

日本

(中国料理)

横浜中華街発展会協同組合	
「亜洲飯店」	東京都立川市

(韓国料理)

「鳳仙花」	東京都港区
焼き肉レストラン「どん」	東京都渋谷区
「高麗苑」	東京都板橋区

(日本料理)

木澤昭夫	新潟県上越市
小林　隆	神奈川県川崎市

OVERSEAS

HONG KONG	Timothy Tsang, Betty Tsang
TAIWAN	Bo Shi Lin
KOREA	Kim In Gi, Joung Chae Sang, Kim Too Ran
AUSTRIA	Rupert Rupp, Josef Schlager
FRANCE	Marie Luz MIGNARD
BELGIUM	Jean Rouffa
SPAIN	Pedro Garcia
ITALY	Mara Gironi, Daniela Margiotta, Elio Barattieri
PORTUGAL	Cristina Barreto, Augusto Fonseca

中国料理便覧／評論社
中国料理／辻学園出版事業部
中国料理用語辞典／日本経済新聞社
くわしいやさしい中華料理／グラフ社
中華のおかず入門／主婦と生活社
洋風・中華・朝鮮・エスニック　おかず百科／フジテレビジョン
香港食大王／講談社
中國菜／味全食譜
麺／味全食譜
四川菜／味全文化教育基金曾
上海菜／味全文化教育基金曾
飲茶食譜／味全文化教育基金曾

チョ・カムヨンの食べたい作りたい朝鮮料理／ＮＨＫ出版
作ってみたい韓国料理の本／グラフ社
焼肉料理／旭屋出版
趙　重玉　韓国の家庭料理／中央公論者
ジョン・キョンファのおいしいおかず／柴田書店
世界を食べる旅　韓国／講談社
Practical KOREAN COOKING ／ HOLLYM
HOMESTYLE KOREAN COOKING IN PICTURES ／ SHUFUNOTOMO CO.,LTD.
KOREAN COOKING FOR EVERYONE ／ JOIE,INC.

日本料理／辻学園出版事業部
お菓子／辻学園出版事業部
外国人に教える日本料理の楽しみ／はまの出版
調理法別和風のおかず入門／主婦と生活社
らくらく和食／集英社
和風のおかず百科／フジテレビジョン
日本酒ハンドブック／池田書店
JAPANESE CUISINE FOR EVERYONE ／ JOIE,INC.
FAVORITE JAPANESE DISHES ／ JOIE,INC.
THE JOY OF JAPANESE COOKING ／ SHUFUNOTOMO CO.,LTD.

料理食材大事典／主婦の友社
食材図典／小学館
カロリーチェック料理 Book ／辻学園出版事業部
世界のメニューガイド／弘済出版社
食の文化話題事典／ぎょうせい
世界の名酒事典／講談社
お茶の事典／成美堂出版